From ROUSSEAU *to* PROUST

JEAN-JACQUES ROUSSEAU

HAVELOCK ELLIS

From

ROUSSEAU

to

PROUST

Essay Index Reprint Series

BOOKS FOR LIBRARIES PRESS
FREEPORT, NEW YORK

840.9
EL5 f
65559
April 1969

CONTENTS

CONTENTS

ILLUSTRATIONS

✤ ✤ ✤

FROM
ROUSSEAU
TO
PROUST

I

WHEN I was a young schoolboy the Franco-Prussian War was fought. That event probably coloured my feelings towards France for fifty years. The London *Graphic* was then beginning to appear, with its illustrations more vividly realistic than any before, and here I was able to follow the fate of French arms. No doubt my sympathies were further coloured, apart from the attraction of a losing cause, by the fact that my schoolmaster, De Chastelain by name, was of French origin — the Anglicised son of a Frenchman, I believe — and the school itself bore the name of 'The French and German College,' though the German element was negligible.

It was not till two or three years later, when I was about fourteen, that I became familiar enough with the French language to read it for my own pleasure. Searching among old books that had once belonged to my grandmother, a woman of culture, I came on the *Rêveries* of Rousseau, which was thus the first French book I read for its own sake. Its musical seduction came to me as the revelation of something

3

new, though it was not till many years later that I understood the significance of Rousseau.

So far I had never been in France. I had been twice round the world and knew much about French literature before, in 1883, I reached Paris, accompanied by my nearest friend of early years, Angus Mackay, an acute young critic as well as poet, who later gave his best energies to the Church and died in middle age before making any deep mark on the world. It was a brief visit and limited to those outstanding objects of interest with which one's knowledge of a great city must always begin. A second visit (when I was accompanied by Arthur Symons who then saw Paris for the first time) followed in 1889, the year of the Exposition to celebrate the Centenary of the Revolution, and in 1890, when my medical course was completed and I felt that the next stage in education was to learn something about science and art in France, there followed a more prolonged and more penetrating exploration of Paris. On this occasion also I was accompanied by Arthur Symons, to whom Paris was still an unknown land of heart's desire; but he was furnished with useful letters of introduction which, directly and indirectly, opened for us doors of literature and art, for of science I am not here called upon to speak. We settled in the Hôtel Corneille — facing the Odéon and agreeably close to the Luxembourg Gardens — which had been recommended to me by Professor (later Sir) Patrick Geddes, and we paid, if I remember rightly, forty-five francs a month each for our rooms. This hotel, since considerably renovated, is not only situated in a district historically interesting, but, as I gradually learnt, had its own historical and literary associations, being familiarly known to Balzac and to Baudelaire among other notable persons.

We were not exploring at random. We had neither of us come to gaze at the idols of the crowd or to seek out the venerated figures who still survived to enjoy a fame won in the generation before, and for us faded. It is true, we called upon Coppée in his pleasantly countrified suburban house, and he came forward, arms outstretched, to greet us with all his rather feminine charm; but we were not interested in his

work. True, also, we saw Meissonier, with his little stocky
body and his long grey beard, seated on varnishing day in a
corner of the New Salon over which he presided, but we
passed by his pictures. Neither Anatole France nor Zola
concerned us, and when we saw the genially gross Sarcey in
the middle of the first circle at the theatre, rotating his huge
body and broad smile to beam on his friends to right and left,
it was only as an object of amusement. We ostentatiously
avoided alike the Opéra and the Folies-Bergères, as both temples of convention, though some years later I was present at the
Opéra with my wife for events that are still memorable to me,
for Rameau and for Debussy, perhaps above all for Dukas's
Ariane et Barbe Bleue. In music there was then, or a little later,
the Concert Rouge in the Rue de Tournon near by, where
interesting things not yet to be heard in England could be
enjoyed for the price of a *consommation*, and on special occasions there was the Sunday afternoon Concert Lamoureux.
Here I once had the rare experience of hearing so popular an
idol as Sarah Bernhardt hissed. The concert was preceded by
a recital the famous actress had consented to give of a pretentious and high-strung religious mystery play lately written
by Haraucourt. It was recited in monotonous and duly
solemn tones for what seemed an interminable time while the
audience grew restless, until at last the reciter's voice —
which long before my time had ceased to receive the epithet
'golden' once applied to it — was drowned by cries of '*La
musique! La musique!*' Haraucourt rushed forward from his
stall; actress and author fell into each other's arms and embraced; the first part of the programme was concluded.

We represented the young generation and were concerned
only with those figures who were leaders or prominent representatives of the young generation, however *démodés* and
vieux jeu some of them may appear forty years later when
they are all dead and a new generation has found new orienta-
tions. Such figures were Mallarmé, Rodin, Verlaine, Huysmans, Carrière, Henri de Régnier, Charles Morice, Odilon-
Redon, Remy de Gourmont, and others equally notable of
whom one or other of us caught but a glimpse — such as

Taine and Edmond de Goncourt — and still others whose names are now almost or quite forgotten. We had looked forward to meeting Villiers de l'Isle Adam, but he died just before our arrival. Renan was still alive, though much of an invalid, but he was already a familiar figure to me, for I had attended the course of Hibbert Lectures he had delivered in London a few years earlier.

To return to my own personal attitude, I must go back a few years and refer to a work which, on its first publication in 1885 and the following year, I had most carefully read and eagerly absorbed, the two volumes of *Essais de Psychologie Contemporaine*. Bourget, the author of that memorable book, later became a pillar of the Church, the apostle of conservatism, and the acute critic of all the tendencies of his time. He has even (I am told) carefully toned down in a later edition the more daring utterances in those famous *Essais*. The earlier Bourget was a champion and leader of the youth of his time, though even by 1889 he seemed to me to have fallen behind, and in my first book, *The New Spirit*, published in that year, I put on the title-page a motto from the *Essais*, but thought well to refrain from indicating its source. In the early eighties — I have seen nothing he wrote since — I read the stories in which with a new analytic refinement he presented problems in the psychology of love and above all the *Essais*. Here he discussed, with fine critical insight and admirable literary felicity, among others, Baudelaire and Stendhal and Flaubert and the Goncourts and Tourgueneff, precisely the figures which were then emerging from the conflicts of their own time to become the classics of us of the new generation. It was Bourget, more than anyone, who swept away the last obscuring mists. Any critic thenceforth who disputed the significance of those figures was thereby marked as himself a negligible relic of the past.

Bourget, who dated the Preface of his *Essais* from Oxford, assumed no narrowly French outlook, but one that may be said to be equally congenial to that of my generation in England. He was not concerned, he declared, with literary criticism in the usual sense. For him the processes of art were

EDMOND DE GONCOURT

simply *signs*. He was writing notes for the use of 'the historian of the Moral Life in the second half of the nineteenth century,' using the word 'moral' in the French sense, meaning, as he said, that 'the *book* is the great initiator'; for it presents the modes of feeling and of action which the young generation greedily absorbs, the modes which, when the first stage of life passes into the second and more adult stage, cannot but be influential in moulding their activities. And at the end Bourget seeks to reply to the question whether civilisation has merely complicated man's misery and refined his barbarism, finding, he says, 'sometimes a reply of pain and sometimes of faith and hope.' It is well to recall these *Essais* here, for they admirably represented (distinguishing, I repeat, the former from the later Bourget) the mood in which at that period I faced literature and approached the land in which it seemed to me so acutely alive.

The literary France that I went forth to find was, as I viewed it, largely a continuation of that described by Bourget, the chief later influence being that commonly called of Symbolism which then for a moment touched French poetry. This so-called Symbolist Movement — it is an ill-defined name which is better dropped — is sometimes said to be embodied in Verlaine, who, at all events for me, stood alone among French poets of that time, with indeed few peers at any time in France. There was Rimbaud indeed (whom one then coupled with Corbière), Verlaine's comrade, but he had mysteriously disappeared when little more than a boy, and his work, striking as it was, seemed less important than it seems today when, with a technique that then appeared too daring, it stands out as a great inspiring force. To the English mind, especially, Verlaine was, as he remains today, peculiarly congenial, for he stood at the furthest extreme from that pseudo-classical French rhetoric that offends us; there was in and over his verse the broken haunting music, the iridescent mist, of England — where indeed some of the best of it had been written — and his genuine sympathy with English poetry aided his native genius in making a deep and irresistible appeal.

The echoes of an earlier pseudo-classical and romantically rhetorical age were indeed still heard in France, and some of those who carried them on not only survived but even displayed a high degree of virtuosity with their instruments. Such a one was Catulle Mendès, a man who came into touch with the younger generation, but had mixed with some of the most notable persons of his own, and himself attained a high degree of virtuosity in literature. It was that sort of quality which lies in presenting a superb mask with nothing behind it, a quality supremely well illustrated by Gabriele d'Annunzio and for some of us without deep appeal. Catulle Mendès was at that period no longer the fair Apollo — a rare type among Jews — which he had been for those of his own generation; there was a fixed lassitude in his pallid face and heavy body; and with languid interest I listened as he discoursed languidly one day of the famous people he had known.

Verlaine at that time seemed to dominate French imaginative literature as Rodin dominated French plastic art, each with an intimate and lyrical quality, each, curiously enough, with the same complete defect of architectonic constructive power, and both of them destined to be overshadowed for a time by men who followed them, yet both surely, with all their limitations, remaining in their own spheres unapproachable.

It was at an early stage that, together with Arthur Symons, and guided by Charles Morice, I sought out Verlaine. Morice had not long before published an admirably intelligent and appreciative little book about Verlaine, the first ever published and perhaps still the best.[1] We had shared the expense of inviting him to dinner at our favourite restaurant, the Boulant in the Boul' Mich, where we frequented a corner

---

[1] Morice had abilities of his own as poet as well as critic, but seemed more concerned to proclaim the genius of others than to affirm himself, and, as he possessed a fine and persuasive eloquence together with his art of divination, he was a real influence in his time. He gave of himself freely and received but little, living and dying poor. An appreciative book has been written about him, but, as we might perhaps expect with so selfless a man, there is little in it that is biographical.

8

ruled over by Céline, a waitress of gracious dignity and a personality of her own, who remained at that post for many years later, where I would greet her as an old friend when passing through Paris, until at last she was no longer there and I heard from a fellow-waitress that she had retired. After dinner, which Morice devoured with a fine appetite (to be the banner-bearer of the new generation does not enable one to put much butter on one's bread), he led us down the Boulevard to the café which stood at the corner near the quays, where at that time Verlaine was usually to be found in the evening with the traditional glass of absinthe. Near him were seated several men of his group, notably Moréas. For me there was nothing attractive about Moréas either as personality or poet (but his best work was done later), and his loud metallic Greek voice and accent, his dark sinister features and *staccato* movements, were antipathetic. Not so Verlaine. The descriptions one sometimes finds of Verlaine are so unpleasant that I suspect, and sometimes am sure, that the writers never met him. He was certainly an ambiguous figure for respectable society, to which he had no entry; but at that period at all events, and as I met him, there could be no more pleasant companion, simple, unaffected, and genial. Symons, in his *Mes Souvenirs*, written long after, has described this occasion, in his own manner, indeed, but his account here of Verlaine's appearance and behaviour is as accurate as it is vivid, and I can endorse it at every point.

He invited us to come on a subsequent evening to the room he then occupied at the Hôtel des Mines, some distance up the Boulevard opposite the Ecole des Mines. This hotel was, and remained many years later, a dingy and primitive place with many small gloomy rooms, for Paris hotels, until recent times, were sometimes among the most unpleasantly antiquated I have known anywhere. (In the South they are often antique, but with lofty if ragged nobility.) Here we duly appeared and inquired at the concierge's bureau for M. Verlaine; I must admit that the young woman, when she told us he had not yet returned, looked sour at the mention

of his name. We strolled along the Boulevard and soon saw
the poet jovially approaching us, as with lame leg and stick
he noisily clumped along the pavement, accompanied by an
insignificant little man who seemed an attached friend. We
returned to the hotel and Verlaine led us to his room, where
we were soon joined by a tall pale youth. As ever, Verlaine
played the part of genial host in his bare and sordid abode.
He drew forth a purse, produced from it a two-franc piece
— all it contained, I fear — saying in English, in honour of
his guests: 'I have — *money;* I — will have — *pleasure!*' The
little man was sent out, again in compliment to supposed
English tastes, for a small bottle of rum and glasses, and on
his return I handed round my cigarette-case. At first, I think,
the conversation was of Verlaine's experiences, some twenty
years earlier, in England, and then we talked of poetry; Verlaine dismissed rather summarily most of the French classics,
but when Racine's name was mentioned his tone suddenly
changed to deep appreciation. There was no call for more
drink. It is a subject with which Verlaine's name is often
(no doubt too correctly) associated; but though he usually
had a glass in front of him, he seemed to me as abstemious
over it as most Frenchmen; in my early days in Paris I constantly wondered at the ability of the Frenchman to spend
an hour over a *bock* which an Englishman would swallow at
a draught.

The thought of Verlaine leads to Mallarmé, for, unlike as
were the two men in character and art and environment, they
were contemporaries, associated in the same movement of
Symbolism, and both furnished with rather similar memories of England, though it is in Verlaine's work that these
may be more easily detected. I no longer recall how contact
with Mallarmé was secured, but I well remember climbing
up with Symons to the little apartment in the Rue de Rome,
the neatly kept home of a family man of fine taste who had
to exercise a rigid economy. It was Tuesday evening, his reception day, and he opened the door to us, a small quiet man
with a pleasant smile, a figure at once arousing a sympathetic response. These famous Tuesday evening gatherings

— at that period the social focus of French poetic art —
correspond to nothing in London. But England had known
such centres in earlier centuries when the young pioneers of
great movements, literary or social, gathered round a Master
who preached to them a new gospel. Ben Jonson at the
tavern, Samuel Johnson at the tea-party, Samuel Parr at the
dinner table, were all the dominating figures of groups,
literary, conservative, or radical, to mould the coming generation. But these groups were formed, as it were, on the
monarchic constitutional pattern under which they arose;
the King thundered insolently among subjects who meekly
bowed their heads. Mallarmé belonged to a democratic dis-
pensation; we listened devoutly to his words, but there was
no assumption of superiority, his gentle voice was never
raised; one could not imagine him thundering. The scene of
these gatherings was the small dining-room almost filled by
the long oblong table at which we sat, with Mallarmé at the
head, his back to the door, Henri de Régnier at one hand,
and Gabriel Mourey, the translator of Swinburne, at the
other, while at the lower end of the table were Symons and I.
The bowl of tobacco was passed up and down, and we made
cigarettes at need. We did not meet Madame Mallarmé and
the daughters, but (as I learnt later from Mrs. Moulton, the
poet, who knew the Mallarmés) they were in the next room,
quiet as mice, able to hear our voices, and even to make mischievous comments. On this occasion the tone of the gathering was perhaps unusually subdued. A few days earlier a
young poet of promise, Ephraïm Mikhaël (but his real name
was Georges Michel) had died in Paris under rather pathetic
circumstances, and all I can recall of the conversation was
that, apart from some discussion of English poets, especially
Swinburne, it was mainly concerned with Mikhaël, whose
death, on the fifth of May, serves to date this meeting.

A man of letters of the first rank of that time in Paris,
though not the leader of a movement nor the soul of a *cénacle*,
personally impressed me more deeply than the amiable Mallarmé. That was Huysmans. Introduced by Gourmont, who
was then in close touch with him, though later they had a

misunderstanding, I met Huysmans (of whom I have written at some length in my book of *Affirmations*) on various occasions. We visited him at his government office; we accompanied him to a café to take a vermouth for, he said, his digestion; above all I have spent an evening with him in the apartment of his friend and Gourmont's, Madame Courières, a tall and gracious person, in earlier years, it is said, the favourite model of a famous sculptor; she was Gourmont's 'Sixtine' and also perhaps the original of Madame Chantelouve in *Là-Bas*, which had just then been published. It was a tiny room and the walls at every possible and impossible spot were covered by knick-knacks and bric-à-brac. Here Huysmans sat and quietly talked, in response to remarks that we made, not often initiating conversation nor yet addressing any particular person, recalling absurd little incidents in his experience which illustrated the pathetic imbecility of mankind, and uttering opinions which could sometimes be very damning. But he always spoke gently, and however atrocious he might find the world it always seemed to him — as to Edward Carpenter who would in conversation judge it rather similarly — still worth a smile.

When I look back, Huysmans remains for me, of all the men I have ever known, perhaps the most unalloyed embodiment of genius. I am thinking of his personality, not of his work, though that seems to me of permanent value. If the man of genius is the supremely well-tempered man who yet has working in his constitution a strange ferment which produces on the physical side a certain fragility and on the spiritual side a new creative energy; and if — as I would also say — he is one who, with a temperament which thus freshly blends morbidity and health in hitherto unknown proportions, is set at an angle to the world and mankind at which no man was ever set before, so that he sees everything anew, then I think that genius is well illustrated by Huysmans. In appearance he was slender and rather tall, with an air of refined distinction, almost of asceticism, not the rigid and repressed moral sort, but suggesting an intellectual and temperamental source. In relation to health he tended to be dyspeptic, but though not robust there was nothing weakly about him. His finely strung nature was held in natural control; he was a man of the North to whom Southern excitability was not congenial, and I can believe the report that he was a model government official, and in private life, as his friends assured us, most impeccably careful and elegantly bourgeois. Yet his duties may well have furnished a wholesome balance to an organism which seemed a psycho-physical unity exquisitely poised for the finest responses of sensation and intellect, and at the same time held (as his friend Dr. Maurice de Fleury has left on record) a distinct morbid element of paranoiac and cyclothymic nature. Though his civility was, De Fleury remarks, 'sometimes stupefying,' he was capable of the most violent abuse of quite honourable persons. It was because he felt the human soul more and more empty and uninteresting, he wrote to De Fleury, that he preferred now and again 'to roll in liturgical waves far from Time and the World.' [1] It must not, at the same time, be supposed that such an organic adaptation involved an inhuman attitude to life. Beneath it, however slightly obvious on the surface, there was tender humanity and boundless charity, and when his friends were suffering or dying it was Huysmans who was at the bedside to succour. His own passage through life he has described in a series of books of unequal value. At the time of which I speak he was about to enter what was perhaps the most memorable and fascinating stage of it, that recorded in *En Route*.

The name of Remy de Gourmont has appeared here more than once, as indeed may be natural, for of all the men I came in touch with during those months in Paris, it was with

---

[1] I am not here concerned with Huysmans as a religious mystic, but I should like to quote the opinion of an authority of the first order on that point. M. Seillière had remarked that Léon Bloy was a better Catholic than Huysmans. But the Abbé Brémond opposed that view. Bloy, he truly says, was the exact opposite of a mystic; he was the very type of the 'illuminé' or visionary. 'The mystic experience has nothing in it which resembles vision or revelation or prophecy.' In the 'orasion de quiétude' nothing is *learnt*. And Brémond is enthusiastic over the beauty of the religious and mystic characteristics of Huysmans. (*Nouvelles Littéraires*, 8 Oct., 1932.) The confusion of the mystic with the visionary is common.

Gourmont alone that the relation continued, remaining un-impaired even to his death twenty-five years later. He was not one of those whom I had come to Paris to see, and his early work indeed, however brilliant, with its rather fever-ishly cerebral imaginative qualities, was not of a kind to appeal to me. But he was remarkably friendly and helpful from the outset. Already much of a recluse, at that time liv-ing in the Rue du Bac, in a little study lined high with books, he would call in at the hotel to furnish us with news or in-formation, and sometimes to accompany us on a little excur-sion, once to the famous Gingerbread Fair at Vincennes where we were all three photographed in a group. A rather small grave reserved man, with the traits of his Norman race, not an active talker, there was no doubt a certain irritable suscepti-bility beneath; I recall, when one evening we were together on the Parvis Notre-Dame and a woman approached and lightly touched his arm, the subdued indignation of the re-proof with which he turned to her: '*On ne touche pas!*' The posthumously published *Letters to the Amazon* were for many the revelation of an unknown side to his character. For the most part his life was lived in the world of books and he would move in that world with intellectual muscles that were singularly supple and vigorous, as may be admitted by one who prefers to regard books, not as the world of life, but as the steps to be trodden on the approach to life. Gourmont began his career with a position in the Bibliothèque Nation-ale; nothing could have better suited one who was so essen-tially a man of books. It was about the time I began to know him that an article he had published, an innocent little out-burst about 'patriotism as a toy,' which proved a shock to the solemn anti-German traditions of France, caused his dis-missal. So he set himself seriously and methodically to the life of letters outside a library, largely in association on the publishing side with M. Alfred Vallette, the director of the activities of the *Mercure de France*, whom I recall as a solid, cautious, and capable business man, and found just the same, except for whitened hair, and still at the same post, when I had occasion to visit him in his office in the Rue de Condé thirty-five years later. Gourmont's intellectual grip continued to grow stronger, ever closer to the world of life, and his style more brilliant, during the years that followed, so that by the beginning of the century he seemed to be the finest contemporary French critic and was already gaining an audience wherever the influence of France penetrates. Varied as his work was, it seems as a critic that he was at his best, and that on the series of *Promenades Littéraires* and allied volumes his reputation may most surely rest.

In the period of which I am speaking, however, good criticism was lacking in France. There was indeed Gourmont's own youthful work, the two volumes of *Livre des Masques*, remarkable for their insight and judgment concerning writers still largely at the stage of promise. The age was creative rather than critical. Even the most notable critics of the immediately preceding period had themselves been creative. That was true not only of Bourget in his *Essais*, but still more of a more powerful spirit, Taine. His history of English literature was a creative evocation such as had not before been witnessed; it was comparable in this respect to Michelet's *History of France*. The fascination of elemental passion for the cool and deliberate scholar put Taine equally apart from the unprejudiced analyst in Sainte-Beuve's manner and the rigid academician in Brunetière's, making him the ideal historian of the natural and primitive art of England, and when he turned to French literature in his admirable *Essais de Critique et d'Histoire* it was in the same spirit.

'The critic,' Taine declared, 'is the naturalist of the soul. He accepts its various forms; he condemns none and describes all.' It is a difficult function to perform, and Taine himself sometimes failed to live up to it. But in the immediately succeeding period the academic professional critics, of whom Brunetière was the outstanding type and representative, were having it their own way, fitting all literature into pigeonholes, and dismissing altogether or ignoring those literary manifestations which could not be cut down and trimmed to fit frames made in the eighteenth century. With such critics, however useful for pedagogical purposes, I was not concerned.

I should like, before going on, however, to say more about
Taine, even though, when I reached Paris, his work may be
said to have been done. Before I was born, indeed, in the
Preface to his *Essais de Critique et d'Histoire* he had put forth
ideas, then revolutionary, which are still alive and active
in the world. When we analyse a person or an age or a civilisation, he here explains, we find that all the parts hang together like the organs of a plant or an animal. Each part of
an age, for instance, presupposes all the other parts, so that
it is impossible to alter one without altering the others.
(Here we already have the germinal idea which Spengler
more ambiguously developed half a century later.) Man is
an organised mechanism, a system, not a mere pile of uncon-
nected fragments. All parts are governed by a few forces,
sometimes only one force. (It is a revolutionary idea, perhaps questionable, but it is the idea on which Freud seized.)
To know man it is these forces which have to be separated
out; the source has to be reached. Even though this may
seem to lead to but dry and ugly results, 'it is not my object
to amuse,' Taine declared. 'And if I write coldly,' he added,
'that is my fault; accuse the writer, not the method. For the
forces that govern men are all human. The passions of
history are our own passions, our very substance and being.
The method is the method of all science, from Aristotle down.
I need only to ask pardon for the worker.' He was already
speaking, in the modern spirit, for those daring spirits of
today who still are only pioneers.

Among critics outside these academic ranks, however,
putting aside Taine, it was not easy to find in Paris any of
significance or insight. There was Lemaître, and to him I
could attach no value; it is hard to tell how he could have
exerted any influence. Enough to have seen and heard him.
I went to the Odéon when he gave there an address on Ibsen.
What he said I do not recall, though well I recall the famous
performance of *Ghosts* by Antoine at his own theatre (he was
not yet at the Odéon), before it reached England. Lemaître
was small and fragile and deformed; that was a primary
fact in his spiritual evolution, not the only fact, for in some

men what seems the like physical impediment may result in a robust masculine protest. But in Lemaître, no doubt, it furnished the favourable condition for turning towards literature a man who may have had no native literary gift, and, beyond that, was the foundation on which arose his special critical temperament: that absence of all vigorous affirmation, the weak morbidly sensitive appreciativeness soaked in malicious doubt, the envious attitude of the feeble man in the presence of strength. When I sat in the Odéon, and listened to that gentle voice and witnessed that sly smile, I had ample opportunity to realise how strange it is we are so slow to understand that a man is what his organism is, that it is foolish to judge a critic's work when we have caught no glimpse of the embodied soul that criticism expresses. Yet surely a skilled intelligence might have deduced Lemaître's soul even from his writings. It is easy now; *esprit de coquette* someone has lately called him, always ready to flirt and to befool.

A more representative critic of 1890, though certainly far from a great critic, was Charles Morice, already mentioned, with his *Littérature de Tout à l'Heure*. He had not the solid intellect or the wide culture needed for permanently fine achievement in any direction, and died at length without having made any deep mark. But for his own time he performed a real service. With a mind perhaps too extravagantly sensitive to be well-balanced, he was eagerly receptive to new movements; he could recognise the personalities incarnating new moods of creative art which had not yet penetrated the callous epiderm of conventional opinion; and he knew how to write of what he had so vividly seen. He was a Provençal and had all the emotional excitability of mind we associate with the South, although, as a matter of fact, it is thence that so many grave and deep philosophers have emerged. I think of him as I once saw him on varnishing day at the New Salon, with the tall awkward lanky form, the vulturine head, the waving arms, rushing through the rooms, looking swiftly to right and to left, as though he would seize all that the new men were producing in a single swoop.

I have passed over many memorable experiences of that

long and fruitful summer in Paris, but they would not modify
the total picture. Such was the Paris of 1890. So at all events
it appeared to a youthful and ardent spiritual adventurer
who was privileged to come into contact with many of its
chief representatives, some of them now reckoned among the
immortals.

2

IN THE FOOTSTEPS OF ROUSSEAU

NO ONE who wanders through the land of Savoy can fail to meet the traces of Rousseau's presence. After a time, if we follow up these traces, we begin to perceive a real bond between Rousseau and this region, and not only has the man helped us to understand the land, but the land helps us to understand the man. It is certainly for us today a delightful land, not less so because it is a little outside the modern tourist's usual tracks. Once, it is true, this was the only highroad to Italy; the marks of the civilising presence of the Romans are still visible all along the route, while even today the P. & O. express traveller is borne through Savoy to the Mont Cenis Tunnel on his way to the south. But for the most part the modern tourist may traverse Europe many times in many directions and yet never find himself in Savoy.[1]

It is a land apart, formed by Nature to be the home of an independent State, so that only within the last half-century has it found its final place in the great nationality of France. French it now most certainly is, notwithstanding its old connection with Italy, yet with a certain individuality. Anyone familiar with Provence and other regions of Southern France here finds himself in a different land among a different people. He has left behind not only the Mediterranean olives, but the typical Mediterranean people, the slender, long-headed Ligurian race, nervous and restless and loquacious, a little overweighted by the ancient Roman traditions among which they live. Here we are among people of the round-headed Alpine race, a less artistic but also a less lazy race,

[1] It may be well to point out here that the present essay was first published as far back as November, 1904, in the *Fortnightly Review*, and, though in part revised, I have thought it best to leave it substantially unchanged.

honest, hospitable, industrious, of at least as genuinely French quality as the Provençals, yet with a pleasant tinge of Italian and Spanish elements. Subtle reminiscences of Italy and Spain, sometimes too intangible to describe, frequently meet the traveller who knows those lands. Chambéry, especially, the capital, where the Spaniards once ruled, has still to some extent withstood the tendency to imitate Paris, which has spoilt most French provincial towns. Its narrow and sombre streets, with their quaint and solid architecture, haunt us with reminiscences which seem trans-Pyrenean as well as trans-Alpine. Its women, too, still have a singular distinction and beauty that is not altogether French, or even Savoisian, and we remember how Rousseau, recalling the days when he gave music-lessons to the girls of Chambéry, could not think of one who was not charming, and how Casanova in old age dwelt on his stay here and the amorous escapades that had befallen him. Savoy, however, is less a land of passion than the neighbouring province of Dauphiny, very closely allied in race, to which we may preferably turn to find notable love-stories. No part of France has produced so many tragic dramas of passion as the records of history and private memoirs have revealed during the past three centuries in Grenoble and its neighbourhood; it is scarcely an accident that Stendhal, the acute psychologist of love, was a man of Grenoble, and that Laclos is thought here to have found his characters. The land of Savoy and its people are alike marked rather by graciousness and gentleness than by temperamental ardour or rugged strength; passion here tends to become mystical, as in Jeanne de Chantal and that almost sensuously devout saint who wrote the *Traité de l'Amour de Dieu*.

It is true that Mont Blanc stands on the frontier of Savoy, but the general character of the land is not mountainous; its heights are for the most part variegated and often beautifully coloured hills on which the snow only begins to lie in late autumn or early winter, and their lower slopes are clothed with vineyards. The general aspect of the land is undulating and park-like; its trees are singularly beautiful, in these mild and windless valleys retaining their foliage in every shade of green and crimson and brown until late in November, which in Savoy is sometimes a delightful month. Its lakes, again, Annecy and Bourget, are exquisite haunts of peace; one can well understand how Taine chose for himself a grave that overlooks the one, and how the famous monastery of Hautecombe appropriated the central site on the shores of the other.

The special note of Savoy seems to be a gracious harmony between the land and its people. These park-like stretches undulating afar seem, to the casual glance, left idly to the hands of Nature in her mildest moods; nowhere do we catch sight of those rough edges and ugly scars which mark the progress of Man across the earth's fair surface. Yet at every available point Man has settled himself here, from the higher regions where villages are hidden in gorges, and châlets are scattered over summer pastures, down to warmer, more luxuriant and prosperous districts. In this gracious harmony may be said to lie the peculiar charm of Savoy, its *amenity*, as we may most specifically term it, a quality which exerts a singularly soothing and yet tonic influence on the stranger who wanders hither from less happily situated lands. The qualities of Savoy find their finest representative in one of the greatest of her children, who was at the same time one of the most admirable of saints. François de Sales belonged to an old aristocratic family long settled at Annecy in the very heart of the land. In his serenity and his fervour, his cheerful humanity, his unfailing amenity, François de Sales sums up all Savoy.

We quickly learn to appreciate the qualities of Savoy if we cross its border and enter Switzerland to reach Geneva and the cantons on the opposite side of Lake Leman. One might have supposed that the great lake whose shores are divided so equally between Savoy and Switzerland would have reduced to uniformity the qualities of the peoples who live around it. It is by no means so. The Rhône, which enters one end of the lake and emerges at the other, has served, if not as a racial boundary, at all events as a national and religious frontier of the first importance. When we reach

Geneva, on the very borders of Savoy, we enter the great city — strongly placed on two hills at the point where the Rhône leaves the lake — which was the stronghold of Calvin. Even in the early nineteenth century, with its lofty houses — resembling those of the other great Calvinistic city, Edinburgh — Geneva seemed to Stendhal to look like a prison. Today it has superficially taken on the air of a Swiss Paris, but its neighbours in Catholic Savoy still speak with dismay of the Geneva Sabbath. Nor is it likely that the people of this city will quickly lose the characteristics which caused it to play a part of the first importance in the spiritual history of Europe during three centuries. Joachim du Bellay in the sixteenth century drew a very unattractive picture of the people of Geneva, and even their modern admirers admit the absence of charm. A certain angularity and sharpness of character, an exaggerated *amour-propre*, a jealous pride of citizenship in the 'Protestant Rome,' a lurking tendency to suspicion, an ineradicably bourgeois disposition, a discontent which under varying circumstances may be noble or ignoble — such qualities have not been favourable to the cultivation of art and beauty, though they have here always been associated with a certain fervid intensity, with a singularly penetrating and subtle critical faculty, and a marked devotion to science.

It is interesting to note that these qualities which still survive today are not the characters of any definite race so much as the results of a stringent process of human selection. Calvin and Voltaire, the two greatest representative Protestants of Geneva — so we may fairly call them, unlike as they were in many respects — were in no sense Swiss, since each belonged to remote provinces of France. The Lake of Geneva drained away from France all those elements which could not adapt themselves to the rule of the Church. The people of Geneva thus constituted a peculiarly elect society, on the material side earning its livelihood as tradesmen or artisans, especially as expert watchmakers and jewellers, and on the spiritual side retaining that alert intelligence, the wakeful suspicion and exaggerated egoism, the unconquerable independence, which had been strong enough to break the bonds that tied them to their own people.

Rousseau, like every man of supreme genius, transcends the qualities of the people from whom he sprang. His exquisitely sensitive temperament, his eloquence, his instinctive thirst for beauty were not characteristic of Geneva, yet it is easy to see that fundamentally he belonged to his own city. Even the sensuous elements in his temperament were acute merely because they rested on a basis of perverted sensibility, while the native angularity and suspiciousness of the child of Geneva in his morbidly sensitive temperament at last reached a degree which was sometimes unquestionably insane. He could scarcely have escaped the influence of his native town, for his ancestry — now accurately known — was typically Genevan. We can today trace his descent much better than he could himself — for even his account of his grandfather is confused and incorrect — back to the sixteenth century, and we find it made up in part of refugees — tradesmen, dyers, tanners, more especially watchmakers — from all parts of France, and in part of families of local origin, sometimes of good citizen class, sometimes from among the peasantry. The Rousseaus had reached a certain height of middle-class prosperity three generations earlier than Jean-Jacques, and were now a decaying family, both as regards material well-being and constitutional stamina. From his mother, Susanna Bernard, whom he never knew, Rousseau inherited his refined aptitudes for art and music and literature, while from his restless and eccentric father he derived the nervous irritability of his temperament. There is always an incalculable element in genius, but when we know this ancestry — selected from the most robust and independent middle-class elements of France, mingled with the rustic manual labourers of Lake Leman, whose tough fibres were now half mellowed into sensitive receptiveness — we know all that we can know concerning the hereditary soil which seems so curiously adapted for the nourishment of this unique plant.

In later years, Rousseau declared that Lake Leman is the most beautiful spot in the world. We may well doubt, however, whether that was the impression made on him in child-hood. With children of this temperament nervous sensibility is far too much exercised, too much tortured, by the immediate incidents of daily life to grow receptive to the beauty of Nature. In his early years the child Rousseau was learning the lessons which would later bring him to the feet of Nature, but it is seldom that Nature appears to us in the familiar en-vironment of our early lives. It was in Savoy, and not at Geneva, that Rousseau learnt those secrets which he after-wards imparted to all the world.

When at the age of sixteen the young engraver's apprentice ran away from Geneva into Catholic Savoy, leaving all his friends behind him, he might have been regarded as a fitting inmate for a reformatory training school. The most saga-cious observer could not have divined that here was the man destined to mould the spiritual life of Europe. His heredity indeed was there — but that was not altogether promising — and his exalted nervous sensibility — but that was largely perverted — and for the rest he was without education, without ideals, worse still, he had some of the instincts of the street arab. It was under the influence of a woman that out of this seemingly unpromising material the Rousseau we know developed.

Madame de Warens lives in the memory of those who have but a casual acquaintance with the facts of Rousseau's life solely on account of the laxity of her opinions and practice.[1] It is from her worshipper alone — much as we now know of her from other sources — that we learn this feature of her character, and it is a feature that has its own bearing and weight. But we misunderstand alike the woman and her influence if we concentrate our attention on it. Madame de Warens had not the temperament of strength either in intel-

---

[1] 'Laxity' seems the proper term to use, for Rousseau is doubtless correct when he insists that her benevolence played a larger part here than ardour of tempera-ment. The men she chose for her favours were not brilliant lovers (we cannot regard the author of the *Nouvelle Héloïse* as an exception) and were of lower social rank than herself. She might have said with her eminent contemporary, Ma-demoiselle Gaussin, 'What would you have? It gives them so much pleasure and costs me so little.'

lectual matters or in practical matters, notwithstanding the one bold action of her life, less bold than it looked, in leaving her husband and changing her religion, but like many another woman who achieves personal charm and personal influence, though she could not fight her own way to the sun, she involuntarily radiated on those around her every ray of sunshine that reached her. Ineffective as her conduct of her own life must be admitted to be — a woman who had broken away from a childless home, abandoned her religion, failed in business enterprises, and was one day to die in abject poverty — she combined more or less harmoniously various winning qualities. Her most obvious characteristic was a benevolence of nature too native and reckless to be called a virtue, while the generosity and affectionate sympathy which expended itself on everything that came near her seems never to have exhausted her own sunny cheerfulness and childlike readiness for enjoyment.

Such as she was, Madame de Warens was the first well-bred and cultivated woman with whom the youthful Rousseau had ever been in familiar intercourse. The middle-class feminine society of Geneva was intelligent and capable enough, and how strenuous, not to say priggish, its maidens could be in theological disputation, Casanova has given an amusing example. Madame de Warens was a woman of another nature and another social world. But there was more than this; there was, in a sense, an affinity between her and the youth she took under her protection. On his side, from the first moment he saw her, his habitual constraint and timidity, he tells us, fell from him. On her side, the obvious link of benevolence was, as Rousseau himself explained, reinforced by unused maternal instincts.[1] But below this, on both sides, there was a certain affinity of temperament which could scarcely have been so clear to either as it is to us. Both

[1] When Rousseau refers, as he frequently does, to Madame de Warens as 'Maman,' however, we must not suppose that this necessarily corresponds to the English 'Mamma.' It was the title applied to the mistress of the house when one was familiar with her. As Ritter points out, Voltaire so called his niece (Madame Denis) when she was keeping house for him at Ferney. At the same time, as he came to use it, Rousseau often gave it an intimately affectionate significance.

alike belonged to the same Protestant side of Lake Leman, they had alike lost their mothers at birth, both had abandoned their early faith and had forsaken their homes to seek refuge in the same Catholic land of Savoy. In both cases alike, moreover, this restlessness and instability were clearly associated with a lack of nervous balance. Thus, on her side there was something more than the gratification of benevolent and maternal instincts, and on his side something more than the fascination that a charming woman of the world of twenty-eight can exercise on an untrained youth of sixteen; there was a real and profound affinity.

It is certain that when young Rousseau drifted back from Turin, after the failure of her first attempt to provide for his future, and had been installed in the spare room of her own house at Annecy — 'People may say what they like!' he overheard her remark to the servant — her faith in him withstood every test. Faith was certainly needed. The runaway apprentice from Geneva was awkward, physically undeveloped,[1] short-sighted, slow of speech, ill-mannered, excessively timid. At a much later period, Casanova, who went to see Rousseau, reports that he showed no signs either of personal or intellectual distinction, that he was conspicuously deficient in fine manners, and could not be called *un homme aimable*. It is a portrait by an unsympathetic observer, for Casanova regarded Rousseau as a morbid weakling, but we cannot deny it a considerable element of truth. Throughout his later life, it is true, Rousseau evoked unbounded love and admiration notwithstanding his morbid suspicions, and we may, for instance, recall the affectionate enthusiasm and reverence with which the illegitimate daughter of the Prince de Conti — whose education, down to the minutest details, he had directed — spoke of him in her *Mémoires*. But we have to remember that all these people saw him through the atmosphere created by his fame and the passionate eloquence

[1] When Rousseau's coffin was opened some years ago, Dr. Monod estimated his height (by Rollet's method) as 1.52m., or about 5 feet. It must be remembered that in those days the average height seems to have been somewhat lower than it is now, and Rousseau was not commonly referred to as very short, though he now would be.

of his writings. Madame de Warens had only her own intuitions to rely on, and whatever gleams of genius may have been revealed in the brown eyes of the runaway apprentice, all her intuition was needed to retain faith in so unpromising a subject. It seemed that every effort she made for his advancement failed, and every man of experience whose advice she asked reported unfavourably of the awkward youth whose timidity was apt to rebound to the opposite extreme of insolence and presumption.

Yet she was furnishing the best conditions for his development. As often happens in the case of men of original genius, he was not teachable by direct methods; they struck at once against a hard and impenetrable surface. But to the indirect influences of its environment, such an organism becomes sensitive, alive, absorbent; and Madame de Warens provided precisely the influences which Rousseau needed. When he met her his education, not only his moral and emotional training, but even his training in intellectual discipline — for his development was extraordinarily slow — can scarcely be said to have begun. When he left her, more than ten years later, he had received not merely his initiation in the life of sentiment, but in these peaceful surroundings he was able to complete his intellectual and moral apprenticeship. Though ten years more were to pass before, at the age of forty, the moment of inspiration came, he was already prepared to take his place among the teachers of Europe.[1]

There was another educational influence of the first significance which Rousseau experienced to the utmost in Savoy, and that was the influence of scenery. This semi-Alpine land, with its gentle elevations and deep gorges, its varied and delicately tinted vegetation, its streams and torrents and cascades, is to the modern man a land of perpetual charm. But in the eighteenth century, though it lay on the highroad to Italy traversed by all the ' men of taste,' it attracted no attention; it was regarded with something of the horror which all felt

[1] I do not enter into the details of Rousseau's life and his numerous escapades during the years he was in touch with Madame de Warens. They are well dealt with in the light of recent investigation by Mr. A. L. Sells in his excellent *Early Life and Adventures of J. J. Rousseau* (1929).

for the Alps. The medieval dread of Nature was breaking up in the region of ideas, but still persisted in relation to scenery. Even the most sensitive and poetic individuals were for the most part children of their age in this matter. Gray spoke with repulsion of the most exquisite landscapes, and Goldsmith's enthusiasm for scenery only burst forth in the flower gardens of Holland. The versatile and observant Casanova, who knew all Europe, said nothing of its natural aspects; he stayed in one of the most happily situated of the valleys of Savoy, and refers to it as a *vilain endroit*. It would, indeed, be a mistake to suppose that all were equally insensitive. But the love of untamed Nature, if it existed, remained, on the whole, an inarticulate love, and even when articulate, it had never modified the sensibilities of men generally. For us today, when we are tired or sad, natural scenery is as the soothing contact of healing waters. But before the middle of the eighteenth century no Moses had yet struck the rock that seemed so desolate, and no healing waters had gushed forth.

Rousseau had been born by Lake Leman, but he was a city child, whose chief outlook had been onto the blank grey walls of the lofty houses of Geneva. His flight into Savoy involved a change in this respect which was of the first importance in its influence on his life. At Annecy his window in Madame de Warens's house looked out over a stream and a garden towards the open country, and her charm and the spring's became, as he said, deliciously confused in his mind. His walking tour to Turin, about this time, occurring at perhaps the happiest moment of his life, doubtless had its weight in bringing to consciousness that secret of the emotional significance of Nature which he had discovered, and was afterwards to communicate. All the treasures of Savoy were unfolded before him during that happy week of exaltation, when he felt himself following in the path of Hannibal on the road to Italy, and this ever-changing scene of delight, these perpetual hills and valleys and rocky streams and shady orchards, seemed to him the fitting home of a life of leisurely charm, joyous and yet peaceful, voluptuous and yet simple. His sensitive organism responded at once beneath the influence of Nature, as beneath that of the woman whose temperament was so fitted to his own. To the men of that period only a plain seemed beautiful. 'Never has a land of plains, however beautiful it may be, seemed beautiful in my eyes,' wrote Rousseau, bringing a new sensation into literature, if not into life. 'I need torrents, rocks, pines, dark forests, mountains, rough paths to climb, by precipices that fill me with fear.' It was the country which he found in perfection around Chambéry, and it was the country he soon found the best stimulus to work. 'I have never been able to do anything with a pen in my hand in front of a table and paper; I write in my brain as I walk among rocks or in woods.' This child of an industrious race of craftsmen and peasants needed the auto-intoxication of bodily activity in order to attain intellectual activity. In the open country, on the mountains, enjoying the simple fare and the freedom of little inns, afar from everything that recalled the miseries of daily life, the people and the things that imposed constraint and timidity, he inhaled a new power, audacity, and resolution. The ineffective Jean-Jacques, escaping from the good-natured ridicule of bourgeois society, would soon speak with the authority of an apostle.

These, then, were the great formative and educative influences in the life and work of Rousseau: a highly intelligent and cultivated woman, and the consoling and inspiring scenery of the happy land of Savoy. We have to note one other influence which was distinctly beneficial and emancipating in its moral effects. This was an illness, more or less persistent in its effects, from which he suffered at the age of twenty-four. The symptoms are obscure, and might best be described as largely of the nature of what was later vaguely termed neurasthenia, associated with slight chronic inflammation of the ear,[1] though it seemed to him at the time that the termination would be fatal. But, as he tells us, 'I only began to live when I looked upon myself as dead.' His conceptions of life were ennobled and deepened, he began to formulate his re-

[1] This is substantially the opinion of Régis. Courtade, in his study of Rousseau's partial deafness, considers that his troubles were due to Ménière's Disease, the same disorder from which it is now supposed that Swift suffered.

ligious ideas (being helped herein by Madame de Warens, he said, more than by all the theologians), and the crudities and meannesses which had marked his unamiable adolescence began to fall away. His restless and irritable temperament grew calm, and with the prospect of speedy death before his eyes he was even better able to give himself up to the enjoyment of the moment. Spring came, and with surprise he found himself still alive; it seemed to him, indeed, that he had risen again in Paradise when he was carried into the country, where he was never ill, to his beloved haunt at Les Charmettes.

It was at this pleasant spot on the outskirts of Chambéry, in the heart of Savoy — whither he came every year with the first nightingales, only to go when the leaves in the still atmosphere had taken on their deep and lovely autumn tints — that Rousseau received the final seal of his mission. Here he spent his happiest years, the years of his early manhood, carrying on that education of himself which was after, in *Emile*, to make him one of the world's great educationalists, and discovering and developing the mysterious gift of words. When in old age he wrote the *Confessions*, his memory still retained the impression of the period he had spent in this spot, a period of work and of laziness, sometimes with the spade, and always with a book, in garden and orchard and vineyard and among the hills, alone or with his beloved companion, who was, he said, mother and friend and mistress all in one. It was those 'peaceful but brief moments,' he wrote towards the end of his life, 'which give me the right to say I have lived.' [1]

---

[1] Much doubt has been thrown on the dates in Rousseau's account of his Charmettes experience. His memory certainly often played him false, and some say, relying on a *bail* dated 6th July, 1738, that that must have been the year that Rousseau was there, and not, as he says, 1736; others would admit 1736, though not at Les Charmettes, but some other property. Albert Schinz and Isabel Lawrence in a brief and precise article (*Revue d'Histoire Littéraire*, 1928) put forward a theory which seemed to accord with the psychological facts and dispose of the documentary objection. They stated that it is true Madame de Warens in 1738 rented the Charmettes *domaine* for purposes of exploitation, but the proprietor M. Noeray (Rousseau calls him Noiret), being an officer, was often absent, and it was easy for Madame de Warens, with Rousseau in poor health, to have

The little valley of Les Charmettes, though close to Chambéry, is as solitary and retired, Rousseau remarks, as though a hundred leagues away from the city. We may say the same today as we climb the gradual ascent of the lonely road, noting the stream and the trees and the scattered dwellings as Rousseau described them. Nothing seems to be changed. The little house that we seek stands on its little terrace, above the road, on the slope of the hill; we push open the iron gate, ascend a few steps to a small grass plot, and pull the chain of a bell suspended beside the door, and the loud clang that follows leaves the silence of this peaceful spot unruffled. Again we ring, and at length a woman hurries down from a farm building beyond, and draws out the doorkey from under the ivy that covers the gatepost. We enter the vestibule, with its broad flight of stone steps leading to the single storey above, turn to the right into the large square kitchen and dining-room, with its floor of red tiles and its ancient sideboards, and pass on into the salon, a smaller oblong room, still bearing about it an air of faded antique coquetry, the seal of the eighteenth century, while one notes the little *clavecin* that now scarcely responds to the touch, the faintly traced paintings of flowers, such as our great-grandmothers executed, over the doors and windows, the mirrors, the pictures. A door opens from the salon on this side of the house onto the terrace and into the garden, and beyond this the vineyard spreads along the faint slope of the hill. We return to the broad staircase of the small dwelling, and ascend, to find on the right the narrow room which was Rousseau's, with its little alcove, while in front the landing — which is still, as it was for Madame de Warens, a tiny oratory — leads into her bedroom, with its wooden floor eaten by age. In one corner is a bureau, with old music and books flung carelessly into it, one almost believes by Madame de Warens

rented the *house* alone at an earlier date, without *bail*, for a few weeks. In 1737, a M. Renauld rented the *domaine* which need not have prevented Madame de Warens staying in the house. Then later she rented a neighbouring farm to exploit, and finally exchanged it in 1738 for Les Charmettes. Still more recently, however, in the light of freshly discovered documents, André Monglond (*Jeunesses*, p. 29) would reject this theory and explanation.

herself. In another corner is the little bed, with its ancient canopy, and its worn pink-lined coverlet slowly falling to pieces. A decayed charm still seems to hang about the room, and in one respect at all events it has lost nothing; from its windows we gaze across the red roofs of Chambéry below, towards the green slope, diversified by grey cliffs, of the mountains beyond, not too near to oppress, not too far to lose the beauty of their various colouring and contour. No scene of more peaceful and soothing enchantment could be imagined as we look upon it from these windows, while the sunset casts the magic of its reflection northwards over the already enchanted hills; we realise that here, as nowhere else, we enter into communion with the great apostle of Nature whose novitiate was spent in the solitude *à deux* of this hermitage. The house altogether, embalmed as it is in the dust of its own natural decay, has about it an atmosphere in which ghosts may move. No ghosts ever haunt our well-kept English show places, from which, with the energy of our race, we carefully scrape off all the precious patina of antiquity. But this spot is still haunted, and here the careless, vivacious little blue-eyed woman, and the youth whose genius has made her immortal, alike become, for the first time, real persons.[1]

Les Charmettes is a shrine from which the glory has departed. Rousseau no longer arouses our passionate enthusiasm. Once he was part of a volcanic eruption which covered Europe. Now his ideas and his books leave us calm, often cold. Where our forefathers saw burning lava we only find scoriae. Yet for the historian of morals Rousseau must always remain a personality of the first significance, the Colum-

---

[1] I here leave untouched the record of the ineffaceable impression made upon me when I walked out from Chambéry to Les Charmettes with my wife on a beautiful day towards the end of October, 1902. Since then the place has become State property in the charge of a curator and is a sort of Museum. What its condition now is I do not know, but in the eyes of M. Maurice Bedel it is very unsatisfactory. In an Open Letter to the curator (*Nouvelles Littéraires*, 7 May, 1932) he describes the house as neglected and going to ruin, the old bed cover falling to rags, the window fastenings broken, the garden neglected, and the petticoats of the woman in charge hanging there to dry, rubbish lying about, while a stream of visitors arrive in all sorts of vehicles. The curator subsequently sought to repel these charges, so far as they concerned him.

bus of a new emotional world. His figure is dimmed to us by the more vivid figures of those to whom he showed the way, of Byron and Shelley and Madame de Staël, who all carried further the movement he had initiated, and were all associated with the lake that washes his native city and his beloved land of Savoy, while Wordsworth, among his own lakes and in a land somewhat akin to Savoy, carried the same movement to its ultimate point. These prophets of Nature, with their two regions of hill and lake, will always occupy a place of chief importance in the history of European sentiment. In this gracious land of Savoy it is worth while, for a few moments, to trace the footsteps of the morbid and suffering man who was their leader.

3

PERHAPS there is no woman of the eighteenth century whom we know so well by name and yet differ about so widely. Indeed among all the notable figures of that century few, if any, have been discussed with so much confidence, on so slender a basis of facts. There is no doubt about her significance. She is the woman who meant more than any other for the man whom it is possible to regard as the chief spiritual force of modern times. It is of minor significance that she also, more than any other, may be regarded as the original of the heroine of *La Nouvelle Héloïse*, a novel, however little read and little readable now, which once moved the world of readers as no other novel has ever done, and may, indeed, still be said to live in the writings of novelists who perhaps never heard of it. We can never forget how Madame de Warens initiated into love and life the youthful Rousseau who was himself to become the initiator of coming generations.

If we realise all that Rousseau stands for in our world — whether for good or, as so many think, for evil — we need to know, as precisely as possible, what it was he met at that spot at Annecy which, even in old age, he still desired to see surrounded with railings of gold, and only to be approached on their knees by those who revere the monuments of human salvation. If we can imagine Rousseau looking down on earth today, one may well suppose that it is not the extent of his fame, or his infamy, in the world that touches him but the fulfilment of that extravagant wish, exactly two centuries after the event (in 1928), in the delicately wrought and gilded iron-work which now encloses what is judged to have been that spot. Indeed, it records a memorable event in

MADAME DE WARENS

our civilisation, if, as Michelet put it, Rousseau's genius was born of Madame de Warens.

Yet, even for Rousseau, this woman was evidently always something of a mystery. He says much that is in her favour, much that is not; we cannot safely estimate her from his narrative. She was not only a person of peculiar temperament, but the first woman of breeding and culture and social attraction with whom he had come into intimate contact. He was evidently dazzled from the first moment when the brilliant fair-haired and blue-eyed figure so graciously received the runaway youth in a foreign land. It may well be that he never came to see her in any clear light, while it is certain that at some points, intentionally as well as unintentionally, she misled him. Today we know much more about her than Rousseau could know, and she has been the subject of numerous volumes. Yet still she appears a different person to different investigators. For some she is an enlightened religious mystic, for others a mean superstitious little creature with an ill-regulated imagination; for some almost an erotomaniac, for others, on the contrary, a typical example of sexual anaesthesia. Even in discrepant aspects of character there may be elements of truth. But considerable discrimination is needed if we are to bring out a really harmonious picture from the data now accumulated around this woman.

The chief authorities for our new knowledge of Madame de Warens are a few men of letters and research in Switzerland and in Savoy, more especially De Montet as regards her early life in the Vaud country, Mugnier concerning her later life in Savoy, Eugène Ritter for her religious opinions and their sources; while more recently Benedetto from the Italian side has gone over the field in detail in a less friendly and somewhat debunking spirit, though even he at the end admits that, after all, there was real love in Rousseau's transfiguration of Madame de Warens, and that it was she, above all others he loved or was loved by, whom Rousseau made the ideal woman.

Françoise-Louise de la Tour belonged to the aristocratic family who possessed Châtelard with its picturesque old castle on the hillside near Vevey, a familiar sight to the foreign colony now dwelling near by at Montreux and Clarens. She was born in March, 1699, the second of three children and the only survivor. Her mother died in childbirth when Françoise was still an infant, and she was sent to her father's two sisters who lived at Le Basset close by, old maids who, especially the elder, became devoted to the child, and fully took a mother's place. Her father married again and she remained with her aunts to the age of ten.

Many of us today are familiar with the Lake of Geneva's stretch of shore between Vevey and Chillon. It long since grew civilised and commonplace. Along the main road are fashionable shops and crowds of tourists from many lands; even when we look up at the solemn Alps we find them dotted with big hotels. Yet it is a pleasant spot still, and with an abstracting imagination we can picture it as it was a century and more ago when the great champions and apostles of the new Romantic Movement — Byron and Shelley, Victor Hugo and George Sand, with the rest — came hither as pilgrims to the region whence their inspiration sprang. We may even be able to evoke the vision of what was seen here, a century still earlier, when the man from whom that inspiration chiefly emanated came on this scene to concentrate there his enthusiasm. It was in a delicious corner of that district that Françoise spent her early life. An undulating tableland on the sloping heights above the Clarens Bay was the site of the little estate.[1] This tableland is an oasis of greenery amid surrounding vineyards, with fine trees and glimpses of the great lake below the gracious descent of the green slopes, and behind, the majestic circle of the mountains which are the background to its limpid waters. The house, called Le Basset, was, though comfortable, a rather humble dwelling with a wooden gallery outside onto which the doors and windows of the upper floor opened, as one may still see in old houses in that region. There yet remain a few of the splendid chestnuts which once formed a wood called 'le bosquet de

[1] I have not seen it and the crumbling house disappeared nearly half a century ago, but I follow the description of de Montet who saw it just before.

Clarens,' celebrated by Rousseau in the *Nouvelle Héloïse*, and now often called 'le bosquet de Julie.' Madame de Warens in character, tastes, and feelings, corresponds to Julie, although the heroine of the novel lived on a somewhat more magnificent scale. This was so not only because the scenes of the real girl's life had been passed through an exalted imagination but also because Madame de Warens herself was never absolutely accurate regarding the details of the past, always willing to magnify events and to leave out of account anything unfavourable to herself. It is a reticence which, like much else in her life, has not in the end proved altogether wise; for, as we shall see, it led Rousseau, by trusting to his imagination or to gossip, to defame unduly the woman to whom he owed so much and whom he so sincerely worshipped.

We know, however, all the essential facts of young Françoise's life, and it is not difficult to reconstruct. At that time it was usual for the rural aristocracy to live in this simple fashion and they were not on that account the less considered. Françoise seems to have been a wild and indocile child who was rather spoilt by her aunts, doubtless charmed by her pretty face, her precociously alert intelligence, and that spirit of independence which was from the first a note of her character. But during the winter months the aunts occupied themselves with her education and not without success. When she was nine years old, her father's new wife, in a letter still extant, tells of the progress Françoise has made in household and other affairs under her aunts' care, 'especially the elder who has a wonderful gift of education. Just imagine! She has so well fixed Françoise's wildness that she has already read all the books at Le Basset!' We discern in the child the mixed traits of the woman.

But Françoise's 'wildness' was scarcely 'fixed,' in spite of her love for her aunts. They were necessarily much absorbed in the care of the estate, and the child had ample opportunities to cultivate her refractory spirit of independence among the young villagers over whom she could play the mistress. When she was ten one of the aunts died and she was brought to the paternal home. On her father's death shortly after, her stepmother decided that it would be best to send her to school at Lausanne. Here no doubt she acquired various accomplishments, though she never resigned herself to learn how to spell correctly, scarcely indeed a general accomplishment then, and difficult for many now. When at fourteen her education was considered complete, it seems to have been felt that she still needed to be kept under control and a husband was speedily found for her.

At this point, however, some reference must be made to what may well be regarded as an important early influence. The importance has by some been exaggerated and by others denied. Yet it has significance, and must not be passed over.

The ladies of Le Basset were on intimate terms with Magny, an old man who enjoyed a reverential esteem in the Pays de Vaud, although he was the leader there of the pietistic movement, by no means an orthodox position in a strictly Calvinistic land. Magny was in touch with the German mystical movement of that day which was bringing a new freedom and emotional depth into religion. An indifference to forms, a belief in intuition and impulse, a tendency to sum up the doctrines of religion in Saint Augustine's formula: 'Love, and do what you like' — such were the characteristics of the new movement. They could not but appeal to a girl of Françoise's temperament. In the 'Confessions of a beautiful soul' in *Wilhelm Meister*, Goethe recorded the inner life of a woman who had fallen under the influence of Moravian pietism, and like the woman of the 'beautiful soul,' Madame de Warens could have said: 'Nothing appears to me in the form of a law; it is an impulse that leads me; I follow my feelings and know as little of restraint as of repentance.' But the 'beautiful soul' added that the impulse that led her always led her right, and that Madame could scarcely have ventured to claim; the elements of her nature were less happily tempered.[1]

---

[2] Benedetto is rather sceptical of the genuine nature of Madame de Warens's religious tendencies, but P. M. Masson who has more recently dealt with the subject with full knowledge in his valuable work, *La Formation Religieux de Rousseau* (1916), sees no good reasons for doubt.

To have been bathed in this atmosphere before her feelings had been moulded into any rigid shape cannot but have affected the youthful Françoise. Her pietism remained rudimentary, but it so genuinely harmonised with her own temperament that she may never have realised how much she owed to Magny. It is impossible not to attach weight to her early association with him. It was so close that at the age of fourteen he acted as her tutor and then became her trustee. Later he felt entitled to behave as her spiritual guardian and would write to admonish her from time to time. On one such occasion she replied: 'I do things with an indifference which sometimes surprises me.'

Her vague pietism certainly never became deep or definite, and it would seem that she never mentioned Magny's name to Rousseau. Yet the religious ideas she transmitted to the youthful Jean-Jacques were such as she may well have absorbed from her early teacher. Together, certainly, with other influences, it is these German religious ideas, filtered first through Magny and then through Madame de Warens, which reappear glorified in the *Vicaire Savoyard*, and elsewhere in Rousseau's writings, as a mighty force which was to sweep away the cold deism of that age and almost to become a part of the modern spirit.

However uncertain her religious spirit, Françoise de la Tour had an eager thirst for knowledge, hardly satisfied by the modicum of instruction in which a girl's education consisted, and she gratified this by devouring the medical and natural history books which had belonged to her grandfather, a doctor. Thus she acquired the taste for concocting drugs and for amateur doctoring which never left her and at one time induced her to urge Rousseau to become a doctor, without effect, though he acquired a love for botanising. She later secured her husband's copy of Bayle's famous *Dictionary*, an extensive work, which dealt with the whole sphere of knowledge in a free-spirited and entertaining manner, and it became her chief intellectual pleasure. For housewifely duties and domestic economy, all the efforts of aunts and stepmother could impart no aptitude; that was one chief source of the misfortunes she was plunged into throughout life.

Even at the age of fourteen, before her marriage, Françoise de la Tour was famed in the neighbourhood of Vevey for her gay and independent spirit, as well (so at least it was reported) as for the lively parties she presided over, with games and music and dancing. She associated much, indeed, with the peasant girls of the neighbourhood; it was thus she acquired, and, as we know, retained, the love of being surrounded by inferiors, and a delight in their admiration and subservience. She certainly caused some anxiety to the family. That may have been the reason why she was put under Magny's care. That also may have been why in 1713, when still only fourteen, a husband was found for her. There could be no difficulty over that, for not only was Françoise a brilliant and seductive personality, but she could bring her husband a substantial dowry, and Magny (when the two previous trustees disagreed over the marriage settlement) was appointed sole trustee.

The husband was a man of importance, and of solid if not exactly high character; he always possessed the esteem of his fellow-citizens who placed him in numerous positions of local responsibility, and for a short time he was appointed tutor to a young German prince, which indicates that he was a man of some culture, as is also indicated by his purchase of Bayle's expensive *Dictionary* and by the style of his letters.

This Captain Sébastien-Isaac de Loys was of good family and had been a soldier serving in Sweden and elsewhere. We know him as De Warens (sometimes De Vuarens) from the little village of which he possessed the lordship for fifteen years when he sold it. Madame de Warens claimed the title of 'Baroness,' and sometimes attributed the title of 'Baron' to her father, incorrectly, though he was of noble family; all she was entitled to be called was 'Dame de Warens,' and that not after the property had been disposed of. In Rousseau's famous novel the petty lordship of Warens is magnified into the barony of D'Etanges and little Chailly figures as the domain of Clarens.

The young wife was twenty years younger than her husband who certainly had a far greater influence in moulding her ideas than she led Rousseau to suspect. In some respects he admirably complemented her character, for he possessed all the stability, prudence, and common-sense which she lacked. Consciously or unconsciously, also, he cannot but have carried further an education which hitherto had been rather elementary and uneven. But in other respects, as Benedetto has pointed out, his character has sometimes been too highly rated by biographers, and he may even have fostered the young girl's defects. There are underlying elements of coarseness and vulgarity discernible in his conduct, and a tendency to moral indifference rather similar to his wife's. If Magny had preached freedom on the spiritual plane, De Warens scarcely had strict principles on the intellectual and moral planes. Bayle and Saint-Evremond, the writers in whom, certainly first by her husband's guidance, Madame delighted, could easily be associated with an attitude of refined and sceptical laxity. Thus the partners suited each other and lived for some time in harmony. They settled at Vevey where many French Huguenots had settled after the Revocation of the Edict of Nantes, and spent the autumn at Chailly — the vine district which was part of the bride's dowry — in order to oversee the grape harvest.

Her husband was violently in love with his young bride who was already growing into that early maturity of which she was to preserve the fresh bloom so long. We do not need to rely on Rousseau for the description of her charm, there is confirmation from independent sources. We hear especially of her beautiful blue eyes and dazzling complexion and fair hair (the *cheveux cendrés* so much admired in France) which she knew how to dress piquantly. She was short rather than tall and inclined to be a little too plump. Her voice was musical (they called it 'argentine') and she possessed a spirit of gaiety, of radiant vivacity. We hear from the first of her gracious air with strangers, and ready adaptability, the charm that won the boy Rousseau's heart from the first moment he met her in Annecy. Even Benedetto, the least sympathetic of her biographers, admits her 'sovereign talent of fascination.'

It is in 1715, when still but a girl of sixteen, that Madame first steps into public life and at once clearly reveals herself. By marriage she had lost her rights of citizenship at Vevey, and her husband possessed no such rights there; consequently she was unable to sell her wine in the town, for that was a privilege reserved to legalised citizens. She induced her husband to apply for these rights. But in the meantime, without waiting for the results of the application — and probably without consulting her husband, whose conduct as a citizen was always correct — she forthwith began to sell her wine in the town. It is an episode characteristic of the woman's conduct throughout life. Her eager impetuosity could never wait for events to ripen; her plans must be carried out at once, recklessly, even, if need be, unscrupulously. The results, of course, were not usually happy. They were not so on the present occasion. The town council, which would certainly have granted the desired privilege, felt called upon to reprimand M. de Warens and to threaten more severe measures. Young Madame's pride was hurt, all the more, doubtless, because she was in the wrong. Feeling her social position shaken, she agreed to an old wish of her husband to settle at Lausanne — persuading him, however, first to secure the Vevey citizenship — in the course of 1718. De Warens, being a native of Lausanne, was received with distinction. But living proved expensive there — as, in Madame de Warens's experience, indeed, it proved everywhere — and she persuaded her husband to secure further resources from his father. This led to quarrels and unpleasantness, and as Madame felt no attachment to Lausanne, they returned to Vevey where her husband received an official position, and the wife distinguished herself by her generosity and philanthropy.

At this point we have to consider a difficult and delicate question. Rousseau states definitely in the *Confessions* that young Madame de Warens was seduced by a certain M. de Tavel, who to effect his object had first persuaded her that morality and modesty were merely conventions, and that she afterwards, 'it is said,' became the mistress of a Swiss minister, one Perret. Both De Montet and Mugnier throw doubt on this statement, though Benedetto thinks it possible on the ground that De Tavel seems certainly to have been on friendly relations with the young wife. The question arises: How did Rousseau know? In after years he went to Vevey and the neighbourhood; during his stay there he associated mainly with the society that met in the parlours of small inns, and while such gossip as he might hear there concerning a woman who had abandoned both her husband and her religion would certainly be scandalous, it would certainly also be worthless. It is known that up even to her final departure from Switzerland Madame de Warens enjoyed the highest consideration, and as a rigid puritanical inquisition then ruled at Vevey this could not have been possible had anything been publicly known of such episodes as Rousseau tells of, for in that case she would have been called before the bar of the Consistory. Her husband, in the end, had much fault to find — with her fondness for industrial enterprises, her extravagant generosity, the vanity that led her into exaggeration and falsehood, her independence and dislike of advice, her leaning to pietism, the ease with which she made acquaintance with people who flattered her, he even called her at last 'an accomplished comedian' — but he never hinted that he suspected her of infidelity. If, therefore, rumours of immorality afterwards gathered around the name of the apostate and fugitive, they could scarcely have proceeded from any reliable source.

We must fall back on the supposition that Rousseau's statements are founded on the confidences of Madame de Warens herself. But here we have to remember the unquestionable fact, clearly to be seen in the *Confessions*, that, even with Rousseau, Madame de Warens was never communicative regarding those matters of her personal life, however remote, which might show her in an unfavourable light. It must be added that neither De Tavel nor Perret are unknown persons; the former was a colonel, an old friend of De Warens, but very seldom at Vevey, though a native of that place; the latter was a clergyman, twenty-five years older than Madame de Warens, and a man of high position and unspotted reputation.

It seems most reasonable to conclude that Rousseau's statements must be regarded as an effort of constructive imagination founded on slight data which seemed to him sufficient basis for an episode enabling him to explain Madame de Warens's character, but which, in the light of our further knowledge today, cannot be unreservedly accepted. It is probable enough that De Tavel on his visits to Vevey brought a knowledge of the new revolutionary moral maxims of Paris which the intelligent and inquisitive young woman was interested to learn, and that eventually these maxims mingled with the pietistic teaching of Magny — in a way that venerable teacher would have been far from approving — to prepare her for that indifference for conventions which her conduct subsequently showed. But that De Tavel sought to apply these maxims may well have been an ingenious supposition by which Rousseau supplemented the reticence of his informant. Had De Tavel been the cynical libertine which Rousseau's statements imply, his intimate friend, De Warens, would scarcely have regarded him as a fit associate for his wife. We know that in several cases Rousseau has, on altogether inadequate grounds, attributed acts of early misconduct to other people, including the original of the Vicaire Savoyard, whom he highly esteemed, and it must not unduly surprise us that he has done so in the case of Madame de Warens. That he himself was a little uncertain about his statement as to De Tavel is suggested by the fact that he coupled it with the quite wanton rumour about Perret.

De Tavel has so often served, even in the hands of the most serious historians, as a stock example of the depravity of the eighteenth century, that it is time to insist that the one episode by which his name survives is probably a legend. Statements of the kind which Rousseau attributed to De Tavel were often made during the eighteenth century by philosophers in the seclusion of their studies; one may be permitted to doubt whether they proved dangerous even in that century. 'One may be amused by a lover's wit,' remarks Madame de Lursay in Crébillon's *Egarements du Coeur* a few years later, 'but it is not that which proves seductive; it is his embarrassment, the difficulty he finds in expressing himself, the confusion in his speech — that is what makes him dangerous!'

We now reach the circumstances that led up to the most decisive episode in the life of Madame de Warens — her abandonment of her home and her religion. In 1724 a young Frenchman, Elie Laffon, son of a refugee French Protestant minister, had arrived at Vevey, and, in accordance with the industrial traditions of the Huguenots, he proposed to start a factory of silk stockings. Madame de Warens, who had once been a pupil of Laffon's sister, soon heard of the scheme and entered into it with enthusiasm. She was, as we know, attracted to business enterprises at an early age, and remained so to the end, the ardour of her commercial scheming always rendered more acute by her continual lack of money. Laffon needed assistance and capital, and without asking advice of her husband Madame engaged herself to take control of the whole business. De Warens opposed the scheme from the first, but his wife's influence over him was still great; she induced him, against his own better judgment, to borrow money in all directions and to make many sacrifices.

It is needless to follow the history of the silk stocking factory, now known in all its details; the issue could not be doubtful. Madame had no real business capacity, and she even appropriated some of the money obtained for the factory to her own personal uses; Laffon with equally little business capacity seems to have followed her example. Things went from bad to worse, but Madame was too proud to confess failure. At last the strain began to affect her nerves. In 1725 she had to go across the lake to Aix-les-Bains, for treatment and distraction.

It was a fateful visit. She felt, in passing from Switzerland to Savoy — though Gray's letters show that this was by no means the universal sentiment even at that time — as still today we feel in some degree, a delightful sense of contrast between the asperity of the one land and its people and the larger and more cheerful atmosphere of the other. Aix, as we learn from Casanova's account of his stay there, was then on a humble scale what it has since become on a more magnificent and cosmopolitan scale, a region supremely well fitted to be the haunt of pleasure-seeker and health-seeker alike, and Madame de Warens, with her over-sanguine and volatile temperament, here soon recovered. She met during her stay a certain Madame de Bonnevaux, a connection of her husband, who belonged to Savoy and was a Catholic; by her she was taken to Chambéry for the first time, and Madame de Bonnevaux would not have failed to make her realise how different was the tolerant Catholicism of Savoy from the austere Calvinism of the Vaud country. It is not necessary to suppose that at this moment Madame de Warens conceived the idea of flight, but when again at home she could not help knowing that a more delightful and congenial land lay on the other side of the lake, and when the stress of life became unbearable that land appeared as a harbour of refuge. She was not so much converted to Catholicism as to the religion of Savoy, and her husband doubtless felt this when in later years he used to refer to his divorced wife as 'la Savoyarde.' On reaching Vevey she openly declared how charmed she was with Savoy and how disgusted with the Pays de Vaud. The almost hopeless confusion into which she had plunged her affairs furnished ample cause for such disgust. The strain of pretending to her husband and her acquaintances that all was going well, and nothing now needed but a little more capital, became more severe than ever.

In the spring of 1726 she realised that the crash was approaching. Her pride would still not allow her to confess even to her husband, or to humiliate herself in the public eye. She preferred a secret flight — although that placed her husband in a much worse financial position than if she had stayed beside him — and with more or less certain knowledge of honours and pensions bestowed by the King of Sardinia on distinguished Swiss converts to Catholicism she decided to cross the lake for ever. Having persuaded a doctor that she needed to visit the baths at Amphion in Savoy, she collected together as much furniture, linen, and plate as possible, together with the goods and money remaining at the factory, and had them conveyed to the boat; she always carried so much luggage when she travelled that this excited no notice. Her husband saw her off, one day in July, when accompanied by a servant-maid she crossed the lake and went direct to Evian, where the King was then residing. At the earliest possible moment, when the King was going to Mass with a few of his lords and Bishop Bernex of Annecy, she seized the prelate's cassock and falling on her knees said: '*In manus tuas, Domine, commendo spirituum meum.*' The Bishop raised her up and after Mass had a long conversation with her in his rooms. This time her plans had come off. She had left Vevey behind with all its torturing worries; her conversion was effected; she was being treated with distinction, soon to receive a pension, while the Bishop was warmly congratulated on the brilliant conquest he had made for the Church.

The matter has sometimes been left at that. But, as Benedetto has specially sought to make clear, there is more to be said. The anxiety on the part of the government of Savoy to regain both the old civil and ecclesiastical authority over Geneva led King and Bishop to work together to gain influential converts and then undertake to reward them, at the same time, if possible, using them. Madame de Warens appeared an important convert and a general sensation was caused by her capture. But, even when we bear that in mind, the pension awarded her seems extravagant. It was larger even than the fee received by a senator.

If the terms of the decree conferring the pension are looked into, it would appear that it was really not so much a pension as a salary and that it involved duties. These, there is reason to believe, were twofold, on the one hand to further the work of effecting conversions among fugitive Swiss immigrants from across the lake (which throws a light on her reception of the boy Rousseau), and on the other hand to act, when required, as a political spy, a position for which her brilliant social qualities seemed to fit her.

The conversion may not be entirely explained on merely prudential grounds. Madame de Warens was not always guided by prudential considerations and the step she had taken cost her anguish and sleepless nights. It was true that she had not been a convinced Calvinist; her religious beliefs, new and old, seem loosely held. Her old friend Magny came to see her shortly after her conversion, and declared on his return, to the astonishment of everyone, that he was entirely at rest in regard to her spiritual state; the testimony may be less to the credit of her genuine religious belief and genuine sincerity than to the skill her husband attributed to her as a comedian.[1] The good Magny was seventy-six years of age, and no doubt eager to think well of his clever and vivacious young pupil. Perhaps the remorse which she found it hard to stifle had reference more to the husband she had abandoned than to the religion she had exchanged. There had indeed been no children of the union, though two children had been adopted, but it could scarcely be said that the marriage was altogether unhappy; the couple had drifted apart simply because the husband, who had begun by idolising his wife and allowing her to rule his actions, was now realising the abyss into which her impetuous recklessness, her vanity, and her business incapacity, had plunged him, while she, on her side, had no real sympathy with his strict and, as it seemed to her, narrow conceptions of honour and duty.

Her husband paid her two visits in Savoy. At the first visit, to Evian, immediately after her conversion, she refrained from mentioning that episode. She asked him to send her his copy of Bayle's *Dictionary*,[2] and with it his own English gold-headed cane to use when she went out; these com-

---

[1] But it must be remembered, as Masson points out, not only that Magny accepted the inner promptings of the Holy Spirit as valid, but that there were Catholic tendencies in his pietism.

[2] It is significant of her tolerant religious spirit that even at this moment of conversion she desired to possess this famous masterpiece of scepticism.

missions he fulfilled. Once more he came to see her at the Convent of the Visitation at Annecy. She received him in bed, he wrote, to hide her confusion, and he was himself so overcome that at first he could not speak. When he began to talk of the fatal step which, as he now knew, she had taken, she pointed to a corner of the room, and on raising the tapestry he saw a little cupboard with an opening into the cloisters, and they spoke in whispers as they amicably settled their affairs before parting for ever. He noted with surprise, however, as he afterwards wrote, the slight importance which she seemed to attach to the forms of religion, the cavalier manner in which she treated him, her sudden changes from sorrow to joy, her strange proposition that since he was always tolerant in religious matters he too should become a Catholic. They parted, never to meet again. De Warens returned to Vevey and by his own skill and the good will of his fellow-citizens slowly retrieved his financial position. At one moment, indeed, fearing ruin, he fled to England, and wrote from Islington to his brother a long letter, detailing the history of his separation from his wife, which is, after the *Confessions*, the most valuable document we possess in the light it throws on Madame de Warens's history and character. Finding he could not obtain in England any position suited to his rank, he returned home, and finally retired to Lausanne where he died in 1754. At the instigation of his family he had obtained a formal divorce on the ground of his wife's 'malicious desertion and abjuration of Protestantism,' but he never married again.

When Madame de Warens settled in the delightful little town of Annecy — in a house to the west of the present episcopal residence, overlooking the Thion Canal — she was nearly twenty-seven years of age. She was, her husband remarks, a woman of great intelligence, of much strength of will, and a delightful companion. Her faithful friend, De Conzié, who first knew her at this time, speaks of her charming laughter, her vivacious eyes, her intelligence, as giving an uncommon energy to everything she said, while she seemed to be entirely without affectation or insincerity.

It is not altogether easy to confirm all we hear of Madame de Warens's appearance by turning to portraits. There are various alleged portraits extant, and there has been much difference of opinion as to which are genuine, and of uncertainty as to what has become of others which are known to have existed. Even as early as 1790 (not long after Rousseau's death) Madame de Charrière took much trouble to find one of the portraits, writing to several people, including Gibbon, who were supposed to possess it, but without success. A miniature in the Musée de Cluny has been accepted by good authorities, but now seems doubtful, as also a pastel by La Tour and a painting attributed to Largillière. A rather indifferent engraving of a portrait which disappeared more than a century ago is, however, almost beyond dispute; that at all events is the opinion of Benedetto, on what seem good grounds. It corresponds to the descriptions we have and represents a handsome woman with large eyes and vivacious expression and well-formed hands playing an instrument which looks like an organ. We know that she played the harpsichord and also sang.

There is one point in regard to Madame de Warens's temperament which is of importance in the light it sheds on her life and actions, though so far it has never attracted attention. De Warens mentions, briefly and incidentally, without insistence, that his wife was hysterical ('sujette aux vapeurs'). The fact is significant; it explains the intelligent but too impetuous and ill-regulated activity which marked her whole life; it gives us the clue to that thread of slight mental anomaly and ill-balance which was fated to plunge her into difficulties at every step. We are not entirely dependent on her husband for our knowledge of this constitutional peculiarity. Rousseau also, equally unsuspecting the significance of his statement as an index of abnormal nervous sensibility, mentions that at dinner she was so overcome by the odour of the dishes that she could seldom begin till he had finished, when he would begin again to keep her company. This statement of Rousseau's is disputed by writers who say that Madame kept a good table and therefore was fond of good living, but

I see no ground to dispute it. It confirms our suspicion that, like Rousseau himself, who was so irresistibly attracted to her, Madame de Warens, even though but in slight degree, was a constitutionally abnormal person.

She had the temperament of the extravert, full of romantic and ambitious dreams which, with alarming versatility, and a show of brilliancy without solid foundation, she was always seeking to transform into reality, and always failing to achieve her object. Benedetto calls her a kind of superior Madame Bovary, with more vigour, and somewhat better equipment, and, one may add, more success.

In spite of her real or alleged lovers, I do not think she can be called sensual. Like many women of somewhat similar temperament she probably found satisfaction in an affection which took on maternal shapes and in the gratified vanity of a dominant nature. She possessed a high degree of what we should now call Narcissism, magnifying herself and everything connected with herself, suppressing anything that might hurt her pride. For the youthful Rousseau, fresh from Puritanic Geneva, she could not but be at once not only a revelation but also an enigma. He never quite unravelled it, and she never aided him to do so. That is why his picture of her is so incoherent and contradictory. So that he represents her as at once the 'best of women' and the victim of vulgar tastes. He fitted her into his typical picture of human nature, which indeed his contemplation of her may have helped him to formulate: the human being who is born virtuous and led by external circumstances to vice.

We have seen that the evidence as to Madame de Warens's infidelity to her husband rests on a weak foundation and may safely be rejected. The evidence regarding the divorced wife is usually considered to be less doubtful. Very shortly after settling at Annecy she was reported as living on intimate terms with her servant, the faithful steward of her affairs, Claude Anet. Rousseau has done full justice to the estimable and upright character of this young man; except his extreme devotion to his mistress no reproach has ever been cast on him. He was born at Montreux and belonged to a family which had long served the La Tour family. At the period we have now reached he was twenty-one years of age. It is probable that he already cherished devotion for Madame at Vevey; he prepared for his flight at the time that she was leaving; he left Switzerland soon afterwards to join her, and with her he abjured Protestantism. One is inclined at first to suspect (with M. Mugnier) that we have here an elopement, but on the whole the suspicion seems unnecessary and the financial ruin which hung over Madame amply accounts for her flight. It is clear that she gladly availed herself of Anet's devotion, and accepted his sacrifices at a moment when she sorely needed them. When later she felt her loneliness in a foreign country, and knew that by the law of her own country, though not that of her new religion, she was a divorced woman, the close association with Claude Anet may have induced a warmer emotion than that of gratitude. The relationship, whatever it was, remained a secret, for though Savoy was a freer country than austere and inquisitorial Switzerland, social feeling would not have tolerated a lady whose steward was apparently her lover.

It may be noted that the three men whom we may regard as Madame de Warens's lovers — Anet, Rousseau, and Wintzenried — were all Swiss Protestants who had abjured their religion; they were all younger than herself, and all of lower social class. She never really changed under the influences of life; what she was in early youth she remained in age; in the mature woman we still see the little girl at Le Basset who delighted to lord it over the peasant children around her.

Rousseau, an unpromising runaway youth of sixteen, reached Annecy on Palm Sunday, 1728, and met Madame de Warens as, with her stick in hand — the gold-headed cane, no doubt, that we know of — she was entering the church of the Cordeliers. It was a memorable day in his life, and a more memorable one in hers than she was ever to know. As regards the years that followed at Annecy, the earlier years at Chambéry, and the occupation of Les Charmettes, Rousseau's *Confessions*, however untrustworthy in detail, remain the prime authority for Madame de Warens's life; it was, as we may by other evidence conclude, the happiest and the most peaceful stage of her existence, as well as supremely important to Rousseau. The incomparable pages which he has devoted to these years are on the whole so faithful in spirit though often so inaccurate in fact — partly by defects of memory and partly by unconscious self-deception — that the story need never be told again; no reader of the *Confessions* ever forgets it, and when he visits the secluded valley of Les Charmettes and enters the little house, which is scarcely changed since Rousseau left it, he seems to be returning to a spot he had known long before.

It is perfectly true that the story, regarded as an idyll, has been sadly battered of recent years by the critics, often pedantically minute in their approach, sometimes unmistakably malevolent. There can be no doubt that official documents do not always support Rousseau's narrative and sometimes definitely contradict it. It has even been plausibly argued, on the basis of such evidence, that Jean-Jacques's intimacy with Madame de Warens, if intimacy there had been, had practically ceased when he came to live at Les Charmettes; that when there he was little more than a care-taker, though with fine opportunities for study and meditation of which he fully availed himself, since Wintzenried, more capable than Rousseau as an overseer for his mistress's business affairs, had largely taken Rousseau's place in her regard and affections, and that she was really pushing Rousseau into the background, though he continued to cling to her.

An instructive document for facts, dates, and small details of Madame de Warens's farming activities, has lately been discovered by a M. Rey Jouvin in an old house perched on a height between Savoy and Dauphiny, a parchment notebook fastened by a leather ribbon. This document is nothing less than the *Journal* of the accounts of Les Charmettes kept by Wintzenried from 2 October, 1737, to 1739, and afterwards casually used from time to time by Madame de Warens herself.

This document has been studied by M. André Monglond.[1]

[1] A. Monglond, 'Le Journal des Charmettes,' *Jeunesses*, 1933.

A precious journal, he remarks, which throws a crude light on the sixth book of the *Confessions*, those pages which for a century and a half have fascinated so many pilgrims to Les Charmettes. Here we learn the little details of the rural life in which Rousseau was plunged during his formative years, and we see in naked realism exactly how Madame de Warens treated her dependents and servants. All through, the part that Rousseau played is minimised.

We must, however, remember that at the point when the *Journal* begins, Rousseau had just set out for Montpellier. He was not a newcomer; for more than six years he had been a guest of Madame de Warens, sometimes an independent one paying for himself, and for four years she may have been so intimate with him as to appear his mistress. He still returned to her again and again, while she seemed ever ready to encourage him to become independent. But clearly the idyll is not destroyed, and M. Monglond, while ruthless in criticism of details, makes no attempt to destroy it.

It is, indeed, a hopeless task to attempt to destroy the central emotional core of this supremely important epoch in Rousseau's life. If we succeeded, his whole significance in the world would become almost unintelligible. That central core of emotional fact is the intimate contact of a crude and undeveloped youth of marvellous latent genius with the first woman of distinction he had ever met, and the consequent awakening of his own immense sensibility, with, in addition, the shock of the discovery of the world of Nature and of culture. That little woman, however unworthily, was the key to that complex revelation.

The precise facts and dates are irrelevant. Even Rousseau himself thought them so. He had no record of most of them, and in old age, when he wrote the *Confessions*, they became confused in memory. At the end of the fifth book he is careful to say when giving a date to the possession of Les Charmettes, ' as far as I can recall times and dates.' And at the end of his life, in the fourth 'Promenade' of his *Rêveries*, we find: 'I wrote my *Confessions* when I was already old.... I wrote them from memory; that memory often failed me or furnished but imperfect recollections, and I filled up the space by details supplied by imagination to supplement those recollections.... I loved to expatiate on the happy moments of my life, and I sometimes embellished them with ornaments supplied by tender regrets. I said things I had forgotten as it seemed to me they ought to have been, and as perhaps in fact they were. ... I sometimes lent strange charms to truth.' Nothing could be more candid. We cannot hold Rousseau to an accuracy of detail which he never himself claimed.

In 1744, after Rousseau had finally left Savoy to settle in Paris, the Spaniards had come to occupy Chambéry; Madame de Warens for a time lost her pension and with her usual energy and skill in initiative she started a soap factory, and also, it appears, a chocolate factory, sending some of both products as a present to Rousseau. At the same time she began coal-mining and iron-mining operations, trying to establish a company. But, as we know, she could never carry through the schemes she was so clever in planning, and these new enterprises went through all the same stages to ruin as the silk stocking factory of twenty years earlier. Rousseau, himself struggling with difficulties of all kinds, sent her small sums from time to time. In 1754 she writes to him reproachfully that she is in the state mentioned in the *Imitation* wherein that fails us on which we had placed our chief hopes. 'In spite of this,' she concludes, 'I am and all my life will remain your loving mother.' Less than a month later she writes to the Court of Turin that she is 'without bread and without credit,' and solicits a loan from the King as her pension is engaged by industrial obligations. In the same year, as Rousseau tells us, he came with Thérèse to see her at Chambéry; he was afflicted at her condition and made the impracticable proposition that she should live with them in Paris. Of her jewels but one ring was now left, and this she wished to place on Thérèse's hand. It was the last time Rousseau ever saw her. In 1761 the *Nouvelle Héloïse* appeared and fascinated the attention of the world. By this time the woman who was its real heroine was old, poor, forgotten; some years before, she had become a chronic invalid; we do not know whether she ever read the famous novel she had so largely inspired or even heard of its fame. The year afterwards she died, and it was some months before Rousseau received the news of her death in a letter from De Conzié; she had left nothing behind her, wrote De Conzié, but the evidence of her piety and her poverty.

Sixteen years later Rousseau also died. The last words he ever wrote, the concluding lines of his *Rêveries*, were devoted to the memory of his first meeting, exactly fifty years earlier, with that 'best of women' to whom he owed those 'four or five years wherein I enjoyed a century of life and of pure and full happiness.'

Madame de Warens has seemed, to many who only know her through the *Confessions*, an enigma, almost a monstrosity. When all the facts of her life are before us, and we have patiently reconstructed them — and, where we cannot reconstruct, divined — we realise how little that is enigmatic remains. She was simply a restless, impetuous, erring, and suffering woman, of unusual intelligence, perhaps somewhat hysterical — less so than some women who have played a noble part in practical affairs, less than many women whom we revere for their spiritual graces. Her life, when we understand it, was the natural outcome of her special constitution in reaction with circumstances. She presents, indeed, with the genius left out, much the same mixture of good and evil which the world has found so baffling in Rousseau himself. The explanation of the supposed enigma becomes therefore an interesting psychological study.

But Madame de Warens is something more than a mere subject for psychological study such as we might more profitably exercise nearer home. She is the only person who can claim to be the teacher of the man who was himself the greatest teacher of his century. When he came to her he was a vagabond apprentice in whom none could see any good. She raised him, succoured him, cherished him, surrounded him with her conscious and unconscious influence; she was the only education he ever received. When he left her he was no longer the worthless apprentice of an engraver, but the supreme master of all those arts which most powerfully evoke the ideals and emotions of mankind. And, as it has been well said, the golden age which Rousseau wished to bring back to earth was simply a generalisation of the life he had himself lived at Les Charmettes. We may or may not now open his books. For most people the immortal *Confessions* alone remain. Nevertheless Rousseau once moved the world, and whether or not we know it, his influence lives in us. When the curious critic takes up innumerable counters from among our current sentiments and beliefs, and seeks to decipher the effaced image and superscription, it is the pupil of Madame de Warens that he finds.

4

IT IS not easy to discuss the period of French literature which begins with Rousseau and what is conventionally termed the Romantic Movement, without considering the attitude in that period to Nature. Since Nature really includes everything, not excepting Man himself, that is a large subject. We need not discuss it here. But it seems indispensable to investigate, however briefly, one aspect of it: the love of wild Nature.

The origin of the love of Nature in scenery has been obscured by confused and conflicting statements. We are told, on the one hand, that the beauty of wild Nature was discovered by Rousseau and the leaders of the Romantic Movement during the following half-century. We are told, on the other hand, that the love of even the wildest landscape has existed in all ages. There is a certain amount of truth in both these statements, but they are not illuminative, because they fail to bring us to the causes of the love of Nature. It is useless to pile up miscellaneous quotations showing the appreciation, or the lack of appreciation, of natural scenery. We may, perhaps, reach the root of the matter, and reconcile opposing assertions, by analysing the significance of our accumulated facts.

By the love of wild Nature we properly mean the attraction to any kind of scenery — sky, mountain, ocean, forest, desert — untouched by Man. Scenery mixed with Man, to some extent moulded by him, and so presenting a suitable home, cannot fail always to have been agreeable from the most primitive times, whether or not its agreeableness found expression or even became definitely conscious. The love of wild

Nature is a love of scenery from which Man is excluded, of scenery which seems, though perhaps mistakenly, without utility for Man. In the strict sense, therefore, such feeling may be described as originally both unsociable and luxurious. It tended to draw men away from their fellows and away from the useful arts of life.

It is this fact which determines the attitude of savages towards natural scenery. If the savage took what civilised man might consider a strictly practical view of his life, he would doubtless have no feeling whatever for the wild. But it so happens that savages nearly everywhere believe that the external world holds beings and influences which have an effect on their practical life. Even mountain and sea and sky may be peopled by beings whose operations on Man may be beneficent or maleficent. Here we have at the outset the germinal possibility alike of the love and the horror of wild natural scenery. Mountains especially have seemed to primitive men the home of the divine.

This, indeed, we find the more clearly the farther back we go in the tradition which, directly or indirectly, we of European stocks inherit. The Babylonians regarded the earth itself as a huge mountain ('the mountain house'), and the mountains as the natural abode of the gods; the transference of the gods, or some of them, to 'the heavens' — where they still remained even for Christianity — being, as Morris Jastrow remarked in his *Religion of Babylonia*, a later scholastic theory. So that the Babylonian temple was, as Jensen first pointed out in his *Kosmologie*, an imitation of a mountain, a miniature of the cosmic 'mountain house,' and really a 'high place.'

It is a significant fact that the monotheistic Jews found their Jehovah amid the thunders of Sinai, while the polytheistic Greeks equally placed their gods on the top of their highest mountain, Olympus. 'A cave eaten by time in the flank of a mountain,' said Seneca, 'fills the soul with the feeling of the existence of a high power.' Many of the most ancient and sacred shrines in the Christian world are caves in the mountain or the rock, and it is probable that many of these have inherited their sacredness from older faiths, and in earlier days were hallowed as Delphi was hallowed.

It is held, as by Sir William Ramsay, a great authority in the archaeology of the Near East, that the ancient holy repute of mountains especially influenced the early Christians in their selection of religious sites. 'During many years of study,' he remarks in his *The Thousand and One Churches*, written in association with Gertrude Bell, 'I have relied on the principle that the Pagan religious centres were found in places where the divine power, which resided specially in the bosom of the earth, the Great Mother of all, was revealed to men by natural phenomena of an impressive kind, valuable minerals or other mysterious exhibitions of the life and riches of the underworld.'

If we go as far as Japan we find not only that Fusiyama is a national religious symbol, but that there are everywhere shrines and temples on the summits of mountains, with pilgrims frequenting them in the hope that they may there the more readily fall into spiritual trances. A distinguished Japanese has stated that his countrymen never climb a mountain save with a religious object. Yet while primitive animism and its later supernatural developments tended to complicate the savage feeling that the useful is beautiful and the useless is ugly, on the whole they ranged themselves in harmony with it. The stern home of a fierce god might become attractive if the traditions changed and the god won more of his people's love. Or the rugged shrine, like Delphi, might, by its sacred and patriotic associations, and even by the inevitable humanising results of much frequentation, slowly acquire the effect of beauty. But in the main it would seem, and more especially among genuinely primitive peoples, spiritual influences were divided: good spirits dwell in the places which men found useful and beautiful, and chiefly loved to frequent; evil demons infested those spots which had little or nothing to give to men, and which, therefore, were seldom willingly visited.[1]

[1] Robertson Smith (*Religion of the Semites*, p. 114) speaks of the results of his Semitic studies in words which have a precise though undesigned accuracy in

This sharp distinction in the primitive man's sense of natural beauty — his acceptance of the useful, homely, and familiar, his rejection of the useless, wild, and unfamiliar — is illustrated even by those primitive peoples who have had the finest sense of natural beauty. This is notably the case as regards the early Celts. The old Celtic literature reveals a delightful sense of beauty, not only in human beings and the objects of daily life, but in natural scenery. This Celtic appreciation of Nature was well shown, as Alfred Nutt remarked, in an admiration of the western isles of Scotland, and he added that Deirdre's farewell to Alba (Scotland) in the *Woe of the Sons of Usnach*, the most famous and vital legend of the Ultonian cycle, is 'the germ of medieval Gaelic nature poetry; indeed, of all nature poetry written in any European vernacular for over a thousand years.' Yet this 'Farewell' strictly insists on the homely features of the 'lovable lands' to which it refers — the 'grassy estuary,' the 'fish and venison,' the 'cuckoo's note on bending bough,' the 'clear white sand beneath the waves.' The things that Deirdre regrets are either the things which are useful to life or the things which have become lovable through their association with life. So far as there is here any advance on the strictly primitive view, it is in the charmingly aesthetic vision of the things belonging to this second group. The same points may be illustrated by an allied passage, again addressed to a Scotch island, from the Ossianic *Colloquy with the Ancients*:

Arran of the many stags, the sea impinges upon her very shoulders! an island in which whole companies were fed, and with ridges among which blue spears are reddened! Skittish deer are on her pinnacles, soft blackberries on her waving heather; cool

reference to the primitive feeling for natural beauty. 'The earth,' he remarks, 'may be said to be parcelled out between demons and wild beasts on the one hand and God and men on the other. To the former belong the untrodden wilderness with all its unknown perils, the wastes and jungles that lie outside the familiar tracks and pasture ground of the tribe, and which only the boldest men venture upon without terror; to the latter belong the regions that man knows and habitually frequents, and within which he has established relations, not only with his human neighbours, but with the supernatural beings that have their haunts side by side with him.'

water there is in her rivers, and mast upon her russet oaks! Grey-
hounds there were in her and beagles; blackberries and sloes of
the dark blackthorn; dwellings with their backs set close against
her woods, and the deer fed scattered by her oaken thickets! A
crimson cup grew on her rocks, in all her glades a faultless grass;
over her crags, affording friendly refuge, leaping went on and
fawns were skipping! Smooth were her level spots, her wild
swine were fat, cheerful her fields, her nuts hung on her forest-
hazel boughs, and there was sailing of long galleys past her!
Right pleasant their condition all when the fair weather set in;
under her rivers' brinks trout lie; the sea-gulls wheeling round her
grand cliff answer one the other — at every fitting time delectable
is Arran! [1]

There is, indeed, here, and in many other passages that
could be quoted, an exquisite delight in natural things, but
of the modern love of wild things there is no slightest trace.
Nor in the *Mabinogion* also, where the Celtic spirit attains its
finest and most romantic expression, can I find any expression
of the beauty of wildness.

If we turn to the classic literature from which we must
trace our own literary descent much more directly than from
the racially nearer Celts, we find the same attitude in a more
definite and conscious shape. The Greeks and Romans, as
Friedländer says, had as real, living, and profound a feeling
for Nature as the moderns, but it was narrower. The landscape beauty that appealed to the classic mind was easy and
luxuriant, pleasant to all the senses and good to rest in. A
mountain might have its awful solemnity or its religious
sacredness, but it was generally agreed that it could not be
beautiful. Even Lucretius, though he seems to have been attracted to wild and solitary places, admits that mountains
and deep forests, being infested by wild beasts, are places of
horror that had better be avoided. A beautiful place was one
that was agreeable to live in, or, at all events, that had become agreeable through the habit of living in it. From habit,
said Cicero, in the *De Amicitiâ*, every place one lives in becomes pleasing, 'even though it is a mountain or a forest.'

[1] I quote from the translation of S. H. O'Grady, *Silva Gadelica*, p. 109.

It is an instructive remark, and reveals an assumption that underlies all the ancient feeling towards landscape.

We may test the feelings of the ancients in the matter by their attitude towards the Vale of Tempe, the great cleft between Olympus and Ossa. This ravine has both the mountain solemnity of high cliffs and the softer charm of fine vegetation. To the early Greek Herodotus, the pass was merely a difficult route, and afterwards to the early Roman Livy it was a terrifying and horrible spot. But later the Vale of Tempe became a favourite touring ground for Romans, and Aelian in the reign of Hadrian has a long and enthusiastic passage about its beauties and the charms it offers to the traveller who rests there; he says not a word of its horrors, ignoring those sterner aspects which had terrified the men of earlier antiquity. The modern traveller, on the other hand, is chiefly impressed by the grandeur and sublimity of the spot, but he views it not, like Livy, with horror, but with something of the same pleasure which had been aroused in Aelian by its softer and more luxuriant aspects.[1]

The example of the Vale of Tempe shows that there was an advance in the enjoyment of Nature as we pass from early Greek to later Roman times. Gebhart considers that the charming and luxuriant landscape of Italy was more fitted to win men to the love of Nature than the more terrifying and dramatic aspects of some parts of Greece. The feeling of the Greeks for moderation and equipoise held them aloof from the excesses of their natural scenery and fixed their attention on man. Neither of the famous sentences on the portal of Delphi — 'Nothing too much' and 'Know thyself' — were calculated to draw men's thoughts to wild Nature. 'My dear Phaedrus, fields and trees have nothing to teach me!' The Greeks' love of Nature remained platonic.

Rohde has well described the special character of the feeling for Nature developed among the later Greeks and its total unlikeness from the modern feeling for wild Nature. It was

[1] This contrast between the ancient and modern ways of viewing the Vale of Tempe was long since pointed out by E. M. Cope, 'The Taste for the Picturesque among the Greeks,' *Cambridge Essays*, 1856.

idyllic and sentimental, craving for a softened and restrained Nature. 'The ideal for this kind of sensitiveness is Nature as a garden,' and Rohde remarks that Greek descriptions of their favourite ideal recall the so-called English-garden art as practised in eighteenth-century France.

The Roman temperament, more massive, more violent, more melancholy, felt other impulses as it attained to complete self-consciousness. There seems, as Freshfield pointed out, a real significance in Nero's choice of the semi-Alpine site of Subiaco — the wildest spot near Rome — for his summer palace, and, it may be added, in Marcus Aurelius's strong desire to seek retreats on the seashore or in the mountains. As men grew more individualistic and more abnormal, craving new and stronger stimulation, wild Nature lost something of its horror and began to become even agreeable.

At one important point the Romans showed an aesthetic appreciation which allies them to the moderns. The Greeks felt no admiration for the sea, not even Homer, though it was so frequent a factor in their lives. The Romans of classic days, and later sometimes the Byzantines, developed, as Hennig has especially emphasized, a remarkable understanding of the aesthetic aspect of the sea. They were originally drawn to it, no doubt, by the need for its refreshing coolness in summer. Then, as now, the heat and dust of cities drove men from the cities to the seaside. Every rich and cultured Roman had his villa by the sea, and Baia, especially, became, as Hennig remarks, the ancient Monte Carlo.

After Roman days the sea as a source of health and refreshment and beauty was completely neglected and forgotten. It was not till the middle of the eighteenth century that seabathing, first notably in England at Margate, began to become, with many precautions against danger and indecency, a fashion. It was not till the nineteenth century that the sea became a romantic passion. Indeed Remy de Gourmont remarks that if we ask what was the most original creation of that century we should perhaps have to answer: the sea. Byron and Chateaubriand were here conspicuous pioneers. Up till then, as Madame de Sévigné bears witness, a plunge in the sea was only known as a remedy for people bitten by a mad dog, and Mont Saint-Michel was until 1850 merely a place scarcely good enough even to lodge criminals.

We may say that in classic days delight in landscape developed with increasing culture, and that this progress involved a growing tendency to ignore the wildness which at an earlier period had seemed to possess only unmitigated horror. The new pleasure in landscapes more or less associated with scenes of sombre grandeur seems seldom at first to have really involved a conscious pleasure in that grandeur. In a passage which, as Matthew Arnold pointed out, is probably unparalleled in classic literature, Marcus Aurelius said that things that come in the course of Nature have beauty in them and give pleasure, like the ears of corn bending down and the lion's eyebrows and the foam flowing from the mouth of wild boars. In this passage, which is Stoic in its sentiment, lies the germ of the modern feeling for the wild, but in classic days it remained for the most part an undeveloped germ. At the best it represented the stage of transition towards a new feeling that was about to grow up in the world.

It may now become clear that there is a connection between the love of wild Nature and religion. That love generally, as found among primitive peoples, first takes the form of awe. So long as a people remains primitive it stays as awe. The terrifying aspects of Nature seem to early man associated with the activities of superior beings; terrifying spots seem the abode of gods to be reverenced, or of demons to be placated. As these aspects and spots became less terrifying, because a little better understood, they are found less disagreeable. In the still devout eyes of superior minds, however, they begin to become attractive. To an intellectual pagan of no creed but still a mystic in temper, such as Marcus Aurelius, there comes a comprehensive vision of all Nature as beautiful.

At what may be a rather earlier date we find in the New Testament but a single precept concerning pure aesthetic beauty in Nature.[1] But that is attributed to Jesus himself in the famous remark concerning 'the lilies of the field,' in which

[1] In the Old Testament, however, we must not forget Psalm CIV.

he found a natural beauty independent of human touch or any human utility. It scarcely seems that this essential source of our sense of the beauty of wild Nature is sufficiently emphasised. It is rooted in the primitive fear and veneration of divine beings. It is first sensitively felt by devout worshippers, and then by the mystics. Religion is the womb of aesthetics.

There can be little doubt that the love of the wild in Nature received a powerful impetus from influences associated with the development of Christianity. It was, indeed, merely a by-product of Christianity, regarded simply as a creed, for there is nothing in the doctrine of Christianity which implies direct approval or disapproval of any aspects of wild Nature. Christian doctrine may be said to encourage indifference towards Nature altogether, abstracting man's attention from the external world and concentrating it on the problems of the soul. The last book of the New Testament, the *Revelation* sometimes associated with the name of the Apostle John, is significant from this point of view. The author of this book states that he is writing in Patmos — a barren land of volcanic origin — but it can scarcely be said that his book either reflects any love of the natural conditions around him or represents any reaction against his environment leading to the recall of scenery the writer had known in the past. Imagery was essential to his purpose, but the imagery he prefers is purely imaginary and, so far as possible, deliberately selected from the mineral world. His 'New Jerusalem' is a gorgeous palace blazing with metal and jewels. There are no trees there, no flowers or fruits, no sunshine, no hills, and we are expressly told that there was no sea, so that the natural objects which were most familiar to the writer's vision must have been peculiarly repulsive to him. The New Jerusalem might be a goldsmith's Paradise.

The first and most obvious way in which Christianity contributed to develop the love of the wild was by driving men out into the wilds. It was a necessary and inevitable result, among sensitive and receptive men often tinged by culture, that some should be found to respond to this new environment

66

and find beauty there. That was, indeed, an extension of the fact recognised by Cicero that the least attractive places through familiarity often grow pleasing. It was not, it is true, an invariable fact, either among Christians or pagans. The seer of the New Jerusalem saw nothing in his island home, just as a very different person, Ovid, was altogether blind to the beauty that surrounded him in exile on the Black Sea. But the new outburst of Christianity led to a prodigious exodus from the cities, into the wildest and most desert spots of emotional, highstrung young people who thus cut themselves off from the excitements of urban life, and often from the pleasures of social intercourse. They had not gone into the desert to find the beauty of the desert, but there can be little doubt that they often found that beauty, usually for the first time. So far as can be seen, indeed, the Christian hermits who swarmed out of the Roman world into the solitudes of Egypt first discovered the beauty of the African desert. Jerome was perhaps the most distinguished of these, and it is highly improbable that any earlier or non-Christian writer had ever broken out into such an eulogy of the desert as we find again and again in Jerome's delightful Epistles. 'O desert,' he exclaims, when writing to the monk Heliodorus, 'blooming with Christ's flowers! O Solitude, from which are brought the stones to build the Apocalyptic city of the Great King! O familiar retreat delighting in God! How long will you let the houses press you down? How long will you shut yourself up in the prison of smoky cities? Believe me, I know nothing more brilliant than the light here. Here one lays aside the burden of the body and flies up into the pure and splendid aether.' There is here, it is true, no deliberate aesthetic attentiveness to the special quality of the desert's beauty, but it is clearly and accurately felt. Jerome and those who obeyed the same impulse had, at the very least, for the first time, woven beautiful associations into their memories of the desert.

It was not alone through a new familiarity with wild Nature that Christianity enlarged the conception of beautiful scenery. There was another reason which has already been implied, but it is significant enough to be emphasised. A sensitiveness to the attraction of the wild lay in the special temperament of many of those who were most strongly drawn into the fold of Christianity. That is the really decisive moment in generating the love of the wild. It is necessary to point this out clearly, because it seems to be ignored alike by those who imagine that that love is simply a result of civilisation, a statement that is only partially true, and those who fancy that it is a normal and general characteristic of humanity in all ages.

The people who call themselves Christians today, being for the most part born into Christianity, are, as we know, average members of society. It was not so at the beginning of the Christian era. A new faith so profoundly subversive of the accepted religious creeds and the established social order, inevitably attracted a considerable proportion of abnormal people, of the highly emotional, the exalted, the romantic, the people who, in relation to the society of their time were, and in no necessarily bad sense, anti-social. Such people are often of the finest character and the highest intelligence; this mental state was once minutely analysed by Pierre Janet who termed this condition psychasthenia. These people are instinctively repelled by the ordinary social environment in which they live; they cannot adjust themselves to the ordinary routine of life; its banalities crush and offend them; the 'real world' of their average fellow-men seems to them unreal, and they are conscious of a painful sense of inadequacy in relation to it; they seek for new and stronger stimulants, for new and deeper narcotics, a new Heaven and a new earth. There were many of them, we are able to divine — though the precise evidence is usually obscure — who were powerfully attracted to Christianity, and found there all that they craved. It was among such that the love of the wild found its earliest Christian apostles; it has been among such that in later centuries the fuller and more complete forms of that love have been first of all proclaimed.

There can be little doubt, indeed, that the same tendency existed in earlier than Christian days among the Romans. A passage in Seneca's treatise, *De Tranquillitate*, is significant on this connection:

> There are some things which please our bodies though accompanied with a certain painful feeling..:. Let us visit uncultivated lands; let us roam over the Bruttian and Lucanian passes (of Southern Italy); let something pleasant yet be sought amid these desert places where our eyes, accustomed to the luxurious, may be rested by the wide desolation of rough places.

It is noteworthy also that in his tragedies Seneca insists on the horrors, indeed, but also on the fascination, of forests and other fantastic and solitary spots. Much the same may be said of Lucan. The spirit of Christianity was beginning to make itself felt among people who knew nothing of Christianity. The men of hypersensitive and abnormal temperament, Seneca and Lucan and Cicero — who must also be named in this connection — were tortured by the evils and injustices of the later Roman world; they turned from the wildness of man to the wildness of Nature with a sense of peace and joy that had never before been known. Earlier than these men, the great and sombre Lucretius, the Roman Dante — pursuing an isolated course in literature and in life, and dying, as legend reported, insane — reveals a love of the solitary and wild which led him to symbolise his own path in poetry as that of untrodden mountains and intact fountains and new flowers.

In the third-century treatise, 'On the Public Shows,' attributed to Cyprian, Bishop of Carthage, there is a memorable passage contrasting the shows of Nature with the shows of the theatre, which illustrates the way in which the solitary and, one may say, anti-social temper of the early Christian turned from the urban amusements of the day to find relief and delight in the most varied natural phenomena: sunrise and sunset, the waxing and waning moon, the course of the seasons, the troops of stars, the heavy mass of the earth balanced by mountains, the rivers and their sources, the seas with their waves and shores, the mere air, and in the air the birds, in the water the fishes, on earth man.

Let these, I say, and other divine works, be the exhibitions for faithful Christian. What theatre built by hands could be compared with such works as these? Though reared with immense piles of stones the mountain crests are loftier; though the roofs glitter with gold they will be surpassed by the brightness of the starry firmament.

Saint Augustine, also, though in a less didactic spirit, towards the end of the *De Civitate Dei*, enumerates and expatiates on 'the manifold and various loveliness of sky and earth and sea.' He makes, indeed, no mention of mountains, which he had little familiarity with, but he is enthusiastic over the sea, which he had often crossed or gazed on as he paced the fantastic mosaic esplanade of the harbour at Carthage, the emblem of his own turbulent and passionate, yet massive, spirit — 'so grand a spectacle when it arranges itself as it were in vestures of various colours, now running through every shade of green and again becoming purple or blue. Is it not delightful,' he adds, 'to look at it in storm?' Saint Basil also, who lived at Pontus, within sight of the Euxine, speaks appreciatively in his *Hexamoron* of that sea which Ovid had found so dreary. We are clearly beginning to witness the development of a feeling for the beauty of the terrible which we found only the first hints of in the pagan Roman world.

In the attractive chapter at the beginning of the second volume of his *Kosmos*, in which Alexander von Humboldt first outlined the subject which concerns us here, he called attention to the letter in which Saint Basil, writing in 360 to Gregory of Nazianzen, described the scenery around his hut on a mountain summit in Armenia, overlooking the plain through which the river Iris impetuously rushed. This passage Humboldt regarded as the most remarkable natural description in all ancient literature. Biese, indeed, is less enthusiastic about Basil's landscape picture, remarking that a similar tone may be found in the Greek anthology and in Pliny the Younger. Yet the passage has its significance, for it expresses the delight in his wild surroundings felt by a man, not writing as an artist or a tourist, who had really come to live amid the solitary magnificence of Nature, and enjoyed describing in

detail the spectacle presented to him and the peace and solitude of his lofty home, only disturbed now and again by
hunters seeking stags or goats or hares. To that extent it
represents a new attitude resulting from the special circumstance of Christian life and the special types of men who were
attracted to that life.

In the same century Gregory of Nyssa even more definitely
and precisely refers, as an early nineteenth century romantic
might, to the pleasurable melancholy evoked by natural
scenery. This fourth century indeed, as Hennig remarks,
presents the climax of the early Christian feeling for Nature.

In the same century the Gallic poet Ausonius, who was in
the line of the old classic poets, carried further the same spirit,
and Dill remarks in his *Roman Society* that he was indeed almost the only Roman poet who (in his poem on the Moselle)
transferred to verse the subtle and secret charm which Nature
has to modern eyes.

During many succeeding centuries we may trace a close association between ascetic moments of Christian life and scenery that was sometimes beautifully or romantically wild. It
by no means follows that the spot was in the first place sought
out because it possessed these qualities. There were several
circumstances which led to this association. In the first place,
utility came in for consideration. The pious hermit, however
rigid his life, could not dispense with wood and water and
shelter, and these were most easily obtainable in a forest-
clad mountain. Ordericus Vitalis, the twelfth-century Anglo-
Norman monk, writing of a chapel in Normandy — supposed
to have been founded much earlier — in which he had himself
lived, says: 'The site is pleasant and well suited to a hermit's
life. A little river flows through a wild valley; the summit
of the hill is clothed with a forest, the thick foliage of which
forms a screen from the blasts of the wind. The chapel stands
on a slope between the road and the stream. A fountain bursts
out before the door.' Nowadays, when the question of wild
beasts has been practically eliminated, this picture seems as
pleasant, even to a school-girl, as it seemed to the hardy
monk, yet this was a scene from which the men of classic times

would have shrunk in horror. A good deal of ground had been traversed in those first thousand years of Christianity.

It is remarkable how many of the most famous and sacred religious shrines of Christianity are situated in spots which, though not beautiful according to the ancient standards of landscape beauty, appeal strongly to us. No doubt in many cases the Christians were carrying on the old pagan traditions which associated divine influence with rugged and terrible spots, and in not a few cases also they were simply conquering for the new religion shrines which had already been hallowed by an earlier religion. But this cannot always be demonstrated, and merely pushes the problem further back; we simply have to admit that the religious men of the earlier faith were moved by the same feelings. The Spanish shrine of Montserrat, one of the most famous goals of mediaeval pilgrimage, has been the place of Christian worship for more than a thousand years, and a pagan shrine before that; this rocky shrine near the top of a mountain is the kind of sacred place which Seneca speaks of with horror, yet the modern lover of natural beauty justifies the choice of the early men of religion, and finds it one of the most fascinating spots in Europe.[1] Sainte-Beaume, the cave in a rocky height, which legend made the picturesque and secluded scene of Mary Magdalene's repentance, was certainly the home of ascetics at a very early period. Rocamadour, again in France, is another delightful and romantic spot fixed on by religious men to become a famous shrine, though it is only now beginning to be generally recognised as a shrine of natural beauty. The Benedictines found their first home in the peculiarly wild and picturesque Apennine height of Monte Cassino, which dominates all the country round.

In the Alpine region, Freshfield, who knew it well, remarks that the choicest Alpine sites — Chamonix, Engelberg, Disentis, Einsiedlen, the Grand Chartreuse — were all seized on

---

[1] I may perhaps refer to the chapter 'Montserrat' in my *Soul of Spain*, though today much of the unspoilt fascination of that spot I experienced has been vulgarised away, and the visitor must not expect to find it exactly as I found it on my first visit some thirty years ago.

by religious recluses. Wherever we go we constantly find that the most solemnly and beautifully wild spots have been dedicated to religion at remote periods, when, to the general eye, though it may not have been so to the religious men who discovered or invented their sanctity, they had no beauty at all.

There was another reason why, as Christian asceticism became organised on a large scale, it tended to be associated with what we now regard as beautiful spots: such spots were cheaper. Pious benefactors, more or less gladly, for the good of their souls or for other motives, made gifts of land for the erection of religious houses. But they preferred to give land that was too uncultivated, too wild, too remote or inaccessible, to be of much good to themselves. And if the land had to be bought, there was the same reason for selecting the same kind of spot. For the more practical and social religious Orders, it is true, such spots were usually unsuitable. The Benedictines, for instance, with their manifold human activities, generally, though not always, preferred to live in towns, and, of course, the various Orders of friars, whose work was entirely among the people, were compelled to dwell among the people, like the Salvation Army today. But the contemplative Orders not only felt no such necessity, but were obviously better able to carry out their own special mission of working for the world by prayer and meditation when living in secluded spots. The demands of ascetic religion thus coincided with the demands of the more modern aesthetic love of landscape. When Bruno, in the eleventh century, established his ardent and solitary monks at the Grande Chartreuse, the primary consideration was a spot hard of access suited to continuous worship and peace. But the love of wild Nature would, on purely aesthetic grounds, have selected exactly such a spot. In England we are familiar with the fact that the Cistercians, a contemplative Order, have left the beautiful ruins of their abbeys in what now seem to us the most exquisite and romantic spots in the land, as at Fountains, at Furness, at Llanthony. Yet the contemporaries of the monks who selected these beautiful sites were astonished at the courage of those who dared to penetrate such horrible wildernesses, infested by wild beasts and far from the haunts of men. This is, for instance, clearly brought out by the old chroniclers as regards Furness, and again as regards Clairvaux, a beautiful valley, open to the sun, furnishing a most admirable site, but described by a contemporary of Saint Bernard as merely 'a dreary spot enclosed by gloomy woods and rugged mountains.'

It is certainly true that a large part of the beauty we now find in these spots was the actual creation of the monks who planted themselves there. They cultivated and humanised these wild and remote haunts of untamed Nature. But they could not alter the essential features of the natural sites they selected. Today we have to recognise that, however hard the task they undertook, they exercised the soundest judgment from every point of view, and we can well believe they sometimes smiled in their cowls when they heard laymen marvel at their courage. The spots they secured or selected were not only cheap in hard cash, because despised, and secluded and often situated among the hills, but they had the further advantage that they were well wooded and that a stream ran through their midst. Often, also, as at Furness, the buildings were admirably placed in a kind of natural amphitheatre, so as to receive at once both the maximum of sunshine and of shelter. In addition to all this, we may well believe that the men of the contemplative Orders, who showed what it is difficult not to regard as a deliberate predilection for romantically beautiful and wild spots, had a conscious appreciation of the scenery they lived amongst.[1] They had themselves been bred in some similar scene, so that the spot at the outset had something of that quality of familiarity which, in Cicero's eye, could alone render any wooded and mountainous place pleasing.[2]

[1] This is suggested by the attractive names the Cistercians gave to their houses, Clairvaux, Bonmont, etc. Ordericus Vitalis, who refers to this point, remarks that 'the very names incited the hearers to hasten to places whose names bespoke the blessedness to be found in them.'

[2] The Cistercians settled in Llanthony and found themselves at home there. But when the Austin Canons, who were accustomed to towns, were removed

THE LOVE OF WILD NATURE

For fifteen centuries, it seems probable, the love of wild, natural scenery was cherished by a long succession of Christian ascetics, whose cult of Nature was for the most part silent, perhaps, indeed, most often unconscious, since it was not their vocation, and scarcely perhaps their interest, to cultivate deliberately the aesthetic perception of landscape. But from time to time they refer to it. Odo of Cluny in his journeys across the Alps reveals that he was a pioneer in their appreciation. 'Believe one who knows,' wrote again Saint Bernard to Murdac of Fountains, 'you will find more in forests than in books; wood and rocks will teach you what you cannot hear from the masters in the schools.'

With Francis of Assisi, indeed, and his 'Hymn to the Sun,' the love of Nature grew more eloquent. Francis had his mountain height of Verna — 'his Tabor and his Calvary' — a place of exquisite beauty which arouses the enthusiasm of all his biographers. The Franciscan feeling for natural things in the thirteenth century — though it cannot be quite disassociated from the ancient ascetic feeling — has something of the charm of a new revelation. Outside the cloister, however, there seems little genuine love of wild Nature.

The Renaissance changed this condition of things. But the change thus effected was by no means of a startling or revolutionary character. It was simply a revival of the late classical feeling for landscape, carried out by cultivated Italian ecclesiastics, and reintroducing a deliberate and consciously aesthetic enjoyment of agreeable scenery such as had appealed to the Romans of the Empire. That ecclesiastics like Bembo, Aeneas Sylvius (afterwards Pius II), and especially Petrarch took a leading part in this movement is an added indication of the closeness of the religious life to natural scenery; while the fact that these ecclesiastics were Italians shows that we are in the presence of a genuine revival of ancient feeling. The Italians were the pioneers in the modern discovery of landscape, just

from Colchester to Llanthony they were unable to like it at all and were finally transferred to Gloucester. 'We may believe,' remarks Freeman, who records this episode, 'that the very presence of the hills, which is to us the chief charm of the spot, was to them a matter of horror.'

75

as they were the natural and inevitable pioneers in the discovery of classic civilisation generally. The evidence was clearly and concisely summarised by Burckhardt, who regards Petrarch — 'one of the first completely modern men' — as the full and definite representative of the revived admiration for landscape, while Aeneas Sylvius was the first who not only enjoyed mountain landscape, but described it enthusiastically in detail (in his *Commentaries*), though Aretino was the first to describe sunset effects. We might expect to find Leonardo da Vinci among these pioneers, and his name is, indeed, sometimes mentioned in this connection. It is, however, difficult to find among his writings any passage that can be definitely quoted in evidence. He clearly possessed a minute and impartial knowledge of Nature; he was evidently familiar with mountains; he describes atmospheric effects elaborately; but he approaches Nature less in the aesthetic spirit than in the searching scientific spirit. It is true that in the background of some of his pictures he introduces fantastic rock scenery, and it is difficult not to believe that his profound study of Nature involved a real love for wild Nature.

At an early date, even from the thirteenth century on, Italian painters may be said to precede the poets in the study of Nature for her own sake. From the conventions of Giotto there is a gradual progression (it has been interestingly traced by Emma Gurney Salter in her *Nature in Italian Art*) to a magnificent culmination in Venetian art. Giorgione here specially comes before us, as notably in 'The Tempest' which Roger Fry seemed inclined to regard as the most beautiful picture in the world. Tintoretto also already reveals a tendency to dramatise nature in romantic or melancholy shapes which forecast the '*Sturm und Drang*' poets of the early nineteenth century.[1]

At an early date, also, in the backgrounds of Flemish painters, we seem to detect this love of Nature. It was the painters

---

[1] The rise of the love of Nature in English landscape painting during the eighteenth century is studied by Myra Reynolds in *The Treatment of Nature in English Poetry*, Chap. VI (pp. 273–326). An earlier study of wider scope, Josiah Gilbert's *Landscape in Art before Claude and Salvator* (1885), is full and valuable.

of the Netherlands who came first in presenting landscape, no longer as a mere background, but for its own sake. Patinir at an early date made the landscape important and figures small, and later Rubens gave free scope to his love of landscape. Jacob Ruisdael and Gaspar Poussin showed an absorption in wild scenery apart from man which we find no traces of in literature, while Salvator Rosa pictorially expressed the romantic in its most extravagant forms long before the Romantic school arose. But at that time pictures other than religious were inaccessible to all but a few amateurs, and these pioneers in art had no influence on life.

II

This Renaissance movement towards Nature was a revival, in a more elaborate and more intense form, of the classic enjoyment of landscape, continuing, we may say, the tradition of Pliny the Younger. It was not primarily an attraction towards wild Nature, such as we seem to discern in the earlier ascetic Christian movement. But it embraced elements of the love of the wild, and these were notably shown in a new and actively adventurous love of mountains. The Italians had themselves, as Burckhardt points out, prepared the way for this feeling by freeing Nature from sin and the influence of demons. Dante, at an earlier date, was a notable pioneer in this field. Though he showed no appreciation for mountains at a distance, he was, as he clearly shows, familiar with mountain-climbing. In his enjoyment of mountains Dante was, indeed, a unique figure. He experienced, in a more conscious way, the medieval ascetic attraction to wild Nature combined with the Renaissance inquisitive adventurous taste for exploring it. Petrarch possessed, in a high degree, the normal Renaissance feeling for landscape; that is to say, the revived feeling of the late Romans, and in addition he had a certain taste for mountain-climbing, which was no longer so rare and abnormal as in Dante's day; he climbed Mount Ventoux, near Avignon, and he described his delight in this little achievement. The Swiss, from Renaissance days onwards, showed from time to time an enthusiastic admiration for the Alps in the shadow of which they live. Conrad Gesner, man of letters and botanist in the sixteenth century, wrote an account of his *Ascent of Pilatus*, and was an important pioneer in mountain climbing and the love of mountain scenery. At a much later date (1729) another eminent Swiss, who was a bad poet and a great physiologist, Haller, wrote his poem on the Alps. Marti, in 1558, and Simler, in 1574 (as Coolidge has shown in his monumental work), were full of admiration for the peaks, chasms, precipices, and glaciers of their native mountains, '*deliciae nostrae, nostrique amores*,' as Marti called them. It is not difficult to account for the enthusiasm of these Swiss writers; it was the result of familiarity heightened by patriotism. Much more remarkable and more genuinely novel is the attitude of the Spanish soldier and poet from Valencia, Cristobal de Virues, in face of the Alps, which he had to cross as one of the leaders of the Spanish army which marched from Milan across the Saint Gothard to Flanders on foot in 1604. A Southerner from the Mediterranean is not predisposed to sympathy with the Alps, and for the soldier they have always been, not objects for admiration, but hostile barriers to be overcome. Virues, who wrote a letter to his brother full of enthusiastic description of the Alps, represents a new attitude. He feels, indeed, the horror of the scene, but with something almost like pleasure, and he expressed these feelings in a sonnet on the Saint Gothard Pass which is accounted one of the earliest poems inspired by the Alps.

Such opinions as these, however, must not be taken as representing the typical attitude towards the Alps of even the finest minds of Europe at that period. For most travellers the Alps still remained what they had been for Livy and for Ammianus, a scene of unmitigated horror which no one could approach for the sake of pleasure. By the beginning of the eighteenth century this feeling, far from diminishing, had gained in strength, and it affected even those who were most sensitive to natural beauty. In 1621, Howell, who, as a Welshman, might have been expected to be appreciative of mountains, and who possessed an alert mind receptive to new impressions, wrote of the 'high and hideous' Alps, 'uncouth huge, monstrous excrescences of Nature,' unlike 'our mountains in Wales, which bear always something useful to man or beast, some grass at least.' Howell is still in this matter, we see, at the standpoint of the savage who can find no beauty where there is no use; the fascination of·the wild has no meaning to him. Pepys, half a century later (in 1668), experienced something of the same feelings when merely going across Salisbury Plain, where he encountered 'some great hills, even to fright us.'

Addison, at the beginning of the eighteenth century, represents, it as probable, a slight but yet definite advance, so far as England is concerned, in the love of wild landscape. He was predisposed to a sympathetic appreciation of the natural beauties he met with during his 'grand tour' through Italy and Switzerland by the fact that he was by birth and heredity a Westmoreland man, and already familiar with the hills, waterfalls, and lakes of his own region, that region which was a century later the home of the Lake School, though for most people in Addison's time it probably was, as to Roger North, a land of 'hideous mountains.' Addison was abroad from 1701 to 1703, and in 1705 he published his *Remarks on Several Parts of Italy, etc.* It can scarcely be said that he really admired wild Nature, but he went beyond the taste for cultivated Nature which ruled in his time, and was attracted by the beauty of natural disorder. At Albano the scene seemed to him 'the most agreeable confusion imaginable.' He admired the Lake of Geneva half a century before that lake became the birthplace of the feeling for romantic beauty, and the Alps, as seen from the Savoy side of the lake, he wrote, 'fill the Mind with an agreeable kind of Horror, and form one of the most irregular misshapen Scenes in the World.' This attitude very accurately represents a state of transition; natural wildness was beginning to arouse an agreeable tone of emotion, and yet it was still felt to be intrinsically ugly and repellent.

With Gray, a little later in the eighteenth century (in 1739), we hear a somewhat new voice, that of a man who was to some extent a pioneer in his vision of Nature. Gray was a poet, a sensitive, solitary man of neurotic heredity, predisposed to this task. There is a note of enthusiasm in his feeling towards wild Nature which we scarcely hear in any other equally notable writer of his time. He went up to the monastery of the Grande Chartreuse and wrote: 'Not a precipice, not a torrent, not a cliff, but is pregnant with religion and poetry.' If he had been born in Saint Bruno's day, he declared, he would himself have been among his disciples. It was, he said, 'one of the most solemn, the most romantic, and the most astonishing scenes I ever beheld.' He still hesitated amid Alpine scenes on a large scale. 'Mount Cenis, I confess,' he wrote, 'carries the permission mountains have of being frightful rather too far, and its horrors were accompanied by too much danger to give one time to reflect upon their beauties.' Yet even the apologetic form in which this sentence is thrown indicates a new attitude. We are here carried far beyond the usual eighteenth century tourist whose enthusiasm for the picturesque generally reached its climax when he had climbed the few feet which lead up to the ruined little temple at Tivoli.

In this movement towards the appreciation of wild Nature England was at this period distinctly ahead of France.[1] There the attitude towards mountains remained one of unmitigated repulsion. Misson, in 1687, spoke of the Alps as 'ces affreuses montagnes,' and compared the line of their summits — for the first time, as Remy de Gourmont believes — to the foam-covered waves of an extremely angry sea. In the *Voyage* of Chapelle and Bachaumont in the same century, they have nothing to say about the Pyrenees; they scarcely seem to have looked at them, for Nature only appealed to them on a small scale, when dainty and pleasant. They visited Sainte-Beaume, 'an almost inaccessible spot,' they said, 'and which cannot be viewed without terror'; they hastened away as soon as

[1] Myra Reynolds points out, in her *Nature in English Poetry*, that the beginnings of English enthusiasm for the mountain scenery of the Lakes may be found before the *Nouvelle Héloïse* in Dalton's poems (1755) and Amory's novel (1756), while Ossian began in 1760; about the same time, Warton, she considers, was 'the first of the romantic poets to advocate a return to Nature in the sense in which Rousseau used the phrase.'

possible. What pleased them best in their whole tour was a place in the environs of Toulouse, kept 'as neat as a garden,' and they were much impressed by a fountain they found there which rose to a great height. It was the age of beautifully ordered and symmetric gardens; the monstrous disorder of wild and sterile Nature could inspire no emotion but antipathy. Its very existence, indeed, seemed to call for explanation. Malebranche declared that the irregularities of the earth's surface, like the uncertainty of its seasons, both so painful to philosophical geometricians, are due to the fact that God has intended that our thoughts should be fixed on the world to come, and not on a world which is the abode of sinners, a world which He has ordained to be given up to disorder, as indicated by the irregularities of its rocks and the cliffs of its coasts. That was a view of the matter which Rousseau rendered for ever impossible.

There were at least two reasons why the men of the seventeenth and early eighteenth centuries, more especially in France, should have adopted an attitude towards wild Nature so unlike that which subsequently prevailed. There was, in the first place, their high cultivation of the social instincts. They cultivated sociability, the art of fine human relationships, with an ardour that almost amounted to passion. It never occurred to them to turn from man to the silence and solemnity of wild Nature, for Nature in those aspects had no voice for them; Nature only spoke to them in the beautifully ordered alleys and fountains of Versailles.

There was probably another and more subtle reason why it was peculiarly difficult for the men of that age to approach sympathetically the rugged wildness and confusion of Nature, and that was the sudden rise and popular expansion of geometrical and mathematical studies during the latter half of the seventeenth century. The interests and ideals of men in one field are apt to spread, unknown even to themselves, into other fields of thought and taste with which they seem to have nothing in common. As we look back at that period today it is difficult not to see that there was a real relationship between the geometrical studies then in the ascendant

and the love of orderly and regular gardens, the horror of disorderly and confused Nature which was expressed in so simple-
minded a spirit by Malebranche, the geometrical philosopher.

For the most part, however, we need no subtle or complex
causes to account for the indifference to Nature, to the posi-
tive distaste for even the most exquisite landscapes. It was
just stolid insensitiveness, the absence of a new sense that had
not yet been stimulated or aroused. Dr. Johnson is here, as in
so many other similar respects, a choicely typical figure. As
late as 1773, he set out with Boswell for the Hebrides. Even
on the lovely shores of Loch Ness, all he could say was that
'these journeys are useless labours since it is easy to sit at
home and conceive rocks and heaths and waterfalls.'

Even after Rousseau, indeed, Madame de Staël, who was
herself so prominent a figure in the Romantic Movement,
could say that she preferred the gutter in the Rue du Bac to
country fields, 'which always smelt of the dunghill'; and
the Marquise de Courcelles would only consent to marriage
on the definite stipulation that her husband never took her
into the country.

III

This attitude towards Nature had become so completely
dominant, at all events in France — for in England, as we
have seen, a new movement had already begun to make itself
felt — that scarcely a discordant voice could be heard. That
was the opportunity of Rousseau. With his new vision and
the magic of his impassioned eloquence, he created a new
feeling for Nature, a new sensibility, almost a new sense.
The attitude of men towards Nature was suddenly and permanently changed.

In 1759 appeared *La Nouvelle Héloïse* (described in the sub-
title as *Lettres de Deux Amants Habitants d'une Petite Ville au
Pied des Alpes*), Rousseau's most popular book, perhaps, indeed, the most influential novel that was ever written; and in
Letter XXIII of the first Part he describes an expedition in
the Haut Valais, which well illustrates the qualities he had

found in Nature and taught others to see. It can scarcely be said that Rousseau admired aspects of Nature which had never been admired before. In late classic days, in early Christian days, and at the Renaissance, there were certainly men who would have found beautiful most of the things that Rousseau found beautiful. But their admiration had remained inarticulate, or else received only tepid and conventional expression.

Even Rousseau's attitude to Nature has sometimes been belittled. Thus Mornet, in his substantial work on *Le Sentiment de la Nature en France*, points out that Rousseau lived in the midst of scenery which might enrapture a painter and yet was only a mediocre painter. He remembered not so much the things themselves as the emotions they gave him. It was the total impression — the temperature, the odour, the air — that impressed him. His details are vague and sometimes inaccurate. Such descriptions as he gives in the *Nouvelle Héloïse* are commonplace and dull, and though so great a master of style, his epithets are ordinary and repetitive, at the best appealing to the ear rather than to the eye.

But, as Mornet himself seems faintly to realise as he goes on, it was precisely on the emotional side that Rousseau's revolution was effected. Precise descriptions could be found elsewhere, and would have effected nothing. It could not have made Rousseau, as he has been called, one of those rare beings whose revolutionary originality so changes the aspects of life that the world's history, so to speak, begins anew. Only a change in the human spirit can do that.

Charlier, in his penetrating study of the feeling for Nature in the Romantic period, has discussed Rousseau's attitude with finer insight. He points out that Rousseau seems intuitively to discover the right expression and is singularly happy in noting effects of light and colour contrast. He never forces the emphasis or the detail. There is a frequent lack of precision; he may use commonplace epithets like 'delicious.' What is marvellous is, Charlier remarks, how much Rousseau can do with such expressions, and he seeks to explain how it is. He concludes that if, since Rousseau, Nature has been painted with more detailed and incisive realism, 'never perhaps has Nature been so much loved.'

Rousseau's immense motive power lay in the fact that he had found a reason for loving Nature, and that he could express that love in the clearest, the most fervent, the most winning of ways. He preached Nature as a gospel; and Nature in mountain and Nature in unsophisticated man were to him one. He had, as he described himself in the *Confessions*, an almost morbid passion for walking. It was only in walking that ideas came to him; he could not write before a table: 'I write in my brain as I walk among rocks or in woods.' He found locomotion the prime stimulant and sedative of his restless and tortured organism: 'I need torrents, rocks, pines, dark forests, mountains, rough paths to climb, by precipices that fill me with fear.' Solitude, motion, the spectacle of Nature unpolluted by the hand of man, the tonic resistance of steep climbs, the exhilaration of keen air — these were the things that more than anything else in the world brought joy and peace to Rousseau. In proclaiming them to mankind he knew of what he was speaking.

There was thus a double reason why Rousseau became to his generation the revealer of Nature. In the first place, he was Swiss, and thus belonged to a people traditionally and patriotically attached to those wild aspects of Nature with which they had grown familiar. It is true they had never given adequate expression to that attachment. It may well have been, indeed, that Rousseau also would not have become the apostle of a new vision of wild landscape if he had not in youth been transferred to the other side of the lake and learnt to know the slightly different landscape of Savoy, for over-familiarity dulls rather than heightens the perceptions.

Apart from this predisposing factor of race and birthplace there was another and decisive factor: his abnormal and even morbid personal organisation. This was undoubtedly congenital, as his *Confessions* clearly show. Inapt for the ordinary duties and relationships of life, awkward and unsociable, with a timidity that sometimes rebounded to the opposite extreme of insolence, and beneath this unpromising exterior seething with emotions and aspirations, young Rousseau, suffering, tormented, diseased — 'the prince of psychastheniacs,' as Janet called him — was predestinate to the love of wild Nature. Here, amid the strong and beautiful impressions of a wildness untouched by man, his restless, exhausted nervous system was at once stimulated and soothed; he found the peace and joy which the world of civilised men could never give to one of his temperament. And the might of his genius — his exquisite sensibility, his acute analysis, his entrancing eloquence — enabled him to transfer his vision to the brains of his fellow-men, and to inoculate the world with his own emotion. Henceforth it was felt to be at least in bad taste to apply to mountains that epithet of 'horrible' which had been the conventionally correct description for over a thousand years, while for some, as for Shelley at the sight of Mont Blanc, that feeling of horror was now replaced by 'a sentiment of ecstatic wonder, not unallied to madness.'

It must be noted, however, that, even as that remark of Shelley's indicates, the mountain represents an extreme form of wild Nature which is not far from inspiring what may be termed 'horror.' It was later than Rousseau that Madame de Staël, herself Swiss, referred to Switzerland as 'une magnifique horreur.' A friend, who is himself a distinguished landscape painter, while agreeing with my view that the love of wild Nature is fostered by the anti-social spirit, adds (and I would agree): 'To my mind the attraction or the repulsion exercised by mountains, when of the magnitude of the Alps, is of a specific kind, and I can imagine a genuine lover of the wild being repelled by them. I understand the epithet of "horrible" applied to them simply on account of their overpowering bulk. I have myself the experience as of being *imprisoned* when amid the Alps, far more than in the most crowded city, and it is with a sense of liberation and freedom that I descend into the open plains. Lofty mountains feed the sense of the sublime, but is not that in a way an anti-social sentiment?'

It must be added that Rousseau himself was not an alpinist or mountain-climber as understood today; it was only with the lower slopes that he was familiar, and even then it was not there that he spent his happiest moments. It was 'a place of delight,' he wrote to Meister of his hermitage, 'a solitude filled with all the marvels of art and yet a solitude. I had the most pleasant outlooks. I was enchanted by the murmur of several cascades. Morning and evening I breathed the sweet odour of oranges and flowers. In this retreat I think I had the most cheerful ideas and imaginations I have ever had in my life.' And of what spot was he speaking? The little hermitage, far from mountains, at Montmorency in the neighbourhood of Paris, which Madame d'Epinay had lent to her 'bear.' The Précieuses (as Charlier remarks) had once passed through this very region and seen nothing of interest. It had, indeed, a century earlier, actually been a refuge for hermits. The first time Rousseau saw it he exclaimed: 'Ah! what a delicious dwelling! It is the refuge made for me!' Madame d'Epinay repaired it, unknown to him, and then brought him to it, smiling: 'My bear, here is your refuge!' And it was here that much of his best work was done. One may see it still, a little ruined neglected building, apparently untouched for years. When I was there (which is now a quarter of a century ago) only the walls remained, with a half-effaced inscription, and the roses. They bloom deliciously over the crumbling walls and the birds sing all day. It stands in the grounds of a small rustic café, supplying cider and beer ('*On peut apporter son manger*'). The hermitage is sheltered against the south side of a small height and is open to the sun all day; on the height grow huge and ancient chestnut trees. It is of such a scene that we must think in the first place when we associate Rousseau with 'wild Nature,' even though he could find stimulation in more savage spots. Or we may think of the Lac de Bienne which he found 'wild and romantic' enough, and to understand fully his new love of Nature we should read the exquisite Fifth Promenade of the *Rêveries* in which at the end of his life he described his stay there.

We must, however, remember not only that Rousseau was not himself what the alpinist of today would consider a real mountain man, but that our general conception of mountains

86

is distorted by the prominence which Alps and alpinists have come to assume in the picture of Europe. In this connection a memorable successor of Rousseau — and though influenced by him a man of wider outlook in this field and a more scientific culture — Ramond de Carbonnières, must not be overlooked. A pioneer in the more human approach to mountains, he was less occupied with the Alps than with the Pyrenees; 'the great poet of the Pyrenees' he has been called. Though his name may seldom now be heard, his high place was long ago fully recognised, as by Sainte-Beuve and Michelet, and has lately been reaffirmed.[1]

Ramond's *Observations faites dans les Pyrénées*, published in the fateful year of 1789, has been termed 'the birth certificate of the Pyrenees,' previously as remote and little known as Tahiti. Ramond was not only singularly various in his outlook and a man of scientific culture, but was able to bring an almost scientific precision into the analysis of the emotions aroused by the mountains. In this first revelation of the special qualities of the Pyrenees, Ramond clearly realised the characteristics which for some of us (among whom I must myself be counted) render the Pyrenees so much more sympathetic than the Alps. 'Here,' said Ramond, 'we are far from the summits stretching beyond summits in desolation, from the abysses the eye dares not plumb, and the solitudes where the memory of the habitable world grows faint.' Here we are not out of the world, we dominate it, we observe it; the home of man is still beneath our eyes. Ramond was influenced by Rousseau, but he was emancipated from the philosophic conventions of his age, and when he described the vigour and freedom and fine character of the Pyrenean shepherds he spoke of what he intimately knew. Ramond de Carbonnières was a powerful influence on many distinguished writers who followed him, on Senancour and on Chateaubriand.

How instinctively the craving for wild Nature makes itself felt in the men of Rousseau's more special temperament is wit-

---

[1] This has been done, for instance, by G. Charlier, 'Le Sentiment de la Nature chez les Romantiques Français,' *Mémoires, Academie Royale de Belgique*, 2d Series, tome IX, 1913, and in a long essay in Monglond's *Jeunesses*, 1933.

nessed by Restif de la Bretonne, the 'gutter Rousseau' ('*le Rousseau du ruisseau*'). Born some twenty years later than Rousseau, and with a like abnormal nervous organisation, and a like impulse to war with the civilised society of his time, it was Restif's lot, unlike Rousseau's, to spend all his life, after childhood, in Paris. Yet we find in him the same spontaneous cry after the savagery of Nature. The environs of Paris, he declares — writing of himself as a boy of fourteen in his autobiography, *Monsieur Nicolas* — charming as they were, satisfied no desire of his heart: 'I would like to have lived in a wood, in some half savage spot, so long as the castle was far away. I have felt what few have experienced, but what a savage would have felt if brought to France, on seeing our beautiful things.' And then he speaks of English gardens, which, it must be remembered, for the men of his time represented the beginning of a new movement towards unfettered Nature in scenery. 'Ah, if I had then seen an English garden! I should have fallen into ecstasy, I could not have left it!... I would have fled to America if I had had the means, not to make my fortune, but to become a savage. It was the only kind of life that suited me; to civilise me was to do violence to my nature.'

Rousseau, like Restif, was not only anti-social in relation to the society of his own day; he was abnormal to a degree that may properly be termed morbid. That was why he was peculiarly fitted to be receptive to natural influences and to become the discoverer of new aspects of wild Nature. But all the pioneers of the approach to Nature, if we consider the matter, have been, so far as we are in a position to discover the facts, men of a more or less abnormal temperament, placed in a position of hostility to the society of their time.[1] Lu-

---

[1] Douglas Freshfield (as in his presidential address to the Geographical Section of the British Association in 1904), prejudiced by his own personal tastes, sought to show that the love of mountains is 'a healthy, primitive, and almost universal human instinct.' Otto Pfister, with sounder psychological insight, has pointed out (*Love in Children and its Aberrations*, p. 216) that it is the reserved and introverted boy, lacking the ability for affectionate adaptation to his environment, who displays fondness for the savage grandeur of mountain scenery, finding therein the symbolism of his own longings; our reactions to landscape depend on the symbolism we interpolate.

cretius, Jerome and the other conspicuous early Christians, Dante, the extreme ascetics of the contemplative Orders — these were not people of the *homme moyen sensuel type*, who instinctively accept the world as they find it. For the most part, also, they have had the temperament of genius which so often causes a man to view the world at a different angle from his fellows, to reverse the emotional values of life, *in tristitia hilaris, in hilaritate tristis*. The men who followed Rousseau, to complete the movement to which he had given the chief impetus, showed the same characteristics, notably the two great poets who in England finally completed it, Byron and Wordsworth. Byron was, after Goethe, undoubtedly the most brilliant and influential of the distinguished poets who came to the school of Rousseau on the shores of Lake Leman to learn his lesson and to proclaim it to the world. By the force of his temperament, and the immense prestige of his genius, he effectually acclimatised in England, indeed in Europe, the new gospel of Nature. At the same time Wordsworth, a more subtle and a more profound revolutionary, quietly elaborated on the heights of his own lake country the spiritual significance of that gospel of Nature, and left little further to be said.

The result was that the old habit and fashion of speaking of mountains and wild Nature as 'hideous' was replaced by the new convention of speaking of them as 'romantic.' That, indeed, was an essential part of the great Romantic Movement. It is sometimes said that Addison, on his foreign tour, was the first to apply the word 'romantic' in a favourable sense to natural scenery. That is scarcely correct. The word was current at least nearly half a century before. I find that it occurs twice in Pepys's *Diary*. In 1666, Pepys visited Windsor and wrote enthusiastically that 'It is the most romantique castle that is in the world.' Next year he refers contemptuously to 'romantic lies.' The word was applied to something that seemed to belong to the region of romance, of fiction, and in its favourable sense it was for a long time most commonly applied to landscape containing a castle in ruins as being a scene suitable for a novel. It lost its stricter meaning as the interest in Nature grew wider, but in Addison it still indicates a scene for a story. His vessel put into Cassis, not far from Sainte-Beaume, on the voyage to Genoa, and he writes: 'We were here shown at a distance the Desarts that have been rendered so famous by the Presence of Mary Magdalene, who is said to have wept away the rest of her life among these solitary Rocks and Mountains. It is so Romantic a Scene that it has always probably given occasion to such Chimerical Relations.' Goethe, in Friedländer's opinion, probably adopted the word from Tobler's translation of Thomson's *Seasons* (1765). As its use grew general and conventionalised, it became applicable to any scene of wild Nature, which commended itself to the spectator, though it is probable that in the use of the epithet there was an underlying feeling that the scene described as 'romantic' constituted a fitting background for a delightful story.

We may perhaps find the climax of the movement we are here concerned with in Ruskin. He grasped it comprehensively, he largely devoted his life to it, he presented the peculiar type of temperament which is specially drawn to wild Nature. He was, finally, the last really popular and influential champion of the romantic in Nature. He has himself described the attitude which he herein shared with his great comrades. 'There is,' he declared, 'a sense of the material beauty, both of inanimate nature, the lower animals, and human beings, which in the iridescence, colour-depth, and morbid (I use the word deliberately) mystery and softness of it — with other qualities indescribable by any single words, and only to be analysed by extreme care — is found, to the full, only in five men that I know of in modern times; namely, Rousseau, Shelley, Byron, Turner, and myself, differing totally and throughout the entire group of us from the delight in clear-struck beauty of Angelico and the Trecentisti, and separated, much more singularly, from the cheerful joys of Chaucer, Shakespeare, and Scott... all this love of impending mountains, coiled thunder-clouds, and dangerous sea, being joined in us with a sulky, almost ferine, love of retreat in valleys of Charmettes, gulphs of Spezzia, ravines of Olym-

pus, low lodgings in Chelsea, and close brushwood at Conis-
ton.' It is Ruskin, we must not forget, who leads us on to
Proust, and in such words as these we feel the direction.

The movement which led to the consecration of wild Nature
in mountains fully ran its course in Byron and Wordsworth
and Ruskin. There was no further progress along that path.
No poet, eager to shun the ways of man, no pioneer in the
love of wild Nature, would nowadays dream of finding inspiration on the shores of the Lake of Geneva, or of writing a
poem on the distant prospect of Mont Blanc. Comfortable
and pleasant those regions have become to the average man,
and Chamonix is almost a railway centre. Rousseau and
Byron and Shelley would now certainly hasten away in horror. In the nineteenth century the pioneer in the love of wild
Nature began to seek beauty, not in the ruggedness of mountains, but, reverting to the early Christian feeling associated
with Jerome, in the dreariness of plains and deserts. We already find a hint of this in Shelley's *Julian and Maddalo*, when,
writing at Venice of the Lido, he says:

> 'I love all waste
> And solitary places where we taste
> The pleasure of believing what we see
> Is boundless, as we wish our souls to be.'

Shelley was impartial in his love of all aspects of wild and
unfettered Nature, though for the most part of the school of
Rousseau, whose genius seemed to him almost more than human. A more characteristic example of this modern form of
the love of wild Nature is perhaps furnished by George Borrow, who, it has been said, 'could draw more poetry from a
wide-spreading marsh, with its straggling rushes, than from
the most beautiful scenery, and would stand and look at it
with rapture.' In American Thoreau, as well as in English
Doughty, this fascination became highly developed. Thoreau
was in love with wildness: 'Life consists with wildness,' he
declared. 'The most alive is the wildest.' And he found the
wildness he sought by no means supremely, if indeed at all,

in mountains, but in dreary wastes. 'My spirits,' he wrote in his journal, 'infallibly rise in proportion to the outward dreariness. Give me the ocean, the desert, or the wilderness!' These men had the abnormal temperament, the instinctive antagonism to the society of their time, which we find among the mountain men of the earlier love of wild Nature, but their passion sought a different outlet. The difference is well described in the introductory chapter of Hardy's *Return of the Native*. It is a question, remarked Hardy, whether the exclusive reign of the orthodoxly beautiful landscape is not approaching its last quarter. 'The new Vale of Tempe may be a gaunt waste in Thule: human souls may find themselves in closer and closer harmony with external things wearing a sombreness distasteful to our race when it was young. The time is coming when the tourist will find the chastened sublimity of a moor most in keeping with his moods, and Heidelburg and Baden be passed unheeded as he hastens from the Alps to the sand-dunes of Scheveningen.' It is doubtless true that the marsh and the moor and the desert never exerted the same potent fascination and poetic reverence as the scenes which stirred the lovers of wild Nature a century earlier.

When we glance back over the great field of human emotion we have here rapidly traversed, it becomes possible to see what amount of truth there is in the opposing views which have been maintained concerning the evolution of the love of wild Nature. While it is by no means true that the attraction to mountains is, as Freshfield had supposed, 'a healthy, primitive and almost universal human instinct,' the more widely current view that that attraction dates from little more than a century back is still further opposed to the truth. A psychological interpretation of the facts shows us that while there have probably always and everywhere been a few persons who have ascended mountains or gone out into the desert, the pioneers in such movements have been temperamentally exceptional persons, and by their abnormal constitution instinctively thrown into a state of more or less violent and indignant opposition to the moral and aesthetic ideals

of their time. They have gone into the mountains to seek
peace for themselves and a new inspiration for life, and they
have returned with a new table of commandments.

> 'Thou hast a voice, great Mountain, to repeal
> Large codes of fraud and woe; not understood
> By all, but which the wise, and great, and good
> Interpret, or make felt, or deeply feel.'

For the men of this make the natural terrors of the wild
become a source of joy and strength, and they return to mankind from their Sinai with the authority of law-givers. These
ardent and passionate explorers pave the way for the mob
that follows them, but the mob feels none of their emotion.
'Nature is for them merely a spectacle,' it has been truly said;
'they go to the Righi as they go to the Opera.' Even the
mountain-climber is often, perhaps usually, untouched by
the passion for wild Nature, and quite incapable of entering
into the emotion of Rousseau or Wordsworth. Sir Leslie
Stephen was a prominent and enthusiastic alpinist. But he
wrote: 'Scenery, even the wildest that is really enjoyable,
derives half its charm from the occult sense of the human life
and social forms moulded upon it; the Alps would be unbear-
ably stern but for the picturesque society preserved among
their folds.' Thereby Stephen betrayed the fact that he was
in feeling a man of the early eighteenth century. The appeal
of wild Nature can only be perfectly felt by men who are, by
temperament and circumstance, rebels against the laws and
conventions of their time. It is a passion that arises in ages
of splendid individualism. The representative men of such
a period experience what Nietzsche describes as that 'sympathy for the horrible and questionable which arises when
one is oneself horrible and questionable.' That is why, in an
age like the present, when the instincts of social and urban
development are dominant over those of revolutionary individualism, the search for wild Nature sometimes — though
by no means always — seems to be a spiritual adventure which
constitutes an almost closed chapter in the history of the human soul. We are drawn today to the more humanised and

socialised forms of Nature, mixed with personal intercourse and deliberate art. We witness the revived love of beautiful gardens.[1]

---

[1] These words were written more than a quarter of a century ago. I leave it to the reader to decide whether they are now more true, or less true, than when they were written.

5

THE BICENTENARY OF ROUSSEAU

I

TWO centuries after his birth,[1] Jean-Jacques Rousseau continues to exert a potent and disturbing influence; we still have among us his ardent advocates, his bitter enemies. For the most part, during the century that follows the death of any mere writer of books, he falls back into the historic background; the battles that may once have raged around him have subsided; and those persons who are still sufficiently interested to like or dislike his work combine to adjust him in the niche, large or small, which he is henceforth destined to occupy. It is so even with the greatest. Less than a century has passed since Goethe died; for some he is in the modern world 'the master of those who know'; for others he is 'a colossal sentimentalist'; but each party recognises it has something big to deal with and there is no longer any inclination to fall into violent dispute. Not so with Rousseau. This man, who filled the second half of the eighteenth century, who inspired most of the literary and even social movements of the nineteenth century, remains a living and even distracting force in the twentieth century. At the present time there is probably more written about Rousseau than about any contemporary man of letters with the possible exception of Tolstoy, and Tolstoy, we may remember, was an avowed disciple of Rousseau. We have made up our minds about Voltaire, even about Diderot, but we have not made up our minds about

[1] This essay was written in celebration of the bicentenary of Rousseau's birth on 28th June, 1712, and published in the *Atlantic Monthly* for June, 1912 (as well as in the *Mercure de France* for September), under the title of 'Rousseau Today.' It is here reprinted with only a few slight verbal changes, since it seemed of interest to preserve the tone and outlook of the 'today' when the essay was written.

Rousseau. According to the point of view, and the special group of alleged facts on which attention is concentrated, Rousseau figures as the meanest of mankind, as a degenerate pervert, as an unfortunate lunatic, as a suffering and struggling man of genius, as the noble pioneer of all the great humanitarian and progressive movements in the modern world, and as the seductive and empty rhetorician who is leading society astray from the orderly paths of civilisation into the abyss of anarchy.

It is not the least remarkable feature of this polemical literature that often it most magnifies the influence of Rousseau when it is most hostile to that influence. Mrs. Frederika Macdonald, who brings twenty years of scholarship and patient research in archives to the service of the thesis that Rousseau was the victim of a deliberate conspiracy on the part of so-called friends, is content to fix her attention on the human fate of a much-suffering and greatly abused hero. Thomas Davidson, the erratic philosopher and 'wandering scholar,' who wrote a book to prove that Rousseau incarnated all the evil and disorderly elements in modern thought and modern life, yet leaves on the reader the impression of a mighty force which it would be idle to combat: 'the father of Democracy,' 'the father of modern political science,' 'the father of modern pedagogy,' 'the parent of Socialism,' and the completest exemplification of the 'tendencies and aspirations comprehended under the one term individualism,' until it seems that there can be nothing left for anyone else to father. Pierre Lasserre, again, who in *Le Romantisme Français* has with fine literary skill and relentless logic comprehensively attacked the Romantic Movement, regards Rousseau and the Romantic Movement as identical, alike as 'the genius of evil,' 'the modern disease,' 'the most subversive torrent that has ever been unchained among men,' until, as Remy de Gourmont's *alter ego*, M. Delarue, put it, we begin to wonder how such a flood of horrors as the nineteenth century can ever have had any existence except in the imagination of a morbid brain. The prestige of Rousseau has thus been maintained, not only by those who reverence his name, but equally by those who look upon him as the incarnation of evil, alike whether they are representatives of the ancient objective hierarchical 'classical' mode of thinking, of which Davidson was a belated survivor, or whether they represent a new objective systematisation, as was the case with Comte, who, it may be recalled, had devised, for the purpose of expressing everything he most objected to, the adjective 'Roussien.' The antagonists of Rousseau have been inspired in their attack by the conviction that they were defending the sacred cause of civilisation. And yet, such is the irony of things, they have laid themselves open to the charge that they are themselves attacking the movements and the personages who are in modern times the banner-bearers, the very incarnation, of civilisation.

II

Since those who revile the name of Rousseau are at one with those who adore it in magnifying the extent of his influence, it becomes easier than it would otherwise be to estimate what our modern world presumably owes to Rousseau. It may be interesting to touch on two of these things: the Revolution and Romanticism.

The whole Revolution, say its friends and its enemies alike, was Rousseau; Berthelot, the great man of science, declared it in solemn admiration a quarter of a century ago. Lasserre, the acute critic, declares it in bitter indignation today. Rousseau was not, indeed, consciously working towards the Revolution, and he would have loathed its protagonists who acted in his name, just as Jesus would have loathed the scribes and Pharisees who have masqueraded in his Church. But, as we look back, it is easy to see how Rousseau's work, and Rousseau's alone among the men of his generation pointed to revolution. They appealed to intelligence, to good sense, to fine feeling, to elevated humanitarianism; but it is not these things of which revolutions are made. Rousseau appealed to fundamental instincts, to soaring aspirations, to blind passions, to the volcanic eruptive elements in human nature, and we are at once amid the forces of revolution. No wonder that all the men of the Revolution fed themselves on Rousseau's words. Not a single revolutionary, Mallet du Pan noted in 1789, but was carried away by Rousseau's doctrines, and burning to realise them. Marat was seen in public enthusiastically reading aloud the *Social Contract*, and Charlotte Corday, who slew him, was equally the fervent disciple of Rousseau. There was one other man beside Rousseau who had a supreme part in moulding the Revolution, at all events so far as concerns its final outcome. It is interesting to hear that this man, Napoleon, declared to Lord Holland that without 'that bad man' Rousseau there would have been no Revolution. Since the Christianisation of the Roman Empire there have been four great movements of the human spirit in Christendom — the Renaissance, the Reformation, the Counter-Reformation, and the Revolution. Three of these movements have been so diffused in time and space that we are scarcely justified in closely associating even one of them with the influence of a single man. But the Revolution, incalculably vast as its results have been, was narrowly circumscribed. It is comparatively easy to measure it, and when so measured its friends and its foes ascribe it — so far as any complex social-economic movement can be associated with one man — to Rousseau.

Mainly by virtue of his relation to the Revolution, Rousseau is claimed as the pioneer of Modern Democracy, alike in its direction towards Socialism and its direction towards Anarchism. For both these democratic movements — the collectivistic as well as the individualistic — rest on those natural instincts which it was Rousseau's mission to proclaim. The democracy which insists that the whole shall embody every unit, and the democracy which insists that each unit shall have its own rights against the whole, alike appeal to deep emotional reasons to which the humblest respond. 'There would have been no Republic without Rousseau,' says Lemaître. Republicanism, Socialism, Anarchism — these are the three democratic movements which have been slowly permeating and transforming the political societies of men since the Great Revolution of 1789, and we are asked to believe that the germs of all were scattered abroad by this one man, Rousseau.

The chorus of voices which acclaims or accuses Rousseau as the creator of Romanticism is even greater than that which finds in him the inventor of Revolutionary Democracy. The Revolutionary Movement and the Romantic Movement are one, we are told, and Rousseau was responsible for both. What, it may be asked, is Romanticism? There is not much agreement on this point. Lasserre, one of its ablest and most absolute opponents, tells us that it is 'a general revolution of the human soul' which may be described as 'a system of feeling and acting conformably to the supposed primitive nature of mankind,' and since we do not know what the primitive nature of mankind is, Romanticism becomes, in opposition to the classical spirit in general and the Gallic spirit in particular, 'absolute individualism in thought and feeling,' or in other words, 'a disorder of the feelings and ideas which overturns the whole economy of civilised human nature.' This definition is itself individualistic — and therefore on the theory Romantic — but it may, for the moment, serve. Fortunately, though there is no agreement as to what Romanticism is, there is less dispute as to the writers who may be termed Romantic.

It is a remarkable fact that though Rousseau so largely filled the second half of the eighteenth century he had little influence on its literature in France. He was the adored prophet, preacher, teacher, but not the inspired and inspiring artist with a new revelation of Nature peculiarly apt for literary uses. Beaumarchais, who here dominated that period, belongs to altogether another tradition. Only Bernardin de Saint-Pierre was the follower, as he was also the friend, of Rousseau, and *Paul and Virginia* opens the great literary tradition of Rousseau. The first notable names in French literature which we can at all associate with Rousseau are dubious names, more dubious perhaps than they deserve to be, but still distinctly dubious. It is highly probable that the *Confessions* moved Casanova to write his own immortal *Mémoires*. It is certain that they inspired that interesting picture of an

99

unwholesome mind, the *Monsieur Nicolas* of Restif de la Bretonne, the 'Rousseau du ruisseau,' as he has been wittily and
accurately termed. We must even recognise that Rousseau
was the adored exemplar of the Marquis de Sade, who, in
Aline et Valcour, makes Valcour, here speaking probably for
his author, assert that Rousseau encouraged him to devote
himself to literature and philosophy. 'It was in the conversation of this deep philosopher, of this true friend of Nature and
of Man, that I acquired my dominant passion for literature
and the arts.'

In Germany, earlier than elsewhere, the influence of Rousseau was profoundly felt by men of an altogether different
type of character. In France, Rousseau could only be potent
by stimulating a revolutionary reaction against everything
which had long been regarded as the classic norm from which
no deviation was possible; that was why the morbid and unsound personalities in literature, rightly finding a real point
of contact with Rousseau, felt his influence first. But an altogether different tradition, if we look beyond cosmopolitan
aristocratic circles, prevailed in Germany. Here the subjective emotionalism of Rousseau, his constant appeal to the
ultimate standard of Nature, were so congenial to the Teu-
tonic spirit that they acted as an immediate liberating force.
Rousseau was Kant's supreme master; only one portrait, Rousseau's, hung on the walls of the philosopher's simple study;
all his doctrines in the three Critiques may be regarded
(Thomas Davidson has ingeniously argued) as a formal
crystallisation of Rousseau's fluid eloquence. Fichte also was
largely moulded by Rousseau, as were Herder and Lessing.
Goethe in the final stages of his long development aimed at
serenely objective Neo-classic ideals which were far indeed
from Rousseau, but at the outset he was as thorough a disciple as Kant. He went on pilgrimage to the beautiful island
in the Lake of Bienne once hallowed by Rousseau's presence;
his Werther is manifestly the younger brother of Saint-Preux,
and it may be, as some have claimed, that without Rousseau
there could have been no *Faust*.

It was not until the nineteenth century that the Romantic

Movement finally burst into magnificent life in France. Chateaubriand appears as the quintessence of Romanticism, a more pure embodiment of its literary quality than even Rousseau himself. Senancour, especially as he shows himself in his *Obermann*, was an equally typical and much more genuine representative of the Movement. Madame de Staël, one of the first to write about Rousseau, was penetrated by his spirit, and became the revealer to France of Romantic Germany. Alfred de Musset was a Romantic through Byron, rather than directly from Rousseau. Victor Hugo, Lamartine, George Sand, even at times Balzac, all belonged to Romanticism. Michelet, writing history by the sole light of his own personal emotions, was peculiarly a Romantic. Flaubert, in a later generation, was Romantic on one side, altogether alien from Romanticism, as were his fundamental ideals. But during the first half of the nineteenth century in France, with the possible exception of Stendhal — for even he was really affected by the movement — it is not easy to name any notable figure in literature who was outside Romanticism. Rousseau's influence had become so all-pervading that, like the universal pressure of the air, it was sometimes unperceived by those who were experiencing it. Louis Dumur has pointed out that Alfred de Musset in his *Confession d'un Enfant du Siècle*, when trying to discover the sources of Romanticism, never so much as mentions Rousseau.

The attitude of England towards Romanticism and towards Rousseau was different from either that of Germany or of France. The Germans were made conscious by Rousseau of their own unconscious impulses. The French were forced to undergo a violent conversion. But the English were Romanticists already from the outset and here the Romantic Movement could effect no revolution. All Rousseau's literary inspirations and aesthetic ideals had come, directly or indirectly, from England: Richardson's *Clarissa*, Kent's English garden, Locke's philosophy, English independence and English freedom, these were the things which had aroused the emulation or stirred the enthusiasm of Rousseau. English influence equally stimulated also the great apostle of Romanticism, and Chateaubriand composed *Atala* and *René* in Hyde Park. These splendid flowers were therefore easily acceptable in England for they were clearly raised from English seeds. Rousseau's influence recognised and unrecognised, reached English Romanticism, but Rousseau was here only giving back in a more highly developed form what he had himself received from England.

If we look beyond the Romantic Movement in its narrower literary sense, we still find that the influence of Rousseau remains just as plainly visible, in Russia, for instance. It is unnecessary to say that the greatest writer of modern times in Russia, the greatest writer in the world of his day, was from his earliest years a disciple of Rousseau; Tolstoy read and re-read the twenty volumes of Rousseau's works until some of the pages became so familiar that it seemed to him he had written them himself; he wore Rousseau's portrait next his skin as the devout Russian wears the cross; it was, he himself said, worship rather than admiration which he experienced for Rousseau; even shortly before his death he wrote that the two chief formative influences of his life had been Rousseau and the Gospels.

If we turn away from the apostles and the propagandists of avowed emotional revolution, we have not yet escaped Rousseau. The austere Emerson equally has his roots in Rousseau, if he was not actually, as Davidson termed him, 'the most loyal disciple Rousseau ever had.' The Transcendentalist was here at one with the Positivist. George Eliot, equally alien in temperament, was an equally ardent admirer of the *Confessions*; Rousseau, she said, 'quickened' her mind, not by imparting any new beliefs, but by 'the mighty rushing wind of his inspiration'; he 'made man and nature a fresh world of thought and feeling to me.' It was an accurate characterisation of the kind of power by which Rousseau has so often held the souls of men and women.

In the twentieth century the same potent force is still quickening ardent and aspiring souls who strive to create new ideals. Moreover, Rousseau is still the precursor even of those who are unconscious of his influence. He had long ago anticipated our latest philosophies. William James is counted the founder of Pragmatism, but the conception of 'truth' as 'practical truth' or 'cash value' rather than 'science,' was so clearly set forth in *Emile* and the second half of the *Nouvelle Héloïse*, that Schinz has been able to argue that 'the greatest of the Pragmatists is — and will probably remain — Jean-Jacques Rousseau.' So also with the fashionable Bergsonian philosophy of the day, with its depreciation of reason and its insistence on the vital force of instinct. That also is laid down, with a less subtle elaboration but not with less emphasis, by Rousseau.

Even those for whom Rousseau is nothing but a poison have not escaped the operation of that seductive venom. Nietzsche, the most conspicuous and influential thinker of these latter days, was absolutely opposed to Rousseau. Rousseau's 'Nature,' his 'good man,' his sentiment, his weaknesses, especially his lack of aristocratic culture and his plebeianism — against all these things Nietzsche's hatred was implacable. Yet Rousseau was in his own blood. 'Nietzsche,' says Alois Riehl, 'is the antipodes of Rousseau, and yet his spiritual relation. He is the Rousseau of our time.'

III

In thus estimating the hold of Rousseau over the things which have been counted precious since the days in which he lived, we have the authority even of those who rebel against his influence. But there is always a fallacy involved in such attempts to fasten an unlimited responsibility upon any human figure, not excepting the greatest. Even the supreme man of genius, as Dumur truly says, is no aerolite from another sphere, no bolt from the blue. The most absolute innovator has found the terms of his fruitful ideas in ancient tradition. The most potent revolutionary owes his power to the fact that in his day certain conditions, especially economic and social conditions, combine to produce a vacuum his spirit is peculiarly fitted to fill. The name of Darwin is immortally associated with the idea of evolution, but the idea had been slowly germinating through thousands of years, sometimes in brains of as great a calibre as his own, until the moment arrived when at last fruition was possible, and the cautious, deliberate Darwin calmly completed the work of the ages. Even the great movement of Christianity, which sometimes seem to us so mighty as to be beyond the reach of reason to fathom, is seen to be necessary and inevitable when we realise the conditions under which it arose and see the figure of Jesus slowly hammered and annealed into the shape which best satisfied the deepest cravings of an epoch. Rousseau — again alike by friends and foes — has been counted, like Jesus, a prophet issuing with a new law from the desert into a decadent civilisation he was destined to dissolve and renew; he has been regarded as a great reformer of Christianity such as Luther was, the incarnation of a new wave of Christianity, adding to the renovation of its essential qualities — its abandonment to emotion, its magnification of the poor and humble, its insistence on charity — a new set of notes, a trend towards political realisation, a fresh ideal of natural beauty, a justification of passion, a refinement of voluptuous sentiment, which adjusted Christianity to the modern soul as it had never been adjusted before. Luther had de-Catholicised Christianity; Rousseau, who in his own person united the two traditions, while yet retaining the plebeian and individualistic basis which Luther established, re-Catholicised Christianity on a new plane, even though in the end he stood aloof from Christianity, and created a Church whose dogmas rested on the universal authority of instincts and emotions.

Yet, just as we can counterpart every Christian rite and dogma outside Christianity, so also it is easy to duplicate every tenet and tendency in Rousseau. Marivaux, within narrower limits and with a more restrained method, was a sympathetic and original moralist, a delicate artist, a subtle psychologist, to a degree that Rousseau never attained; in his earliest work Rousseau was frankly an imitator of Marivaux. The Abbé Prévost, again, more than any man had let the flood of early English romanticism into France, had translated *Clarissa*, and himself written novels of wild and sombre romantic passion; Rousseau knew Prévost, he was profoundly affected by his novels. Locke, in another sphere, had set forth epoch-making reflections on political government, and had written an enlightened treatise on education; the author of the *Social Contract* and *Emile* clearly reveals how much he owed to 'the wise Locke.' Before ever he began to write, Rousseau had soaked his mind in books and meditated on them in his perpetual long walks; he was brought up on romances, he had read everything he could find, English travel books especially, about savages in 'the state of Nature'; he had absorbed all that matters in the literature of the seventeenth century, though he knew comparatively little of the literature of his own century; without any guidance, by unerring instinct, he had seized on the things that fed his own mood, from Plutarch to Petrarch. Even without going outside the pale of Catholic Christianity, he could, had he known it, have found the authority for every intimate and daring impulse of his own heart.[1]

The ideas and the emotions, therefore, which Rousseau manifested were by no means unique. The temperament he had inherited furnished the most exquisitely fertile of all conceivable soils for these seeds to flourish in. But the seeds were not new seeds and for the most part we can trace with precision the exact source from which each of them reached Rousseau. Moreover, when we come, calmly and critically, to measure and to weigh the ideas and the emotions we find in Rousseau's books, it happens, as often as not, that they fail to stand our tests. If we explore the *Social Contract*, we find that every page swarms with bold propositions for which no proof is, or can be, supplied. Rousseau had borrowed Hobbes's conception of sovereignty and Locke's conception of popular

[1] 'Whence but in Christianity had Rousseau drawn his ideas on equality, on simplicity of life and poverty of spirit as the conditions of happiness?' asks Remy de Gourmont (*Dialogues des Amateurs*, xliii). 'Who but the preachers have declaimed for fifteen hundred years before Rousseau against luxury and the vices of civilization, and intellectual corruption? The divagations of Jean-Jacques concerning the state of nature are foolish, but not more so than those of Fénelon. His diatribes against civilisation are mad, but not more so than those of Saint Bernard. And who gave the example not merely of cursing society but of fleeing from it except the monks? Rousseau is wholesome compared to a Bruno or a Rancé. And what is the anarchism of Rousseau compared to that of Francis of Assisi?'

government and amalgamated them into the image of a Sovereign People which can do no wrong and governs by its own direct *fiat*, in such a way that the will of each finds its part in the will of all. No doubt it is a magnificent idea and it is still alive in the world moulding political institutions; it is responsible for the establishment of the Referendum which has had a certain vogue in new political constitutions and we are constantly endeavouring, however much in vain, to approach its realisation. But when we examine Rousseau's exposition of this idea, we find that verbal logic takes the place of inductive reasoning, that impassioned declamation is the agent of persuasion, and that the very lucidity of the statement only brings out more clearly the glaring inconsistencies and absurdities which the argument involves.

If we turn to a very different book, though not less famous and in its own way not less influential, we encounter the same experience. *La Nouvelle Héloïse*, in the effect it has had on the writing of novels, is second to none, except *Don Quixote*. Schopenhauer, himself a great literary artist, counted *La Nouvelle Héloïse* among the four great novels of the world. Shelley, who was a fine critic as well as a great poet, was enraptured by the 'sublime genius and more than human sensibility' displayed in this book, as well as by 'the divine beauty of Rousseau's imagination,' as he realised it on sailing across the famous lake which is the scene of the novel. A more modern French critic finds that 'Julie has the tongue of an apostle, she is our greatest orator after Bossuet.' That is a eulogy which may well serve to condemn any novel, but it is probably the most favourable judgment which from the modern standpoint can be bestowed upon Rousseau's novel. This novel so unlike a novel yet re-created the novel; that is admitted. Today *La Nouvelle Héloïse*, for all the fine passages we may discover in it, is far less agreeable to read than the best of those novels by Marivaux, Prévost, and the younger Crébillon which it replaced in popular esteem. Its sentimental rhetoric is now tedious; as a story it fails to enchain us; of subtle characterisation or dramatic vigour we find nothing;

as a work of art it is incomparably inferior to *Clarissa Harlowe* on which it was modelled.

If we look more broadly at Rousseau's work, the results of critical examination are similar. The world's great teachers are, for the most part, impressive by the substantial unity of the message they have proclaimed; we feel a convincing harmony between that message and the personality behind it. So it is with Marcus Aurelius and so with Thoreau. It is so, also, on what may seem a lower ethical plane, with Rousseau's chief contemporaries, with Voltaire and with Diderot. It is not clearly so with Rousseau. He often seems like an exquisite instrument, giving forth a music which responds to the varying emotions of the hand that strikes it. He is the supreme individualist, and yet his doctrines furnish the foundations for socialism, even in its oppressive forms. He is the champion of the rights of passion, and yet he was the leader in a movement of revolt against licentiousness, of return to domesticity and the felicities of family life and maternal devotion to children. He was opposed to the emancipation of women, even to the education of women side by side with men; he is denounced by the advocates of women's rights who see in the philosophers whom he opposed the pioneers of their own movement, and yet he was acclaimed as the liberator of womanhood; noble women, from Madame Roland onwards, were his enthusiastic disciples, the literary promulgators of his genius are headed by two distinguished women, Madame de Staël and Madame de Charrière.

Still more discordant seems to many the clash of Rousseau's doctrines with Rousseau's life. The uncompromising champion of virtue was nearly forty years old before he learnt how to earn his own living honestly. The regenerator of love was a solitary sensuous sentimentalist. The author of *Emile*, the gospel of childhood, put away his own children — if indeed he ever really had any — as foundlings.

When we thus critically survey Rousseau's books and personality, it is difficult to avoid the conclusion that, to a large extent, Rousseau has represented a backward movement in civilisation. His influence has tended to depreciate the value of the mighty instrument of reason by which civilisation is mainly wrought; it has consecrated prejudice under the sacred names of Nature and instinct; it has opened the way to the triumph of plebeianism and the sanctification of mob-rule; it has tended, by casting off the restraints on emotion, to an unwholesome divorce between the extravagancies of feeling and the limitations of life.

<h2 style="text-align:center">IV</h2>

It is on this note, at all events, that so many discussions of Rousseau finally rest: Rousseau was a 'degenerate' from birth, and his teaching is the disorganisation of civilised society. Yet, even if we believe that there are elements of truth in such a view, we can scarcely choose this standpoint for our final survey of Rousseau. When we bear in mind that the most aspiring efforts of the noblest souls during more than a century have been directly or indirectly inspired by this man, it becomes clear that to attaint Rousseau is to stain our own human nature, to place ourselves in the ranks of the Yahoos. For, there can be no doubt, unreasonable as it may be to regard Rousseau or any other man as the primary cause of any great social movement, it is he, more than any man, who has moulded the form of our spiritual activities and shaped our ideals. His passions have become the atmosphere in which we move. Since the days of feverish activity which Rousseau spent in his little hermitage at Montmorency, not merely our aims in politics, but our feeling for religion, our feeling for love, our feeling for Nature, have been renovated. They would have been renovated even if Rousseau had never lived, though perhaps not so thoroughly, yet, as things are, the new forms they have assumed have been determined by this solitary dreamer. 'Religion,' said Butler in the orderly and reasonable eighteenth-century manner, 'is a useful piece of information concerning a distant region of which otherwise we should have had no explanation': the mystic enthusiasm of the Vicaire Savoyard would alone have sufficed to sweep away for ever so pedestrian a conception of religion. Before Rousseau, love was a highly refined form of social intercourse, a species of gallantry conducted with self-restraint and all the formalities of its special etiquette; any extravagancy, whether in feeling, in speech, or in action, was banished. But when Saint-Preux, oppressed by his high-strung passions, came to the rock at Meillerie to pour forth in solitude the flood of his sentimental tears, all the witty refinements of eighteenth-century gallantry, for good or for evil, were finally swept away; extravagancy was free to lay down the law in love. It was Rousseau who enabled Mirabeau in his first letter to Julie Danvers (whom he had never seen) to declare: 'I, also, am a lover, have emptied the cup of sensibility to the dregs, and could give a thousand lives for what I love': it was Rousseau who laid down a new etiquette of love which every petty poet and novelist still adheres to.[1] Finally, Rousseau renovated our feeling for Nature. The geometrically minded eighteenth century could see nothing beautiful in Nature until trimmed into symmetry by the hands of man; even for Madame de Staël the Alps were merely 'a magnificent horror.' But Rousseau, who told Bernardin de Saint-Pierre that he 'would rather be among the arrows of the Parthians than among the glances of men,' only breathed freely and thought freely in the solitude of mountains and forests and torrents, and here also he has inoculated mankind with the virus of his own passion. In all these ways (as indeed Höffding has pointed out in what is, so far as I know, the most profound statement of Rousseau's philosophic position), Rousseau stood, in opposition to our artificial and inharmonious civilisation, for the worth of life as a whole, the simple undivided rights of life, the rights of instinct, the rights of emotion. This was his assertion of Nature. This was the way in which he renovated life, and

---

[1] 'To oppose the *Nouvelle Héloïse* to Crébillon's *Sofa*,' Remy de Gourmont well says, 'was to effect in the domain of feeling the revolution which Descartes effected in the intellectual world. Before Descartes there were intellectual persons: there were impassioned persons before Jean-Jacques: but they both created methods, and there is nothing fruitful but methods. Descartes and Rousseau are both alike out of date; maybe, but their methods are immortal. Whoever thinks starts from Descartes and his sceptical inquiry, whoever loves starts from Rousseau and his optimistic fever.'

effected a spiritual revolution which no mere man of letters has ever effected, a revolution only comparable to that effected by Christianity, of which indeed it was but a modern renascence.

Yet the man who wielded, and continues to wield, this enormous power over the world cannot be called one of its great men. In intellect, one sometimes thinks, he was not conspicuously above the average; in what we conventionally call moral character, he was at the outset conspicuously below it. Ill-born and ill-bred, morbidly shy and suspicious, defective in virility, he was inapt for all the social ends of life, mentally and physically a self-torturing invalid. No man more absolutely than Rousseau has ever illustrated the truth of Hinton's profound saying that the affinities of genius are not with strength but with weakness, that the supreme man of genius is the man who opposes no obstacle to the forces of Nature of which he is the channel.[1] Or, as St. Paul had declared long previously in a passage which seems to bear the same sense, it is the despised and rejected things of the world, even the things which are not, that God has chosen to put to nought the things that are.

It may, indeed, be pointed out to those who insist on the ludicrous, mean, and contemptible incidents in Rousseau's early life — only known to us through his own narration of them — that, as Lemaître said in a book that is, for the most part, superficial as well as unsympathetic, Rousseau's life was a process of moral evolution, a continuous purification completed by 'insanity,' or, as Rousseau himself put it, 'a purification in the furnace of adversity.' It is this process which largely gives the clue alike to his intellect and to his moral contradictions. Rousseau's abandonment to emotion was always checked by his timidity, by the perpetual searching suspicion which he applied to himself as well as to others.

[1] 'So far from genius being greatness and indicating power,' said Hinton (*Art of Thinking*, p. 237), 'it is emphatically the reverse. The men of talent are the men of power; they are the strong. The affinities of genius are with weakness. His faculty is that he opposes no obstacles: that his strength is taken out of the way, and Nature operates through him. The truth is "loosened" in his mind, and falls by its own weight and not by his energy.'

That is how it comes to pass that we may find in his writings the warrant for the most contradictory doctrines. It was so in the political field. In 1754 in the *Discours sur l'Inégalité*, he proclaimed that revolt of the non-possessors against the possessors of property which has since fermented so mightily in the world. But towards the end of his life, in the Constitution for Poland which he prepared at the request of the Poles, he had become in these matters a timid opportunist: 'I do not say that we must leave things as they are; but I do say that we must only touch them with extreme circumspection.' The contrast between Rousseau's apparent abandonment of his children and the fervour which in *Emile* he expended over the parental training of children has often been set forth to his discredit. But, as he himself viewed the matter, that gospel of childhood was simply the atonement for his own neglect. He displayed throughout a very passion of expiation. Born defective, beset on every side, he was yet of those who, according to the ancient metaphor of Saint Augustine, make of their dead selves the rungs of a ladder to rise to higher things. To some he seems to have been a kind of moral imbecile. But Thérèse, the mistress-wife who had been at his side during the whole of the period of his literary life and knew his weaknesses as no other could know them, said after his death: 'If he was not a saint, who ever was?' To view Rousseau rightly, we must see him, on the one hand, as the essential instrument of genius, a reed stirred to magnificent music by all the mighty winds of the spirit, and on the other hand, as a much-suffering man, scourged more than most men by human frailties, and yet for ever struggling to aspire. In this double capacity, at once the type of genius and the type of humanity, we learn to understand something of the magic of Rousseau's influence; we learn to understand how it is that before this shrine the most unlike persons in the world — the Marquis de Sade as well as Emerson, Charlotte Corday as well as Kant — have alike bowed in reverence.

Rousseau was a creature of clay. He was also a devouring flame. But of such blended fire and clay, in the end, the most exquisite products of the divine potter's art are formed. Under that stress Rousseau's character was slowly purified to the highest issues. Under that same stress was finally woven the delicate and iridescent texture of the finest style which French speech has ever assumed. The great traditions of the literary art of France — through Montaigne, Pascal, La Bruyère — reached at last in the furnace of this man's tortured soul their ultimate perfection of sensitive and intimate beauty. This style, which is the man himself, the style of the *Confessions* and the *Rêveries*, alone serves to make these books immortal. Here in his art the consuming fire and the soft clay of Rousseau's temperament are burnt to shapes of a beauty that is miraculous and stirs the depths of the soul. What indeed can we say, in the end, of all the operation of this man's spirit on the world save that it is a miracle, with effects that immeasurably transcend their causes? The water, if not the very mud, is turned into wine, and a few small loaves and fishes suffice for the feeding of the nations.

6

THE MAKING OF ROUSSEAU

WHEN we consider the immense influence which, by the testimony alike of friends and foes, Rousseau has exerted over our modern world, the inadequacy of the means whereby that influence has been exerted seems scarcely less than miraculous. The French Revolution, the ideals of Democracy and Socialism and Communism, the Romantic Movement in literature, the revival of the love of wild Nature, our latter-day preoccupation with education — one man is, with more or less reason, declared to be the 'father' of all these things. And that man has plausibly been termed a 'degenerate,' a morbid solitary dreamer, a lifelong invalid physically and mentally, if not absolutely a lunatic. To unravel the process by which so marvellous a result was attained out of such apparently unpromising material is, even on account of its difficulty, a singularly fascinating task. To achieve it is to solve a unique problem in the spiritual history of the world. A problem in spiritual chemistry is, as it were, set before us; we are permitted, for the first time, to look into the alembic in which human ideals are made. In earlier ages this was not possible; we have only been able to see the figures of religious creators dimly reflected in their stupendous creations.[1] We see Rousseau in all his nakedness; for once the most subtle problems of the human spirit are set before us to investigate.

Rousseau was sometimes proud to describe himself as 'a citizen of Geneva,' and for more than a century before his birth Geneva had been the great nervous ganglion of Northern Europe: here were concentrated, as in no other city to the same

[1] I do not overlook Dr. Binet-Sanglé's remarkable work, *La Folie de Jésus*. But, notwithstanding the great skill with which the investigation is carried out, it has to be admitted that the facts are disputed and therefore the interpretation cannot be altogether convincing.

degree before or since, the highest aspirations of its human individual soul in the theocratic direction, its most strenuous ideals of human character, the most concentrated and prolonged effort that has ever been known to wind up the pitch of human moral effort to its point of highest tension. Rousseau was the forerunner of the Revolution, but Calvin had already produced a Revolution of an even more fundamental character at Geneva; and we must never forget that Calvin was the fellow-townsman of Robespierre. Rousseau was born in the house of revolutionaries and was himself from the outset of their family.

In the middle of the sixteenth century, in the days of Henri II, Didier Rousseau, a Protestant of Paris, left his native country and sought refuge in the city of Geneva. He combined the occupations of wine-seller and book-seller, and was without doubt a man of character and intelligence. He established himself in an inn at Geneva, and became a fairly prosperous citizen. Late in life he found a good wife in a lower middle-class girl of Savoy. Jean-Jacques, we may be sure, knew nothing of this ancestor. But though four generations came between them, the spirit of Didier still remained latent in the stock and revived in Jean-Jacques with the same results; like his ancestor the book-seller, the book-writer was led by this same free spirit of independence to become also an exile, and even at one period to follow the same path from Paris to Switzerland.

It must be admitted that at Rousseau's birth the firm fibre which we may assume in the earlier members of the family was exceedingly softened; even the characteristic individualism of Geneva had become eccentric in the Rousseaus. At the best we can only say, in Mendelian phraseology, that the stern Calvinistic elements in the family character were no longer dominant but recessive; and perhaps the later development of Rousseau's character may be held to indicate that the sternness was only latent. The physical vigour of the family and its worldly prosperity seem alike to have reached a climax in Jean-Jacques's great-grandfather, the first of the family to become a watchmaker, who married into a good family and at the age of seventy-eight left a considerable fortune among his surviving ten children. His son David, Rousseau's grandfather, began to show various signs of worldly, if not indeed biological, ineffectiveness; of his fourteen children all but three died at an early age; his pecuniary means were small, if indeed he was not in old age suffering from actual poverty; and though he was selected to occupy a minor magisterial post, which permitted him to continue his vocation as watchmaker, he was eventually deprived of this for having, during the seditions of 1707, shown what was considered to be undue leniency, two of his brothers being also admonished at different times for expressing opinions displeasing to the government. Isaac, Jean-Jacques's father, presents in addition to ineffectiveness, for the first time in the family, a definite though vague morbid element. He was vigorous, fond of hunting and of good cheer, by no means unlovable.[1] But he was unstable, with no sense of responsibility for his family, extremely irritable, violent and quarrelsome. He was several times fined and reprimanded by the Consistory, once for sending a challenge to an English gentleman who, he declared, had insulted him, and he finally had to flee from Geneva and settle in Nyon on account of his threatening attitude towards a farmer on whose fields he had trespassed. After completing his apprenticeship as a watchmaker, he took it into his head for a time to learn the violin and be a dancing-master.[2] Again, after only a year of marriage to an attractive wife he was

[1] In this he resembled his famous son, who, though Casanova failed to find him 'un homme aimable,' undoubtedly exerted considerable personal attraction throughout his life. The son resembled the father also in personal appearance, and a friend of the latter declared in 1754 that Jean-Jacques was recognisably his father's son.

[2] Geneva was not a musical city, and it is probably one of the anomalous characteristics of the Rousseaus that they had developed a love of music; several of them played the violin, many of them were fond of singing. On the maternal side, also, there were musical tastes. This is a highly significant fact when we remember that Rousseau in early life proposed to earn his living by music; later he became a respectable musical composer, even an innovator in musical ideas, and eventually decided to adopt music-copying as his means of livelihood; while his supreme genius in literature was more specially manifested by the art with which he brought a new music into prose. He had, as Kretschmer remarks, 'something of a genuinely musical nature.'

really devoted to, he suddenly went off to Constantinople and remained there for six years, only returning, at the entreaty of his faithful wife, after the death of his mother-in-law with whom he had quarrelled. At the same time he showed much sensitiveness and was very romantic. He was clearly unbalanced, though in no extreme degree, what French alienists call *déséquilibré*. It is interesting to note that another member of the family, a nephew to this man and cousin to Jean-Jacques, who was a consul in Persia, showed somewhat the same traits.

It cannot be maintained that Rousseau's mother represented a strain which adequately corrected the lack of balance beginning to manifest itself in the paternal line. Suzanne Bernard was indeed not only conspicuously attractive, but she was charming and highly intelligent, a lover of poetry (she wrote verse herself) and an accomplished musician. She was, moreover, a girl of high spirit, and had once, though a pastor's niece and living in his house, dressed up as a peasant and gone to see the performance of a farce, although the theatre was sternly disapproved in Geneva; when the Consistory sent for her in order to administer reproof, she repeatedly failed to appear, and at last, on final appeal to the City Council, an usher was sent to bring her before the Consistory which administered a severe censure. Again, on another occasion, she sinned against Genevan morals by persisting to receive the visits of a married man belonging to the aristocracy of the city. There is no charge of real misconduct, but such behaviour was seriously improper; it came before the Consistory many times, and the offending visitor was at last compelled to make his apologies to that assembly. Suzanne thus seems to have been as spirited and independent as the man she married and the immortal son she gave birth to.

In her ancestry, however, there were other and less satisfactory elements. The Bernards belonged to the wealthy and cultured aristocracy of Geneva. But Suzanne's father, left an orphan at an early age, had proved a *mauvais sujet*, with nothing in him of the spirit of Geneva, and specially reckless and uncontrolled in his conduct with women. On four separate occasions he was brought before the Consistory and the Council for incontinence, forced to acknowledge his sin upon his knees, fined, sent to prison — but all without any genuine repentance. Even when, at the age of twenty-three he married, Suzanne, his eldest child, was born only a few months later. His wife seems to have been attached to him, and there were several other children, but the father died at the age of thirty; thus it is probable that Rousseau knew little or nothing about this grandfather, nor, it is clear, was he acquainted with the history of his father's sister, Theodora, who at the fairly mature age of twenty-seven, formed a relationship with his mother's brother, Gabriel Bernard, a youth much younger than herself, married him, and a few days later gave birth to a child; the Consistory, shocked at this 'scandalous anticipation of marriage,' as they termed it, forthwith excommunicated the young couple, not re-admitting them to the Sacrament until after due repentance. Rousseau, however, in evident good faith, boasts of the pure morals of his family, and especially refers to his devout Aunt Theodora and her 'love of psalm-singing.'

It is easier to us than it was for Rousseau himself to see that much of his spontaneous, instinctive, and uncontrollable emotional temperament was inherited, not only through his father, but also through his mother, the two families having so strong an affinity for each other in their instability that two unions took place between them. Suzanne, however, notwithstanding her early escapades, made a good and faithful wife, though she never married till thirty and was not even then easily won. Jean-Jacques, her second child, was born ten months after the father's return from his long sojourn in Constantinople. She died of puerperal fever a week later.

It is necessary to accumulate these details of Rousseau's ancestry because they are all of them significant. We see that he belonged on both sides to ancient and excellent stocks which in his more immediate progenitors, paternal and maternal, had begun to show a tendency to be unsound, eccentric, ill-regulated, obtrusively wayward. Together these two stocks could not fail to furnish the temperament responsible for the temptations into which in his early life young Rousseau fell. His vices were rooted in his ancestry. All that was new was the incommunicable quality of genius.

We can, indeed, assert, in the light of the facts now revealed, that the very qualities which in Rousseau became genius were essentially present in the stocks he came out of. In one of the earliest criticisms of Rousseau's genius, shortly after his death, Madame de Charrière acutely said that his genius ultimately lay in the fact that Rousseau was a dreamer and a musician. It is clear, indeed, that Rousseau derived from the families he belonged to not only these unstable, reckless, and inconsequent tendencies that pointed towards viciousness and towards madness,[1] but also the aptitude for dreaming and for music. His life was the slow, the exceedingly slow, development of these aptitudes. It was, further, the even slower reinforcement of these aptitudes by the purification and invigoration of character which also lay in the ancestral germs he bore within him, though more remote and less easily realisable. Rousseau was the product of stocks, grown wild and wanton and sentimental, which had already something of the 'romanticism' which he was to bring to a new focus. But, further back, those same stocks had been the unbending champions of spiritual freedom, the stern preachers of Puritan morality. Moreover, they were workers, craftsmen, tradesmen, and men of affairs. Rousseau's four great-grandfathers were a Genevan citizen who was a prosperous watchmaker (a highly honourable occupation to which only citizens were admitted), a master tanner, a draper or cloth merchant, and a lawyer; beyond this his forefathers belonged in part to the local peasantry and in part to the solid ancient bourgeois aristocracy of Geneva. Rousseau's genius is the final result, the slowly achieved synthetic fusion of apparently incongruous elements.

The prospects for his fate were not promising at his birth. His parents were no longer young, and so delicate was he at birth that he was not expected to live; the death of his mother

---

[1] A cousin on the Rousseau side, born in Persia, appears to have had hallucinatory tendencies, perhaps delusions of persecution.

a few days later, a loss always serious, seemed an especial handicap in a family on whom parental responsibilities sat so lightly, a trait Rousseau may himself have inherited. Several of the family had not easily been persuaded, even in puritanic Geneva, to assure the advantages of legitimacy to their off-spring. Jean-Jacques's grandfather Rousseau, though living during his childhood, is never so much as mentioned in the *Confessions*, and evidently had no claim on his grandson's gratitude; the father, Isaac, when compelled to expatriate himself from Geneva to neighbouring Nyon, showed no anxiety about the children he left behind. His elder son had run away from home and disappeared in Germany. So it came about that Jean-Jacques's early years were very diversified, that he had no orderly training, that he was innocent of all formal 'education.'

Yet as we look back today we can see that Rousseau really had the best possible education. To apply to such a child with such an inheritance — a delicate, wayward, sensitive child — the heavy, conventional, cast-iron 'education' which he would nowadays be compelled by law to receive might perhaps have served to crush him for ever; at the best it would have meant that the long years of his school-life were wasted. Such a child with such a mission in the world could only have de-veloped under those free and peculiar conditions which are described in the early pages of the *Confessions*. If those condi-tions failed to repress his natural perversions or to correct his natural weaknesses, they were, we can scarcely doubt, indis-pensable for the development of his natural sensibilities and his natural powers. It was not perhaps their least benefit that they encouraged no precocious mental development and saved him from the sad fate of those sensitive and abnormal youths who (like Weininger in later days) are thrust into an intellec-tual forcing house. The influence of Rousseau on the world is bound up with the fact that he was intellectually the least precocious of great men.

As with many people who succeed in escaping, almost or altogether, the bondage of formal education and become in-stead their own schoolmasters, Rousseau's education may be said to have been of lifelong duration. It certainly continued for forty years and was in active progress while *Emile* was being written. It may be said to have become more stringent as the years went on, for Rousseau was constantly making more severe demands on himself. The period of early indulgent training was at the outset before he had taken himself in hand and was most marked when he was still in his father's charge. Father and son read ancient romances together until far on into the night, until the dawn appeared. 'I am even more of a child than you,' the father said on one of these occasions. In later years Rousseau was opposed to the early cultivation of the imagination in children. For good or for evil his own childhood was given up to the cultivation of the sensibility with which he was born.

The influence of Genevan Puritanism on his sensitive temperament in early life seems small; indeed, the families he sprang from furnished an immediate environment which might almost be regarded as representing a reaction against Puritanism. At this early period, also, he was not able to appreciate the natural influence of the neighbouring lake scenery which later inspired him so mightily. At the age of eight he was put in charge of the pastor Lambercier at Bossey at the foot of Mount Salève outside Geneva; it was the impression on another aspect of his sensibility which gave importance to his stay there. He precociously woke to the charm of sexual emotion, under the influence of the childish physical chastisement inflicted by Mlle. Lambercier, the pastor's sister. Thus his sentimentality received an impetus in a perverse direction, placing him in a permanently masochistic attitude towards the opposite sex, though that attitude became less marked after early youth and ultimately, by self-control, was to some extent conquered.

Sentimentally and sexually, we see, the child Rousseau was precocious. Born weak, of failing and abnormal stocks, with arthritic and neuropathic heredity, subject from early life to various nervous disabilities, in addition, so he tells us, to pleurisies and quinsies, he was an apt subject for such precocity. But, as often happens, precocity in such a case may

be followed by a much retarded development. If Rousseau
began to develop early, he ceased developing very late. His
full intellectual stature was scarcely attained even by middle
age; he was always educating himself, on the moral and artistic sides still developing even at his death. Moreover, he
remained to some extent a child throughout life. Shy, timid,
awkward, suspicious, unsociable because inapt for society,
yet frank, independent, outspoken even to rudeness on occasions, his resemblance to a child was constantly noted. It is
a schizoid trait significant at once of neurotic heredity and of
genius.

Young Rousseau's purely formal education, we see, was
clearly a negligible quantity. His real education — putting
aside the training in emotional experience which was so fundamental and significant — was an education in the world of
books, and an education in wandering (after the manner of his
forefathers on both sides) over the actual world. As regards
books, it was fitting that the boy who was to become a great
master of words and a supreme artist in the expression of intimate emotion should have been from the outset soaked in
literature. He began, as we know, in his earliest childhood,
with D'Urfé's *Astrée* and the old romances of amorous chiv-
alry. He went on to absorb nearly the whole available serious literature of the seventeenth century in France. This study
was of fully as much value to him as the earlier bath of romantic sentiment. It largely gave to his work that almost
unconscious savour of freshness and vigour which he could
not have acquired from the unduly refined and desiccated
literature of the French eighteenth century. He went outside
French literature to Plutarch to obtain what he imagined to
be a genuinely classical standard of 'virtue' against which to
measure the defects and vices of his own time, and he went to
Italy, especially to Petrarch, to reach a genuine wellspring of
poetry, for he detested French poetry, and could not indeed
fail to be repelled by its rhetorical aloofness from native emotion. Again he went far afield to garner in all the books he
could find of voyages and travels, especially those of English
origin, which the activity of circumnavigators was beginning

to multiply; thus he obtained the data which enabled him to formulate his conception of 'primitive man' and to bring it into line with his conception of ancient virtue. Finally, in his own century, he fastened on the works of Prévost and Marivaux. Prévost was clearly a predecessor, and was doubly useful to Rousseau who was well acquainted with him personally. In the first place Prévost knew England well and had translated *Clarissa* and other English books into French, so that Rousseau was brought into contact with all that was most sympathetic and most stimulating to him in current English literature, while at the same time the form of the future *Nouvelle Héloïse* was fixed on Richardson's lines. In the second place, Prévost's own novels displayed a sombre, romantic, melancholy, extravagantly emotional character which Rousseau could not fail to find akin to his own temperament, though he was too little of a novelist to derive much inspiration from them.[1]

These adventures in the world of books, however, extensive as they may have been, even at an early stage, were still only at the beginning when at the age of sixteen, an engraver's apprentice, he fled with his little bundle from Geneva, crossed over to Catholic Savoy, and on Palm Sunday in March, 1728, at the spot he later desired to see surrounded by a railing of gold, met Madame de Warens on her way from her house to church. His relations with this, for him, and indeed for many others, adorable woman have been a constant puzzle for later ages, and remain so still. Even the house to which pilgrims have gone for over a century as to a sacred shrine was probably not Rousseau's home until his 'idyll' had become a dream. I have already dealt with some of these problems. But on one point there is no question: Madame de Warens was an influence of the first importance in the making of Rousseau; she not only aided him on the side of intellectual development; she awakened his love-life; she moulded his attitude towards

[1] Miss Marguerite Reichenburg in a doctoral thesis has been able to prepare a table of the books possessed, read, or mentioned by Rousseau, and finds they amount to nearly seven hundred, ancient and modern, and in various languages. He was specially attracted to religious and scientific works.

women; she became a leading part of the emotional and sentimental inspiration he let loose in the world.

One other event followed, though at a long interval, to
complete the making of Rousseau, but it was decisive, and
without it all that went before would have been in vain.
That event was the realisation of the vocation, the message
which determined the mission. It was what, in religious
phraseology, is called 'conversion.' [1]

Nearly every great religious teacher of whom we have definite knowledge has received, in some shape or another, such
a call. It has sometimes even seemed to take on an hallucinatory shape, especially the shape of a mysterious voice. We
find indications of such manifestations in the Bible, even apart
from the most precise and typical, that by which Saul of
Tarsus was in a moment changed from being the ruthless per-
secutor of Christians, to become eventually the greatest
apostle of Christianity. He was on the road to Damascus;
suddenly he heard a voice reproaching him for his persecutory
spirit; he seemed to see a great light; he fell to the ground.
Psychologically it was in essentials exactly what happened to
Rousseau in October, 1749.

Thirteen years later (January, 1762) Rousseau described the
episode in a letter to M. de Malesherbes:

> I was on my way to see Diderot, then a prisoner at Vincennes; [2]
> I had taken in my pocket a *Mercure de France* and I glanced at it as
> I walked. I came on the question set for discussion by the Academy
> of Dijon which gave occasion for my first essay. If ever anything
> could resemble a sudden inspiration, it was the movement which
> took place in me at that moment; all at once I felt my mind daz-
> zled by a thousand lights; crowds of ideas appeared there at the
> same time with an inexpressible force and confusion; I felt my

[1] Strictly speaking, the process of 'conversion' does not determine vocation.
But the realisation of a mission, at all events in exceptional persons, has often been
a swiftly ensuing result.

[2] Diderot had been arrested for his *Lettre sur les Aveugles*, greatly to the indignation of Rousseau, who even wrote a wild letter (which received no reply) to Madame de Pompadour demanding to be incarcerated with his friend. But Diderot's
confinement was now easy; he had been removed from the prison of Vincennes
to the Château and was free to enjoy the park and meet his friends.

head seized by giddiness, like that of drunkenness; a violent palpi-
tation oppressed me, my breast heaved. Not being able to breathe
while walking, I let myself fall down under one of the trees in the
avenue and spent there a half-hour of such agitation that on rising
I found the front of my vest bathed with tears I had no idea I had
shed. Oh, dear Sir, if I could ever write a quarter of what I saw
and felt beneath that tree, how clearly could I present all the contradictions of the social system, with what force I could reveal all
the abuses of our institutions, with what simplicity I could show
that man is naturally good, and that it is through these institutions alone that men become wicked.

The event of that day, he declares, must always remain present
to him even if he were to live for ever.

In Book VIII of the *Confessions*, Rousseau again speaks of
this memorable episode. He has now forgotten some of the
details, he says, but he remembers that the season was very
hot, that the trees offered little shade, and that he usually
walked very fast. It was, indeed, to encourage himself to
linger that he had taken the *Mercure* in which he fell on that
arresting question: *Whether the progress of the sciences and arts
has contributed to corrupt or to purify morals.* 'At that instant I
saw another universe and I became another man.' He adds
that on reaching Vincennes his agitation resembled delirium
and was noted by Diderot to whom he confided the cause,
and Diderot encouraged him to compete for the prize.

Again, still later, close to the end of his life, in the third
Promenade of his *Rêveries*, Rousseau once more refers to this
turning-point in his life at the age of forty, but now without
details, setting forth the change, internal and external, which
took place in its broadest and most significant outlines:

A great revolution had taken place in my life; another moral
world was unveiled before my gaze. It is from that epoch that I
can date my complete renunciation of the world, and the keen
taste for solitude which has never left me since that time. The
work I was undertaking could only be executed in absolute retreat;
it demanded long and peaceful meditation which is impossible in
the tumult of society.

This 'revolution,' this 'inspiration,' as Rousseau terms it, was strictly of the nature of religious 'conversion.' That has seemed doubtful to some, since no Christian faith, nor indeed any fixed religious creed, appeared as the agent to effect the change.

But that is to take too narrow a view of religion. It is a sad mistake to suppose that traditional creeds or conventional faiths are of the essence of religion. In the broad and full sense, religion is concerned with the attitude of a man towards his universe; it is the establishment of a harmonious relationship between the Self and the Not-Self. In persons of a low stage of culture, in or out of civilisation, this process is mixed up with creeds which usually involve supernatural elements, or a faith in the beings commonly termed 'gods.' Nothing of this kind is necessarily involved when we are concerned with persons of a higher type. 'Conversion' may thus be associated with any or no degree of intellectual development. It leads a Salvationist to feel safe in the arms of Jesus; it led John Stuart Mill to find peace far away from any theological creed.

The significance of Rousseau — who is significant in so many respects — in this respect is that he, first in the modern framework of conventional Christendom, presents a typical picture of 'conversion' altogether apart from any conventional religious creeds. But the process remained the same as though it were along conventional lines. It differed certainly in occurring at a later age than usual. But then, as I have already pointed out, Rousseau's whole development was slow and late. Conversion, however, is never as sudden as it appears. The explosion is sudden, but the impulses and influences, which have come together in readiness for the inflammatory match, were accumulated gradually; or, we may say, that there was the eruption, suffocating but delicious, of subterranean forces which had slowly accumulated below.

Though Rousseau had reached the age of forty he had not yet found either himself or his vocation; he had never, though almost naturally a writer, even published a book. So far, as he remarked, he had only written for himself. He was wavering, discontented, torn in various directions, a stranger in the

world. The three or four years before the illumination of Vincennes were probably, Masson believes, 'the most artificial
and the most feverishly worldly of his life.' [1] His happiest moments had been earlier, with Nature or with books, but he
had not felt that that was life. It had only seemed a preparation. And for what? He had come to Paris; he had tried to
mix in society and been not ill received though his temperament and his training had here been no fitting preparation.
This timid, melancholy, impassioned creature had tried to
become 'a man of taste,' 'a polished gentleman,' an ordinary
representative of 'good sense' in a thoroughly sceptical and
cynical circle. He had especially associated himself with
Diderot and the encyclopaedists and was working for them;
but their rationalistic environment was completely aloof from
the sphere of emotion and sentiment to which Rousseau's
nature instinctively drew him. He was trying to adapt himself to Parisian civilisation, yet still remaining, as he later
put it, discontented alike with himself and with others, unconsciously seeking, all the time, to break the bonds by which
he was binding himself to a society he esteemed so little. All
the elements for a spiritual revolution were there. Only a
touch was needed and they would fall into a new order,
crystallise in a definite and permanent shape.

The Academy's question applied that touch. The sudden
illuminating flash came; nearly always in such states there is
a sense of being bathed in light. The Parisian civilisation he
had been trying to adapt himself to was false and alien. His
universe was that of Nature and simplicity and native emotion, to which he had always been innately, even if unconsciously, drawn. Now he suddenly realised his universe and
could accept it. Now he could work for it, however humble
and ineffective a worker he might prove to be. He saw a universe in which he was at home. He felt a vocation that was
for ever fixed.

[1] Professor P. M. Masson's careful and elaborate study of Rousseau's religion,
in three volumes, *La Religion de J.-J. Rousseau*, is essential for all who seek to know
Rousseau's religious place in the world and his work in bringing back to it 'this
old word of religion.' I am here quoting from the first volume, *La Formation
Religieuse de Rousseau*.

It is true that the months immediately following this tre-
mendous moment of effervescence were comparatively peaceful and indeed coincided with what was probably the happiest
period of Rousseau's 'conjugal' life with Thérèse, as the pair
just then became comfortably settled, with Thérèse's mother
managing the household. It was indeed largely to Madame
Levasseur that, lying in bed, he with much difficulty dictated his
Academy *Discours sur les Sciences et les Arts* of which he was never
proud as a literary production. Nor did he for a moment
anticipate that what he supposed would be dismissed as a wild
paradox could meet with success. It was therefore a thunder-
clap when in the following July he learnt that he had received
the Academy's prize — a prize swiftly followed by celebrity.

Undoubtedly Rousseau experienced many other sudden
changes of attitude and mood, both before and after the illumination of Vincennes. He said of himself that he was 'more
changeable than a chameleon.' But no other psychic revolution in his life went so deep, or was so permanent. It was the
final stage in the making of Rousseau. Similarly we may take
little account of his varying attitudes towards the current religious faiths of his age, Protestant or Catholic, an attitude of
agreement or disagreement, of sympathy or antipathy, the
most significant being, no doubt, that expressed by his *Vicaire
Savoyard*. All these varying attitudes were superficial. The
Vicaire Savoyard aspired, he said, to be himself, without
contradiction, without sharing, with no need but of himself
to attain happiness. And Masson concludes: 'In the Paradise
of Jean-Jacques, even God is discreetly effaced, to give place
to Jean-Jacques.'

If we meditate on that saying, we may perhaps understand
how it has come about that the most revolutionary figure in
the religious western world since Jesus has been Jean-Jacques
Rousseau, each taking the place of God.

Yet the world becomes a stranger mystery than ever when
we contemplate its 'Saviours.' Sometimes it even seems doubtful whether they ever existed at all, and when we know their
lives intimately how vague and dubious and complex they
are apt to appear!

7

I

WHEN we consider the almost boundless significance which, for good or for evil, is on all sides accorded to Rousseau, it is astonishing to realise that the chief source of reliable knowledge about him has always been neglected. I refer, of course, to his letters.

Of all the great leading figures in our modern world Rousseau — whatever else may be doubtful about him — may fairly be said to stand first in the art of letter-writing: I mean in the modern world, for in the ancient world, not to mention Cicero, we have at all events Saint Jerome who was really a letter-writer of the same class as Rousseau. But in the modern world the men of this type had not before the eighteenth century yet learnt to pour themselves forth in letters. There is, for instance, Shakespeare. We are told by Ben Jonson with what facility his pen moved, and we may judge for ourselves the swiftness with which his thoughts and emotions seem to flow. He should surely have been a supreme letter-writer. But we look in vain for the traces of even a single letter. The traces may be lost. But his great contemporary, Bacon, wrote many letters. I once read all those that remain, and with care, in the hope of finding some intimate revelation of the man. But the evidence proved mostly negative. They are formal and distant even when addressed to his dearest friends, written much as we write today to friends living under certain European governments which take an anxiously paternal interest in the correspondence of their subjects. If there were any good letter-writers, they were such as in themselves we count of small personal importance; Madame de Sévigné is the stock example, or, in English, Howell.

Rousseau was both a dominating personality and a supreme letter-writer, whose art herein enabled him to put himself into his letters. Voltaire wrote letters well and copiously. But they take no such place in his works as Rousseau's letters take in his.

Rousseau was not only a great master in the art of letter-writing. He took that art as seriously as it had ever been taken and placed it on a higher plane. It became the chosen medium for conveying his message. He had nothing but contempt for ephemeral writing (he refers slightingly to periodical literature, 'which shines at the toilet-table in the morning and expires in the privy in the evening'), and we find little that is ephemeral in these letters he wrote from day to day. And since his temperament was intensely personal, and other persons also peculiarly real to him, he became naturally a pioneer in writing personal letters. He was willing to put the whole of his true self into a letter, even to a comparatively unknown correspondent, and to make drafts and keep copies of his letters, as well as to preserve those sent to him. That explains why so many letters of Rousseau's survive. It is also the ground on which we may claim that in Rousseau's letters we have the chief source of knowledge concerning his temperament and his opinions. They are a higher authority than even the *Confessions* which were written in old age, and largely in the absence of verifying documents. The letters furnish a continuous and intimate record, from the period when he left Les Charmettes to the very end.

Yet until today no editor has seriously undertaken to present a scholarly and fairly complete edition of these epoch-making letters. The books about Rousseau are endless; they appear every year. Yet the main foundation on which such books should be based has been imperfect, if not unsound. Collections of his letters have certainly been put forward, but they have been partial, incomplete, inaccurate, the editing perfunctory and unscholarly. The recent publication of the *Correspondance Générale de J.-J. Rousseau* — of the man, that is to say, who not merely presents the fascinating personal picture of perpetual oscillation between the extravagance of a madman and a martyr, but also gave the greatest shock to French literature it has ever received and has proved the most revolutionary figure in our modern world [1] — cannot but be a significant fact. It may not seem so — as one critic has remarked — to the swarming millions who find their supreme interests in the sporting field or the wireless. But since history began, and doubtless before, these masses have been equally unconscious of the current events which in the end mould their own lives.

The *Confessions* of Rousseau is one of the world's immortal books. But it has called forth critics, who on the one hand have hurled abuse at the head of its author or on the other hand exhausted themselves in ingenious attempts to explain away his sincerity or his veracity.

In these twenty volumes we find the complete justification of Rousseau. The *Confessions* remain. But it is true that they were written late in life and largely present the outlook of but one phase under special circumstances, and moreover, as he was himself prepared to admit, with inaccuracies of detail, for his idealising imagination was vivid and his memory had grown weak. Here, in the correspondence, we have the complete man in all his phases and moods, each at the moment of experience.

I have described Rousseau as 'the most spiritually naked person who has appeared in our civilisation.' The final proof of that description is in these letters. Here we find him, not, as we may sometimes suspect in the *Confessions*, refashioning more or less unconsciously the past to the pattern of the present, but in his immediate reactions to that past, swift, direct, passionately intimate, and there is no possibility of doubt concerning his naked sincerity. We see him, moreover, in all his different attitudes to very unlike friends and correspondents, and in all his varied responses to the things in life which emotionally or intellectually interested him. And even when we put aside this primary and essential value of these letters as the revelation of a supremely significant personality, many

---

[1] I am here deliberately echoing the judgment of one of the most competent and cautious critics in this matter, P. M. Masson in his *Religion de Rousseau*.

notable aspects remain. We still have here a highly important document for literary history (including the light thrown on Rousseau's own books), on the history of science, of morals, and indeed of history in general.

The editorial incubation of this great work, as we might expect, has been slow and laborious. We owe its inception to Théophile Dufour, a scholar who was Director of the Archives and the Public Library of Geneva. Apart from his official duties, he cherished an enthusiastic but scholarly devotion to Rousseau. At a comparatively early period in life he set himself, as a life-work, the highly necessary task of preparing a final and complete edition of Rousseau's letters.

To this great task he devoted himself with the most patient, careful, and wide-ranging activity during fifty years, bringing together, collating, annotating, commenting letters many of which had been dispersed and thought lost. Unfortunately he never lived to see the final result in the twenty volumes slowly but steadily published during over ten years in admirable shape by the house of Armand Colin.[1] Dufour's task was

[1] In 1933, before the *Correspondance* was completely published, Dufour's daughter, Madame Noëlle Roger, produced a book, *Jean-Jacques le Promeneur Solitaire*, making a picture of Rousseau as the letters and other recent investigations reveal him. It is popular in style, superficial, and sometimes slurring over difficult points (though the scholar's daughter comes out in the abundant reference notes of the Appendix), but provides the best approach to the man Rousseau for those who do not know him. There is real feminine intuition, moreover, as in the discussion of the insoluble question of Rousseau's alleged five children sent to the Foundlings, and various considerations are brought forward to suggest that Rousseau's story is imaginary, though this conclusion is admitted to be quite uncertain, Madame Roger points out that in any case it was usual to send illegitimate infants to the Foundlings and many thousands were so sent every year in Paris, of which the population was considerably below a million. The wealthy Madame Tencin so disposed of her infant who was destined to become the famous d'Alembert. I may add, as possibly bearing on the question, that we cannot assume that Thérèse was strictly faithful to Rousseau. We now know that Boswell, according to his own very precise statement, had relations with Thérèse when conducting her over to England. I may also recall that, when in the first year (1754) that Thérèse joined Rousseau in Geneva, he wished to be admitted to the Protestant sacrament of his native city, members of the Consistory objected because Thérèse was known to sleep in his room. Rousseau, when told of this, replied: 'If those people knew my situation, they would be convinced that I am not in a condition to realise their suspicions'; and he referred to his long-standing urethral troubles. It is Rousseau's friend De Luc, his intermediary with the Consistory, who records this incident.

fortunately taken up, and its worthy appearance assured, by M. Pierre-Paul Plan, working with a complete understanding and wide learning, which have enabled him to add additional discoveries of his own.

A so far final collection, it contains over four thousand letters, not including the doubtful rejected documents relegated to appendices. That is to say, it comprises three times as many letters as the then complete edition published a century earlier, in 1824. It also brings together many attractive pictures of Rousseau and his correspondents, some of them reproduced for the first time, including a sanguine by Caresme, with face lean and deeply wrinkled, done near the end of Rousseau's life.

We realise in this great collection the extent and the variety of the interests of the man who was for so many years choosing to earn his living by industriously copying music at forty *sous* a day. A special and enthusiastic interest was botany. He was often the guest of the great naturalist Jussieu at the Jardin des Plantes, and in these letters he appears under a delightful aspect as the initiator in the science of plants of Madame Delessert and her daughter.

It is especially during his last years that, returning to an early love, he sometimes seems almost predominantly a field naturalist. Some of the longest of the late letters are devoted to botany; we constantly find him botanising, always in his immediate neighbourhood, not much interested in more remote problems of botany; and when the Duchess of Portland, thinking to interest him, sends a consignment of exotic plants, he writes politely to decline the gift as of no use to him.

Even more notable is the extent and variety of the personal friendships, with people of high rank or of low, cultivated by this lunatic, as he has seemed to many chiefly to be, by this unsociable enemy to civilisation as he more certainly was. He often seemed a 'bear' to visitors whom he disliked or with whom he could not get into touch.[1] Under such circum-

---

[1] 'Bear' was the familiar nickname often used by Rousseau's friends and accepted by himself. Thus we find Madame d'Epinay addressing him as 'My Bear,' and writing to Saint-Lambert: 'The Bear has had a tooth extracted. If

stances he had no hesitation in writing to them to request that, as he politely phrased it, they would no longer honour him with their visits, and he was prepared to do so even to ladies high in the social scale when he found them pretentious or artificial.

We are often, indeed, reminded that he regarded his century as 'an age of humbug when the greatest rascals are always talking about the public welfare,' and that, as he wrote to the Abbé Raynal in 1753, he accepted the comparison of the human race generally to 'a flock of sheep, following example rather than reason, each of them far more afraid of being ridiculous than of being mad or wicked.' But he once received, without knowing who he was, a visit from the Prince de Ligne, an aristocrat of the highest rank and supreme man of the world, who seems to have conquered the Bear by his charm. Directly after, we find the Prince writing to Rousseau, with the greatest consideration, to offer him a dwelling on his own estate — which would be Beloeil, famous for its beauty and its gardens — and proposing all sorts of arrangements to suit Rousseau's special tastes. 'You will have the key of my books and my gardens; you will see me or you will not see me. You will have a very small country house all to yourself, a quarter of a league from mine; you will plant, you will sow; you will do just what you please.... Like you, I do not love either thrones or dominations; you will reign over no one and no one will reign over you.' And he concludes: 'And if all this does not suit you, take it that I have said nothing. I will continue to read you and admire you without telling you so.' It may not be surprising that we hear no more; a few weeks later Rousseau was dead.

Rousseau is commonly regarded as a perpetually sombre and melancholy and suspicious creature, regarding himself as the victim of general persecution. No doubt there is truth in that view. We again and again find him in that state, sometimes it seems hopelessly, and to some degree it is natural enough, for the pioneer is always exposed to ridicule or con-

it were only that which he has against the human race!' And we find Rousseau sending to the same lady 'la révérence de l'ours.'

tempt or detestation, and the persecution of Rousseau was often real. Yet we also find this same person on easy and familiar and hospitable terms with innumerable friends, and even full of playful banter. I open a volume almost at random and find him at the Hermitage writing to his friend Lenieps, the Paris banker, to say how pleased he will be to receive him at his 'délicieux séjour' and hopes he will come to dinner; 'I have wine and rustic foods, and if my rural fare does not suit you, you can bring your own.' Then at the end he adds: 'My respects to your daughter. But I warn her that I do not like to be kissed by letter; it is far better to make a merit of that pious deed, and to come on pilgrimage to visit the devout hermit, as if a relic.'

It has been a great satisfaction to receive these volumes as they appeared, a cherished possession, even though I can by no means claim to have mastered them. Yet, however incompletely studied, there can be no manner of doubt that they, rather than the *Confessions*, furnish the real and trustworthy life of Rousseau. I have elsewhere suggested that in some respects we may find a real analogy between Rousseau's revelation and Proust's. It is true. There is probably even more than an analogy, a real relationship, in personal temperament and its morbid directions. Duffner in his medical study of Proust places him in the schizoid or schizothymic group, and definitely relates him in this respect to Rousseau. This does not involve insanity; but it represents a psychic temperament which becomes exaggerated in insanity. Bleuler termed it *autism*, a living in oneself, which often involves two widely contrasting aspects of personality. But Rousseau represents this state in a far more decided shape. No psychologist has brought this out with more penetrating insight than Kretschmer alike in his study of general temperament and in that on genius.[1]

Kretschmer emphasises the contradictory elements in Rousseau's temperament. 'The most complete geniuses,' he remarks, 'like Goethe, Shakespeare, or Rousseau, are usually complex constructs and syntheses, inferior in constitutional

[1] E. Kretschmer, *Physique and Character; Der Geniale Mensch.*

purity to many of the smaller fry.' But in Rousseau we can
trace this tendency precisely in a schizoid temperament. He
was a romantic in at least one aspect of his schizothymic
temperament; that is to say he was an artist fleeing without
struggle into a world of phantasy and combining the heroic
and the complementary idyllic moods, in him fairly balanced
but both extreme. 'In great ages of upheaval, when the impossible seems the solely possible, and there is no use for
realists, such men are the heroes.'

In *Der Geniale Mensch* Kretschmer devotes nearly his whole
chapter on 'The Prophet' to Rousseau, whom he classes in the
first place with Hoelderlin as belonging to the great group of
sensitives, dominated by a self-feeling not to be confused with
possessive egotism, full of extravagant tenderness, yet suspicious of the outside world, always too vulnerable to even the
small shocks of everyday life. Here was a foundation on
which the contradictory forces in Rousseau's nature easily
found root. 'The delirium of persecution and the cloak of the
prophet are both two aspects of the same thing.' We see at
once the reason of what in modern slang would be called his
inferiority complex as well as of his lofty sense of a prophetic
mission. He complained that the seemingly wise things he
did would soon after appear to him mere *sottises*. In 1735 he
wrote to his father that, 'subject to extreme weaknesses, more
full of defects than anyone in the world, I feel that there are
vices in me to correct.' It was a genuine admission, and, in
one form or another, it is made again and again by the man
who penetrated to the core of the world's weakness and laid
down the laws for its reformation. But, as Kretschmer acutely
points out, it is precisely that inner tension between weakness
and pride that is the source of the sensitive man's spiritual
greatness, for the most powerful psychic forces are produced,
like steam, from fire and water, hostile elements that cannot
be unified, but exist tense in the breast of one and the same
man. By force of them he predominates in human society
over the normal man, who is merely healthy and strong, and
holds no such contrasting elements. Such is the great reformer — shy and sensitive, wounded by touches the normal

man does not even perceive — while the virtuous and sinless would-be reformer, the man all of a piece, appears and vanishes, leaving little trace.

We see the schizoid resemblance with Proust, but on the same foundation we also see the wide difference. They were both copious correspondents. But if nothing remained of Proust but his letters (in that case, it is true, they would never have remained!), a touch of contempt would have clung, even if sometimes smilingly, to Proust's memory. If nothing remained of Rousseau but his letters, he would still have been recognised as one of the greatest figures of his century, clearly revealed without any disguise.

It is an admirable feature of this *Correspondance* that in association with Rousseau's letters those to which they are a reply, as those to which they gave rise, are also, when extant, reproduced. This adds to the illumination thrown on Rousseau's character and situation on various memorable occasions.

There is, for instance, that stage of his friendship with Madame d'Epinay when in 1755 she offered him the charming retreat at the Hermitage of Montmorency which brought him joy, though the end was much confusion and trouble in personal relationships. It has always been an attractive spot. In Napoleon's only recently published letters to Marie-Louise he writes in May, 1813, on the eve of the great battle of Bautzen: 'I hope you enjoyed yourself at Saint-Leu. The valley of Montmorency is very beautiful at this season, though I fancy the time when it is pleasantest is the beginning of June when the cherries are ripe.' So we need not wonder that Rousseau, who was so sensitive to beauty, found it 'delicious,' even though it was in April, and not May, that he first arrived there. The negotiations with Madame d'Epinay, to whom the property belonged, had begun in March. Rousseau had been feeling he could no longer stand life in Paris and had some idea of returning to Geneva. About the 16th of March Madame d'Epinay writes to 'my dear Rousseau' to make, with much delicate precaution, a proposition. In short: 'I have a little house which is at your orders. You have often heard me speak of the Hermitage which is at the entrance of

MARCEL PROUST

the Montmorency forest, and with the most beautiful view. There are five rooms, a kitchen, a cellar, an acre of vegetable ground, a spring, and for garden the forest: You are the master, my dear friend, to dispose of this dwelling, if you decide to stay in France.' She proceeds with careful consideration to propose assisting him by an advance on the sales of his last book. She seems to have sent this letter by express messenger, and on the same or the following day he replies, in a not entirely gracious way, telling her that she is consulting her heart rather than either her fortune or his disposition: ' You badly misunderstand your interests if you wish to make a valet of a friend.' He adds: 'I am not troubled about either living or dying; the doubt that cruelly troubles me is what I must do during what remains to me to assure for myself the most perfect independence.' There speaks Rousseau in the spirit which so often made him appear rude and ungrateful. The trouble is, he says, where to find independence. He would prefer to stay in France, and he admits he would find life sweeter near his correspondent. He will decide in a week, ' but be very sure it is not reasons of interest which will decide me, for I have never feared lacking bread, and at the worst I know how to do without it. For the rest, I do not refuse to hear what you have to say to me provided you remember that I am not to sell.' Madame d'Epinay replies briefly at once: ' Your letter made me laugh at first, but then I felt sorry for you. It must be a very awkward mind that is angry at proposals dictated by a friendship that ought to be known to you, and to suppose that I have the foolish pride of wanting dependent creatures.' And she asks him not to decide in his present mood. Then Rousseau, evidently at once: 'I hasten to send you two words for I cannot endure that you should think me angry or misconstrue my expressions. I only took the word "valet" for the degradation in which the abandonment of my principles would necessarily throw me; I thought we understood each other better than we seem to; must people who think and feel like you and me explain these things? The independence I mean is not that of work. I wish to earn my living, I find pleasure in it; but I will not be subjected to any other duty if I can help it.... I wish to work, but according to my own taste, and even to do nothing when it so pleases me, without blame from anywhere, except my stomach.'[1] It was probably the 22d of March that Rousseau wrote: 'At last, Madame, I have taken my decision, and, as you may suppose, it is you who have won. I will, then, go to pass the Easter holidays [Easter was the 18th of April that year] at the Hermitage, and will remain as long as I find myself comfortable there and you may be able to put up with me; my plans extend no further than that. I will come and see you tomorrow and we will talk about it, but always, privately, I beg of you.'

In her *Mémoires*, Madame d'Epinay says that this letter gave her so much pleasure that she could not help showing it in presence of Grimm who happened to be with her, and he observed (though at that time Rousseau regarded him as an 'old friend') that she had made a great mistake in giving Rousseau the Hermitage. The short letters that immediately follow are friendly and familiar on both sides, and Madame d'Epinay seems to have conducted him personally to the Hermitage. On the 12th of April he writes to her from there: 'Although the weather has been unfavourable, since I arrived here, I have just passed three of the sweetest and most peaceful days of my life.... You will find everything in delightful order. Every time I enter my room I look round respectfully for the inhabitant of a place so well furnished.' And a few days later: 'You will be glad to learn, Madame, that this place charms me more and more. Unless you or I greatly change I shall never leave it.' And he ends: 'Good-bye, my good friend and not "Madame" as I have twice inadvertently scrawled. But what need of the correction, and what does the difference of the words matter when the heart gives them both the same meaning?'

[1] In her *Mémoires*, long afterwards, Madame d'Epinay refers to this attitude of Rousseau, and says that she had explained to him that his principles would have been excellent were he free, but were blameworthy when it was a question of exposing to want two women (Thérèse and her mother) who had sacrificed everything for him; but he had replied that they were as free as he was himself and that he did not beg anyone to stay with him or to follow him. A sophism, comments Madame d'Epinay.

It seems worth while to summarise an episode now fully set forth in the *Correspondance* since nothing could be more revealingly characteristic of the man Rousseau: his fierce and aggressive independence, his sincerity and his sensitiveness, yet at the same time his impracticability, his lack of consideration for the feelings of others sometimes approaching callousness, and mixed up with it all a fundamental tenderness and almost childlike simplicity.[1]

We see also those swift transitions and contradictions which marked not only the man in his daily life but the philosopher. Throughout these volumes we find, indeed, the extravagant propositions which are familiar to those who only know Rousseau's work at second or third hand, but also we find the judicious and penetrating observations by which, when brought up to the concrete point, he always knew how to qualify abstract statements. Those who find only extravagance in Rousseau might do well to remember that a thinker who so profoundly admired Montesquieu could scarcely have been fundamentally extravagant. He had a way of stating great truths, and even opposite truths, without qualification. Such, for instance, is the principle of the natural 'goodness of man,' and such the principle of man's fundamentally evil nature. He asserts them both, and there is truth in both. Whenever it comes to the point, he was quite able to express, and with complete felicity, the concordance of both truths in actual life. He could even do so when this involved opposing views of the same person. Thus he writes judicially, in a familiar letter, of Voltaire, who 'with the finest pen of his age yet possesses a heart apt always to create misfortune for

[1] It was his helpful kindness of heart that had in the first place won him Thérèse's devotion in 1754. When seriously ill, Madame Dupin obtained for him the assistance of Thérèse's mother, Madame Levasseur, who had a high reputation as a nurse, and his nurse persuaded him, when restored, to remove from lodgings to her house. A little later Thérèse met with an accident in a Paris street; she was passing two men fighting and a kick from one of them accidentally hit her, brought her to the ground in a faint, and caused injury. She was carried to her married sister's where she lived, but at Rousseau's entreaty she was removed to her mother's and with skilled medical aid she recovered, aided by the zealous co-operation of Rousseau, returning to the daughter the benefit he had received from the mother. In gratitude, as she shortly after told De Luc, Thérèse vowed herself to his service till death.

himself and sometimes for others.' When the Academy *Discours* was published in 1755, Voltaire wrote to Rousseau: 'You make me want to walk on all fours when I read your book. But as it is more than sixty years since I lost that habit, it is impossible for me to resume it. Literature,' he continues, as in opposition to Rousseau, 'fortifies and rectifies the spirit, consoles it, and is the source of your glory even when you write against it.' In his reply Rousseau writes, in the same tone, of literature as 'the only pleasure which remains to me. Do not return to all fours,' he adds: 'no one would succeed less, and in your case that return would be a mistake at once so great and so harmful that only God could effect it and only the Devil desire it.'

It is the swiftness and sincerity of Rousseau's actions and reactions, his temperamental vitality and spiritual independence, the penetrating insight and the extravagant impulses, which largely constitute the fascination of these letters and could not possibly be displayed on the same scale in the *Confessions*. In his letters we understand how he sometimes felt that he was always doing things that seemed wise and afterwards turned out to be follies.

In almost the last of his intimate letters extant, written to Comte Duprat in 1778, a few months before his death, he hopes to accept a proposal made by the Comte. But he adds: 'It is a castle in Spain, and of all such as I have built in my life I have never seen one realised.'

II

But we cannot leave it at that. If Rousseau had really been only, as at that moment it seemed to him, the builder of insubstantial castles in the air he would still remain a memorable figure, a great architect of such castles. He would have been not only a master in literature but a wonderful adventurer, a spiritual Casanova, exploiting a rich and extraordinary personality on the highest plane, in search of that El Dorado of the soul which somewhere beneath the horizon men have always vaguely divined.

Dr. Glover, one of our most illuminating historians of early Christianity, has in his book, *The Influence of Christ in the Ancient World*, sought to show how it was that Christianity conquered. That ancient world — Greek and Roman and Jewish alike — had reached a barrier it could not break through. Genius and inspiration were feeble, there was no new vitalising religion; the Romans, great rulers but allowing little space for spiritual expansion, had come to set up order and routine, to govern almost too well. 'Solitary hearts lost faith and nerve and a new impulse was needed, something or other to hearten men.' The Christians, often illiterate and clogged by the old religious traditions which they partly absorbed, conquered the world by the new life they infused into men's thoughts and aspirations. 'Christianity squared best with the world's best intelligence because it liberated the human mind and gave it a chance to develop.'

Much the same situation was again arising nearly two thousand years later in the eighteenth century, in the first place in France. The old flame of Christianity had died down; it seemed little more than ashes, no longer able to set light to any lofty aspiration. The reign of 'good sense' had set in, with the social routines it demanded, all extravagance was ridiculed, progress was felt to lie along narrowly rational lines. A great part of the wide-ranging human spirit was stifled. Once more solitary hearts lost faith and nerve; a new impulse was needed. It proved to be the opportunity of a unique person, the one who had seemed to himself no more than a builder of castles in the air.

Not, indeed, that that belief was absurd, even at the end of Rousseau's life. Supposing we knew nothing whatever of Christianity but the four Gospels, would we not say that here are castles in the air? Could we possibly conceive of a world-wide religion on such a foundation? That was actually the feeling of the polite and learned Roman world, and we can well understand the fierce controversies (so well described by P. de Labriolle, their historian today) which went on even for centuries afterwards.

Just the same controversies were aroused by Rousseau over

the ashes of Christianity (though he had taken elements from it just as the Christians had from paganism) and still continue centuries after his death: I read just now: 'Abuse of Rousseau is more frequent than understanding, especially today when he is represented as the cause of all our woes. He is indeed become almost the personal Devil of the new religion of "Humanism," and the number of people in the United States who have been taught to shudder at the word "Rousseauism," without having read, say, a single chapter of *Emile*, must by now be immense.' And if we turn to England I find Dr. Inge declaring that 'the influence of this sentimental rhetorician has perhaps been more pernicious than that of any man who has ever lived.... Without Rousseau there might have been no Karl Marx and no Bolshevism.' And yet only a few lines lower down this same eloquent moralist pleads for the renovation of economics, for greater simplicity and the reduction of waste, pointing out that in our civilisation today myriads of men are wasting their whole labour on producing things that nobody ought to want, supplying luxuries for the vulgar, the senseless, and the selfish, though the money spent on such barbarous indulgences would bring poverty to an end and restore war-stricken nations — and all the time completely unaware that he is preaching the gospel of Rousseau!

But it is interesting to see this reference to Marxism. Others have pointed out, as is easy, that Marx's theories were not built upon any foundation supplied by Rousseau, but were a natural product of the Industrial Revolution and might well have appeared had Rousseau never existed. Rousseau may be, and has been, more truly regarded as the source of another line of socialistic thought culminating in Henry George, since it was he who, in the essay on the *Causes of Inequality*, first insisted that economic inequality began with the unjust appropriation of land which should be common property. Yet another book of Rousseau's, the famous *Social Contract*, really may be brought into line with Communism.

This has been made clear in a recent essay by Mr. Middleton Murry, 'Rousseau Revisited,' printed in his privately issued periodical, *The Wanderer* (August and September, 1934). Mr.

Murry has of recent years become converted to Communism, though without entering the rigid sectarian Church of the Russian Bolshevists. He has also during nearly twenty years become increasingly and intimately aware of a spiritual message in Rousseau. In this latest essay he feels that he is at last able to make that message clear.

He finds it in the *Contrat Social*. At Oxford he had listened to the exposition of that famous work, and it had seemed to him, as it has to many of us, 'the dullest of dull books.' But now he knows it to be 'one of the most exciting.' He goes so far as to justify Dr. Inge in placing Rousseau at the source of Marxism. No one, Mr. Murry says, will accuse him of minimising the significance or the validity of the *Communist Manifesto*. But he is now convinced that it cannot be understood either in its expansions or its limitations, except by those who understand the great previous charter of Social Revolution, namely the *Contrat Social*.

The fundamental idea, as Murry views it, of this work is that unless society becomes a moral entity it becomes a madhouse. Unless Society should 'advance to Nature' it must degenerate. This did not mean men becoming either savage or licentious; it meant being obedient to those natural impulses which could be universalised, those which express a 'general will.' It was the spirit, not the form, of democracy which he valued. He foresaw the dangers of industrialism; he warned men against capitalistic society. He showed the remedy in what is 'the greatest attempt of the European mind to create a consciousness of the social whole.'

Mr. Middleton Murry concludes that Rousseau is one of the chief architects of the society of the future and 'his doctrine of the utmost importance for the achievement of that social Revolution which we all have at heart.'

It seems to me worth while to refer to this brilliant exposition of the significance of Rousseau, as a social philosopher, still today. It justifies alike the friends and the enemies of Rousseau. It may lead us to understand why, today even more than ever, they seem to feel justified in flying at each other's throats.

Rousseau, it is true, found himself from time to time in sympathetic, if superficial, touch with Catholics or with Protestants, and even seemed to identify himself with the one or the other. But, deep down, after his 'conversion,' there was always this fundamental difference: what Christianity desired to do by magic, and formulas involving a supernatural agency, he sought on a completely natural foundation. Man's regeneration was not to be based on a supernatural process but on a natural relation to a natural human society. In that difference there was the whole distinction between the old world and the new. The religions of today — from those of Communism (however Marxists may rebel!) to those of abstract mysticism — are all on Rousseau's pattern. That is why Rousseau dominates our spiritual world.

For my own part, however, while I am far from wishing to belittle the philosophic significance of Rousseau, it has never been that significance on which I have chosen to insist. The philosophy was the outcome of the man, and it is the unique and puzzling phenomena, still profoundly human, presented by the man to which I am drawn.

That is why I attach such high importance to the *Correspondance*. All the man's varying and opposing impulses are seen here at their moment of appearance in full flower. If I may once more echo Kretschmer's penetrating estimate, it seems indeed, almost incredible that the same breast should harbour this sanguine and sunny soul side by side with earnestness so sombre, and a temperament so sensitive to any pin-prick. But it was part of his greatness that he was not the model of the abstract and faultless moralist. He fought against what he had himself lived, and it is his double nature which has rendered him so lovable. In the face of wretchedness he never quite lost his smile; he enjoyed life while he disdained it; he understood and tenderly delighted in the actual world which he demonstrated to be impossible. That is the central contrast of his personality, the essence of his genius. It is that (as Kretschmer reminds us) which renders possible the judgment of Schopenhauer that on Rousseau alone has Nature bestowed the gift to be a moralist without being a bore.

But I could continue indefinitely to write about the letters of Rousseau. I will only say, in leaving him, that if in these difficult times any among my readers is ever sentenced to exile on a desert island and permitted to carry with him a limited number of literary works, I would recommend the inclusion, to count as one work, of the twenty volumes of this *Correspondance*. They contain, moreover, much praise of solitude.

RESTIF DE LA BRETONNE

I

A GUTTER Rousseau — *le Rousseau du ruisseau* — is the description commonly applied to Restif de la Bretonne. There is enough truth in that pun, however inadequate, to make it a fair starting-point for the discussion of a remarkable figure in a remarkable epoch which he most vividly illustrates. Restif always lived in contact with the pavement; he was plebeian in spirit as well as in life, and it was, indeed, because he was so close in feeling to the streets, as he was earlier to the countryside, that he was able to produce pictures of everyday life in town and country such as we seek in vain among more distinguished writers of his time. Rousseau, on the other hand — springing from craftsmen of old citizen stock — was in spirit, however he sometimes fell short, of more aristocratic temper, and rose by long efforts of strenuous aspiration, which we may follow step by step, to heights beyond even the discernment of Restif. Yet there were not lacking links of fraternity, and Restif shared with his greater contemporary not only some personal weaknesses and an excessive sensibility but a generous humanitarian ardour, though, for all his innate plebeianism, we can scarcely say he had a saner vision of what society can yield than came to the man of soaring genius. Rousseau (who was yet a moralist in spite of himself) once declared: 'I am an observer, not a moralist; I am the botanist who describes the plant, not the physician who prescribes its uses.' Restif similarly, but in his more arrogant way, said of *Monsieur Nicolas*: 'I here present a book of natural history which places me above Buffon.' He was an ostentatious and effusive moralist, but it is in description, in the vivid presentation of reality, that he was really admirable and even a pioneer. A large sphere of activity is indeed possible to the 'Rousseau of the Gutter,' especially when he happens to be an artist. Restif made the utmost of his possibilities good and bad; he drained his cup of life, unscrupulously and indiscriminately, to the last dregs.

From an early period there were those who put forward other claims for Restif de la Bretonne. His fellow-countrymen found for him names like the 'Voltaire of Chambermaids,' the 'Rousseau of the Market,' the 'Teniers of Fiction,' and *Monsieur Nicolas* was called the '*Liaisons Dangereuses* of the lower classes.' Some of his books were widely popular in his time, especially among the middle-class people with whom he was so closely in touch, though they no doubt fell into the hands of all sorts of people; they were to be found (to Michelet's surprise) in the private library of Marie Antoinette, and (to Sainte-Beuve's surprise) were admired by Mlle. de Lespinasse. Even outside France, in Germany, before the eighteenth century was out, Restif was taken seriously. So fine and learned a critical intelligence as Wilhelm von Humboldt wrote to Goethe from Paris in 1799 that *Monsieur Nicolas* is the truest and most living book there is (though he had no means of judging its truth), adding that he who had not read it will never understand the French character. A year earlier Schiller had called Goethe's attention to this book as of 'incalculable value' and spoken with more critical discernment of its real qualities; he justly dwelt on the vivacity of the narrative, the multiplicity of the figures, especially of women, and the vivid presentation of the life and customs of a certain section of the contemporary French population; he put it in the same class as Cellini's autobiography. Wieland and Tieck and Lavater regarded Restif de la Bretonne as a phenomenon of the first importance. I do not find that he aroused much interest in England, where attention was concentrated on the greater figure of Rousseau, and the forty-two editions of his *Paysan Perverti*, which the credulous Restif believed to have been issued in London were sheer imagination. In 1790, *Pictures of Life*, translated from one of his less important books, was published in London in two volumes, without Restif's name, but I have not been able to find that any other of his books appeared in English until at last *Monsieur Nicolas* has been translated in full by Mrs. Powys Mathers.[1] In France itself Restif's popularity evaporated under the stress of the new movements initiated by the Revolution, even before his death, in 1809, which indeed attracted a moment's attention to him again, and even a moment's respect, followed by immediate oblivion.

During the whole of the first half of the nineteenth century the name and works of the 'ignoble' Restif, as Sainte-Beuve called him, were treated with indifference or with contempt in France. 'His books are nearly all forgotten today,' a French writer said in 1828. The eighteenth century was in the shade, except in so far as it had been the prelude to the Great Revolution or to the grandiose movement of Romanticism. The only people interested in Restif were third-class writers who found him a rich mine to steal from, and it was to their interest to say as little as possible about him.

At the end of the first half of the nineteenth century, a more just conception of the previous century began to be formed, and Restif was one of the first to profit by it. At almost the same moment two distinguished but very unlike people, the refined critic Charles Monselet and the delicate poet Gérard de Nerval, both independently became interested in Restif and wrote of him prominently with enthusiastic appreciation. Monselet in 1854, in what may be considered, though slight and superficial, the first modern book on Restif, described him as ' the strangest figure that ever appeared on the threshold of literature.' A little earlier Gérard de Nerval, himself a strange and fascinating figure, wrote a romancing biography of Restif which he included in *Les Illuminés*. There was indeed an extraordinary affinity between these two eccentric spirits who were yet so unlike, and Gérard de Nerval's biographer, Aristide Marie, can write that 'it is impossible to exaggerate the

[1] *Monsieur Nicolas, or the Human Heart Unveiled.* Translated by R. Crowdy Mathers. Edited with an Introduction by Havelock Ellis. Six volumes, 1931. The Introduction corresponds in substance to the present essay.

degree to which Restif's autobiographical novels modelled the soul and influenced the life of Gérard de Nerval.' It is no mean testimony in favour of the earthly minded Restif that he should have been so cherished by that delicate and etherial spirit, who even seems to have derived from Restif a doctrine of 'erotic predestination' and the 'transfusion of souls,' the doctrine according to which the same soul may be loved through different bodies.

In 1883 appeared the excellent reprint of *Monsieur Nicolas* by Liseux. The neglected volumes of Restif's early editions with their charming illustrations soon fetched high prices; reprints of fragments of his work appeared; and a period began of what Octave Uzanne called Restifomania. Paul Lacroix in 1875 had already thought it worth while to publish a bibliography and iconography of Restif. It was not, however, till after 1889, when Binet first formulated the conception of erotic fetichism, that Restif became, not only an object of scholarly investigation but also of fierce controversy. In various medical publications he was brought forward as a typical example of the sexual perversion of shoe fetichism. Champions of Restif, thereupon, arose to defend him from this imputation and to assert his normality. Grand-Carteret, who had brought out an abridged edition of *Monsieur Nicolas*, protested indignantly on behalf of this 'great and calumniated Nicolas-Edme Restif,' and declared: 'If Restif was a fetichist the whole eighteenth century was fetichist with him.' Even from the medical side Dr. Louis Barras in 1913 put forth a lengthy monograph, not very scientific in tone, entitled: *Le Fétichisme: Restif de la Bretonne fut-il Fétichiste?* in which he likewise argued that Restif's fetichism was 'the fetichism of everybody.'

We owe the longest and most substantial study of Restif to the late Dr. Iwan Bloch who in 1906, under the pseudonym of 'Eugen Dühren,' published in Berlin his *Rétif de la Bretonne: Der Mensch, der Schriftsteller, der Reformator*, and followed it up with a smaller volume of bibliography. Bloch was admirably equipped for this task, not only by his receptive Jewish enthusiasm but by his scientific training, his Germanic thoroughness, and his specialised knowledge in the field of sex literature where Restif is so often to be found. He has no hesitation about describing his hero as a shoe fetichist, even of the most typical kind, but he is equally sure that this is but one of Restif's many aspects and, taken altogether, he places him confidently on a high pedestal. 'In Rétif de la Bretonne,' he asserts, 'the spirit of the French people, in a certain sense, has been vividly embodied.' Nor is Bloch by any means alone in this judgment of Restif's place in the world, and one of his latest champions has even termed him 'the greatest writer of the eighteenth century.' Finally, in 1928, this champion, M. Funck-Brentano, in his *Retif de la Bretonne* (published under the editorial care of M. Emile Magne), has produced a scholarly biography of Restif based on a fresh examination of the sources, and testifying to the serious place which Restif now takes in French literature.[1]

Restif himself would certainly have accepted the highest estimates of that place. He never hesitated to put forth large claims for himself, and to put them forth with emphasis. The unhappiness of his later years was heightened by the failure of his world to take him at his own valuation. It is certain that no man was ever more present in his work than Restif was in the copious writings he was constantly pouring out. Alike in the books put forth as truth, which were in part fiction, and in the books put forth as fiction, which were in part truth, Restif himself was always there: now he exaggerates; again he conceals; he disguises himself in embroidered garments; he is always there. But he is there in such a copious and manifold and elusive way that we need to examine his manifestations with critical care in order to define the essential Restif.

II

Nicolas-Anne Edme Retif was born at Sacy, a village near Auxerre in Burgundy on the 23d of October, 1734, and baptised

[1] In 1934 a special Restif Exhibition was organised at the Musée Carnavalet by M. Vaudoyer, the new curator.

the same day, which seems to indicate that his life was de-
spaired of. Retif was his correct family name, not Restif or
even Rétif. He himself, however, adopted the form Restif,
which he had found in an old history of Auxerre, and he added
'de la Bretonne' from the name of a farmhouse at Sacy into
which the family moved when he was a child of eight. This
farmhouse still belongs to descendants of the family and in the
chief room now hangs a portrait of its most famous member.

Although he sometimes liked to dwell on his peasant origin,
Restif's home was not that of peasants in the humble sense.
At that period the condition of the peasantry had sunk very
low, to an unheard-of degree of misery, the contemporary
Marquis d'Argenson states. The peasants were haggard figures
in rags, and their mud hovels, Arthur Young tells, would in
England only be considered fit for pig-sties. Restif's father
was a well-to-do farmer and vine-yard cultivator, living in a
community which enjoyed many privileges and considerable
self-government; he had once been a clerk in Paris; he was
only a peasant in the sense that he himself worked on the
land with his family and his thirteen menservants and maid-
servants. Joseph Delteil, the distinguished writer of today,
is similarly, like Restif's father, a *vigneron* and proud of the
fact. His position corresponded to that of the yeoman in
England at the same date. In addition to labour on the land
he exercised the functions of village notary and justice of the
peace. No doubt he was a man of admirable character, and
his literary son often celebrated his virtues, notably in *La Vie
de mon Père*, a romancing and sentimentalised version of his
father's life and a charming though highly idealised picture
of rural conditions, which has seemed to some to be Restif's
masterpiece. He married twice, having seven children by each
marriage. The first wife we may fairly regard as a peasant woman. Not so the second, Barbe Ferlet, of whom Nicolas was
the eldest child. Although young she had already been a
widow, and belonged to a Burgundian family, which was
well connected, while she had herself, Restif states, once
been in the service of the Princesse d'Auvergne in Paris. That
may be an important detail. It would explain how it was

that her eldest boy was not brought up in rough and rustic ways; we may understand his frequent emphasis on personal cleanliness, hardly characteristic of ordinary life in his time and land, his prescription of three baths a week, and his remark in describing the type of the 'untidy wife' in *Les Parisiennes*, when he was himself approaching old age: 'the unfortunate thing is that the exterior is always the symbol of the interior; the woman who is untidy, disorderly, and dirty has the same defects in her soul.' There may have spoken the son of the Princess's lady's maid, though it is to be feared that Restif kept these fine sentiments as a prescription for women: he himself, we are told, paid in later life no attention to the cares of the toilet, and constantly wore the same old clothes with but little trace of linen beneath. But as a boy he seems to have been brought up in such fine-gentlemanly ways that the other village boys nick-named him 'Monsieur Nicolas,' and so furnished the title for his most memorable work.

There was more about Barbe Ferlet, however, than the mere refinements of training in an aristocratic house. We may perhaps find in her a chief element of her most notable child's heredity. We search his character in vain for much indication of his father's solid virtues, though the elder Restif's father is displayed as a harsh, morbid, and dissolute character which may well have had its significance in the heredity. But we may easily find much of the mischievous and petulant vivacity attributed to his mother, though that characteristic hardly appears in the account he wrote of her in the form of a story, 'La Femme de Laboureur,' in *Les Contemporaines*, where she is represented as embodying Restif's own ideal of the perfect wife: 'She regarded her husband as her Head, her Guide, her Master, and her Father; she was far from that dangerous and criminal system of equality which can only be put forth by libertines in towns.' Bibi, as she was familiarly named, had evidently to undergo a severe discipline such as her son never felt called upon to submit to.

Monsieur Nicolas's morbid nervous sensibility, whether it was from his mother or his paternal grandfather that he inherited it, appeared at an early age. He was, if we may trust his own account, until smallpox destroyed his good looks a very beautiful child — with fine eyes, curly hair, and a delicate pale complexion — but subject to night-terrors which were not calmed by putting him to sleep at the foot of his parents' bed. He was attacked by terrifying visions in the dark, and he felt his hair standing on end with fright if he had to go outside the door after nightfall. This nervous over-excitability soon manifested itself in sexual precocity (he claims to have become a father at the age of ten and a half) and was continued throughout life in a constant preoccupation with matters of sex. It was apt to overflow in an attraction to sexual aberrations (nakedly and outrageously illustrated by his *Anti-Justine*), of which the most innocent and the most frequently recurring was shoe-fetichism. The dispute as to the extent to which he became the victim of this aberration is unprofitable. It is evident that, in the adoration of his preferred symbol of womanhood, he went beyond the limits that may fairly be called normal, and that he exhibited the germs, even more than the germs, of a variety of perversions, but it is also clear that he hardly reached that extreme of perversion when the symbol becomes more important than the woman. Here, no doubt, the robust solidity of his paternal heredity came to the support of his nervous temperament. Restif's prolific extravagancies were confined within a firm framework which preserved him from destruction; even on the intellectual plane, it is curious to note how his Utopian schemes of social reform were generally fitted into a system of old-fashioned conventional notions, based on the traditions he had inherited, and with a perpetual ostentatious insistence on 'virtue' which, in spite of what we know of his life, we need not consider altogether hypocritical, or merely due to awareness of its popularity among the middle-class audience he addressed. Fundamentally Restif always retained the traditional morality. He abandoned the Christian creed but not Christian morals. That inculcation of Jansenist teaching in boyhood of which he speaks with admirable insight in *Monsieur Nicolas* left upon him an ineffaceable mark.

As a small child Monsieur Nicolas was sent to the village

school, but he learnt little there, though he made acquaintance with the rod, for his precocity was all in sensibility and not in intelligence. His associations with his girl friends — often such as the moralist must consider extremely unwholesome for a child — were the chief educative influence at this early period, though they were blended with a growing delight in the lovely natural scenery of his homeland; indeed, Restif has sometimes seemed to suggest to the spectator a Gilles de Rais in Arcadia. He made no progress in study until he was taken in hand by his eldest half-brother, a priest who belonged to the severe Jansenist party in religion. When he was twelve, a venerable member of the Restif family, a sagacious old lawyer, arrived on a visit to Sacy, and after examining young Nicolas at his father's request pronounced against making him a farmer and in favour of giving him a superior education. Therewith the fate of Nicolas was decided. He was taken to Paris and placed at the Bicêtre asylum, where was then a choir school, with the organisation of a religious confraternity of Jansenist character, in which another of his half-brothers, Abbé Thomas, had just been appointed to a post. So Monsieur Nicolas became, with a name borrowed from a famous Father of the Church whom the Jansenists regarded as their special patron, 'Brother Augustine,' and himself for a brief period a devoted Jansenist.

In 1747, however, when Nicolas was fourteen years old, the Jansenists fell out of favour in the State, the Bicêtre seminary was put into other hands, and Nicolas was taken for the completion of his education to the parsonage of Courgis, a village near Auxerre, where his eldest brother, Abbé Nicolas-Edme, had become the village priest and was now joined by Abbé Thomas. The small parsonage, close to the church and the cemetery, still stands exactly as in Monsieur Nicolas's time, sheltered by a great and venerable elm said to have been planted in the days of Henry IV.

It was in the church at Courgis that, on Easter Sunday 1748, young Nicolas first saw Jeannette Rousseau, the local notary's daughter, a girl ten years older than himself, and the vision produced so powerful an impression on the boy's exalted sensibility that he ever afterwards considered that on that day he had met his fate. Jeannette Rousseau was his Laura, his Yvonne de Galais, though Restif's earthly and facile temperament easily found 'accommodations' for his ideal in an endless stream of women who embodied one or others of her perfections. Jeannette was the source of Restif's famous metaphysical doctrine of fidelity, by love for the same soul in a succession of different bodies. The vision of the original ideal remained, and when forty years later Restif learnt that Jeannette Rousseau at the age of sixty-four was still unmarried, he even for a moment schemed to make her his wife. This series of events, however, is described in detail in *Monsieur Nicolas*, with much reticence and much exaggeration, no doubt many added embroideries, which the critical reader may discern, for, as his latest and most competent biographer, M. Funck-Brentano, remarks, 'we must accept with reserve the narrative of Monsieur Nicolas's love-scenes in his autobiography.'

In 1751, Nicolas was taken to Auxerre and apprenticed to the local printer, Fournier, whose wife, under the name of 'Madame Parangon,' played an important part in Restif's life. Fournier (though not to be confused with the more eminent Parisian printer of that name) was a printer of some distinction, enjoying special privileges, and his house and printing establishment were situated close to the famous Tour de l'Horloge in the centre of that charming and interesting old Burgundian town on the broad and peaceful Yonne. Auxerre has scarcely yet learned to be proud of its association with Restif de la Bretonne; one may not easily see or hear his name there, even when one is staying at the old Hôtel de la Fontaine close to his early home, but there is much still to recall him; indeed the house, now a chemist's shop, still remains, little changed from Restif's time. 'How pretty the girls are at Auxerre!' suddenly exclaimed young Nicolas as he gazed out of the window on to the street at his arrival, and I confess that I have found myself independently making precisely the same remark more than one hundred and seventy years later, though with none of the results that followed in the case of that impressionable boy.

Restif was now seventeen, of middle height, not specially good-looking, but with large dark eyes, long brown curly hair, thick eyebrows, and red lips; he could be ardent and vivacious in speech but he was generally silent, very wild and shy, hating society and easily blushing when addressed, 'the modest girl' one of his cousins called him. In spite of his extreme sensibility, his disorderly imaginations, and his lack of courage, he was not without physical strength and possessed much agility. We may perhaps accept his own assurance that girls found him attractive. There is no doubt that he found them attractive. In old age he prepared a calendar of the women who had fascinated him, one lady saint for each day of the year, and when every day was filled up there were still many women left out. In portraits that show him in early manhood we still see a rather pleasant face with large sensitive eyes; the bird of prey's head which we more commonly associate with him belongs to later life. At the same time Cubières-Palmézeaux, who knew him well in old age, describes him as of average height with large forehead, and large dark eyes revealing 'the fire of genius,' aquiline nose, black eyebrows descending on the eyelids as years increased and suggesting an eagle or an owl, a hairy chest like a bear, altogether a vigorous laborious sober man, skilful and industrious in his work as a printer, notwithstanding his perpetually effervescent emotional temperament and the always recurring thirst for new debauches combined, in apparent inconsistency, with what seemed fundamental goodness, a moral and physical Hercules, with 'the finest head in the world.'

It was in Auxerre, whither he had returned from Paris to work again with Fournier, that Monsieur Nicolas found a wife. That was an event which he speedily came to regard as one of the unhappiest in his life, though he put down the unhappiness, not to his own nature and conduct, but to his really admirable wife. She was certainly unsuited for the position she too rashly assumed, though it is difficult to say what woman would have been better suited, unless, indeed, some ignorant peasant, humble and subservient to all her master's extravagant impulses.

Agnès Lebègue was a refined and cultured girl far above the average in ability, brought up in easy circumstances as the daughter of a highly esteemed apothecary at Auxerre who had recently suffered severely from legal proceedings which were entirely to his credit. When she married Nicolas in 1760, Agnès was prepared, and quite able, to be a sympathetic helpmate, alike in domestic and intellectual affairs, as well as to further his prospects in the world. Joubert many years later fell in love with her, and if we are tempted to take too seriously Restif's wild and random abuse of his wife we may remember the testimony in her favour thus supplied by that shrewd and delicate spirit. Her troubles began from the first; she had to struggle with the domestic disorder in which from poverty and taste Restif habitually lived, and the marriage was scarcely consummated before she discovered that her husband had become the lover of no less than three of her girl friends. Nevertheless she soon became by her energy and ability the chief and often the sole support of the family, in which four children rapidly appeared, while her husband sometimes earned nothing; she taught; she took in boarders; at one time she became a milliner. If under these circumstances it was not long before the young wife began to lose her youth and her illusions — she never lost her charm — Restif, of whose fundamental goodness his friends so often assure us, might have had the grace to recognise that any faults in the marriage relationship could not be entirely hers; he might also have acknowledged the numerous occasions in his troubled life when he fell back on his despised wife for the assistance she never refused. Her chief defect in his eyes was what he calls her '*fureur du bel esprit.*' She had literary accomplishment; she was skilful in the epistolary art, and in accordance with the custom of many superior women of her time, she wrote letters which were privately circulated among friends. Nothing could be more aloof from what Restif regarded as the proper sphere of woman, at all events of woman as wife. Yet he had ample and manifold reasons for gratitude. It may even have been in emulation of his wife that a few years later his own slumbering literary aptitudes were stimulated into activity, and they took on at first the same epistolary form. The virulent abuse which in public and in private he poured upon his wife 'unveil the human heart' of Restif more than any of his avowed confessions. The 'goodness of heart' which impressed his friends was largely that slipshod emotional generosity which always impresses superficial observers. We may accept Restif's way of becoming an author, as we may accept (to use Funck-Brentano's comparison) Gauguin's way of becoming a painter by abandoning his wife and family to set out for the Pacific. It may be one of Nature's methods for making an artist, but we are not called on to admire it.

At this point we reach a disputed period in Restif's life. In 1798, in old age, we know that he secured a post in the police department as a censor of private correspondence. We can well believe that he found this duty full of interest. But a modern scholar, Grasilier, in his book, *Rétif de la Bretonne Inconnu*, finds reason to believe that, some thirty years earlier, exactly at the period when on becoming an author he threw up work as a printer, Restif entered the service of the secret police. That function would serve to account for his frequent mysterious nocturnal activities, of which *Les Nuits de Paris* was one of the literary by-products. Such duties could hardly have failed to prove congenial to Restif, but Grasilier's arguments have not proved convincing to Funck-Brentano, chiefly on the ground that we can detect no evidence in Restif's writings of the alleged activities. I may remark that I cannot accept this counter-argument as absolutely conclusive. Duties of this kind are necessarily secret, and Restif was quite capable of maintaining secrecy about his own activities when he considered that his interest or his vanity made that desirable. Casanova for many years acted as a political spy, but it is on State archives and not on his confession that we depend for our knowledge of the fact. The point may be left undecided, but Restif's frequent terrors of the police would seem unnecessary if he was himself in their employ.

It was during his nocturnal rambles that Restif initiated the most curious of his methods of autobiographic record, the 'inscriptions' he carved on the stone parapets and walls of the Ile Saint-Louis. These inscriptions were records of important events in his life, which had to be made on the very day or that immediately following, with brief comments in Latin, carved with a key at first, but afterwards with a special tool he had made for the purpose.

The Ile Saint-Louis is a peaceful and delightful spot even today, as those of us well know who have ever dwelt in one of its ancient houses with beautifully panelled rooms and silent court yards. It must have been more charming still in the eighteenth century, and yet more so by contrast with the crowded and filthy Ile de la Cité. But no one ever gained so much joy from the Ile Saint-Louis as Restif. For him it was a sacred spot; his 'beloved Island' was a temple for the most fervid manifestations of his ebullient sentimentality. Sometimes in moments of exaltation he even fell on his knees on the pavement. An amazed and alarmed house-porter once approached him in this posture: 'What are you doing? This is not a church.' Restif solemnly rose and pointed to a bright star: 'Do you not see the starry vault of God's great temple, wretched man? Go and guard your gate.' This went on for years. It was Restif's special delight to seek out the anniversaries of the events he thus commemorated so that he might double and triplicate the joy of the original moment by reviving its memory. It was inevitable that these nocturnal perambulations should attract the attention of street arabs, apparently even more ferocious in those days than they are now, who would lie in wait to play tricks on the strange figure in the long cloak at his inscriptions, sometimes throwing stones or mud, so that Monsieur Nicolas was put to flight. The persecution of these 'little ogres,' as he calls them, at last became intolerable. Restif copied his inscriptions and abandoned his cherished island. The manuscript book was eventually discovered and published in 1889 by M. Paul Cottin as *Mes Inscripcions*. The inscriptions themselves have now all disappeared through renewal of the stone-work. But Monselet records that in 1847 one still remained on the Quai d'Orléans.

Restif impulsively abandoned printing for writing, though for many years after marriage it brought in little or no money, so that he was often dependent on his wife's exertions. Subsequently he sometimes combined the two occupations, composing the book in his head as he composed it in type, just as an author of today may with a typewriter. He became at length an easy and prolific writer and left some two hundred volumes behind him, though so far from being a precocious author. He was thirty-three when he published his first novel, *La Famille Virtueuse* (put forward as 'letters translated from the English'), which had little success and deserved no more; so also his second novel, *Lucile ou les Progrès de la Vertu*, both these books, it will be observed, revealing Restif's ostentatious love of virtue. The third, *Le Pied de Fanchette*, in which all the incidents depended on the heroine's pretty foot, was less virtuous but rather better. Later followed his best novel, *Le Paysan Perverti*, which was really about himself slightly disguised and converted into the hero of a pathetic drama. Thereafter Restif's profuse literary activities are hard to follow. But there are two features which mark nearly all and constitute the entwined threads on which they are strung: they are nearly always inspired by the 'muse' of some woman who at the moment attracted him, and they nearly all contain, with whatever modifications, a foundation of fact in which Restif himself often plays a leading part. That statement itself tells us much about Restif. He could not write romance unless he was supplied with a foundation of fact, and he could not deal with fact without yielding to the temptation to romance. This is what we find whenever we 'unveil the human heart' of Monsieur Nicolas.

It is such interwoven threads of fact and romance which characterise *Les Contemporaines* (or 'Adventures of the Prettiest Women of the Present Age'), perhaps — with all its lapses into carelessness and banality — the most generally attractive of Restif's works outside *Monsieur Nicolas*, and it has indeed been considered one of the most interesting works in the whole range of French literature. It is certainly one of the most extensive, for it is contained in fully forty-two volumes (not counting some further continuations under other names) and it includes seven hundred and sixteen stories and anecdotes. They were written between 1782 and 1786 when Restif had attained the maturity of his powers, and certainly present an invaluable picture of middle-class life during the second half of the eighteenth century, covering, indeed, the most varied aspects of that life. Assézat has enumerated two hundred and eighty-two different occupations as exercised by the heroines of these stories, some of them now extinct, and every story probably has some foundation in fact. The stories are of very various quality, some admirable, others sinking to the depth of platitudinous commonplace. This work contains no adventures, Restif tells in the Introduction, save those that the heroine's story naturally gives rise to. In a note, 'those persons who have subjects to be treated or who have themselves composed their own story' are invited to write to the author at an address given. Restif claims that he is presenting 'events which occur daily in the interior of the home and which by their variety as well as by their singularity will help you to anatomise the human heart.' The reader will find here, he says, 'neither the terrible gloom of English books, which fatigues even while it attracts, nor the butterfly absurdity of ordinary French pamphlets.' In the Preface to the second edition he emphasises the moral lesson of his work. He is, he says, preaching the morality of nature, reason, and good sense; he is 'courageously standing up against the most dangerous of abuses, that most likely to destroy morality and public welfare, the insubordination of women'; he 'prefers truth to his own interest,' in thus 'opening the eyes of women to their own real destination.'

But just as in the episodes of his actual life this moral destination of women is far from clear, so also in his stories it is not too conspicuously displayed. We may take for instance, almost at random, 'L'Amazone ou la Fille qui veut faire un Enfant,' a story with which, as we find in *Monsieur Nicolas*, Restif was himself mixed up. The Amazon is a girl of good position at Dijon — the well-educated daughter of a rich tradesman — who hated marriage and was not attracted to men, but she had strong maternal instincts and wanted a child. She chose a young gardener of good disposition to be the father, imposing secrecy and sending him out of the country directly after, carrying through the whole affair so skilfully, with so high a hand, that all goes well. Restif leaves his feminine readers to draw what moral they like. But his method of inviting stories from strangers led to troubles he had not foreseen. Unscrupulous correspondents gratified private spite by the stories they sent him, on one occasion at least telling him that he need not change the names as they had already been changed, whereas the real names were given. Endless troubles were thus caused and the timorous Monsieur Nicolas was sometimes stopped in the street and insulted by persons who were complete strangers to him. The *Contemporaines* proved, however, an enormous popular success. They were something new in literature and exactly suited to the middle-class audience to which they were addressed. Restif's devoted friend and disciple Milran writes from Cherbourg to say that he prefers Restif to Shakespeare. 'I don't like that barbarian Shakespeare,' he adds, 'who has so many admirers. You are far indeed from so uncivilised a genius.' Restif cannot resist printing this letter, though he adds in a footnote: 'So much the worse for me and my readers. I devour this author and exclaim at every reading, "Blessed be Shakespeare and his translator!"' Restif made very large profits out of *Les Contemporaines*. But he could not help exclaiming: 'Oh! how painful it is to make honey, when one wishes only to extract it from the flowers of truth!'

Les Contemporaines, the climax of Restif's activities in storytelling, gives indications of his moral and social theories. As time went on he became ever more interested, and ever more extravagant, in moral and cosmogonic speculation. Like many distinguished authors who have not been able to reform themselves, he found consolation in seeking to reform mankind. His interest in social reform and in the construction of ideal communities is indeed shown as early as the latter part of *Le Paysan Perverti*. He foresaw in the Southern Continent a 'powerful Empire,' and is by some considered the first to apply to it (in his *Nuits de Paris*, about 1788) its present name of 'Australia,' replacing 'New Holland.' The idea of a sort of phalanstery, which he sketched out, anticipated some of Fourier's ideas, and it is even possible that Fourier may have been inspired by them. The earliest (it was published in 1769) and best known of Restif's books entirely devoted to social reform, was *Le Pornographe*, discussing the reglementation of prostitution, an institution to which throughout life he attached high value and desired to redeem from the contempt in which it is held. A 'pornograph,' it must be understood, is for Restif a student of prostitution, and he attributes the origin of his rules for brothels to an Englishman called Lewis Moore. The book is ingeniously thrown into an epistolary form, and the elaborately detailed regulations are set forth as an incidental part of the sentimental love-story told in the correspondence of a young man with the friend of whose sister he is enamoured. The brothel he desired to set up Restif proposed to call a 'Parthenion,' so as not to wound delicate ears by vulgar words, and he trusted that the inmates would not, like modern prostitutes, be what he called automatised, but retain the fresh sensibility to pleasure which, he believed, prevailed in classic times. Such an institution, he maintained, would be 'the masterpiece of human wisdom, an imitation of Divinity.' He even persuaded himself that the Emperor Joseph II of Austria had adopted and carried out his idea, and the story was spread about (whether or not by Restif) that the Emperor had created him a Baron and sent him his portrait, the democratic author returning the title deed, but retaining the portrait. To the end Restif cherished his moral enthusiasm in this cause. His friend Bonneville once reproached him with describing too minutely the pleasures of prostitution. Restif defended himself. 'Yes,' he said, with heat, 'I am the friend and protector of these houses treated with such contempt. I would far rather go to see a pretty courtesan than make a baby with the wife of my friend or my neighbour.' I do not dispute Restif's honesty, but the method he so highly approved had never saved him from making love copiously in the houses of friends and neighbours, and he seems to have exaggerated the number of babies he thus made.

It was over the sanctity of the home, even more than over that of the brothel, that Restif conceived it his mission to watch. Especially, as we have already seen, he wished to protect the morals of women. 'If my opinion carried any weight,' he said once, 'women would be taught nothing but morality; they would be ignorant of all other sciences.' In *Les Parisiennes* he deplored the tendency of the Parisian girls of his time to marry for the sake of liberty, independence, and pleasure. It is a detestable abuse to which he would put an end by legislation, and he proposed to prohibit the public performance of such pernicious plays as Molière's *Ecole des Maris*. Even frivolity is more compatible with feminine virtue than science, which deprives women of their modesty and their lovableness. But when we know Restif we are not surprised to hear that he had many women of distinguished intelligence among his friends, or that for three years he was anxiously desiring to meet the most eminent intellectual woman of his time, Madame de Staël, and that when at last Mercier took him to see her he returned, his friend Cubières tells us, 'overwhelmed by admiration, love, and enthusiasm.'

Restif's speculations, however, ranged far beyond the sphere of Parisian morals, and became more wildly extravagant with the course of years. Buffon (or Noffub as he sometimes preferred to anagrammatise the name) had been the master from whom he derived the germs of his earlier philosophical ideas. It is needless to add that he was violently opposed to the Church and used to say to Cubières: 'If I were king I would use my power only to abolish Catholicism.' In later life he discovered Cyrano de Bergerac and in that writer's brilliant cosmic expeditions Restif found congenial inspiration for his own adventures in the unknown. He set forth a fantastic theory of evolution; his notions of the eternal recurrence of life are regarded as faintly foreshadowing Nietzsche's; and visions of elaborately Utopian communities were always floating before his eyes. He preceded the astronomers in asserting the movement of the solar system through space;

he imagined flying machines heavier than air, and even anticipated their modern military function of dropping bombs, mingling these suggestions with the wildest absurdities and the feeblest puerilities. It is part of the everlasting inconsistency of Restif de la Bretonne that this dreamer, who only felt at home in the realm of phantasy, and was perpetually seeking idealistic embellishments for the world, has yet left to us the most intimate realistic pictures we possess of his actual world. It was in 1783, when he was fifty years of age — though he had vaguely planned it earlier, even before Rousseau's *Confessions* — that Restif began to write *Monsieur Nicolas*, his most memorable picture of the life of his time. But it was not until 1794 that he began the publication, for the most part composing it on his little printing press with his own hand, and he completed it three years later.

The final stage of life he was now entering was scarcely happy for Restif. The eccentricities of his ill-balanced temperament were becoming more pronounced. His estimate of his own genius went on increasing as well as his bitterness with the world that failed to appreciate his greatness. When the Revolution came the accompanying financial crash destroyed the large profits he had made by *Les Contemporaines*, and ill-health increased his misery. It is true that he was little affected by the political changes. He was indeed arrested at the outset, but a young girl living on the Ile Saint-Louis testified in his favour. 'He is the poor date-carver, a good man,' she said; 'I often liked to follow to see what he wrote. It was all quite harmless.' So he was released, and not long after he became attached to the secret police department (whether or not he had, as Grasilier argues, been working for the police during many years already), with the special duty of dealing with intercepted letters (more especially those in Spanish) in the so-called Cabinet Noir. There were many thousands of letters to read and the work was heavy, but the salary was good and Restif had eight or nine clerks under him. When four years later Fouché, who was now in charge of the police, completely re-organised Restif's department, he was 'suppressed.' He had for a time been full of hope in the revolutionary movement. He detested the tyranny of a proletariat as even worse than that of a monarch, and believed in thorough communism with the abolition of private property. But his enthusiasm for the establishment of this characteristically incoherent scheme of society subsided with the course of events, and the still feverishly active author contented himself with seeking on every side to gain assistance in producing his endless stream of books.

We obtain an amusing glimpse of Restif in the *Mémoires* of the Comte de Tilly, an observer of insight, though he showed so little in guiding his own life. 'One morning, to my great surprise,' Tilly writes, 'there called to see me Mr. Restif de la Bretonne, whom I was not aware that I knew, never having had any relations with him. He reminded me that we had met at the house of the Comtesse de Beauharnais, who maintained what was improperly called "an intellectual bureau," with good company made up of men of the world and men of letters of varying merit; I had been there two or three times. The author of the *Paysan Perverti* said he had often heard of me ['le beau Tilly' had the reputation of 'un homme à bonnes fortunes'] and he had come to ask me to supply him with some "erotic anecdotes" of my life, in a word "some striking adventures" which would occupy an advantageous place in a long work he was meditating, to be written for posterity, and not for his contemporaries, of whom he was "tired." One could not but laugh at the object of such a visit; it would have been absurd to be angry; but I assured him that my life had been one of frightful sterility; at the same time, thanking him for his attention, I begged him to realise that I had taste enough to know what a precious occasion it would have been to reach posterity, and hoped to reserve for him in better times anecdotes worthy of his fresh colours and virginal touch. My compliments charmed him; he was himself still more enchanted by his works; he did not hesitate to declare that the *Paysan Perverti* was a book of the first order, which would last as long as the language which he had "emboldened to speak of everything," and as long as Nature whom he had "caught on the run." He con-

gratulated himself on having been misunderstood by a "taste-
less and petty" generation; the calumnies of journalists and
academicians, unable to measure him, were his first title to
immortality. I replied to everything: "Very true." Then I
bowed and he left.' Tilly was quite able to tell his own
'erotic anecdotes,' and has done so in his *Mémoires* in a way
that Restif could hardly have excelled. It may be added that,
despite the persiflage, his admiration for Restif's works was
genuine; it was Tilly who termed him ' the Teniers of fiction,'
and he claims to have convinced La Harpe, who cherished a
prim academic disapproval of Restif, that ' there is much gold
in this dunghill.'

That was before the Revolution. We have another glimpse
of Restif's attitude to the world, this time from the inside,
at a later period, in correspondence with a lady at Grenoble
in 1797. La Citoyenne Fontaine was a young married woman
who, with her husband, was an enthusiastic admirer of
Restif's books and writes to tell him so. He replies (giving
the address where he lodged with one of his daughters in
later years, 'Rue de la Bûcherie opposite the Rue des Rats')
telling her that all men, except Carnot (who liberally supported him until he fell from power), have deceived him, but
that he has not been deceived by all women: 'Blessed may
they be, these alleviators of my sorrowful existence!' 'I
have just published my *Life*, in order to live,' he remarks,
but complains of his inability to manage his own business
affairs; ' men of letters should not legally reach their majority
until the age of one hundred.' But he still has twenty-six
plans for books, all sketched out, which he is prepared to
write when opportunity offers. He incidentally says that he
is the only one of his family to spell their name 'Restif,'
the others failing to understand that that is the correct
ancient form.

Wearing his large felt hat pressed down over his bushy
eyebrows, Restif would return in the evening to the shop
over which he lived, draw out a little candle from under his
famous long blue cloak fastened at the neck, light it at the
flame over the counter, put it in the lantern and mount the

stairs, without saluting anyone present and often without even answering the remarks that might be made to him. Morose and taciturn, he seldom cared to enter into conversation unless sometimes when he could be induced to talk about himself, then he could grow eloquent, and Cubières tells of 'the old Silenus' once talking for six hours on end about himself in the midst of a group of pretty women who had been careful to ply him with excellent Burgundy and were enchanted by his eloquence. His loud voice, especially in old age, is frequently mentioned. Many observers refer to his old, torn, and stained garments in these later years (he once boasted that he had bought no new clothes for twenty-three years), his neglected, dirty, even repulsive appearance.

He had acquired a distaste for society and was suspicious even of his friends. Yet he had friends, who even tried to excuse his conduct towards his wife, though they could not but take her part against him. Even that fact was an added grievance in his eyes against the woman whose tricks, it seemed to him, had perverted the judgment of his friends, and he referred to her as an 'old coquette' and a 'siren.' 'Has not your sensibility exaggerated your grievance?' wrote his friend La Reynière, trying to put the point as gently as possible. Another friend, Bonneville (whom, I note, Restif characteristically abuses in writing to Madame Fontaine, as 'a rascal called Bonneville who is selling *Monsieur Nicolas* and mocking the old man he cheats'), declared after his death that Restif's *La Femme Infidèle*, which even his latest and most devoted biographer calls 'a criminal book,' was 'an offence that could only have been committed during an attack of delirious frenzy.' But such an apology, which is in place when we are in presence of Rousseau's persecutional delusions, cannot be applied to excuse the atrocious and persistent attacks of Restif on his wife.

Iwan Bloch has suggested that in Restif's impulse to set up his wife and others as images of horror we have in another shape a continuation of his childhood's visions of terrors in the night; he was throughout life perpetually subject to nervous terrors, as his inscriptions clearly show, and they were specially pronounced when he was agitated about his wife, as in 1784. He was haunted by phantoms which sometimes became as real as life. But that explanation hardly mitigates the offence of Restif's violent and public animosity, stimulated by the tender affection which the distinguished Joubert bestowed on a woman, then nearly twenty years older than himself, whom he sought to console. Joubert and his friend Fontanes, two of the finest characters of that age — though Restif calls them 'a disgrace to humanity' — had made the acquaintance of Restif out of admiration for his work and in this way learnt to know his wife. Before long all their sympathy went out to her.

Not altogether crushed by the anxiety and wretchedness of her life, unhappy and beautiful, as described by Beaunier (who has fully and fairly dealt with the episode in *La Jeunesse de Joubert*), she was charming with the double seduction of sadness and gaiety. The tender friendship and intellectual companionship of these distinguished men enabled her to regain self-esteem and brought her new life. On Joubert's side it was more than friendship, and it may well be that she responded to his affection. Her husband succeeded in securing some of her letters to Joubert and published them in the novel *La Femme Infidèle*, in which he presented his version of the story, not hesitating, however, to alter them as his suspicion dictated. The episode came to a natural end, but it was the first and last romance in the life of Joubert, who was of frail constitution and lived to old age as an intellectual recluse, to attain a place in the first rank of French *pensée* writers.

We have ample testimony to Madame Restif's grace, nobility, and intelligence from unimpeachable witnesses, though we may well believe Monselet when he notes that in a pastel of her he has seen in the possession of her grandson, there was in the beautiful face with its powdered head a touch of severity and haughtiness. It was not a fitting mate for a Monsieur Nicolas. She never replied to the outrageous charges he piled upon her, though retort would have been so easy; in his difficulties she never refused the aid he was always ready to accept; after his death she wrote a letter which is the finest testimony in his favour we possess. Brushing aside 'the demon of discord which poisoned the spirit of a man naturally good,' she bears witness to his laboriousness, to his works of public utility, and dwells on his generosity of heart and his unfailing charity to anyone who might be in need.

In spite of all, there was evidently something attractive and winning in Monsieur Nicolas, whether it was his child-like and helpless abandonments or the fire of genius in his eyes. Even in old age, even on a single meeting, it was possible to find him fascinating. The best witness to this is a young German woman, Helmina von Chézy, who played a part in the Romantic movement. Her picture of Restif, whom she met in 1802 at the house of the Comtesse de Beau-harnais, is evidently romanticised, but it deserves to be quoted: 'There was something winning and attractive in his appearance. He was of fairly good height, rather plump, and wore his hair, like Bernardin de St. Pierre, in natural curls falling on his neck; his face was oval, the nose soft, the mouth pleasant, the large eyes full of expression, with a bright and loving glance; his gentle voice struck the heart. He was so charming to me, as a man in the decline of manly vigour ought to treat a young girl. I would gladly have seen him often, but the anathema pronounced by the world frightened me away. Oh, the world, how willingly and hastily it condemns!'

However morose he grew in disposition, however objectionable in appearance, there were always friends to love and tend him, themselves rather eccentric people sometimes, but not seldom people of refinement and intellect, including women, notably the Comtesse Fanny de Beauharnais (aunt of the Empress Josephine) who was continuously helpful during the last years. Restif had become afflicted in health, with hernia and gastric troubles and the results of many earlier venerial infections. But his two daughters, both charming and intelligent — especially the younger, Marion, who had been early left a widow — his son-in-law, and a devoted doctor drew round him to soothe his last discontented days. The

Emperor also (who, when consul, had ordered the seizure of
L'Anti-Justine) was at the end induced to assist the failing
Restif. He died at his lodgings, now No. 16 Rue de la Bûcherie
(near the Quai Saint-Michel), on the 3rd of February, 1806,
in his seventy-second year.

He was buried, not as he had expressed the wish, beside his
father and mother at Sacy, but in the cemetery of Saint-
Catherine, now Montparnasse. Eighteen hundred persons,
including some of distinction, followed the bier, and the
Institut, which had refused to admit him when he was alive,
now sent its representatives.

III

'An assemblage of contrasts' — so Restif de la Bretonne
was described by Cubières-Palmézeau, his first biographer
who knew him well, and was indeed the only biographer who
ever knew him at all. Grimm, another contemporary, a
stolid Philistine but a critic of sound judgment, wrote similarly: 'It is impossible to imagine a stranger complexity than
the mind of Restif, with its extraordinary mixture of platitude
and genius.' This is a central fact about him, whether we are
concerned with the man himself or with his work, which are
indeed one, for the whole man is in his lifelong flood of work
and there is nothing in that work which does not plainly
flow from the man.

That is the key to the opposing estimates, which, from his
own time to ours, have been made of Restif. They have often
thrown less light on him than on his critics. 'That swine
of a Restif!' Brunetière is said to have exclaimed, while
Saintsbury, who might seem to many a conventionally academic English Brunetière, was full of tender admiration for
Restif, finding him even on the moral side at worst 'a sentimental philanthropist,' setting him up on the one hand even
above Laclos, whom he regarded as unworthy of a place in
the history of the French novel, and, on the other hand, even
above Rousseau, who was 'a blackguard.' In his own day La
Harpe and the Institut dismissed Restif, as a writer 'lacking

in taste'; today Beaunier calls him 'a great writer of a sort,' and Funck-Brentano, very bold, 'the greatest writer of the eighteenth century.' It would be easy to bring forward many such flagrantly opposed judgments. From first to last there have been some who saw only the dunghill and others who saw only the gold. It needed a critic as impeccable as Baudelaire to point out that, whatever we may think of his work as a whole, there are some parts of it that form an imperishable element of the literature of his time.

Alike in his life and in his work, Restif combined an extravagantly ostentatious anxiety for morality with an equally extravagant love of sexual licence. He felt the strongest disgust and indignation at what he called 'the abominable productions of the infamous and cruel Marquis de Sade.' Yet he sought to combat them in later life by out-doing de Sade with another form of sadism and *L'Anti-Justine* has been termed 'the most outrageously libertine book in French,' though its author hoped it might be read by wives to their husbands. This incoherent combination of virtue and vice today puzzles us, when we do not put it down to deliberate humbug, and even some readers of his own time may have been disconcerted when they discovered that Monsieur Nicolas's love of moral purity was not incompatible with a sympathetic acceptance of incest.[1] Over and over again he falls in love with some young girl whom he later sees reason to suppose his own daughter, though it is significant that he never comes across a son. But the combination, in milder shapes, especially marked the eighteenth century, not only in France, but also, and at an even earlier date, in England, for it was demanded by the new vigorous lower middle-class public, then pushing itself to the front with un-

---

[1] Monglond has recently pointed out (*Jeunesses*, pp. 130–34) how favourite a subject incest was among French novelists in the immediate pre-romantic period with its love of new sentimental complications. Thus the Abbé Prévost frequently dealt with such a situation as a man falling in love with a girl who turns out to be his daughter, or a brother with apparently his sister. Mercier dealt with the same subject in stories placed among savage races. On the tragic stage there were dramas of incest by the elder Crébillon and by Voltaire. Diderot's *Le Fils Naturel* may also be mentioned.

tamed impulses which thirsted for respectability. We may find it well and typically represented, for instance, by Colley Cibber, of one of whose plays it is possible for a good critic to say that it is 'genuinely moral,' for another critic to say that its atmosphere is 'immoral,' and for a third to say that both are right. Later, Richardson elaborately combined the moral purpose with the sentimental and voluptuous atmosphere in the novels which he wrote for that lower middle-class public to which he himself belonged, and thereby exerted so enormous an influence in France. Since men possess both moral impulses and immoral impulses it may well be that it is precisely this harmonious combination of the two which gives to the eighteenth century in one of its numerous aspects — 'the atrocious eighteenth century, 'as Hügel used to call it — the high rank it takes as a manifestation of the human spirit. Restif, whose devotion to the moral happiness of mankind we cannot doubt, and to whose own fundamental goodness all who knew him testify, yet lived and moved and had his whole being from first to last in an atmosphere which was, pungently and luridly, immoral. With his morbidly sensitive and impetuous temperament he was able to carry this seemingly incompatible combination to so high a point of extravagance that even the eighteenth century itself was sometimes shocked.

Restif possessed as an artist the special qualities which fitted him to reach his public. Beaunier has happily commented on the contrast between the head of Diderot with the fine mouth and the head of Restif with the fine eyes. That bold and inspired head of Diderot's belongs to a man who was forever pouring forth new and brilliant ideas, and all the wrinkles are around the mouth. Restif's head — a blend of the Bourbon with the peasant, Monselet said — belonged to a man who was a spectator of Nature, with vision fixed on her with ruthless inquisitiveness, and all the wrinkles are around the eyes. He was always eager 'to catch Nature on the run,' as he said to Tilly, and what he had caught he was quick to transform into words, words which he was more concerned to gaze at himself than to show to others, so that his first diary was carved in 'inscriptions' for his own secret enjoyment.

To Restif himself it was evidently clear that he was addressing a new audience and in a new way. Even in the notes to his early *Pied de Fanchette* he declared that 'after the king in a monarchy, before all things in a republic, that which is the most sacred, most worthy of respect, most holy, is essentially the people.' He wishes to make 'the people' his heroes, and in support of this resolve he says: 'Our fair-headed (and often red-headed) neighbours whom bawlers call ferocious, and sensible people magnanimous, I mean the English, treat in their books of all classes of people, and with equal respect.' He evidently regarded himself as the pioneer in France of a new kind of writing already existing in England, one may indeed think of Defoe as the great artist and pioneer he was here following — and, as was usual with Restif, he pushed it to a new limit. In France, whatever the excesses of sentiment or licence in literature in Restif's time, there were inviolable rules of convention and decorum in language, inherited from the purification of language effected at the beginning of the century. Rousseau had embodied a new revolution in literature, a return to Nature and to the expression of natural emotion, but it is hardly possible to find a crude word even in his intimate letters. Crébillon *fils* discussed the erotic refinements of his time with complete freedom, and it was impossible for him to be vulgar. All those who accepted either Rousseau or Crébillon as master observed the same rules of dignified reticence. But Restif, as he told Tilly, had deliberately broken these rules. He had 'emboldened the language to speak of everything.' The enrichment due to that liberation from the fetters of the eighteenth century we largely owe to Restif.

This feature of Restif's work, which operated against him among the academic critics of his own day, has probably been the chief cause why some critics of a later day have assigned to him so high a place. The great masters of literature — like Rabelais and Montaigne and Shakespeare and Landor and Huysmans and Proust and Joyce — have often possessed within themselves a plastic force by which, for good or for evil, they were impelled to mould language afresh, to invent new words, to spell old words afresh, to bend language into new constructions, and to make it possible to express what had never been expressed before. In this sense it can hardly be denied that, with all his weaknesses, Restif was, at the best, something of a great master.

It is true that, a few years later, another and very different enrichment of the French language for a while put Restif's achievement into the shade. A new movement, at the head of which stood Hugo, brought in an element of romantic magnificence, which may well have made its champions look upon a Restif as 'ignoble' and lead Hugo himself to go out of the way (as in *Les Misérables*) to disparage Restif. But when a little later Balzac appeared it became clear, and has often been pointed out, that Restif had been his forerunner, as later it was seen he had pioneered Zola. At the same time it also became clear that Restif went back to Marivaux, who happened indeed to be a master in the epistolary fiction which Restif cultivated, and Marivaux's importance is too often misunderstood or under-emphasised. Marivaux, too, in his own different way and with his own unlike temperament, was a pioneer. His sympathies had carried him into fields of observation outside his own class; with a minute and sensitive realism he had described the lives and characters of people of the peasantry and lower-middle-class. So that when Restif by taste and training turned away from the heroes and heroines of the drawing room and the boudoir, who largely occupied the fictional field of the century, it was Marivaux at its very beginning that he reached — even though, as was natural from the different approach, he disliked Marivaux — and *Le Paysan Perverti* owed its title to *Le Paysan Parvenu*. Therewith, for all clear-eyed critics, Restif's position became assured. It was recognised that, whatever his extravagancies and his eccentricities, he had his well-marked and permanent place in one of the great streams of French literature.

Monsieur Nicolas, written after long preparation, when Restif was at the highest point of his matured powers, is by

all critics accepted as his chief claim to permanent remem-
brance. It represents him fully on every side, good and bad.
Here we may see, again and again, how he 'emboldened
language to speak of everything,' and when we contemplate
the pages of his original text, printed by his own hands, we
may trace innumerable personal idiosyncracies of expression
in typography which escape the translator, as well as his
love for new words and new spellings, like for instance
'garson' in place of 'garçon,' for, as he said (quite truly),
this word is a diminutive of 'gars.' By this plastic force on
language he belongs to the class of French masters of literature, with Rabelais at their head, which has later included the
Goncourts and Huysmans and Léon Bloy and Joseph Delteil.
This same force he exerts also in transforming into speech
the things he has seen or felt, so that in his pages we may meet
with experiences, even common and familiar experiences,
which seem never to have been put into speech before. That
is one of the secrets of his fresh vivid direct manner. When
he is at the best in narrative — swift, easy, flexible, familiar
— he belongs less to his own age than to ours.

This mastery of speech has its part in his power of bringing before us the intimate middle class life of his time. All
now recognise his value in this field; here indeed he is unique
and the claim he thus makes on the gratitude of posterity
can never be exaggerated. Elsewhere we seek in vain for
pictures of the everyday life of the people of his time, in
country and in town, which even remotely approach Restif's
in living intimacy of detail. And while such pictures are
scattered through a large part of his work they are nowhere
better represented than in *Monsieur Nicolas.* It was Restif's
distinction that he stood apart from the highly civilised life
of the eighteenth century and approached it from the outside.
When we think of that life and its typical representatives we
think of a highly socialised and conventionalised existence,
carried on, and in literature represented, by aristocrats and
bourgeois within an urban environment. Even Rousseau, who
brought a stream of youthful blood into this rather anaemic
world, and created it anew, was the child of a city, however

remote. But there was no sort of urbanity about Restif. A peasant and a plebeian, he approached this spectacle greedily and yet shyly, and devoured it with all the fresh and undisciplined appetite of his primitive and yet sensitive temperament. And because he had a strain of genius which held him true to that temperament, his writings retain an imperishable vitality.

With the autobiographical claim for *Monsieur Nicolas*, on which Restif insisted most of all, he may again be justified; but this time we must speak with some caution. His place is high, but we do well to hesitate before making that place, as some would have it, supreme. Even if Restif had achieved a perfect autobiography, we should still have to bear in mind that men who are incomparably greater figures in the world have also written the inner history of their own lives. But *Monsieur Nicolas* is far from being a perfect autobiography. The impulsive and capricious Restif allowed himself to be drawn in all sorts of directions away from the main aim when he was writing it and never gave himself a chance of retracing random steps and starting afresh in a straighter line. Thus there are perpetual digressions.

A yet more serious matter is that, while we cannot question the natural spontaneity of his narrative, we can never absolutely trust his ability, or even his strict determination, to distinguish between truth and fiction. All his life he had been writing fiction that was verging on truth and truth that was verging on fiction; he could not but continue to do so even in an autobiography. His complacent credulity was great; he was easily imposed on by others, and in his turn he found it easy to try to impose on others. The fantastic table of descent of the Restif family he put forward as the production of his grandfather, but he printed it on three separate occasions in the course of his life, and when his high descent was questioned he once indignantly declared that the evidence was preserved in the Bibliothèque Royale. Here and elsewhere we are left a little doubtful as to how far Restif was deceiving others, and how far he was himself deceived. Bloch would have us believe that Restif wrote much more veraciously than Rousseau. It is true that Restif, with his mania for 'inscriptions,' could often refer to exact dates and facts in his past life, while Rousseau, trusting mostly to memory, was often a little astray, for memory is never absolutely trustworthy. But we are always sure that Rousseau is conscientious, and the little sins of youth which his tender conscience impels him to set forth in all their heinous details would never have been known if he had not recorded them. Restif is more anxious to soothe his vanity than to confess his sins, and we sometimes know, and can often guess, that he is toning down his misdeeds — when he recognises them as such — or veiling them in sentiment. So it is that he fails to explain how he fled from Auxerre in 1755 before the indignation of Madame Parangon when she discovered how he had deceived her. We note, too, the complacent credulity with which he so easily comes upon illegitimate children of his own in the most unlikely places. And sometimes — as also seems to have happened to Casanova — he is clearly romancing altogether. We may recall, for instance, his narrative of the supposed scene in the Park at Dijon, when he details at length the conversation he claims to have casually overheard, which revealed that Madame Parangon had secretly given birth to a child of which he was himself the father. The claims that have been made for Restif's scrupulous truthfulness can hardly be maintained.

Yet notwithstanding all the defects, even glaring defects, which may be found in *Monsieur Nicolas*, whether as a work of literary art or as a trustworthy document, its right to stand among the great autobiographies, even although not in the first rank, may well be maintained. We really do here possess, as Restif himself asserted, a wonderful piece of 'natural history.' *Monsieur Nicolas* really is the veracious story, told in the most vivid and spontaneous and sometimes brilliant fashion, of an extraordinary man — however far from being admirable — in his intimate reactions with the world in which he lived. It is veracious in a sense deeper than literal truthfulness because it truly brings before us the whole man uncompromisingly, even in his credulity and his vanity and his spitefulness, as well as in his sudden impulses of generosity or humility; it is true to Nature even when it is not true to fact.

The other writings, numerous as they are, of Restif de la Bretonne may be forgotten. *Monsieur Nicolas* will remain the fascinating picture of the ordinary life of a remarkable age, and, against that background, the living picture of an extraordinary man.

9

I

BESENVAL was French in training and tradition, but on his mother's side Polish. That is a fundamental fact we must always bear in mind. So it is as well to state it at the outset.

The Besenvals originated in the Duchy of Savoy, but had settled at Solothurn. In the seventeenth century a Besenval left Switzerland to enter the service of Louis XIV by whom he was ennobled. His son, a Baron and our Besenval's father, distinguished both in war and diplomacy, was for many years Minister of France to Poland. In 1707 he had been sent on important negotiations to Charles XII, then at a serious moment in his headlong career, and to him M. de Besenval proposed various schemes in the interests of France. But, though he was a skilful diplomatist, there were too many influences against him, and Marlborough, who speedily appeared on the scene, negotiated otherwise. Besenval returned to France, and at his death in Paris was a lieutenant-general and the colonel of the regiment of Swiss Guards which his son later commanded.[1] He had married in 1716, when in Warsaw, Countess Catherine Bielinska, who was closely related to the Leczinski family, and therefore to the queen of Louis XV; she was a woman with a charm and wit which, a few years after her marriage, impressed even Voltaire. Their son, Pierre-Victor, the Baron de Besenval we are here concerned with, was born at Solothurn, at the foot of the Jura, when his father was fifty and his mother thirty-seven, in 1721.

[1] G. Syveton, *Au Camp d'Atrandstadt*, 1900, based on the Besenval family archives.

Young Pierre-Victor came into the world with the finest native qualities and under the happiest conditions. These qualities and conditions largely took the place of any formal education. We hear of a tutor, an abbé, but on the whole the world was his teacher, and it seems to us today that there could not have been a better: that is the second significant fact about Besenval. When we first hear of him, at the age of nine, he is already a cadet in his father's regiment, and at the age of fifteen he was in the midst of the campaign of 1735. While still a boy he displayed the Besenval temper of intrepid courage, fearless alike of dangers and of horrors — though, remembering how skilfully he conducted his life, we may hesitate to call him rash — and even at this period, with his combined bravery and charm in leadership, he was the idol of his men. In the years that follow he played an able and brilliant part in many engagements, fortunate and unfortunate, in the Low Countries and elsewhere, and later went through the Seven Years' War. When peace was signed he returned in middle age to Paris, where in due course we find him a lieutenant-general, decorated with the grand cross of Saint Louis, Governor of Hagenau, and Colonel of the Swiss Guards. He showed his fine military qualities not only in war but in peace, by the reforms in discipline and organization which he introduced into the army, not without difficulties and opposition, and his own Swiss regiment became a model for imitation. But there is no reason to suppose that Besenval had the special qualities of a great commander; his insight and aptitude could serve him in whatever position he might be thrown, and he turned from the camp to the Court, with equal relish for the arts of peace as of war, as much at home in the boudoir as in the tent, though with an air of freedom and frankness which seemed *mauvais ton* to some super-refined aristocrats of the old school, like the Duc de Lévis.

We may say, indeed, that it was for civilisation, for society and the arts, that Besenval was best endowed. He regarded war as largely the result of intrigue and ambition; he admired the Quakers, though he did not expect them to multiply; and he was strongly opposed to the hunting of animals.[1] There is a fine portrait of him in early life (still in possession of the family and reproduced by Schmid), wearing armour, which shows a peculiarly attractive face, feminine one might be inclined to say, and with melancholy in the eyes, but it is not weak, and the chin is well formed. Of tall and imposing stature, in old age dignified, and with naturally winning manners, he animated every circle he entered. He was often carried away by his natural impetuosity, even to violence; therein the French strain in him had not modified the high-strung excitability of the Pole. (Warsaw is the only city in Europe where in the best seats of a place of entertainment I have observed a man enter on a furious altercation that the whole house could follow.) But Besenval had the sensitive skill to repair quickly the mistakes he thus made. An incident is significant. He kept in his house an ancient servitor of the family, a certain Blanchard, assigning to him a few trifling duties so that he might not feel himself useless. One day, Blanchard chanced to drop and smash a rare Cape jasmine which Besenval was cultivating. His master overwhelmed him with abuse and next day he declared he would leave the house. 'Leave me?' exclaimed the Baron; 'you, Blanchard? Never, my old friend!' Blanchard insisted. 'In that case,' said Besenval, 'here is the key; you have been here longer than I have; it is for me to go.' And the scene ended in the correct eighteenth-century manner by Blanchard falling at the feet of Besenval who raised and embraced him.

We are not surprised to learn that Besenval was attractive to women, not only in youth, but in age when his whitened head, his epicurean philosophy, and his wide experience made him their trusted confidant. It is the kind of conventional statement we always expect to hear about the men of the eighteenth century. But like many other conventional statements it needs revision. We often forget that, while it is the

---

[1] His essay, 'De la Douleur,' with its pessimistic outlook on human nature and human societies, is singularly unlike what we might expect from a man of Besenval's upbringing and environment. 'We must admit,' he concludes, 'that man is not very good.'

tradition of the Englishman to minimise the extent of his experiences with women, it has been the tradition of the Frenchman, especially in the eighteenth century, to magnify his success in that sphere. In actual fact there may be a difference, but it is a difference that is inconsiderable. The most typical men of the eighteenth century in France are usually marked by fidelity in love. Crébillon, while developing in fiction the psychology of love, was industriously engaged with his official function of censoring improper literature in the respectable society of his plain though excellent English wife. The Chevalier de Nerciat, who is regarded by experts in this field as the most outrageously erotic writer of that age, was said by his son to have been 'nevertheless the best of husbands and of fathers.' The Chevalier de Boufflers, so representative and fascinating a character of the time, displayed for the charming Comtesse de Sabran, whom he married, a romantic attachment of forty years, of which the monument remains in their correspondence and diaries. And Besenval, while it is true that tradition regards him as the real father of the Vicomte de Ségur whom he made his heir, later became for twenty years the devoted friend of his neighbour in the fashionable Rue de Grenelle, the Marquise de la Suze. We know little about her save that, when he was in prison and the mob were clamouring for his head, she had the courage to visit him in the Châtelet, and that at a later period she safely escaped to England. She was a woman of great beauty. A portrait of her exists in which a bust of Besenval (still extant) is seen in the background; and there is also in existence a portrait of Besenval with his head resting on his hand and gazing at a miniature which represents, according to family tradition, Madame de la Suze.

It is no doubt true that Besenval's cherished friends were often among the gay and brilliant young aristocrats whose dissipations he more or less shared, though he never shared in the meaner vices and low intrigues of the Court; he was never among the *courtisans des courtisanes* of the last sordid years of Louis XV. On the contrary, he could be scornful of the hypocrisy and pettiness of Court life. He had attached himself to Choiseul, whom he greatly admired, and when that minister left in disgrace he voluntarily accompanied him.

But when Louis XVI came to the throne, the versatile Besenval became the exquisite embodiment of the tastes which Marie Antoinette was bringing into fashion, some of which he encouraged and perhaps suggested. With his Swiss simplicity, Madame Campan remarked, he would have been capable of singing the 'Ranz des Vaches' with tears in his eyes, while yet he was the most accomplished talker in the circle of the Duchesse de Polignac. The Prince de Ligne, who has set down incomparable pictures of the significant European figures of the dying eighteenth century among whom he moved as an equal, could not fail to write well of Besenval, 'handsome, insolent, and amiable,' whose 'fine and frank air' enabled him to risk all sorts of audacities; 'no one was ever more brilliant than the Baron de Besenval, in war or in the Court, and his writings are as brilliant as their author.'

'His writings?' But nothing has been said of writings. Authorship might well be the last thing to think of in connection with the Baron de Besenval, almost the last thing he would himself think of, for he was as modest about his writings as about what he called his 'good luck' in life, though the truth is that 'Man is his own star,' and by his own personal qualities his fate is mainly wrought. Besenval was a great amateur of life, using that word in its high, and not its vulgar, sense — a lover of life and the arts, with the knowledge and insight of love — and his sensitive and skilful hand marked everything he touched. He was a lover of Nature who never forgot the mountains of his birthplace and later became, it seems, a pioneer in the culture of exotic plants. He was a lover of the arts, an honorary member of the Academy of Painting, and he left behind a valuable collection of pictures. But our knowledge of his activities in these and similar directions is vague. His writings remain, though they were not written for publication and only appeared, through an indiscretion, some years after his death, in the early nineteenth century. They long failed to attract much attention. But it is on them that his reputation rests, and will continue to rest.

The *ancien régime* was now approaching its tragic fall. Besenval, who had become military commandant of the interior provinces of the kingdom, was at the height of his credit, the friend and adviser of Marie Antoinette, who consulted him about all her affairs, small and great. (And when the Queen was ill with measles he was among the few special friends who sat by her bedside to amuse her.) Now over sixty, but retaining his fine and vigorous carriage, he still displayed the moods and habits of his youth, while adequately fulfilling his varied official functions. During the disastrous famine of 1788 it was Besenval's function to preserve order, and he carried out his duties with skill and consideration. Next year he was plunged into the revolutionary troubles, but as he was not in supreme command of his forces his position became difficult, for often he had to await orders which never arrived. For one moment Besenval was in the foreground of history. On the 14th of July, 1789, he was camped with his troops on what is now the Place de la Concorde, in military charge of Paris, including the Bastille. Every hour of that fateful day has been studied, but though Besenval's attitude is still not clear, he seems to have acted in an extremely difficult position with moderation and prudence. From that day on, dangers inevitably arose for him on every side, and as a precaution the King at last ordered him to retire to Switzerland. On the first stage of the journey he was arrested, but Necker, then a popular idol returning from exile, chanced to be near and secured his release. Later he was rearrested and confined in the Châtelet, where his old spirit of gaiety and mockery sustained alike himself and his companions in misfortune. Finally Besenval was brought out for trial. It lasted long; there were one hundred and eighty-five witnesses; crushing charges were brought against him, but his replies were so clear, and the evidence so slight, that in March, 1790, he was acquitted. Thus, by a final stroke of that 'luck' which was not all chance, Besenval escaped the guillotine. His spirit was not killed, but physically he was now a broken man. He tried to live as of old; he gave a dinner party even on the day of his death, the 2d of June, 1791. For a few moments he appeared among the guests, 'the ghost of the commander,' he smilingly said, in allusion to Don Juan, but he felt he had become a painful spectacle and retired. An hour later he was dead.

II

As an author Besenval has usually been best known by his *Mémoires*. Strictly speaking, they are not so much memoirs as episodes, souvenirs of the things that had most deeply touched him, set down, in the spare moments of living, for his own delectation. That is how they come to form so delightful a record, without apology or even explanation, of personal confessions. He tells the doings of other people as freely as his own, and that might make the tone of the *Mémoires* less delightful if we failed to remember their private character, for while everyone is free to confess his own sins we are not free to confess other people's. That has been brought forward in Besenval's justification, but he left the *Mémoires* behind him, and I am not sure that in his free, swift, spontaneous temperament such considerations were prominent. He was apter to retrieve indiscretions than to avoid them, and these are retrieved by their natural good feeling and the absence of malice. In the last part of the *Mémoires* there is much explanation and defence of the part he himself played in public affairs. But it seems likely that this part is spurious, written perhaps by Besenval's literary executor, the Vicomte de Ségur, in his friend's interests. Such is the opinion of Dr. Schmid, and the mistakes in this part of the *Mémoires* concerning matters with which Besenval was familiar clearly suggest a lack of authenticity and would justify the statement of the family at the time of first publication that the *Mémoires* were not genuine, though for the main part they are now undisputed. So also is the fine quality which places them among the best that we have of their period. The Duc de Lévis, in his *Souvenirs et Portraits*, writes unsympathetically of Besenval and of his 'fatal influence' on Marie Antoinette by inducing her to disregard Court etiquette; but he bears witness to the veracity of his *Mémoires*. Besenval writes with frank directness, with swift ease, but skilfully to the point, as one trained to the pen by the sword, the training of so many of the fine writers of Spain, though less often of France. We can understand how these *Mémoires* appealed to Stendhal. It is probably in the pages of Stendhal that most of us (though I can only speak for myself) first met the name of Besenval. I saw it there in youth and the name became imprinted on memory as of one whom I must learn to know. In due course I obtained the *Mémoires* which remained with me. It is only of recent years that I have known the *contes*, now at last brought before the English reader by a skilful translator.[1] In my youth, indeed, hardly anyone can be said to have known them. Like the *Mémoires*, they were not written for publication, and when, in 1881, Uzanne reprinted them from the edition of 1806, he remarked that it would be a surprise to most people that Besenval had ever written any *contes*. They mostly date from his military days. In 1757 he was stationed at Drevenack near Wesel, and a group of officers of cultivated taste formed there a literary club to which each furnished contributions in prose or verse. The chief impetus to Besenval's novels, as he called them, seems to belong to this period, although some, like his 'Amants Soldats,' which is based on a real episode, are much earlier. Twenty years later he sent the chief of them, 'Spleen' (afterwards to be recognised by Stendhal as one of the most charming lesser works of the century), to his friend the Royal Censor, the younger Crébillon, whom he evidently recognised as the finest writer and judge in this kind of literature. He told Crébillon that he had written the story, first entitled 'Le Malheureux,' as one writes a letter, without help and without corrections, to gratify the caprice of the moment and not to set forth personal misfortunes — 'never having had any.' Crébillon's answer, too long to quote here, is a model of sagacity and fine criticism, which might alone suffice to show how far he was from the merely frivolous writer he was once reckoned. He appreciates the fine qualities of the story, under-

---

[1] *Spleen and other Stories.* Translated from the French of Pierre-Victor Baron de Besenval, by H. B. V., 1927.

stands the temperament of Besenval, and gives him excellent advise on style and composition. It is supposed that Besenval then revised 'Spleen,' but the *contes* were not published till long after his death, in 1806, as the fourth volume of his *Mémoires*, with the title of *Mélanges Littéraires et historiques*; and in these changed and disturbed times they attracted little or no attention. Besenval was, indeed, in every respect belittled or slighted (save by the solitary Stendhal) until recent times. It was not till 1913 that Dr. Oswald Schmid turned the light of genuinely critical scholarship on Besenval and published an elaborate study of his life from original documents.[1]

When we survey Besenval's career and activities as a whole, we are inclined to say that he was a man so variously accomplished that on whatever stage of life he found himself he would perform his part well. We see a man, in other words, who was — however gaily, skilfully, and spontaneously — playing at life rather than expressing his own inner self. That is how it came to pass that, though he was brought up in the army and became a brilliantly successful soldier, he easily abandoned the camp for the Court and never cherished any high military ambitions. That again is how, though he achieved the highest social success, he was contemptuous of the courtier's life and realised the empty artificiality of Versailles. 'The perfect type of the French Chevalier,' he has been called in modern times. Yet we see how he transcended that type. The severe simplicity of his ancestry, the highstrung extravagance of the Pole, the contacts of childhood with the mountains of Switzerland, were not needed to make the typical French Chevalier of the eighteenth century. In the sketch he has entitled 'Traduction d'un Ouvrage Chinois sur les Jardins,' he gives rein to his imagination to describe what he doubtless regarded as his ideal of life, amid hills and cascades and gardens, streams and swans, in the company of friends of philosophic taste, where wine cheered the frugal repast.

[1] O. Schmid, 'Der Baron von Besenval,' *Schweizer Studien zur Geschichtswissenschaft*, Bd. V, Heft 3.

There is one field of activity in which Besenval seems no longer to be playing a part. As a writer, it is possible to maintain, he was expressing his real and inner self. His other activities were social; he wrote for himself, not for the public, not even for posterity. When he sent 'Spleen' to Crébillon, he denied that it expressed his own outlook on life. That very denial arouses reflection. Besenval had no creative imagination; his stories are based on real incidents or adventures. Schmid believes that 'Spleen' expresses himself. I am decidedly of the same opinion. When Besenval wrote in his own person, in his essays and *Pensées*, he expressed the same pessimistic sentiments regarding society and man as the stranger in the Tuileries. We have, indeed, but to glance at the early portrait to detect the air of melancholy over that gay and eager face. Besenval was a very different person from Chopin, but it is instructive to remember how in the composer a rather similar racial mixture resulted not only in fine accomplishment, but in a temper of gaiety inextricably interwoven with melancholy. It needs, indeed, little insight to observe how often sadness is concealed beneath the brilliant mask of high spirits.

Crébillon repeatedly referred to Besenval as a moralist. He was a moralist himself, as were nearly all the most characteristic writers of the French eighteenth century who adopted the form of fiction, from Marivaux to Laclos. Indeed one may well agree with Edmond Jaloux that it is in morals that French literature, from Montaigne on, most conspicuously excels, and that ever since the eighteenth century it is in fiction, instead of in essays and maxims, that this tendency has most prominently and most continuously (with a few exceptions such as Flaubert) been manifested.

Born into one of the most formal and conventional periods of social life ever constituted, the eighteenth-century novelists and *conteurs* could not fail to see that the highly polished surface of life was failing to correspond to the vital necessities of the people who were more or less unsuccessfully trying to preserve its veneer; and they exercised on it their satire, playful or fierce, and the more philosophical among them put forward their proposals for re-forming society. The second half of the eighteenth century thus engaged its more serious members in a perpetual debate on morals, evoking among the rest a perpetual resentment that broke out conspicuously against the *Liaisons Dangereuses*; for therein was seen, not the achievement of an austere moralist supremely endowed with the skill to transform morality into art, but an intolerable outrage. Then came the nineteenth century, with its own new and severely standardised respectability, looking back with superior wisdom on the problems which had impassioned its immediate predecessors as merely frivolous, and indecorous as well.

It is because moral problems have for the twentieth century again become vital and serious that we are able to turn with fresh interest to the eighteenth century. We find Besenval, again and again, not with insistence, but in the natural course, touching on the questions which the nineteenth century desired to regard as already answered, but which we today seek, as they sought in the eighteenth century, to face and answer for ourselves. When Besenval speaks of women, for instance, it is without the slightest impulse to idealise or to sentimentalise, but often with a real perception of their position and their problems, as in the 'Aventure de M. de Besenval avec une Dame de Wesel.' Again, near the beginning of the *Mémoires*, he narrates how two officers, living in a garrison and great friends, were frequent visitors at the house of a widowed gentleman with a beautiful daughter of eighteen. She became pregnant. The furious father asked the usual questions, and she replied that it must be one of the two officers, and if not the one, then certainly the other. The officers — recovered from their first surprise at finding themselves rivals, for each had honourably kept his secret — both eagerly offered marriage. But she could not choose between them: all she knew was that she loved them both, and could not sacrifice one to the other. The only escape from this embarrassing situation was to draw lots, with the private condition (carefully concealed from the father) that he who was not to be the husband should remain the lover, and no jealousy be aroused. This treaty was executed, with fidelity and to the happiness of all three, which lasted till, a few years later, there occurred the husband's death, deeply regretted by both survivors who thereupon married each other. But the point to be noted is that it is Besenval the moralist who is interested in this story, which culminates in his characteristic comments: 'It is hard to believe that chance ever brought together three people whose perceptions were so just, who so deeply understood the real value of things, and who were so free from prejudice. If human beings would but place reason before convention, justice before *amour-propre*, and good sense before wit, it would be much easier to live among them.'

Besenval is distinguished among the men of that age by the fact that he is at once a participant and a spectator of life, vividly interested in every activity that fell to his share and yet a detached and critical onlooker. He has been coupled with the Chevalier de Boufflers, who also shared the superficial life of his time and yet preserved a deeper romantic nature of his own. But Besenval was of more penetrating and intellectualised temper. At times he even recalls Stendhal, the great spirit who bridges the ravines of romanticism and links the eighteenth century with our own age. The tone of Besenval is often the tone of Stendhal by whom he was first genuinely appreciated; and if as an artist Besenval was a Stendhal *manqué*, we may perhaps say that in life Stendhal was a Besenval *manqué*. Yet even as writer and artist Besenval had certain advantages. He belongs to an earlier and for us deeply interesting age of which he was in real life the brilliant representative. And at the same time — to come again to the point which we need to emphasise — he was not only the active participant, but the detached spectator; he looks on aloof at the life in which he actively shared. In quality his *Mémoires* have been compared to those of Saint-Simon. They are mere fragments, and cannot fairly be compared to the sustained effort of the earlier and greater writer. But in one aspect they possess an attractive quality which he misses. Saint-Simon stands sternly and bitterly apart from the life he describes; Besenval, who notes down its characteristics with an almost equally pungent vivacity and veracity, allows us to see that he was himself living in it and taking part in it, so that he combines sympathetic intimacy with keen insight. That, we may be sure, was a quality which charmed Stendhal, and it is a quality which we may detect in the *contes* as well as in the *Mémoires*. Maurice Barrès believed that the highest type in life is that of the man who is at once ardent and disillusioned. It is the distinction of Besenval, perhaps alone among the men of his age, that he completely realises this type.

The problem of the fateful part which Besenval played in the events of that epoch-marking day which is now the national holiday of France may be left to historians. But the Besenval, so long neglected or belittled, who has only been studied with care in our own century and now appears as an almost unique figure, still remains. It is the Besenval whom I have had the privilege of introducing for the first time to English readers.

10

ALEXANDRE DE TILLY

I

'YOU will be surprised at the big packet I am sending with this,' wrote Stendhal on the 14th of August, 1828, to his friend in London, Sutton Sharpe, in a letter signed on this occasion, with his love of pseudonyms, 'William Crocodile'; 'don't be afraid. It is the most amusing book that has appeared in France for a year past, the *Mémoires de Tilly*. Tilly was the handsomest man of his time; he blew his brains out in 1812 [really 1816], in Brussels, to punish himself for having been robbed at play. He had many women: nothing surprising in that. *But he loved them*. That is why his book is so little in fashion at the mansions in the suburbs of Paris. Unfortunately, so handsome a man did not know how to write and yet prided himself on being a man of letters. He moralises and generalises on all occasions. By reducing the three volumes to one, we should have a delicious book. I have written an article on Tilly, the first I have done for eighteen months. But an English friend who translates my articles fears to spoil his reputation by writing about such a libertine book as Tilly. Can you give my article to some literary journal in England? If you cannot, send it to Mr. Colburne with the letter I enclose. If you could find an intelligent publisher who has the same esteem that I have for this work, which will have a great reputation in a year or two, I would abridge the original and send it to him, arranged to form two charming little octavo volumes.'

One would be glad to find the article on Tilly's *Mémoires* which Stendhal sent over to London. I have searched the magazines with which he was in touch, the *Athenaeum* and *Colbourne's*, but I have found no trace. Stendhal himself makes no further references to it in the later extant letters to Sutton Sharpe and other English friends. Stendhal knew England and was in touch with the literary world in London, where indeed his genius was discovered half a century before it was clearly discerned in France, and almost the first documented biography of him was written by Paton, in 1874. It is but too probable, however, that English publishers shared the opinion of the English friend who refused to translate an article about such a libertine as Tilly.

Even in France Stendhal's prophecy of the swiftly approaching reputation of Tilly's *Mémoires* was not fulfilled. I happen to have known them myself for over thirty years, but they still seem to be among the least read and least commented memoirs of a century which is now so eagerly and so sympathetically studied. Barrière put an abridged version into his well-known series of eighteenth-century French memoirs, and Iwan Bloch, the scholarly and versatile sexologist, reprinted the early German edition. But until today Standhal's desire to bring out an English edition has remained unfulfilled.[1]

Not only have the *Mémoires* of Tilly been neglected, but such attention as they have received has mostly been of an ambiguous kind. Tilly has been termed the typical *roué* of the eighteenth century, the embodiment in real life of Laclos's Valmont, and since for a century and more after its publication *Les Liaisons Dangereuses* was vituperated and denounced, being only of recent years recognized for the great and significant achievement of art it is, this was not the way to draw favourable attention on Tilly. It may be noted that the comparison was not quite correct. Unlike Valmont, Tilly was, as Jacques Morland has remarked, 'a sentimental roué,' who had fallen under the influence of Rousseau and was by his friends considered 'romantic.'

---

[1] The present essay in substantially the same shape formed the Introduction to the translation of the *Memoirs of Comte Alexandre de Tilly*, by Françoise Delisle (New York, Farrar and Rinehart, 1932; London, Victor Gollancz, 1933).

More than that: attacks were made on the authenticity of the *Mémoires*. To me it seems that careful reading alone furnishes sufficient evidence that they must be genuine. Indeed, a writer who possessed the skill and the knowledge to fake them would too obviously have here been wasting his talents. Many faked memoirs have been produced, most of them easy to see through, and few of them of any interest apart from their assumed authorship. Yet the frivolity with which some would-be acute critics have denied the authenticity of genuine memoirs remains astonishing. Lacroix, as is well known, attributed Casanova's Memoirs to Stendhal. Maurice Tourneux, in a work of repute, *Bibliographie de l'Histoire de Paris pendant la Révolution*, states that the authenticity of Tilly's *Mémoires* is 'anything but certain.' He adds, without giving the slightest evidence for the statement, that a part of the *Mémoires* would be due to Alphonse de Beauchamp, and his work would be finished by Auguste Coué, who was the author with Dittmer of the *Soirées de Neuilly*, four plays published under the name of 'M. de Fongeray.' The climax to these reckless and random attributions is furnished by Dubosc, who suggested, in *L'Intermédiaire des Chercheurs*, in 1918, that 'M. de Fongeray' may well be Stendhal, since the portrait of him in the *Soirées* might easily be a caricature of Stendhal! Certainly it is a fine compliment to Stendhal that the Memoirs both of Casanova and of Tilly, so fine in their different kind yet so unlike, should each have been attributed to him. I may add, since I have examined the copy of the book in the British Museum (neglected and uncut for over a century), that there is no ground for saying that the sketch of 'M. de Fongeray' resembles Stendhal.

It is scarcely necessary to show that Beauchamp and Coué, even if they could have secured the facts which we know to be accurately recorded in the *Mémoires*, give no evidence of possessing the qualities necessary to invent their varied and dramatic episodes; they showed nothing of that 'certain impertinent grace' which, the historian Du Bled remarks, gives to these *Mémoires* so strange a savour and is at the same time so much in the tone of the real Tilly. Beauchamp had in 1824 (the year before Tilly's *Mémoires* first appeared in German) put forward, as anonymous editor, *Mémoires de Fouché*, which led to an action in the law courts and the declaration that they were not genuine. But Beauchamp wrote here of what he knew and it is believed that he was working on real documents and notes of Fouché's. He was a writer of some ability, but his interests were in war and politics and police administration, while Coué was an insignificant collaborator in comedies of which we know little or nothing. It seems a fantastic notion that they possessed the inclination or the skill to write fictitious memoirs of Tilly — whose world was alien to them — for translation into German. Merely to take the interviews narrated in the *Mémoires* with Laclos and Restif de la Bretonne: today, with our present knowledge, we regard the account of these meetings as absolutely convincing. But in the early nineteenth century, when both Laclos and Restif were neglected and condemned, it would have demanded the insight of genius to invent them. It is difficult to guess what motive they could possibly have had to expend so much skill, if they had really possessed it, in constructing the imaginary experiences of an undistinguished aristocrat of the Court of Louis XVI, who had died obscurely abroad by suicide, made no mark, and had long been forgotten. There seemed nothing for them to gain, and it is not easy to see that they gained anything. Nothing was heard of the *Mémoires* until they appeared in 1825, translated into German, in Berlin, which is where we might expect them to appear, since we know that Tilly had long been settled in Berlin, there forming many relationships, but, it seems, compelled to depart suddenly in 1807, leaving his papers behind. The further objection has been brought against the authenticity of the *Mémoires* that they reveal qualities not shown by the earlier unquestioned volume by Tilly, the *Oeuvres Mêlées*, mostly written in youth before the Revolution. This little volume consists miscellaneously of verse and prose, *jeux d'esprit*, poetic epistles, essays and letters, of little or no importance, but all fairly adequate to their usually trifling impulse and object, sufficiently vigorous in those of later date when the Revolution furnished

motives of contempt or indignation. Tilly was here not less
skilful in writing than the *Mémoires* show him to be, for it
may be remarked that the *Mémoires*, with sentences that are
awkwardly constructed and sometimes unduly prolonged, do
not reveal a master of style. It is the vivacity and spontaneity
of the narrative that constitute its quality and its charm, so
far as the personality of the author is concerned. Beyond this,
the *Mémoires* possess a real impersonal value, independently
of their authorship, as a picture of French aristocratic society
of the eighteenth century at its last expiring moment before
the Revolution, for Tilly reveals, as Du Bled points out, 'the
germs of an historian.' This picture is all the more interesting
because at this distance of time we can often see deeper into
the life it presents than was possible for Tilly, who moved on
its surface, and often failed to realise its real significance.

Even when we are convinced of the authenticity of the
Mémoires, it still has to be admitted that, outside them, Tilly
remains a puzzling, mysterious, elusive figure. From his birth
to his death the records we are entitled to expect we fail to
find, and so remain in doubt. Of aristocratic family, occupying a place at Court befitting his rank, and after his expulsion
from France at the Revolution known in England and America
and Germany, surrounded by friends, some of them distinguished, adored by women, of singularly attractive appearance
and commonly known as 'le beau Tilly,' he seems to have left
little mark, so far as easily accessible records extend, and we
even search in vain for his portrait. By an unkind fate, such
notices of him as we can discover are often unfavourable, even
in a grossly calumnious degree, while his friends, though they
seem to have been attached to him, have left no record of their
attachment. To the Prince de Ligne, the most aristocratic
and distinguished of these friends, he dedicated his *Mémoires*.
The two were in fairly close touch at the time Tilly wrote,
and the Prince was enthusiastic over the *Mémoires*. He was a
most acute, impartial, and unprejudiced observer, and his
personal impressions, whether of kings and emperors or of
men of letters and art — Voltaire, Rousseau, Beaumarchais,
Casanova, Gluck, and the rest — are among the most illu-

minating we possess. We would gladly have his impressions
of Tilly whom he seems to have found so fascinating, but so
far as I have searched he nowhere sets them down. There was,
we divine, an element of instability in Tilly's temperament,
a tendency to live in the present, shown even in the reckless
generosity which helped to plunge him into debts and difficulties, and after 1792 a restless vagabondage was not incompatible with his constant longing to return to Paris. It is
only thus, so far as I can see, that we may explain Tilly's
abandonment of the manuscript of the *Mémoires*, with his correspondence and other papers, in Berlin when he fled from that
city in 1807, though he lived for some nine years longer.

II

The doubts and obscurities enwrapping Tilly begin, as I
have said, at his birth, and even before. Concerning his
family varying statements have been made. They were ancient
and noble, belonging to Normandy, and having their original
château near Caen, but settled in Le Mans during the eighteenth century. They seem to have claimed descent from an
Umfroy, Sieur de Tilly, who accompanied William the Con-
queror to England and became, it is said, Castellan of Hast-
ings. The Count Tilly famous in German history as a great
soldier belonged to Tilly in Brabant and is sometimes said to
have been of the same family; he was in nearly all respects extremely unlike the Tilly we are here concerned with. There
were various branches of the family. Our Tilly belonged to
the Tilly-Prémarest branch, but a certain doubt surrounds this
branch because, the author of the *Mémoires* tells us, his ancestors had failed to secure the proper registration of their
titles of nobility. It was perhaps for this reason that another
branch, that of Tilly-Blaru, which had become separate in
the Middle Ages, refused to recognise the Tilly-Prémarest
branch. There was even a duel over this dispute between our
Count Alexandre Tilly and Count Charles de Tilly-Blaru,
which, however, was followed by an amicable relationship.
But another member of Charles's family, the Abbé de Tilly-

Blaru, a pedantic genealogist, would admit no relationship with the 'young intriguer,' as he called Alexandre.

Tilly's father was Jacques, Chevalier (sometimes described as Marquis) de Tilly, of the Royal Garde du Corps, and later Sénéchal d'Epée, or grand bailiff, of Beaumont-le-Vicomte in Maine. It may be noted that there were still ladies of the name of Tilly living at Le Mans under the Second Empire. The Chevalier de Tilly had married, as his first wife, in 1760, a noble lady of Le Mans, Anne-Suzanne Magdeleine le Bourdais de Chassillé; fifteen months later, in August, 1761, she died, a few days after giving birth to that worthless son — as so many have considered him — our hero, the Comte Jacques-Pierre Alexandre de Tilly (though there is no exact agreement as to his baptismal names), generally known as Alexandre de Tilly. As the obscurities that hover over Tilly begin so early, we are not surprised to learn that his act of baptism has not been found in the registers of Le Mans, but there now seems no doubt that he was born in the parish of the Crucifix on the 9th of August. For his childhood and youth we must rely on the *Mémoires*.

The most memorable period of Tilly's life is indeed his boyhood. It is as 'a page of Marie Antoinette' that he is most usually referred to, and that period also, as he himself admits, before he had been spoilt by society and the world, was the time he looked back on with most satisfaction. Doubts have been raised even here. It is said that only young noblemen of unimpeachably high rank could be enrolled among the Queen's twelve pages, and that Tilly's ancestry was open to doubt. It seems, however, to be ascertained that Tilly was really on the list of the Queen's pages. His name is not mentioned by the Comte d'Hézecques, who was one of the royal pages, but he only arrived after Tilly had left, and was, moreover, one of the pages of the King's Chamber, who were distinct from the Queen's pages. It so happened that in the very same year, 1804, when Tilly was writing his *Mémoires*, Hézecques was writing his own reminiscences of the Court, *Souvenirs d'un Page*, though they were not published until 1876 and then at once translated into English. Hézecques's book has nothing of the dashing brilliancy of Tilly's; he was an estimable man, who fought under the new banner of France when the revolutionary storms were passed and died in respectable old age. But he gives an interesting picture of Louis XVI's Court with its rigid etiquette, and he describes the life of the royal pages.

So far as I have discovered, we first hear definitely of Tilly from an outside source when he was twenty-four. There was in those days a certain Reverend Father Nepveu de la Manouil-lère, a canon of Le Mans Cathedral and evidently a man of good birth, who kept a private chronicle in which he entered local events of the day, and set down frankly his opinions, sometimes highly unfavourable, of the most prominent people of the city and its neighbourhood. These *Mémoires* remained unknown until they were edited by the Abbé Esnault in 1877; they alone seem to demonstrate the authenticity of Tilly's *Mémoires*, for they show that the writer of that work was familiar with the social life of Le Mans to a degree which would hardly be possible to an outsider half a century later. The Canon knew all about the Tilly family and held them (at all events on the male side) in low esteem. Under date 15th March, 1785, he refers to our Tilly as 'très mauvais sujet' and in prison for debt. On the following 3d April he records the death of Madame de Chassillé and continues: 'M. de Tilly, aged twenty-four, who is quite mad [*qui est un fou*] has already been imprisoned for debt, and is so still, but will shortly be released.' It was a debt of three thousand livres, we learn, long owing to M. de Saint-Victor and now to be paid out of the property of Madame de Chassillé, who was rich and left her property (thirty-four thousand livres) to be divided equally between her three grandchildren, of whom Tilly was one. Tilly himself avoids mentioning this imprisonment (and his narrative, written many years later, cannot always be reconciled with the dates in the Canon's contemporary chronicle), though he acknowledges his recklessness in piling up debts. 'His father,' the Canon continues, 'a widower, and Seneschal of Beaumont, from which office he deserves to be driven out, is not worth much more, and even less.' I note, however, that in 1782 'M. de Tilly' (I am not sure if it was the father or the son) had been among sixty-six guests whom the Canon invited to a great banquet; the Canon enumerates the attractive dishes at great length, and mentions that there was dancing until three in the morning. The private judgments of the ecclesiastical chronicler are harsh and unqualified, but it cannot be said that they are seriously out of harmony with Tilly's own account of himself and of his father. We need not, however, agree with the opinion of Tilly's *Mémoires* added by Father Esnault in a footnote, that 'it is impossible even for the most benevolent critic not to regret their publication.' The Canon has no more to say about the Tilly family, but about a year later (in April, 1786), he describes the sudden death of the Marquise de Broc. She was, it appears, a woman of great beauty, grace, charm, leading the gay social life of her time, and only twenty-eight years of age. There was a report that she had been poisoned, Father Esnault tells us, and it was noted that she died a few hours after leaving a ball at which she had been offered refreshments by 'the Comte de T****.' The calumnious suspicion was absurd, apart from the fact that a post-mortem examination showed that death was due to abdominal haemorrhage, doubtless the result of a more ordinary cause. But it serves to show that young Tilly's wild life was so notorious that some people at Le Mans thought him capable of anything. Tilly himself wrote at length of Madame de Broc, acknowledging that he was her lover, and giving an account of the circumstances of her death which may well have been unknown to the public.

That his usual avocations were innocent enough, however frivolous, we may gather from the little volume in verse and prose of *Oeuvres Mêlées du Comte Alexandre de Tilly*, which at this very period he had lately published in Paris and Amsterdam. I have not been able to see this first edition, but I am acquainted with the second much enlarged edition which Tilly put forth in Berlin and Paris some twenty years later; and except for one or two pieces of fierce political invective the tone and character of the later issue remain fairly uniform. A modern critic has spoken of the mediocrity of this book when compared with the *Mémoires* so sparkling with wit. But I see no more contrast in this respect than we might anticipate. When writing the *Mémoires*, Tilly found in the varied adventures of his own life the stimulus he needed to bring out his best literary qualities. In the earlier book he is simply concerned to play his part in the world of polite *belles lettres* where the men of rank and leisure, French and English alike, commonly amused their more refined hours. If Tilly cannot here rival the wit and brilliance of Voltaire, or even many a lesser writer, he displays a characteristically spontaneous ease and skill fully adequate to the slight occasions which usually called forth such exercises.

The second edition of the *Oeuvres Mêlées* is preceded by an interesting dedicatory epistle to 'Madame la Comtesse d'An****' evidently Madame d'Angiviller, whom he introduces into the *Mémoires*. He says here, as a little later he also said in his *Mémoires*, that it was she who first encouraged him to cultivate poetry and letters. Tilly's association with Madame d'Angiviller (or Angivillers as it is sometimes spelt) was entirely to his credit. She was the wife of the Inspector of Royal Buildings, the man to whom we owe the transformation of the Louvre into a gallery of pictures and sculpture, and he is said to have won her only after a courtship of twenty years. She is described by the Duc de Lévis as a rather grotesque figure, extremely small, and with nothing beautiful about her but her long hair. But beneath a rather ridiculous exterior, the Duc tells us, she had a fine spirit, high intelligence, and an equally amiable temper. She united wit, animation, and sound judgment, so that one never grew tired of hearing her talk. 'Nearly all the people who formed her social group,' Lévis adds, 'were persons of distinguished intelligence.' At the Revolution her husband, who was a devoted Royalist, fled from France, but she was favourable to the Revolution and remained behind. It seems hardly tactful on Tilly's part to dedicate this volume to Madame d'Angiviller, for his own fiercely anti-Revolutionary sentiments come out strongly in many of his references to what he calls 'the shame of our history and the scourge of humanity.' Such in-

vectives are scattered among poems to charming and aristocratic ladies, written in the light, playful, and accomplished
way on which a *bel esprit* of the age prided himself in achiev-
ing. There are verses addressed to noblemen who were his
friends; in one of special intent 'To my Best Friend' — whom
it may not be too hazardous to assume to be himself — he
deplores the friend's too licentious life and resolves that he
himself will renounce it, to become so virtuous, and so devoted to his wife, if he ever has one, that she will die of boredom. Such resolves, we learn to know, were characteristic
of Tilly, but seldom lasted long. There is a poem on the death
of his friend the Marquis de Senecterre, who died young and
was much addicted to passing amours, Tilly mentions, adding
a poignant note of direct simplicity as he refers to the ease
with which people accept the death of their friends. There
is, again, a long discourse in verse on Chamfort, 'my dear
Chamfort,' of whom we hear more in the *Mémoires*, as also of
Rivarol whom Tilly knew well. Several of the items in this
volume are dated from England, for which he had much admiration; thus in a fragment from a letter to Madame de C.,
dated December, 1783, he speaks of London as 'one of the
most beautiful towns of the world,' being especially impressed by the vast and magnificent streets, with (unlike
Paris) pavements at the side for foot-passengers, showing
that this is a land where the people count for something; he
notes, however, that the English do not form friendly relationships so easily as the French; they give little and ask little.
Two years later, again in England, he sends an invitation in
verse to a friend in France to come to London to see 'a free
people loving virtue and law and maintaining them,' where
also 'the women are worthy of love for their grace, beautiful
complexions, and large eyes'; and he grows enthusiastic over
'the tragic Muse,' Mrs. Siddons, with her magic voice, her
eyes that strike thunderbolts, her heart that seeks the heart,
and with no aid from cosmetics and plaster, or even powdered
hair.

It is mainly on the *Mémoires* that we must rely for Tilly's
story, but I have come across one account of him in the first

storms of the Revolution which must not be neglected because it seems to stand alone even if it tells us little we could not guess. Tilly, as we know from the *Mémoires*, at this period fell in love with Amélie (now more usually and more correctly spelt Emilie) de Sainte-Amaranthe, one of the loveliest and most attractive victims of the Revolution, whose romantic story has often been told. Her mother, of ancient and noble family, remotely connected, indeed, with the English royal family, had led a rather adventurous life and at that time conducted a high-class and aristocratic gambling-house in the Palais Royal. Amélie's beauty, charm, intelligence, and high spirit, to which all who knew her have testified, made a deep impression on Tilly, and his account of his experiences with her is one of the most moving and deeply felt episodes of the *Mémoires*. It so happens that a society woman who moved in the Sainte-Amaranthe group, shortly before her death, in old age, dictated her reminiscences of that family and their tragic fate. This Madame Amandine Rolland was the daughter of a distinguished financier and had thus known many notable persons of Louis XVI's Court. She survived to 1852, though her reminiscences were only published in 1864 under the name of *La Famille Sainte-Amaranthe*, par Madame A. R****. We are here only concerned with her references to Tilly. She speaks of his 'large black eyes constantly turned on Amélie, although his gaze and the flow of his language received no sign of encouragement from her.' Madame Rolland — who says, in agreement with all other witnesses, that Amélie revealed an almost superhuman perfection of beauty in face and figure — then seeks to reproduce the words which Amélie's mother addressed to her:

M. de Tilly has certainly never been one of my preferred friends. I am not dazzled by his brilliant figure, and his mind, which is said to be so interesting, does not amuse me in the least. His behavior to Amélie does not exactly give me the right to shut my door on him, and yet I find ridiculous at least the effusive tenderness he displays for her and talks about to a crowd of his friends. One would say that it is with him a matter of pride and pose. It brings back to me the part, even a thousandfold more ridiculous,

which he played some years before the Revolution when he assumed a far too confident sentimental tone in speaking of the
Queen; his false confidences might have led one to suppose some
august favours for the handsome page. Oh, what a *Cherubino di
amore*, M. de Tilly! Besides, could noble and delicate passion be
experienced by a man who consumes his youth in deplorable liaisons with Miss Adeline and Miss Rosalie? You know, the little
Antonio of *Richard Coeur de Lion*? It is she who reigns now and her
bold tricks of jealousy are really amusing. It is happily quite certain that Amélie does not respond to M. de Tilly's sighs; otherwise my poor child, on a simple suspicion, might be the victim of
a despair both ridiculous and alarming, for the pretty Antonio,
with her fair hair and her gentle face, when in a rage becomes,
they say, a roaring tigress. The end of such storm is, however,
rather comical; Rosalie pays him back by two infidelities for one,
in order, she says, to have the satisfaction of confessing them to
the lover-in-chief, and then it is his turn to rage. But he remains
more enslaved than ever in this pure and worthy relationship.
Lately he definitely announced his intention to emigrate, but he
stopped at Rosalie's little house on the way.

'Then,' adds the author of these reminiscences, 'Madame
de Sainte-Amaranthe thanked me for the interest I had shown
in her long story, which, she said, she might not have told to
people with whom she had been longer associated.' A little
later, at dinner with the Sainte-Amaranthes, M. de Morainville referred to Tilly's departure as certain.

I was opposite Amélie [Madame Rolland tells us] and I looked
at her; the delicious carnation of her cheek was not in the least
heightened. Very certainly, M. de Tilly, the émigré, was for her
only one adorer less, and the crowd of them was too large for her
imagination to be thereby troubled. 'And what will become of
Tilly's widows?' asked M. de Monville, enjoying a slice of pine-
apple. 'His widows?' replied M. de Morainville, laughing 'perhaps Mlle. Adeline will think of him as she says *Il danse fort bien
M. de la France*; then she will redouble her seductions as she continues, *Mais mon André, tu danses bien mieux à mon gré*. As for Rosalie, oh! she is taking her despair seriously in honour of the fugitive. First of all she let all her splendid hair fall loose without
care; then yesterday evening, they say, it was plaited by the
handsome Amédée de K****, lately one of the Duc d'Orléans's

pages.' 'M. de Morainville,' interrupted Madame de Sainte-Amaranthe, 'you are too well versed in the history of the green-room; I bring the session to an end,' and she rose.

We cannot accept literally the old lady's gossip about events which happened as much as sixty years earlier, when she was little more than a girl; it is too suspiciously detailed. It may even have been unconsciously refreshed by the perusal of Tilly's own *Mémoires*. But in the general drift and tone of her story Madame Rolland may be reliable. It is not sympathetic to Tilly, but, as the *Mémoires* show, in that respect it perhaps corresponds to Madame de Sainte-Amaranthe's attitude towards him, nor is there any difficulty in believing that Amélie, whatever her relation with Tilly, refrained from making her mother her confident, while her whole tragic story reveals a singular self-possession and presence of mind. There can, moreover, be little doubt that the narrative correctly presents the attitude of Tilly's social group. The eighteenth century may have been, as we are now commonly pleased to consider it, frivolous, but the eighteenth century itself was not overindulgent to frivolity. If the *roué* flourished that name was derived from the worst criminals. Even Tilly was a severe moralist.

The story of the Sainte-Amaranthes and their fellow-victims of the Red Mass of the 29th Prairial, 1794, has been told many times and it is widely agreed by historians that the profound impression it made, especially the fate of the noble and completely innocent Amélie, was responsible for the revulsion of feeling against Robespierre and his downfall; he slipped, it has been said, in the blood he had himself shed.[1]

It is for his portraits that Tilly is most often cited by the select band of students to whom alone, until recently, his *Mémoires* have been known. He was on familiar terms with various prominent figures of the last days of the *ancien régime*, and they come in and out of his pages. But three portraits are

[1] The chapter on the Red Mass in the book on the Baron de Batz (translated into English), *A Gascon Royalist in Revolutionary Paris*, by Lenôtre, the scholar who has studied so many of the social and personal aspects of the Revolution, presents, it is probable, a reliable account of this episode; he does not reject Tilly's story, though naturally not able to confirm its intimate details.

especially notable, for they bring before us persons whom we still view with curiosity, and it has been possible to say of each that it realises that person more vividly than any other picture we possess. There is first Marie Antoinette with whom Tilly was in daily touch during his first days of impressionable youth, so that he was able to describe her charm without either formality or extravagance. There is Restif de la Bretonne whom we see here, from the outside, but with a fidelity we recognise as exact. The third is Laclos, and this is probably the most interesting of the three portraits, for it is the only real personal portrait we possess of the author of a novel which at length stands unchallenged as one of the masterpieces of literature, and there is, further, an amusing irony in the fact that Tilly, who is still fettered by the old-world notion that *Les Liaisons Dangereuses* was an outrage on morality, has sometimes himself been considered as the embodiment in real life of the accomplished seducer whom Laclos depicted, Valmont *en personne*.

Looking at the *Mémoires* more broadly, we see in them a picture of the last stage of the eighteenth-century aristocratic society circling round the Court in its superficial brilliance, its light-hearted gaiety, the elegant corruption which still left those who moved in it with spirit high enough to mount even the scaffold with a jest. That is the society that Tilly presents and the society he himself embodied, alike in its dissoluteness and its wit and its high spirit, although it was his mixed good and bad fortune to escape the guillotine. Thus Tilly's *Mémoires* make an admirable companion work to Restif de la Bretonne's *Monsieur Nicolas*, where we view with an even greater intimacy the same society from beneath and come in touch with those plebeian and lower middle-class elements which were soon to become so prominent.

In the last chapters of the *Mémoires* we find Tilly in the full swift stream of the Revolution. Here perhaps he appears to better advantage than at any other time of his life, even though — or because — he was on the losing side. It was natural that he should rally to the defence of the Court and espouse the cause of the royal persons with whom he had once been so closely associated. He brought his facile wit and gay insolence to the attack on the Republicans, in the pages of *Les Actes des Apôtres*, which were then playing a prominent part on the literary side of the struggle. He wrote an open letter to the King in which, with what has been held to be sound judgment, he exhorted him to firmness and resolution. Among those whom he attacked he evidently aroused strong resentment, and he believed, rightly or wrongly, that there were attempts to assassinate him. To Condorcet, whom he regarded as a renegade, he addressed an open letter of fierce vituperation, as he believed that he, with Fabre d'Eglantine, had determined on his death. Immediately afterwards he decided that he had better leave France. He made his way slowly to the coast, paid a large sum to be quietly and uncomfortably conveyed across the Channel in a smuggler's boat, and the *Mémoires* close with his arrival in England at the end of August, 1792. He never continued them, though twenty-four years more of life remained to him and many strange adventures. But he was probably wise. The most brilliant and attractive period of his life was over, and if in the *Mémoires* he must often crave our indulgence, in the days that followed his discredit seems sometimes complete.

III

Tilly states at the end of his *Mémoires* that he landed in England at Stockport, proceeded thence by a two hours' drive to Dover, and therefrom to London. Various French writers innocently repeat this statement without knowing that the only English Stockport is at the opposite end of England from Dover, and this statement in the *Mémoires* might seem a more plausible argument against their authenticity than some other little errors that have actually been brought forward. Tilly merely claims to have landed at 'Stockport' and may easily have been mistaken in the name of the place, perhaps a port for none but smugglers, unless we have here an error of transcription, as probably in the name of Mrs. 'Knouth,' the landlady of the British Hotel at Boulogne.

In London, Tilly was no stranger, having made prolonged stays, two or three times before, and he had a good knowledge of English literature; on some occasions, also, he had come into contact with Burke and other distinguished people, even, it seems, the Prince Regent. Many aristocratic French *émigrés*, including old friends of Tilly, especially the Vicomte de Noailles, were already settled in England and on account of their rank and the sympathy felt with their misfortunes often able to mix in good society. But they were naturally in reduced circumstances and compelled to struggle with discomforts and difficulties. We do not know how Tilly, so often in money troubles even at home, contrived to live abroad. The German editor of his *Mémoires*, who had many of Tilly's private papers before him, states that he was everywhere treated with esteem and regard during his four years' stay, but that it is a mystery on what he lived, though he may have been engaged in some business with Noailles, 'and seems to have been fortunate at the gaming table and with women.' But among his papers was preserved a letter written by the Comte de Vaudreuil — once so fascinating and influential a figure at the French Court — and this is worth quoting both for Tilly's sake and for the light it throws on the existence of a noble *émigré*. It was addressed to Tilly from Edinburgh on the 20th November, 1796, without signature but in Vaudreuil's handwriting:

I will begin with myself and describe to you my situation. You know that for a long time Monsieur [that is, the Comte d'Artois, brother of Louis XVI, who later became Charles X] has wished us to come to him in Edinburgh. I have always sought to decline or at least to postpone this, on account of the length and difficulty of the journey, but Monsieur sent a brig to fetch us, and Madame de Vaudreuil and I had to decide on embarking. After a troublesome six-day voyage with seasickness we at last arrived, extremely exhausted. Our lodgings alone cost us four pounds a month. One certainly lives here more cheaply than in London, but it is quite dear enough for people who have altogether only ten pounds a month to spend. Monsieur sends us daily two dishes from the Castle to improve our slender meals. That, however, is all he does for us, or can do, for he is himself in a difficult position. I own (but this is between ourselves) that I had counted on something more, but I have to accept things as they are, for the Prince is not able to pay his own household. I have to do my best with the ten pounds and do not know how I shall get on; my head whirls. How gladly would I come to London, but a seat in the coach costs ten guineas. It is sad. We live in the same island, my good Tilly, and cannot embrace each other; I had so much to say to you, and to confide.... I have received a letter from Alphonse [his son]; he wants money. I am telling him of my sad position, and enclose the letter, to save postage.

We know little of Tilly's reception in English society. But we have definite information concerning his relations with two interesting women in London. The first was a lady not yet forgotten, Lady Elizabeth Craven, daughter of the Earl of Berkeley, married to Lord Craven at an early age and later to the Margrave of Anspach, while the King of Prussia raised her to the rank of Princess Berkeley. In her old age she wrote her own Memoirs, and books have been written about her even in recent years. She was a woman of beauty and real charm as well as intelligence, but she was married at seventeen and had more than one lover afterwards in an almost public manner, so that though her second husband, the Margrave, was a nephew of Frederick the Great, and she herself with the help of his immense wealth was able to maintain a little Court of considerable magnificence in London at Brandenburg House, Hammersmith, her position was ambiguous, and while the Prince Regent visited her, George III and Queen Charlotte stayed away. Horace Walpole, who was at first on friendly terms with her, wrote in 1785 to Sir Horace Mann, the British Minister at Florence, where Lady Craven then was: 'She has, I fear, been *infinitamente* indiscreet, but what is that to you or me? She is very pretty, has parts, and is good-natured to the greatest degree; has not a grain of malice or mischief, and never has been an enemy but to herself.' The famous Lauzun, who had also known her at a rather earlier period of her life wrote that she was 'a very pretty little woman, celebrated for her follies and her misfortunes'; and added that 'gentle, simple, and tender, it was impossible not to feel interest in her.' At a later period she was certainly capable of being inordinately vain and arrogant. She married the Margrave in 1791, immediately after Lord Craven's death.

Tilly seems soon to have found entrance to the cosmopolitan gaieties of Hammersmith, where we hear of him taking part in private theatricals, for the Margravine wrote and performed numerous plays. She was now (in 1793), at forty-three years of age, still very attractive, and we are not surprised to hear of Tilly, though many years younger, making love to her. This episode is minimised by Broadley and Lewis Melville in their work, *The Beautiful Lady Craven*, as 'a mild flirtation.' They quote, however, a letter of hers to Tilly which bears witness to stronger feelings, stating that it is 'the only one which has escaped destruction,' but not stating whence they derived it. Its original source is, no doubt, the German editor's supplement to Tilly's *Mémoires*, and here we find not one, but four love-letters from the Margravine to Tilly, with references to others. Nor do the English authors say anything of the story that Tilly had once at Hammersmith, presumably in a fit of jealous rage, struck the Margravine with his riding-whip. The German editor of 1825, who based himself on Tilly's own papers, knew nothing of this story. Its original source seems to be the French editor of 1828, who, after referring to Tilly's remark in the *Mémoires* in favour of a certain amount of violence in love, continues: 'It has been notorious in London and Hamburg that the Comte de Tilly behaved in this manner with the Margravine of Anspach, and sometimes treated her with singular brutality in her park, using a horse-whip in the presence of witnesses.' Tilly certainly defended such conduct, as we know, referring to a distinguished lady (whether or not the Margravine) who after such an incident confided to a friend that now she felt assured her lover really loved her; and as we know besides that the Margrave placed the horses in the famous stables he owned at the disposition of his guests, it is easy to account for the whip. Nietzsche also has advised that women should be approached with a whip, though we cannot imagine that gentle philosopher following his own advice. Tilly's moods of impulsive violence may be detected in his own pages, and the Margravine's letters show that he thought he had some grievances. We may not absolutely reject the story, and yet I much doubt it. I have not so far met with it in any contemporary record of the times. Horace Walpole, who frequently mentions the Margravine, and could not fail to have heard of such an extraordinary incident, says nothing about it, nor do the biographers of the Margravine. There is no reason to suppose the French editor was ever in London, and, if he was, most of the 'notorious' stories he would hear about the Margravine of Anspach would be the silly gossip, inevitably aroused by so singular and conspicuous a figure, of which she frequently complains.

A few extracts may be given from the Margravine's letters to Tilly:

> How can you call me cruel? I cruel? And to you? I who cannot ever be unkind even to those whom I hate? You are joking, Dearest! So far from putting anything in the way as regards your plans with D—— [of whom Tilly was jealous], I only wanted to warn you to be on your guard. As for the M. [Margrave], he is mad against your nation, but especially against D. M.... But trust me to use my influence over him to secure my happiness. Never was I so necessary to the Margrave. His timid soul takes refuge in mine. When the people in the streets salute me and say 'There she is!' he is delighted.... God is my witness that when I give up the pleasure of seeing you for a few weeks I give up what is dearest to me in the world; but it *must* be, for circumstances prevent. Your journey will give the final touch to my rights over the Margrave; all the others will seem to be in the wrong and you the only one who has not deceived him.... I embrace you. Put a little cross somewhere in a corner of your letter and kiss it, and when I receive it I will kiss it too. Farewell, my dearest, my only friend. Love me well; take care of yourself, body and soul; that will prove that you want to make me happy. Kiss this place.

(Here she has made a circle about the size of a florin.)
In the course of another letter she writes:

> The Margrave goes to Colney-chapel on Sunday and stays till the middle of the week. So I shall be quite free. If you come to

me meanwhile, so that no one knows of it, choose one of two ways which I will indicate to you. Lord Thurlow [the Lord Chancellor and a friend of the Margravine's] will tell you of yesterday's doings with the Margrave. I press you to my troubled heart.

In a third letter she writes:

My tears choke me. I do not think it wise to see you. You do not know *how* I love when I love. You can only have a weak idea of it. Do not believe that I will speak evil of you to the Margrave. Nor do I give myself any trouble to deceive him — very unnecessary trouble, for as soon as you are away I can do what I like with him. I only avoid as much as possible to speak of you to him for fear of betraying myself. My heart is only fifteen, it jumps and beats if I but hear your name. Then I blush and almost swoon.... I am looking for a house in London, for myself alone and for all that my son needs. I will so arrange it that you can come to me unobserved, by day or by night.... But learn, dear friend, to beware of yourself even more than of your enemies. Have *me* as your only friend.

In a further letter she writes:

It is a new torture for me, a deadly martyrdom, to be so near you and not to see you. I am better today, but still far from recovery. I promise to be careful of my health. Why are you silent about your own state? Send me your Henri [Tilly's valet] that I may ask him. I would like to see him if only because he has seen you. Preserve all the strength of your soul to love me as I deserve to be loved. And if ever your heart changes, be chivalrous enough to hide nothing from me. I reckon on this and still more on my and your tenderness. Both promise that you will never change. At the present moment I am much troubled. Farewell.

There were other letters in French and in English, in some of which she defends herself against Tilly's jealousy of D., who, she says, had never been more than a friend. All these letters date from 1793. They are interesting because they furnish evidence, independent of the *Mémoires*, that Tilly could arouse the passionate love of a distinguished, cultured, and high-spirited woman whose beauty, charm, and position brought so many men to her feet. We do not know how the relationship ended. Tilly put the letters in a packet on which he wrote 'Marg. of Ans.' After his death this was found in Berlin among his other papers by the first editor of the *Mémoires*. Perhaps it still lies neglected somewhere.

There is nothing about Tilly in the Margravine's own Memoirs, and we should not expect it, for they were written in old age and with an anxious eye to her own reputation. So we do not know whether it was she who brought the relationship to an end or Tilly's volatile heart. However that may be, we soon find him in close relationship with another woman, this time French, and one in a very different position from the prodigal and magnificent Princess Berkeley.

Charlotte Marie Bobin, married to Dr. Arnould André Roberjot-Lartigues at Port-au-Prince in San Domingo, lived with her daughter, but apart from her husband, in London. Tilly seems to have become acquainted with her through the Prince de Poix, brother of his friend the Vicomte de Noailles and also acquainted with the Margravine. If it may seem characteristic of Tilly to be in the train of a woman of wealth and distinction like the Margravine, it is equally characteristic of him to expend a reckless and almost incredible generosity on a woman in misfortune and poverty. In her financial difficulties, which seem to have been largely due to careless extravagance, she repeatedly applied for help to the Prince and to Tilly. She must have made a deep impression on Tilly, for before the year 1795 was out he had advanced her over sixteen hundred pounds. Whence Tilly, an *émigré* and usually in debt, obtained this large sum is not clear; it is stated by his German editor that he sold or pawned rings, jewels, horses, books, and pistols to obtain money for Madame Lartigues. He very soon wanted the money back. In the same year 1795 he sent a demand to the lady's husband, who replied from Port-au-Prince on the 1st November, 1795, that it was owing to his wife's youthful frivolity and extravagant way of living that these debts were incurred, that the allowance he made her should amply suffice for her needs, and that the disturbed conditions in San Domingo prevented him from doing more.

Next year Tilly took the further step of forwarding to

Dr. Lartigues an acknowledgement of the debt by Madame Lartigues, dated 27th July, 1796, with a request for its acquittal. The document is as follows:

I swear, affirm, and protest that this account of 1649 pounds sterling in English money is exact in justice and truth, as is the eternal gratitude that I and my daughter owe to M. Alexandre de Tilly, who has saved me from perishing of hunger, illness, and misery on various occasions, as respectable witnesses can certify, in the intervals during which I received no allowance (and when I was lost in debt), and especially during the past fourteen months when, with heavy debts, I was receiving no allowance and was abandoned by all my family, and obliged at last for four months to seek the help granted by the English government to the indigent, and that when all my properties are bringing in a full return. I acknowledge, I say, that the said sum of 1649 pounds sterling, in English money, is due to him in the most lawful manner, and that he, Alexandre de Tilly, is authorised before God and man to take by all means possible from whatever I possess, and shall possess, and from whatever my husband possesses or shall possess, the repayment of a debt so sacred.

It does not appear, however, that Dr. Lartigues recognised this debt, and still less that he repaid the loan, for on the 3d December, 1801, Tilly, it is said, wrote with some bitterness from Berlin to the lady, then in Bordeaux, reminding her of the acknowledgement just quoted. She replied on the 20th March, 1802, expressing her gratitude to Tilly and describing her misfortunes since returning from San Domingo, then in a very disturbed state, where she had apparently been to see her husband, of whom, however, she makes no mention.

It was not, as you think, the deadly climate of San Domingo [she writes in the course of this letter] from which I have escaped, but the bloodthirsty fury of the negroes. I have been in the midst of them for two months, with my family and twenty-eight other whites, in constant danger of being massacred. All this time I could not change my linen or obtain food except such as the more human of these inhuman creatures allowed me, and that I gave nearly all to my children and my father whose lives were dearer to me than my own. After two months the monsters left us free and we had to wander through pathless woods, without food or shoes or stockings, even robbed of my last chemise, for nine miles, until we fortunately reached Port-au-Prince. Here for three months I was dependent on the charity of Madame Leclerc [Napoleon's sister, Pauline, then the young wife of Colonel Leclerc, Captain-General of the French forces engaged in suppressing the negro revolt, and afterwards Princess Borghese]. But when the French troops left the island, I went across to New York and there for eight months supported myself with difficulty by dress-making, until Heaven brought it about that my daughter found the best of husbands, and I the noblest of sons-in-law, who has taken care of me and my Alexandre [at this name, that of Tilly, the German editor 'cannot repress a secret suspicion']. Since returning to Bordeaux I have spent six months with him, though his means are limited, and six months with my husband's relations. You may judge, therefore, whether it is possible for me to fulfil my obligations otherwise than by my feelings and words.

We know nothing further of Madame Lartigues.

In the summer of 1797, we find Tilly in Hamburg whither perhaps he went late in the previous year, possibly to escape London creditors. It was one of the centres at which strangers were then seeking refuge from the calamities of war, and as it was at that moment also a chief Continental port for English vessels, it was natural for Tilly to make his way there, even if he was not drawn by the presence of his old friend Rivarol.

While living in Hamburg in July, 1797, Tilly wrote a letter, partly in verse (published in the second edition of his *Oeuvres Mêlées*), to ask Rivarol for the loan of a copy of Rousseau's *Nouvelle Héloïse*, as he wishes to verify a quotation. He here speaks of the novel as ' that enchanting work which at twenty we all know by heart and at forty forget [he was not himself yet forty], where everything is false and empty and sophisticated, yet where everything is true, thanks to the magic of its style.' In the course of the letter Tilly writes:

I passed your door yesterday and was very pleased to find it hermetically closed. I followed the precept of him whose morals were so pure, who says *Pulsate*, and rejoiced that the *aperietur vobis* was not verified. I rejoiced to think that you were face to face with Posterity, at work for her and for yourself. You have conquered all difficulties, and all your rivals, since you have conquered idleness.

In his reply Rivarol writes:

If I had guessed my good fortune yesterday, my door would have been open; it will always be open for you. I close it to bores and to those with whom all time spent is wasted. Knock when you come again twice only, and rather loud, at the downstairs door. Come, if it suits you, just after dinner. It is well for you to preach against idleness, you are yourself the real culprit. Here, as in Paris, you waste your mind and your facility on people with whom you ought at your age to feel disgust, when you know them as well as you do. You are always thirsting for empty pleasures, of which you ought to be weary. You have all that is needed to impart the love of work. Believe me, rest in work, it calls for you, and dissipation is no longer worthy of you.

That was the wise and plain-spoken advice of a discerning friend, even although Rivarol, who left so little to justify his brilliant reputation, scarcely followed his own counsel. We may be sure that the moralist in Tilly admitted its truth. Yet he never outgrew the need for such advice and remained unchanged, save for the worse, until his tragic death.

IV

Late in 1797 we suddenly find Tilly in the New World. It is not, however, a matter for surprise. The gratitude felt in the new American Republic for the assistance derived from France induced many distinguished *émigrés* to follow in the track of Lafayette. Lauzun had gone to America. Friends and relatives of Tilly's including the Vicomte de Noailles, who was Lafayette's brother-in-law, had already gone over. Perhaps Madame Lartigues had stimulated the project. Whatever the motive, Tilly appeared in New York and wrote to apprise Noailles of his arrival. On the 2d November, Noailles writes in reply from Philadelphia: 'Madame de Lartigues told me of your plan to come to us. I took it for a fable as there is nothing *romantic* here. But your letter of

28th October from New York tells me that you have carried out your idea. I shall be pleased to see you again, but I must confess to you that there could not be a more unfavourable moment for undertaking any affairs here.' It may have been the presence of General Noailles (as he was always called in America) which induced Tilly to proceed to Philadelphia. We do not know how he lived during the next twelve months; we hear nothing of any mercantile affairs: as his German editor remarks, the goods that Tilly dealt in were hearts.

In 1799 we find Tilly settled in Philadelphia — we do not know how long he had been there — and in friendly touch with the Bingham family to whom doubtless Noailles had introduced him. Now Philadelphia was at this time a centre of gaiety and splendour, as well as temporarily the capital of the Republic, and William Bingham — who had been born there in 1752 and died at Bath in England in 1804 — was one of its chief citizens and still figures conspicuously in American biographical dictionaries. He was the wealthiest man in Philadelphia and once purchased two million acres in Maine. He was a Senator and had even acted as President of the Senate. His wife was distinguished for her beauty and charm and the magnificent hospitality which her husband's position enabled her to exercise. His eldest daughter, Anne Louisa, had lately (1798) married an afterwards eminent Englishman, Alexander Baring, a financier and statesman (son of Sir Francis Baring, since termed 'the first merchant in Europe of his time'), who later became the first Baron Ashburton and father by Anne Louisa of the second Baron, whose wife, Lady Ashburton, is well known as the friend of Carlyle and sometimes an innocent cause of trouble in the Carlyle household.

We may now turn to the letters found among Tilly's papers by his German editor. We are not surprised to learn that he had quickly sought, and found, favour in the Bingham family, both with mother and daughter, that is, the second daughter, Maria Matilda, still a young girl. We soon find Maria writing little notes on gilt-edged satin paper to Tilly, who carefully preserved them. The first was a formal invitation written in correct French: 'Mr. and Mrs. Bingham beg Monsieur le Comte de Tilly to do them the honour of dining with them *en famille* [this was underlined] next Sunday.' The two notes that followed were in English: 'Miss Bingham presents her compliments to Count Tilly. She takes the liberty of sending him some chocolate, having remarked yesterday, that he approved of it.' In the next: 'Miss Maria Matilda Bingham takes the liberty of offering Count Tilly some fruit just taken from the tree. She hopes it may prove acceptable to Count Tilly in his indisposition.' There were no letters of a more intimate character, the reason being that in the subsequent proceedings they had to be returned to Maria's mother, so that there immediately follows a more alarming document: 'This is to certify that on the 11 day of April in the year of our Lord, one thousand seven hundred and ninety nine, James Alexander Count de Tilly was married to Maria Matilda Bingham. By me Thomas Jones, Minister of the Universal Church in Philadelphia, Pennsylvania.' (It may be noted that Tilly here for the only time used his first baptismal name.)

At this point we may leave for a moment the narrative of Tilly's matrimonial adventure, as set down in his German editor's Supplement, to turn to American records. Here, I have discovered with interest, we may find some rather intimate details concerning Maria Matilda and her family. Philadelphia was at that time, as has already been remarked, a centre of luxury; the Duc de la Rochefoucauld-Liancourt said this luxury recalled that of Europe, with the difference that its women were more beautiful; it was indeed indisputably the leading American city in every respect. Its aristocratic society, surrounding what was at that time the seat of government, constituted the nearest approach to a Court that the Republic has ever tolerated. William Bingham and his father-in-law, Thomas Willing, were at the centre of this society, and his wife was its leader in fashion. Bingham was descended from a good English family long established in Philadelphia; at the age of eighteen he had already been appointed British Consul in Martinique, and his great wealth is said to have been obtained by trade speculation and the ownership of privateers. He founded the first American bank, and Thomas Willing, a wealthy merchant of great ability, was the president of the bank. The marriage of Willing's daughter to Bingham enabled the clan to constitute a ruling oligarchy in Philadelphian society, and the Binghams' mansion — a copy on a more splendid scale of Manchester House in London — became a great social centre; here Washington might often be found at tea. Mrs. Bingham had moved in good society from before her marriage and her sister had even been courted by Louis Philippe, afterwards King of France, but old Willing had forbidden the marriage. Anne, who married Bingham (twelve years her senior) at sixteen, was so beautiful that it was said she 'might sit for the Queen of Beauty.' She certainly seems to have possessed great charm, intelligence, and social distinction, with nothing of either the democrat or the Puritan about her. She spent some years in London in the best English society, associating with the Duchess of Devonshire and other aristocrats, and was said to have brought back with her the bad habit of besprinkling her conversation with oaths and slightly risky anecdotes; but not a word has ever been uttered against her good name, and her husband was devoted to her.

It is in the *Life and Letters of H. G. Otis* that we obtain our only really intimate glimpse of Maria Matilda, and at the very moment of her unlucky matrimonial adventure with Tilly. Otis moved freely among this whole clan and writes familiarly to his wife about them — about Thomas Willing whom he calls 'Old Square Toes' on account of the old-fashioned boots he wore, about the charm and ultrafashionable ways of Mrs. Bingham, and about Maria, only fifteen when she ran away with Tilly, but already, it seems, considered a little wild.

Any reader of the *Mémoires* will know enough of *le beau Tilly* to experience no surprise at his easy conquest of the beautiful and charming young Maria Matilda, who was certainly already surrounded by far more desirable suitors. But up to this moment Tilly's exploits in love and gallantry, however irresponsibly they may have been conducted, have appeared the outcome of genuine attraction towards the objects by whom they are inspired and such as we might expect from a typical young French aristocrat of the late eighteenth century. Here we must evidently recognise designs of a less amiable sort.

The marriage caused profound consternation in the Bingham family directly it was known. It is clear that they had not suspected any matrimonial design on Tilly's part. Whether or not they knew much of Tilly's reputation as a *roué*, and however friendly and hospitably disposed by his personal and social attractions, we soon discover that a marriage alliance with the French count was the last thing desired by the aristocratic clan who had already rejected an alliance with the future King of France. Unfortunately, we cannot help thinking that he himself had realised that beforehand. Tilly must be got rid of at once; and it soon appeared that the simplest and quickest way, and for a man of Bingham's wealth the easiest, was to buy him off. There is nothing to show that the young Countess offered any opposition. It is remarkable that Tilly's friends did not desert him at this unpleasant crisis he had himself brought about, and that even the Binghams, while determined to exclude him from the family at any price, do not appear hostile to him personally. A committee was formed to settle the conditions of the separation, with three friends of Tilly's on one side and three friends of the Binghams on the other. On Tilly's side were Noailles (to whom the affair must have been painful if he was responsible for introducing Tilly), Guillaume Guéroult de Boiseclereau, a cousin of Tilly's on the paternal side, and a Pierre Aurois, probably a business man, while on the other side were Mr. Thomas Willing, connected with the Binghams, a Mr. Francis, who also seems to be connected, and Alexander Baring, Maria's brother-in-law. A certain amount of discussion and arrangement of terms took place before the matter was settled to the satisfaction of both parties. Tilly agreed to the demand of the Binghams that he should at once and for ever renounce all association and communication with his wife, and Mr. Bingham agreed to the demands of Tilly as formulated in the following strange document, drawn up in French, which only too clearly reveals Tilly's motives in contracting this clandestine marriage:

I make the following demands.

1. Five thousand pounds sterling to pay my debts.

2. An annuity of five hundred pounds sterling, to be paid wherever I may wish, in any country, except the United States.

3. Due security that I shall not be disturbed in any manner whatsoever in connection with the circumstances of my marriage.

4. I demand that Mr. Baring shall write to me, or cause the statement to be made to me through General de Noailles, that he pushed me in a moment of agitation, on account of the condition of his wife. [This point is not cleared up by the context, but it is noted that the condition was duly fulfilled through Noailles.] And never, on my honour, in this country or elsewhere, shall I trouble the peace of his family, or his own, even in the most remote manner.

These four articles being accepted and ratified under the responsibility of General de Noailles and Mr. T. Willing, I undertake to leave Philadelphia at once and America directly after.

I undertake on my part to give any security that may be imposed on me, as for example the loss of the annuity or a judgment against me for the sum allocated for payment of my debts, that I will never give any cause whatever for trouble to Mr. Bingham's family or the families of Mr. Willing and Mr. Francis. I will return the Countess of Tilly's letters to her mother, and if at any time it is considered that a divorce would contribute to her happiness, I will agree at the first demand and not ask a shilling of damages. I desire the signature of Mr. Bingham to these articles before two o'clock this afternoon, and before ten o'clock tomorrow morning the absolute fulfilment of these conditions, so that I may leave instantly a country where I have been too unfortunate.

Signed: Philadelphia, the 10th June, 1799.

ALEX. DE TILLY

Mr. Bingham at once signed and sent the following document (which is in English):

Mr. Bingham has received the paper containing certain conditions offered on the part of Monsieur de Tilly — which under certain modifications, not substantially affecting the terms, he will agree to. The necessary Paper, to carry the same into operation, shall be prepared immediately, so that Monsieur de Tilly may leave town tomorrow morning.

Monday morning. WM. BINGHAM

In accordance with the contract Tilly left Philadelphia next morning, and sailed from New York to London in July, never to visit America again.

These details concerning the marriage, the separation that so swiftly followed, and the documents concerning the terms arranged, are all derived from Tilly's own papers, as left behind him in Berlin and first published by the German editor of the *Mémoires*. We can fortunately supplement them by the outside view which I have found in the *Life and Letters of Harrison Gray Otis*.

> It was a shocking and scandalous affair [we are here told by a friend of Otis, who remained anonymous] and created, at the time, prodigious sensation in our highest circles. De Tilly was ready, however, to be bought off. He was bribed to furnish evidence against himself, and the divorce was obtained by influence with the Legislature of Pennsylvania, whether by corruption I am not able to say.

Otis himself, at the time, writes to his wife, on January 18, 1800:

> I just learn that a Bill for divorcing Maria Bingham has passed both Houses at Lancaster, where Mr. Bingham now is. She was, however, every day walking with her mother while the business was pending and in a dress which you would hardly believe it was possible for a lady to wear, at least at this season. A muslin robe and her chemise, and no other article of clothing upon her body! I have been regaled with the sight of her whole legs for five minutes together, and do not know to what height the fashion will be carried. The particulars of her dress I hear from old Mrs. F..., who assures me that her chemise is fringed to look like a petticoat. However, she and the family are evidently dejected.

The divorce appears to have been really a declaration of nullity on the ground of Maria's age and the absence of parental consent. Mrs. Bingham's health had begun to fail at the beginning of 1800 after the birth of a child who did not survive, and the doctors advised a voyage to Madeira. The whole family went in the spring, but the divorce was obtained before they sailed.

In reviewing the peculiar circumstances of Tilly's marriage and separation, we cannot but note how rare a friend he possessed in Noailles, who seems to have been a man of high and honourable character. What Noailles thought of the transaction we may guess, and it is easy to do so when we read a letter he wrote to Tilly only about a fortnight later. Tilly had made to him from New York the hardly tactful suggestion that he should marry one of his sons to the young Countess after a divorce. Noailles replied with a cold and curt air of dignified pride which Tilly must have felt to be cutting: 'I cherish the most tender regard for Maria, and the deepest reverence for Mrs. Bingham, but under no pretext would I agree that one of my children should become the son-in-law of Mr. Bingham; at no price in the world would I put a son of mine in the position of living by the favours of his father-in-law. You may make what use you please of this definite answer.' (We know from other sources that each of the daughters had a marriage portion of one hundred thousand pounds.) At the same time such seems to have been the personal fascination exerted by Tilly that not only Noailles, but even the Bingham family, retained amiable feelings towards him. One is inclined to think that, like the Canon of Le Mans, but in a milder spirit, they regarded him as 'quite mad.' Noailles wrote from Philadelphia to Tilly, three months later, a letter which amid much concerning the state of France at the time contains some personal remarks:

You wish me to deal frankly with you. You know that I have often done so, even to the point of brutality. So listen to me. The family has been considering two proposals. One was a judicial separation, the other a formal divorce. Mr. Bingham and his daughter are in favour of the divorce. This will not take a form offensive for you; the difference of age and your arts of seduction will be recognised. No Frenchman has ever felt offended by the accusation of sweet persuasiveness and irresistible fascination.

Further on in the letter he adds:

All through the summer there have been many wooers round Maria. Her flight from the paternal home has been regarded as nothing more than a rash escapade. She has made much progress in intelligence and knowledge, as well as in accomplishments. Her first attempt to taste marriage has cost her so dearly that it will be hard to persuade her to make a second attempt. She possesses a rare gift for winning hearts. If she ever forms a new tie, it will only be as the result of a passion against which she has long struggled, and with the approval of her father, whose idol she is. ... Since your departure I have not heard your name once mentioned either in the Willing family or the Bingham family. I have communicated your letter to me in part to Mr. Bingham. He leaves you completely free to stay where you please. I should add that Mrs. Bingham cherishes sincere feelings towards you, and good wishes for your health and happiness. I unite my wishes to hers.

Maria later married her brother-in-law Henry Baring. It seemed a promising union, but ended unhappily at an early stage, for we are told by Otis's unnamed friend that Henry Baring, being himself unfaithful, threw his wife into dissipated society and then divorced her on account of an amour with a Captain Webster. She married, for the third time, the Marquis de Blaizel, a Frenchman in the Austrian Army, and Chamberlain of the Emperor. But again Maria was unhappy; the Marquis was a gambler and always in want of money which she could not supply, as Henry Baring had managed to secure the greater part of her fortune. 'I knew her in Paris,' writes Otis's friend, 'then an old woman but quite an amusing one. She had seen the world in many phases and had plenty of anecdotes which she told pleasantly. She was a very amiable, kind-hearted woman. She lived in rather an equivocal position in Paris. She was received at the Austrian Ambassador's, but not at the English Embassy.' That is all I have been able to find about the unfortunate Maria Matilda, and now it is unlikely we shall ever hear those anecdotes 'she told pleasantly,' perhaps sometimes about that early episode with Tilly which alone was destined to preserve her name.

To return to Tilly's papers: there is silence for a time. Then, in 1801, evidently as extravagant as ever and even willing to sacrifice the future to the immediate present, Tilly conceived the idea of compounding his annuity by a lump sum of five thousand pounds down. He persuaded his friends Noailles and Guéroult de Boisclereau to put the proposal before Bingham, who, however, preferred to stand by the original contract, bearing in mind, as he himself said, that he would not be able to rely on Tilly's conduct, especially as he had already, against his promise, written letters both to Maria and to her mother. After Bingham's death in 1804, however, Tilly renewed these attempts with the assistance of a lawyer, Barnett, and finally, after much negotiation, succeeded in 1805 and 1806 in obtaining a composition of the annuity from the representatives of the Bingham family.

That is the end of the most remarkable episode in Tilly's life, an episode unique even in his varied experience, and one which his most indulgent admirers can scarcely view with satisfaction.

V

In August, 1799, Tilly arrived back in London, and we find him applying at the Alien Office for a licence to remain in England. Now for the first time we have a little information concerning his personal appearance. Strangely enough, notwithstanding the admiration aroused by a man who was considered 'one of the handsomest and best built men of his time,' and his own interest in art and intercourse with painters, no authentic portrait of Tilly seems yet to have been traced. In the 1930 Jonquière edition of the *Mémoires* a 'presumed portrait' of Tilly is reproduced, but as no information is given as to why and by whom this is 'presumed,' nor where the picture is preserved, there is no choice but to reject it. In the English passport of 1799, however, found among his papers by his German editor, Tilly is described as thirty-four (really thirty-eight) years of age, five feet five inches in height and with black hair. But the rest of the description had been rendered illegible by Tilly. A later German passport among his papers gives further details: 'thirty-six years of age, of middle height, oval and rather pale face, black hair, large black eyes, regular nose.'

Tilly soon changed his mind about staying in England. In September we find him applying to the English Government, as well as to the Austrian and Danish Ambassadors, for permission to go to Denmark and Germany. First he went to Hamburg, and during the next year or two he seems to have been at Leipzig or the neighbourhood, for he had his English and American letters addressed to a banker in that town.

In 1801 began a new and happier period of Tilly's life. After a stay in Dresden, and then at Teplitz for the sake of the baths — for Tilly often suffered in health and Teplitz was one of the most fashionable spas of the time — he came to Berlin. Frederick the Great, as we know, had set a fashion in Prussia for French culture, and an *émigré*, if of aristocratic birth, a soldier, a lover of *belles-lettres*, and accomplished in the social graces — all of which qualities Tilly possessed — might expect in Berlin more than the mere friendly sympathy and occasional hospitality which was the most the *émigré* usually found in the cities of other lands. Even when we bear this in mind, we are surprised at the high consideration and distinguished position which Tilly seems speedily to have secured in the Court and the society of Berlin.

In 1801 the King of Prussia gave him an appointment as Chamberlain at his Court, while the Emperor Paul of Russia made him a Knight of Malta. This was probably in consequence of the intimate relations which Tilly formed with the Russian Ambassador Baron von Krüdener and his wife, whose reputation has survived till today. Indeed, both the royal family and the high nobility of Berlin seem to have treated Tilly in the most flattering manner, and his German editor found ample evidence of this in the letters left among his papers. Tilly addressed laudatory tributes in verse to the King and Queen, with songs to be sung at Court fêtes, was in touch with the whole royal family, and became an enthusiastic admirer of everything Prussian.

It seems, however, to have been the Baron and Baroness Krüdener with whom Tilly's relations were closest at this time, and he was allowed to use their house as his own. An account of them, found among his papers, helps to illustrate his life at this time. It was written just after Krüdener's sudden death in 1802, and Tilly describes his intellectual powers, the wide extent of his outlook, his straightforwardness combined with diplomatic skill and prudence, though his generous hospitality tended to go beyond the means at his disposal, so that the Emperor he represented had to come to his aid.

M. de Krüdener's death has much moved me [Tilly continues], though I saw less of him during the last six or eight months of his life, on account of absurd calumnies which had been brought to him, calumnies which he sometimes accepted and sometimes rejected. When I first arrived in Berlin he overwhelmed me with marks of interest which later turned to friendship, especially after he had ceased to see much of Rivarol whom he had too much intelligence not to seek, but too much tact not at the same time to avoid, for his ministerial prudence could not sometimes but be alarmed by the political audacities with which that fine wit would amuse himself to embarass the statesman. I was dining with him and a small party on the day when Rivarol was dying [13th April, 1801]. Though then on distant terms with Rivarol, I was none the less shocked by his death. I thought of that extraordinary conversational power now perishing, of the beautiful instrument which had given out such harmonious sounds and was now about to be broken, of that organisation so vast and so alive now reaching the annihilation of the grave. I had never hated him — I seemed to love him still.

After more in praise of Rivarol, Tilly passes without transition to speak of the Baroness, who was without doubt the most remarkable, and certainly the most famous (apart from Marie Antoinette), of the numerous interesting and fascinating women with whom Tilly came in close contact, though the period of her fame belongs to a rather later date.

Julie de Wietinghoff was born in Riga of noble and wealthy parentage in 1766 and was therefore only a few years younger than Tilly. Her father had brought her to Paris when she was nine and introduced her to that advanced philosophical French society, to which he was himself attracted, dominated by Helvétius, Diderot, d'Alembert, and Grimm, in which marriage was regarded mainly as a convention enabling women to follow their own inclinations in freedom. She was only fourteen when she was married to Baron Krüdener, then twenty-six and possessed of great wealth as well as social consideration. The young Baroness is described as full of grace and wit, with a most charming and expressive though not regularly beautiful face, light brown hair that fell in ringlets on her shoulders, and calm blue eyes that seemed, said Diderot, to penetrate alike the past and the future. Krüdener took her to Venice, where for some years he was Russian Minister, and two children were born of a union which proved passionate and stormy and led in 1791 to a separation, though later when Tilly knew them the two had come together again. After returning for some years to her birthplace, the Baroness came in 1798 to Paris, formed an attachment with a young Frenchman, and with him travelled widely through Europe. A little later she published a novel in letters entitled *Valérie*, the hero of which was tormented by a fatal passion for a married woman and kills himself to escape his torments; it was founded on the real history and fate of a secretary of legation of Krüdener's who was hopelessly in love with the Baroness. The novel so well describes her own character and feelings, and was written with so much sentimental energy that it met with wide success which the Baroness proceeded to Dresden and Teplitz to enjoy, as well as to Berlin, where she was introduced to the Queen and admitted to the royal circle.

It was at this time that Tilly learnt to know her, and they entered into correspondence, partly through her daughter Sophie as intermediary. Thus on the 3d July, 1801, she wrote him a long letter from Teplitz, in French of curious orthography, which characteristically brings out her traits as an early representative of the Romantic School.

> By some negligence of Sophie's [she wrote], who insisted on taking charge of one of my letters to you and adding a few words

of her own, you have not received that letter, and I can see from here, Monsieur le Comte, all the accusations which I seem to deserve. So I hasten to tell you that you are quite wrong if you dare to doubt the affectionate feelings and regards of a family which is much devoted to you. The young ladies have received your flowers and adorned themselves with them; they like to owe new graces to you, for they well remember what charm you found in them. Sophie especially would thank you for all those charming bouquets and garlands. But her stupidity has discouraged her and as time passes I charge myself with all the thanks and excuses, and the indulgence I promise in your name. I am forbidden to write, for my nerves are no joke. Will you not come and try the waters here, for they are excellent? You will find beautiful trees and beautiful mountains of which one never grows tired. You will also find the Prince de Ligne who is always cheerful — and a troop of German lords with ridiculous retinues which are always amusing. And besides I hope you will find me and be very pleased to see me, always good and frank for my friends, always in open warfare against the Germans with thirty-two heraldic quarters, always loving what is lovable, true, and simple — demanding nothing, living in my own way, on a very convenient reputation for eccentricity, because then one can do what one likes and imitate the mountain scenery which by its diversity never wearies. But I must no longer try your patience. Keep well and sometimes think of those who are devoted to you and anxious to see you again.

Tilly accepted the Baroness's invitation, and went to Teplitz, where he found the Prince de Ligne, with whom he was already acquainted, though now their relations became closer. With the Baroness the relationship seems to have been one of congenial friendship. Some passages may be extracted from the account he wrote of her:

The Baroness Krüdener was a woman of great intelligence, of many kinds and varieties of intelligence; above all, she was what, had she been a man, would have been called an original. She was in love with solitude, with unrestrained freedom, with the *dolce far niente*. She was, however, fond of the fine arts, and of French literature, and wrote a novel in that language; this described a relationship which had been dear to herself, and though it revealed no strong imaginative power, had a tender melancholic strain. The style shows too much mannerism and research, but where it escapes these dangers it has freshness, maturity, and novelty. It is a wonderful book for a foreigner to write.

A harmony of tastes and opinions often brings us nearer than the inclination of the heart. It is thus simple and easy to explain that Madame de Krüdener showed some interest in me. She should not perhaps have entered with so much warmth into my quarrel with M. de Rivarol which was then occupying Berlin and dividing the public into two parties. But it is not for me to complain of the warmth with which she conducted my defence. M. de Krüdener no doubt thought she showed unnecessary zeal.

Then Tilly proceeds to describe the difficulties and embarrassments that entered into his relations with Krüdener towards the end of the Ambassador's life, and 'the reserve which a man who lives in an attic feels that he must maintain with a man who still possesses a cook and a house.' We are not told the cause of Krüdener's suspicions which— remembering what Tilly himself says of the Baron's shrewdness and judgment — possibly had more foundation than Tilly was willing to admit. And there was no further record of the Baroness found among his papers.

He could scarcely have forseen the new and prominent part she was later to play in the world's affairs. She underwent a religious conversion, admitted, even publicly, the errors of her life, preached among the populace in a spirit midway between that of an English Methodist like Whitefield and a French mystic like Madame Guyon, and was thought by many to possess divine illumination. She foretold the approaching end of the world in a period of great political agitation when the fate of nations was in the balance, for a time found a disciple in the Tsar Alexander himself, and became a figure of European significance. She went from country to country, lavishing her wealth on the poor, and preaching doctrines which were regarded as so revolutionary that she was constantly being expelled by the authorities; finally she died in the Crimea, after her influence had waned, in 1824. She had wandered far out of the orbit of Tilly.

VI

It is at this point in Tilly's career — that is to say during the first four years of his stay in Germany — that we begin to approach the author of these *Mémoires* directly, for here I am able to bring forward an entirely new contribution to the life of Tilly, the first, indeed, to be revealed from a source independent of his early editors. It thus possesses a definite value apart from its intrinsic interest, for it enables us to find indisputable proof of the statements made about Tilly by the original German editor who claimed to have access to his private papers, and it confirms the impressions which we gain from the *Mémoires*.

Tilly tells us, in the course of his narrative, of his duel in 1788 with his 'cousin,' Charles, Comte de Tilly-Blaru, a branch of the Tilly family which had become separate several centuries previously, and was disinclined to accept the claim of our Tilly's branch to belong to the family. Tilly fought the duel in support of this claim, which Tilly-Blaru thereupon agreed to recognise, and a permanent friendship was established, though the cousinship seems to be much more emphasised in the correspondence between them by our Tilly than by Tilly-Blaru. This gentleman, however, who was some ten years older, had much in common with the author of the *Mémoires*, although he has left no record of himself in history. He was an ardent Royalist and fought for Louis XVI; at the same time he occupied himself with *belles-lettres*, and was in correspondence with the Prince de Ligne and other distinguished persons. He found opportunity to return to Paris after the Revolution, but he remained an object of suspicion under every change of government and was watched by the police as a suspect, being once or twice ordered to leave Paris, though he seems to have disobeyed these orders. In consequence a Tilly-Blaru *dossier* was constituted at the Paris Prefecture of Police, and this, being increased by the seizure of his letters and papers, at last included many hundred documents of the most various kinds.

I came on the track of this *dossier* through a reference in the *Intermédiaire des Chercheurs et des Curieux* for 29th February, 1904, which stated that letters from Alexandre de Tilly were here to be found. It is a little troublesome to obtain access to the archives of the Paris Prefecture of Police, but this was achieved, and with the skilful and scholarly aid of the Russian historian, M. Brian-Chaninov, who lives in Paris, I obtained all the information I desired concerning the letters of Alexandre de Tilly to Charles de Tilly-Blaru, twenty-three in number, dating from 1800 to 1803, and written sometimes from Leipzig, sometimes from Berlin, and once from Hamburg whither, it seems, Tilly sometimes had to go to claim money sent from England, probably his American annuity. The letters are all in a friendly and even affectionate tone, although they are usually in response to incessant demands for favours — money, introductions to high personages able to confer situations, etc. For though our Tilly was still in exile, he was now in a superior position and able to exert influence. But incidentally we gain a number of little glimpses into Tilly's situation, tastes, and opinions, and from time to time, also, we find him playing his favourite part of mentor and moralist, though here addressing a man considerably older than himself and at least as well qualified to play the same part. In 1800, Tilly is at Leipzig and writing with reference to a lady who is 'the most intimate friend of the Duke of Weimar,' but that is as near as Tilly ever brings us to Goethe. A little later he is in Berlin, ill, and regrets he cannot approach a great personage as requested. In July of the same year Tilly writes from Hamburg and fulminates against Bonaparte: 'What do you think of Bonaparte, sitting republicanly on the most ancient throne in Europe and creating Kings!' Two months later, from Leipzig, he regrets he cannot respond to the request for a loan: 'At the moment I am in difficulties; I give you my word of honour.' A week afterwards he is discussing the possibilities of returning to France: 'God knows what I shall do, and if I can make up my mind to see once more my Lares.' And later in the same letter: 'Thank you again for all the sentiments you express, and also for all the compliments you pay to my Muse which, however, no

longer has any voice.' In the same month he writes to ask
news of Charles, and is pleased to hear of an improvement in
his situation. He goes on to speak of old age and of the necessity for moderation in all things: 'Here in Berlin there are
many pleasures; I follow them in moderation, and the tem-
perance prescribed to me in part by my ruined health and in
part by the experience of a very full life and that involuntary
regret that always pursues me, far from our country, that I
may perhaps never see again but shall ever bear in memory.'
Then follow letters mainly concerned with Charles's military
career and his requests for intervention in his favour. In a
letter of February, 1801, he seizes on a remark of Charles,
that he was a friend more than a relation, and observes:
'That expression proves to me that you believe yourself
convinced that I do not belong to the same house as you.'
Several letters of little interest follow, one discussing the
recent death of the Tsar Paul and the policy of his successor
in regard to the Order of Malta and the Grand Priory of
Russia. In August he writes of Bonaparte and considers that
Charles exaggerates his qualities. Later in his letters, as
in the *Mémoires*, he becomes more enthusiastic about Bonaparte. In September he writes from Leipzig: 'I confess I have
never advised you to return to France.' He proceeds to tell
of his own position: 'I live in ease, which, however, is far
from being a fortune, with the calm of a happy insolence
which never forsakes me on necessary occasions, though in
the ordinary course of life I am apt to be melancholy. The
fact is that, worn out by everything, I no longer attach importance to anything, am surprised at nothing, and flattered
by nothing, but also allow myself to be subjugated by nothing.
The little Hollenshausen girl grants me her amiability on
credit, and a fine dance at little price. All that has cost me
three louis for fruits and hot water.' In the same letter
he says: 'My health, far from being good, has sent me to
these Neudorff Waters, where the stay and the journey have
still further impaired my fortune.' So he can send nothing
to Charles. In November he writes a friendly letter from
Berlin, and next day he is writing again, this time about

politics, with a growing admiration for Bonaparte. Then there is a year's interval, and, meanwhile, Charles, who had apparently been previously at Weimar, has now returned to France, no doubt as a result of that amnesty to the *émigrés* which specifically excepted Tilly. But the return to Paris meant no peace for Tilly-Blaru; his trouble with the government and the Prefect of Police began almost at once, as his *dossier* shows, and increased as the years passed. In September, 1802, Alexandre writes to ask news of Paris: 'If you wish to give me a real pleasure, you will write me a long letter, with a lively and unprejudiced picture of Paris, of France and of her rulers, a picture of her government, her amusements, her troubles, and her dangers.' In another letter of the same month he says: 'My health is rather better, but I am worn out by rheumatism, the result of my travels and indefinite journeys.' Towards the end of the year he writes appreciatively of Charles's gift for verse (of which we know nothing), but adds: 'While I am on this subject, I will add something I have on my mind: Never write verses except for your mistress or your pocketbook!'

It will be seen that these letters have a real bearing on the life and career of Tilly — all the more valuable because they are the first letters of his to be brought to light — and it is instructive to find that they confirm the reliability of the German editor who — while, he tells us, careful to avoid quoting anything which would compromise Tilly-Blaru — gives numerous brief summaries of the very letters to which we now have our Tilly's replies. They are written from Weimar, Karlsruhe, etc., and most of the favours he begged seem to have come to nothing, but, the German editor states, Tilly — whose extravagance was often associated with an impulse of generosity — had 'in the noblest way' come to Tilly-Blaru's aid in October, 1800.

It may be worth while to quote at length a few of the letters in the Paris *dossier*. Thus Tilly writes from Leipzig on the 6th May, 1801:

I have received your kind and polite assurances contained in your letter, my dear Count, with regard to the interest which you take in what you call my successes: I received them with pleasure because I believe them, just as I believe in the loyalty of your disposition, and attach to your friendship a price which few people nowadays place on that noble sentiment.

Even my enemies could scarcely grieve over the favours which fortune has occasionally shown me, since for long past, partly through troubles, partly through pleasures, the whole course of a full and tumultuous life, my sensibilities are not easily moved. Believe me, I do not pretend to be a beau; in the autumn of my life, far from my country and my friends, I am not easily seducible, or easily impressed.

However that may be, I am sensitive to the voice of your complaints, and the picture of your griefs causes me real grief. If we were talking together I could give you counsel by which I think you might profit; and if I can obtain the necessary light on the project, when I return from Hamburg (in a month's time), were we to pass twenty-four hours together, I could give you an idea which you might be able to utilise. I am only proposing what I think I could carry out, as I will try to prove to you.

As regards the present, and my financial means, they are at zero, and I am going to Hamburg in a few days simply to negotiate a draft on England.

Do not write until you hear from me, my dear Count. In the wandering life I am obliged to lead there can be no fixity in our correspondence. And fixity is the only foundation of prosperity and fortune.

In order to reply to your question as to the stability of Baron de Krüdener's position in Berlin, it is only necessary to refer to the gazette which tells us that the Emperor Alexander has confirmed him in his post. And I may add that he has himself told me so; he is a fine man, a man of wit and intelligence, and with vast and varied knowledge. He is cold, buried in affairs, and, I can see, has not much time to cultivate private correspondence.

Farewell, my dear Count. I did not wish to leave without talking to you, and repeating the assurance of the real and tender friendship which devotes to you for life your relative, the Count Alexandre de Tilly.

From Berlin, six months later, on the 11th November, Tilly writes:

It is long since I had a letter from you, my dear Count, and I have felt regret that our correspondence was languishing: I hope that you received my last letter; it was about the time of my arrival here, rather more than a month ago.

I found an occasion to speak to Baron Krüdener about your plan. 'I am not allowed' he said, 'to send to my Court one who is not actually attached to the Emperor's service; but if the Count de T. B. has business calling him to Russia, and his only object is to save the expenses of the journey he may come here, and at the first departure of a special messenger he will have a place and travel at no expense.' I made clear that that was not the reason of your request, and he repeated the expression of his regret. I am sorry I can report nothing more satisfactory.

I am receiving letters from Paris. The sceptre of B. C. [the Consul Bonaparte] is revealing itself and gradually lengthening, and it will soon reach the proportions of the late Charlemagne. His court is being organised, and his throne will soon be surrounded by *almost* the same courtiers as that of Louis XVI. But the companions of his victories and his fortune will be in the first rank, and the renegades from the monarchy will scarcely be seated even in the second row. Courage and genius seldom reward servitude in the heart and timid inconstancy in the mind. For my own part, I surprise myself thinking that this extraordinary man deserves to restore the heritage of Saint Louis, and such a thought is the false pretext of some and the holy excuse of others.

The good and celebrated Madame Le Brun is here; I offered her a bachelor dinner a few days ago, and was sufficiently inspired by her talent and fine productions to enter the field I had long abandoned by addressing to her the following verses, which I send you because they have had much success here.[1] Farewell, my dear Count; happy are they who do nothing but make verses, who have a soul fresh enough to live in the fields with books and pencils! Far from the quarrels of jealousy, the blows of self-love, the machinations of envy and the fever of great social reunions, with a shepherd's pouch and a flute, shepherd's crook in hand, to wander on the banks of streams, in the green country! One needs also a shepherdess, not to mention a stomach. It is mine that throws me into this melancholy diatribe; I am having a serious

---

[1] He quotes them, but they also appeared later in the second edition of his *Oeuvres Mêlées*: Madame Le Brun is here compared with Titian, Correggio, Domenichino, and Albano.

quarrel with it, and would feel consoled by your affection. Assure him of it who is for you eternally a tender and sincere friend.

In January, 1803, Tilly addressed from Berlin the last of his letters contained in this *dossier*:

A long time has elapsed since you heard of me, my dear Count, and in spite of your wish for an answer you do not consider it my fault.

I had wished to tell you something satisfactory. I have neglected nothing to obtain that result, but unfortunately without success. First of all, I had to keep my room for a long time on account of the severe weather, though, even during my illness, I never lost sight of your interests. I will tell you my efforts and the issue:

To begin with your last proposition: it is only three days since I last made my court to the person whose support you desire; I had the honour of dining with him; he spoke to me with kindness, but it is not in the midst of 23 to 30 people that one can fittingly ask a favour. But I have cornered the person who has most influence over him and best knows what he feels and what he wishes. I will faithfully repeat the reply of this person, who deserves consideration and is essentially good. 'You will not obtain, my dear Count (I was told) what you ask; any intervention of this kind is forbidden by *preliminary arrangements*, one could not ask, even for one's brother, the smallest favour, and if one were to solicit at Petersburg it would be without success. The Imperial Court grants nothing, and nothing is asked of it. You would expose yourself, it was added, to a definite refusal, which would do you neither harm nor good, but would be painful to the giver.'

To pass to the second hope which I had cherished for you and have not yet abandoned, though its realisation requires infinite care: I wrote to the one at Munich on whom I counted for the service I wished to render you, and the reply arrived only 24 hours ago. It appears that the Elector, so complacent a few years ago in this matter, has today many more officers than he needs, and rejects nearly every request; but that with very distinguished and long service, and a good military reputation, there is little doubt that an advantageous position could be obtained by an applicant *on the spot*, especially in circumstances that I could arrange for you. But you may imagine that I am far from proposing that you should follow so uncertain a chance. Please believe that even to obtain this poor response I have made use of an influential person and exercised much care. I am sorry that my genuine friendship for you has not produced better results.

To console you, I would add that there is reason to wager that a time will come (though I must not speak more definitely) when I may be able to explore the ground, and that you may assure yourself that we shall have a better chance of success. If I were with you, I could speak more clearly. The trouble is that you are — and rightly — in a hurry.

I have myself endless troubles. My ex-father-in-law is returning to America without completing the affairs that I have a right to see terminated.[1] I no longer have any hope save in the Vicomte de Noailles, who is, in a way, the guarantor of my arrangements. M. de Poix wrote to me last week that he is expected every day in Paris. Who has not his troubles?

I would like, my dear friend, to offer you consolation more prompt and direct; I repeat that, if the horizon should clear, I will hasten to prepare the way for the reflections of its light to reach you. I embrace you tenderly.

That is the latest letter of Tilly's preserved in the Tilly-Blaru *dossier*, and the whole series shows him in no unamiable light, for it would scarcely seem that there were any motives of self-interest in his long maintained anxiety to serve the interests of his unfortunate 'cousin.' We have here, not only a glimpse into Tilly's life and mind during his stay in Germany but we are brought to the threshold of the *Mémoires*, for it was in this same year, 1803, that he began, at the age of thirty-nine, to write them.

VII

We do not clearly know how it was that at this moment Tilly conceived and carried out — we may be sure that in his impulsive temperament the execution swiftly followed the plan — the one great achievement which has made him memorable. Various circumstances conspired to render the moment favourable. In spite of his endless troubles, this was

[1] As we know, Bingham died at Bath without returning to America; the 'affairs' left uncompleted were probably the composition of the annuity.

really a period of relative peace and comfort in Tilly's restless
and agitated life, and he was enjoying an unusual degree of
consideration. At the same time his days of adventure seemed
over; he felt, as we have seen, that old age was approaching
and that he must study to live moderately on account of his
'ruined health'; his health never seems indeed to have been
robust, and, at all events after he left France, we frequently
hear of indisposition or illness. It may have been this need
of a quieter life that turned his thoughts afresh to literature,
and we know that at this time he was preparing for publication in Berlin the new and much enlarged edition of his *Oeuvres
Mêlées*. The feeling that the best part of his life was over —
a feeling that might well be increased by the news that he had
been definitely forbidden to return to France — may have
furnished the impulse to set down in writing the record of that
past life. The stimulating influence of the Baroness Krüdener,
with her literary and romantic tastes, possibly contributed
to that impulse. And the Prince de Ligne, whom he had now
been associating with — the dedicatee of the *Mémoires* —
was perhaps the most decisive influence of all.

Tilly on his best side could not fail to be attracted to the
Prince de Ligne. He was in personal touch with him, as was
Tilly-Blaru, especially from about 1803 to 1806. They all
belonged to the same aristocratic eighteenth-century world,
the mingled world of courts and camps and salons and *belles-
lettres*, the world of which the Prince de Ligne was the last
and the supreme representative. The Revolution had driven
him from France and his beautiful Belgian home; he was now
living in Vienna and holding high position in the Imperial
army. He and Tilly frequently exchanged letters. The
editor of the first German edition of the *Mémoires*, who claims
to have had the Prince's letters to Tilly in his hands, states
that they are full of attachment, interest, and genuine friendship for Tilly, the highest admiration for his intellectual
gifts, and a just judgment of his qualities and defects of
heart and conduct, while he gives much excellent and sorely
needed advice even on the most practical matters, such as
money, literary style, and publishers, recommending to him

a Dresden publisher with whom he had himself recently made an advantageous contract to issue a few volumes of what he modestly terms his 'bêtises.' Tilly showed his *Mémoires* to the Prince and the latter writes: 'I am most charmed to read you, and seem to hear you speaking, though I would much prefer to hear you, for then I could at the same time see you. Sad that we are separated by a sea of sand! If you ever feel inclined to emerge from it, come here to expiate in our salutary waters *delicta juventutis*, and reward me for the feelings you have inspired.' Nowadays, he adds with reference to the devastation of Europe by war as well as to his own love of gardening, for he had possessed in his Belgian home at Beloeil the most famous of European gardens, 'one scarcely knows where to go when one only desires to see *ruins* in an English garden.' The Prince de Ligne was not only the last great figure of cosmopolitan significance in pre-revolutionary Europe, but a most copious and facile writer, setting down fully for his own pleasure his impressions of himself and of the people he knew. 'The careless and negligent ease of a man of quality,' which Scott attributed to Byron's writings, was possessed in the highest degree by the Prince de Ligne. His style is the *ne plus ultra* of the aristocratic man of the world's familiar conversational tone, quiet, spontaneous, intimate but with a reserve of dignity, completely careless, abounding in flashes of insight but always tending to be too thin and too diffuse. It is hard to believe that it is written and not spoken. It is at the farthest remove from the more formal though also intimate style exemplified by, for instance, the Duc de Lauzun, another great and famous noble of the same period, in his Memoirs. Lauzun has an interesting narrative to tell, but there is always something bald, formal, and pedestrian in his telling of it. He is an inexpert writer and by accident rather than by design he often omits necessary links in the narrative and desirable traits of description. So that we are always less interested than we feel we ought to be.

I would place Tilly as an annalist of manners between Lauzun and the Prince de Ligne, and above both. He has been regarded as personally an inferior sort of Lauzun, and in the life of courts and the adventures of gallantry he had much the same kind of story to tell. But Tilly's sense of life was more vivid, his interests were far wider, and notwithstanding all the defects of his own character, he possessed a singular penetration into events and people, with a genuine literary power to transform his observations into words. Thus, while his standpoint was like Lauzun's, he had much in common with the Prince de Ligne, though with the literary good sense to restrain the aristocratic conversational tone within more reasonable bounds, even while remaining careless and disorderly in style. His manner of writing is sometimes peculiar, at moments a little difficult to follow; when riding his own high horse he is occasionally boring. But we are always carried on; we read to the end, even though the narrative is so broken. For Tilly is always vividly alive; at every moment he is all there, even though at the next moment his mood may have completely changed. And because he is so alive he draws us even though he may often at the same moment repel. It is by this balance of qualities — of historical significance with intimate personal interest, of familiar conversational tone with literary instinct — that Tilly's *Mémoires*, when we look back on them today, possess unique value as a typical picture of the form and spirit of the late French eighteenth century in its aristocratic aspects. We can well understand the Prince de Ligne's admiration. 'Since the Memoirs of Louis XIV's time, and a few of those of the Regent's,' he wrote to Tilly, 'the writers of such things have been mere Versailles chair-porters. It is time that the last beautiful days of France should be in good hands.' 'Your collection,' he is said to have written to Tilly again, 'which I have read with so much pleasure, is made for all ages and all countries, and is in no need of indulgence.'

One would have thought that a work of which the most competent of judges could speak so highly, and as we now see so justly, would have been dealt with in the most reverently careful spirit. Nothing of the kind! It has been left to chance. Tilly wished it to be published after his death with, to prevent offence, the omission of names. On his rather mysterious departure from Berlin in 1807, never to return, leaving his private papers and letters behind him, we do not know in whose hands he placed the Memoirs. For nine years after his death they remained unknown, and his own name was almost forgotten. Then in 1825 to 1827, in Berlin, appeared a German translation in three volumes entitled *Memoiren des Grafen Alexander von T*****. The name of the translator and editor was not given and we do not know how he acquired the manuscript nor how he obtained access to the other papers of Tilly. I have not seen this edition, but it was republished in Berlin in 1909, in Iwan Bloch's *Sexualpsychologische Bibliothek*, as *Die Memoiren des Grafen von Tilly*, edited by Fedor von Zobeltitz, who states in his Preface that the original translator and editor was Friedrich Wilhelm Bruckbräu a Bavarian upper official in the Customs who found time from his duties to write a number of books, verses, rather loose novels, historical or semi-historical books, and (three years after his edition of Tilly) prose translations of Milton's *Paradise Lost* and *Paradise Regained*. In spite of these curiously miscellaneous literary avocations, he was certainly a good and careful translator, with a wide knowledge of French literature and history, which enabled him to supply valuable notes to his translation, while he was careful to give the words of the original in a footnote when he could find no adequate German equivalent. His Supplement, moreover, describing the miscellaneous Tilly papers which came into his hands, is of great value for the light it throws on Tilly's life after 1792 when his own narrative ends. Our chief complaint against Bruckbräu remains that he fails to explain how these papers, as well as the manuscript of the *Mémoires*, came into his hands; and though he lived far into the nineteenth century he never seems to have made good this failure.

In 1828 appeared in Paris, also in three volumes, *Mémoires du Comte Alexandre de Tilly pour servir à l'Histoire des Moeurs de la Fin du 18ᵉ Siècle*, again without any editor's name. This is the standard edition of the *Mémoires*, extremely difficult to find nowadays, and it has served as the main foundation for the

English translation. Here for the first time Tilly's name appears as author of the *Mémoires*, but the French editor's name still remains unknown. Like the German editor, he is competent and well acquainted with the history of Tilly's time, though he is able to add little of importance concerning Tilly himself, and what he does add is not always quite accurate. I conclude he was the publisher of the work and must be added to the number of scholarly French publishers at that time, for, as a supplement to one chapter, he gives a *Note de l'Editeur* (about Mirabeau), stating it is too long for a footnote. There is no publisher's name on the title-page. We must assume that he had Tilly's original manuscript before him, though, like Bruckbräu, he gives no information as to how he obtained it. There can be no doubt that he also had the German edition, and his Supplement concerning Tilly's later life follows, and somewhat amplifies, that of Bruckbräu. But the anonymous French editor is not so reliable and conscientious as the German. The German, though a translator, is clearly anxious to present as nearly as possible what Tilly wrote. The Frenchman has no such anxiety; he wants to improve on Tilly. He adds alluring chapter headings; he omits sentences, even long passages, which do not seem to him interesting; he condenses, sometimes to the point of unintelligibility, and he has a trick of substituting more abstract expressions for Tilly's concrete statements. ('I gave money to the woman who lighted me out' was, in the German version, and surely in Tilly's words, 'I placed money on the candlestick,' and for the description of a lady of title as 'red as a fighting cock and sour as an unripe crab-apple,' we have in the French merely a reference to an acid disposition.) More important are the constant transpositions. Tilly frequently digresses; he will break off an exciting love-adventure in the middle if a point of literary discussion suddenly occurs to him. These transpositions are so extensive and so numerous that it is not easy to compare the French edition with the German. They certainly, on the whole, render the narrative more easy to follow, and the order of the French version has in the English translation been accepted, though many of the omitted passages have been restored, as well as vigorous phrases which were toned down by the French editor.

Then there was a long period of silence. *The Mémoires de Tilly* could not fail to find readers in France, but Stendhal, who in so many other respects then stood alone, seems to have stood alone in his recognition of the significance of Tilly's *Mémoires*, and even he, as we have seen, proposed to abbreviate the work. So far as Tilly was known during the rest of the nineteenth century, it was owing to the inclusion of an abridged version of the *Mémoires* under the title of *Souvenirs* in Volume xxv (the first half of the volume being taken from Lauzun's Memoirs) of Barrière's *Bibliothèque des Mémoires* dealing with French history during the eighteenth century. Barrière attached no great value to 'this awkward imitator of Lauzun,' as he called him, and we cannot find fault with his moral disapprobation; he grudgingly admits the interest of the *Mémoires* and remarks that while they contain 'some very strange episodes,' these were not disputed when the book appeared so soon after Tilly's time, and we may therefore accept them as furnishing the completion of an exact history of the manners of that age.

With the twentieth century a new era opened for Tilly's reputation. When his *Mémoires* first appeared the previous century was sinking from sight under a cloud of obloquy; it was not even seen that the nineteenth century itself, however magnificent, had its roots deep down in the eighteenth. With the coming of the twentieth century the reputation of the eighteenth began to grow clearer and some of its representative figures no longer seemed to demand anything more than moral indignation. If a halo could be reverently placed on the head of Casanova, hitherto objurgated when he was not shunned altogether, there was no longer any reason to despise Tilly. If the last century could accept the dictum that a man was a man 'for a' that,' the new century could take the further step of seeing that — in spite of all the still officially entrenched censors — a writer is a writer 'for a' that.'

So in 1909 Iwan Bloch was able to place a reprint in two

volumes of the earliest edition of Tilly's *Mémoires* at the head of his *Sexualpsychologische Bibliothek*, and the editor, Fedor von Zobeltitz, felt justified in making the highest claims for this 'Song of Songs of Epicurean pessimism,' as he calls it. He places it confidently above Casanova's Memoirs: 'Tilly's Memoirs undoubtedly excel the Italian's in intimate charm and psychological delicacy, in stylistic form and artistic grace, above all in philosophic insight.' That is, indeed, an extravagant and unjustifiable estimate; at none of these points is Tilly's superiority so clearly assured. Zobeltitz is on safer ground when he goes on to assert the value of Tilly's *Mémoires* as a picture of the Court life, and especially the love-life, of a man of the world of that age, of the rich and precious material here brought forward for the study of the women of the French Rococo, of their special psychic constitution, of the spiritual refinements of the art of love in an age which largely devoted its literature to that matter, to the genial wantonness of society at that time, its extraordinary contrasts, its tumultuous progress to inevitable disaster. While Zobeltitz in the main follows the first German editor he states that he has made some corrections and enlargements by comparison with the French edition, but, unfortunately, after the usual custom of Tilly's editors hitherto, he neglects to give any precise indication of these changes.

In France the first French edition of 1828 has lately (1929) been reprinted in two pleasant volumes by the house of Jonquières, with an Introduction and Notes by M. Melchior-Bonnet, and some good portrait illustrations. But on examination this edition proves to be highly unsatisfactory. The text swarms with printers' errors and unintended omissions. The editor's notes are competent and his Introduction most agreeably written, but he has added scarcely anything to the statements about Tilly brought forward by the earlier editors a century before; he has made no fresh examination of the text of the *Mémoires* and he seems to know nothing of the first German edition, and of the problems raised by its variations, or of the doubts thrown on the authenticity of the whole work. The Index also looks most elaborate and useful, but on examination its page-references are found in the large majority completely inaccurate.

It is fully time that a competent French scholar arose to make a scientific study of this whole subject and to produce a really adequate edition of a work which increases in interest as the period it so vividly brings before us recedes into the past. In Belgium M. Félicien Leuridant has brought a scholarly equipment to bear on the life and work of the Prince de Ligne, and Tilly is now beginning to be regarded as worthy of similar careful study. In his *Livres du Second Rayon* (1926), a good modern critic, Emile Henriot, well brings out the significance of Tilly, viewed from the standpoint of today, as coming not far short of the highest rank among annalists of the late eighteenth century, while some of the episodes of the *Mémoires*, as Henriot well insists, are little masterpieces which might have been written by Diderot.

The final edition of Tilly's *Mémoires* must be undertaken by a French scholar working, so far as may be possible, on the original French sources. Yet a considerable claim may be made for the English edition. Not only is new material here brought forward to elucidate Tilly's history, but here, for the first time, an attempt, however imperfect, has been made to compare the two original texts of the *Mémoires*, thus utilising in some degree that primary German version, which, though a translation, is evidently often nearer in substance to what Tilly wrote than the existing French text. Finally the English version reproduces with felicity not only the substance but the spirit and tone of the *Mémoires*: the aristocratic nonchalance of the young nobleman who had been Marie Antoinette's page, his gay impertinence, the amusing solemnity of his misplaced moralisings, his literary affectations, and the peculiar savour of his individual style, with its mingling of wayward impetuosity, stilted awkwardness, occasional seeming obscurity yet really vivid and penetrating vitality, and, piercing through, that sense of an approaching end perhaps more tragic than the guillotine which, unlike so many of his friends and associates, Tilly had escaped.

VIII

That end was now approaching and there is little more to tell. Somewhere about 1803, Tilly had had a love-experience — his last so far as we know — which had a fatal termination and deeply affected him. He refers to it with genuine feeling in the *Mémoires*, which he was just then beginning to write. In this episode there seems to have been passion on both sides, but for some reason the lady committed suicide by drowning herself in the Spree. Bruckbräu describes how he found among Tilly's papers a small black-sealed packet with the inscription in the Count's hand: 'A memorial of great misfortune, of regret, and of eternal sorrow.' It contained, together with various love-favours and souvenirs, a farewell letter from Tilly's Clara — as she seems to have been named — written shortly before her death:

> I assure you, my dear Tilly, that it is from my own impulse, and by my own free will, that I write this to you; I swear that all that I have ever said to my beloved Tilly is true; I swear in God's name that I have never, never deceived him, never betrayed him even in thought. If this oath is false, may God punish me in the most terrible way, by death, or the misfortunes of my worshipped Tilly. May He thrust me away without mercy when I appear before his judgment seat, and may the happiness of my children, now and there, be destroyed. These oaths also cover the future, should I ever deceive you without having first acknowledged that I no longer love you. Then, Tilly, you may make this paper known and shame me before the whole world.

She goes on to reaffirm this oath even more emphatically, signing it 'C. E. P****, *née* St.,' from Berlin, 13th December, 1803. She adds a postscript: 'That story about the hair is also a puzzle to me; but all these sacred oaths are a warrant that it concerns no man that I know.'

It seems to be suggested by this letter that the tragedy was caused by Tilly's unreasonable jealousy. That was evidently Bruckbräu's opinion, for he adds that thenceforward 'a revenging Nemesis' pursued Tilly. The consideration with which he had been received and accepted in the highest circles of Berlin began to melt away, his credit lessened, his debts increased, creditors grew pressing. With Tilly's reckless and extravagant disposition, the composition with Bingham's heirs, which brought him a large lump sum and deprived him of an income, was more a misfortune than a blessing. During 1806 he was making fruitless efforts to return to France. In the spring of 1807 — at some date after 30th April — he left Berlin, abruptly breaking off all relations with that city, and his German editor loses track of him and can tell us no more.

At an earlier point in his Supplement, however, Bruckbräu had mentioned that Tilly was attempting through friends at the Court of the Netherlands to obtain permission from the King to enter the country hoping to settle in Brussels or The Hague, and thence perhaps be able to reach Paris; and he adds that Tilly is amongst a list of persons receiving the Cross of the Legion of Honour. But the abandonment in Berlin, not only of the *Mémoires* but of his personal papers, letters, and treasured souvenirs, seems to indicate that his disappearance was sudden and due to an apprehension of immediate danger. The explanation may lie in the great victory of Jena which at that time had placed Berlin at Napoleon's mercy. Tilly's Prussian protectors fled and he was not himself acceptable to Napoleon. He may well have considered that the safest course lay in flight. The battle was fought in October, 1806, peace between France and Prussia not being arranged until July, 1807, some months after Tilly's disappearance from Berlin. It remains mysterious why Tilly never reclaimed these treasures during the remaining nine years of his life, nor why he never made, so far as we know, any arrangements for their disposal; Bruckbräu, who only brought forward his translation after a further delay of nine years, gives no hint that he was acting in accordance with instructions received from Tilly. Possibly, during the later years of his life, Tilly had no means of returning to Berlin and no friend there to whom he could entrust a confidential mission.

From other sources it would appear that Tilly went to Brussels and only returned to France in 1814 after the Bourbon restoration, again, a little later, going back to Brussels, so that the longing for Paris which had gnawed at his heart for so many years proved but an empty satisfaction when at last he attained it.

It is not hard to understand. Tilly always belonged to the *ancien régime*. He remained at heart, what he still remains in popular repute — so far as he has any repute at all — the former page of Marie Antoinette. But the world he belonged to had vanished. It must have seemed an unrecognisable Paris, a melancholy Versailles, to which he at last came back. The people he had known had nothing in common with the new business-like bourgeois generation industriously building up another and tamer society on the ground swept by the storms of the Revolution and disciplined by the rod of Napoleon.

Moreover, Tilly arrived home late. Most of the *émigrés* had already returned, and made some kind of adaptation to the new order. Tilly was not only late, he was inadaptable. Even at the Court of Marie Antoinette his conduct had called for royal reproof. The 'mad' Tilly of twenty years earlier was now quite hopeless, and there was no longer the old spirit of indulgence for madcap aristocrats, even among their own peers. The worn-out man of the world who continued to lead a life of pleasure and to show a lordly indifference to debts could only be viewed with contempt in the practical nineteenth century. It seems clear that during his last years Tilly had become disreputable. The friends of old days were either dead or they stood carefully aloof. The Prince de Ligne, who had been so amiable, and so full of admiration for the *Mémoires* of which he had accepted the Dedication, was indeed still alive, though still in Austria. He wrote the most interesting reminiscences we possess of Casanova. But M. Félicien Leuridant, who is the chief authority on the Prince and is now engaged in editing his *Correspondence*, tells me that he has nowhere found there even the mention of Tilly. And when by his own hand Tilly died, no one cared enough to record any impressions of a man who now seems to us, with all his weaknesses and defects, so significant a figure.

Thus it is that a cloud still hangs over Tilly's end. We

merely hear a varying rumour. It is even a rumour which only reached vaguely, his first editor, and the writer of the early and rather inaccurate notice of Tilly, before the publication of the *Mémoires*, in the *Biographie Universelle*, who gives a wrong date to the suicide which Stendhal also misdated. We find it altered by the French editor of 1828, who is likely to have received a correct report, and until new documents are discovered, it is his version of Tilly's end, since no friend came forward to contradict it, which we must accept:

He was seen in Paris in 1815, after the second Restoration; but he soon returned to Brussels. There, overcome by misery, he once more took to gambling, and that fatal passion having led him to commit an action which was intolerable to his naturally proud and independent spirit, he died by his own hand on the 26th December, 1816, thus throwing off the burden of a life he could no longer support without dishonour. Such was the deplorable end of a man who by his intellectual and other brilliant qualities would have continued to be the ornament of society if he had known how to master his passions and to avoid the paths of vice.

VICTOR HUGO

A HUNDRED years and more have passed since Victor
Hugo was born. It is but a small space of time when
we consider the number of centuries through which the rich
and various literature of France has flourished. Yet it has
been long enough for this one man, by his own power or as
the representative of the spirit of his time, to arouse the most
conflicting judgments, concerning his achievement. He has
been the supreme poet of France, the adored idol of the men of
letters of his day. His fame has filled France and the world.
At his funeral ten thousand troops were needed to hold back
the multitudes who crowded around. He is still almost the
most popular author in France among the crowd, though for
men of letters he has become 'that abominable rhetorician
whom we have made our national glory.' 'Of all the nine-
teenth-century poets,' declares a fairly typical French author
of today, 'it is Victor Hugo of whom we least think.' Or, if
they think of him, it is with crushing condescension: 'We
must not despise Hugo,' says a critic of today. 'True, he had
no human vocal cords, but consider how superbly he played
on the saxophone!' 'Hugo intoxicated my childhood,' a distinguished writer of today, Abel Bonnard, said to an inter-
viewer. 'When I first read the *Orientales* I seemed to open a
casket full of jewels and every sort of marvellous fruit.' But
today, no longer a child, Bonnard's favourite poet is at the
opposite pole, Paul Valéry.

This conflict of opinion may, or may not, show the futility
of literary criticism. There is, however, another way of
estimating the calibre of a literary personality. We may, for
the moment, ignore his literary output altogether, in order to
consider the man himself who was the primary source and
origin of that output. What the man was, that, we may be

VICTOR HUGO

sure, his work, with blurred outline or added glamour, also was. There are few writers whose personality is so obscured in their work as Victor Hugo; he himself wrote, as early as 1835 (in the preface to *Chants du Crépuscule*), and with more truth than an author always shows in self-analysis, that his personality was only faintly indicated in his books. In gauging that personality, therefore, we only follow the indication he has himself given when we throw aside his books altogether.

In estimating Victor Hugo's achievement and place in the world, we have, indeed, to follow the same course as has been found desirable in the case of an even greater figure of the nineteenth century, Napoleon. We no longer study Napoleon by accepting the opinion of friends or foes, or by gazing at the map of Europe he changed so profoundly; we gather together all the illuminating facts we can find concerning the man, and so at last are learning to reach a reliable estimate of Napoleon's place in the world. And if we are to reach a reliable estimate of Hugo's achievement in literature, we must likewise cast aside the empty and conflicting discussions of critics, and even for a time close his books, to come to the man himself.

The initial fact, that Hugo's work furnishes singularly little self-revelation of the more obvious kind, is itself, one may note, significant. A profound and almost instinctive secretiveness is everywhere characteristic of the peasant, and nowhere more so than in France, a fact which Balzac in *Les Paysans* and Zola in *La Terre* have powerfully illustrated. It is not difficult to account for. Sincerity marks the aristocrat, and secretiveness marks the plebeian, simply because force — which need not be secretive — is the traditional weapon of the lord, and cunning — which must be secretive — is the traditional weapon of the peasant. Now Hugo largely belonged to a race of peasants. He could never have performed his special work in the world if underneath all other elements in his nature there had not been ineradicably rooted the solid and primitive qualities of the French peasant. His grandfather sprang from people who, so far as is known, all cultivated the soil in Lorraine;[1] this grandfather, however, took an upward step in the world, he became a joiner, and married a governess, and that he eminently represented the solid virtues of the French artisan we may judge by the fact that he was 'couronné' on the Fête des Epoux in 1797; all his relations at this time, one notes, were becoming artisans, craftsmen, small tradesmen — bakers, hairdressers, bootmakers, and so on. With Victor's mother, indeed, we are not among the peasants, but among the middle class, but the stolid bourgeois virtues of these pious Breton maternal ancestors could only serve to emphasise the paternal traditions.

We see at once the primary source of that plebeian self-concealment which is so marked in Victor Hugo's work. To call it insincerity is to misunderstand it, for so fundamental an instinct is a massive and solid quality, more allied to a virtue than a vice, and without it we should certainly have had no Victor Hugo. Whenever we look below the surface of his work or his life we come on this solid rock of ancestral peasant and bourgeois nature. When M. Claretie called on Hugo in his old age, he saw the *Petit Journal* lying about, and tells us that he was surprised, adding — sagaciously enough — that he could not tell why. The great poet might speak after the manner of Homer and Aeschylus for others' pleasure; for his own pleasure he shared with the humblest of his fellow-countrymen a devotion to the *Petit Journal*. In the same manner this enthusiastic patriot cautiously invested the large fortune he ultimately amassed in foreign stocks. For Victor Hugo poetry was not an everlasting self-revelation. This descendant of cultivators and craftsmen cultivated the great craft of poetry with the same honest, stolid, fundamentally impersonal spirit in which his forefathers had followed the crafts of carpentering, bootmaking, or hairdressing. Circumstances sometimes forced him to take up what on the surface seemed a revolutionary attitude, but his ideals always remained the same. Even in 1831, when still a young man,

[1] In 1631, Claude Hugo, a grave-digger, who belonged to Damvillier, the home of the poet's family, and was probably an ancestor, is referred to in official documents as 'the Dutchman,' and this perhaps indicates the origin of the family.

he wrote that his poems were 'those of an honest, simple, serious man, who desires liberty, betterment, and progress, but at the same time with all due precautions and due moderation'; and one seems to be listening to the immortal Homais. He displayed the moderation and domesticity of the bourgeois Frenchman even in his liaisons; he was not faithful to his wife, but his devotion (which was really a marriage) to his mistress endured for half a century, though he never allowed that devotion to disturb his friendly relations with his legal wife. A genuinely romantic and aristocratic figure, such a person as Villiers de l'Isle Adam, inheriting the blood and the temper of Crusaders and Templars, could never have played Victor Hugo's part in the world of literature or have wielded his influence. For that was needed all the shrewd caution, the stolid impenetrability, of the essential peasant.

So far, I have said nothing of Hugo's father. It is obvious that when we have made clear in the poet's character the part played by the peasant, the craftsman, the bourgeois, we have only begun the analysis of his personality; we have only set down one of its elements, fundamental as that element may be. Hugo's father brings us to a further stage in his making. In this generation the Hugos seem to have abandoned their village associations, nearly all joined the army, and Joseph-Léopold-Sigisbert Hugo — his name alone indicates the swelling ambitions of the Hugo family, for he was the son of simple Joseph Hugo — became a soldier at the age of fourteen, on the eve of the epoch-marking year of 1789. He was sensitive to the influences of the eventful days in which his youth was passed; at one time he changed his name Léopold to Brutus. He became a lieutenant-general under Napoleon, when generals were springing up from the ranks in all directions, and having written *Mémoires*, in which his own virtues were emphasised, not without some violence to the actual facts, he died at the age of fifty-five. He was a good soldier, with some fine feats of arms to his credit, and fairly won his title of Comte.[1] If not a man of genius, he was clearly an ex-

---

[1] His life has been well written, in the light of freshly discovered documents, by Louis Barthou, *Le Général Hugo*. The poet had impudently asserted that his

ceptional man; with him the Hugo family stepped outside
the narrow parochial limit of those homely vocations and virtues in which its energies had during long ages been slowly
built up, and took part in the life of the world, realising the
existence of ideas. Thus he leads us directly up to his famous son.

It was during the Brutus episode, when he was stationed
at Nantes, that Captain Hugo met his future wife. Her name
was Sophie Trébuchet, and she was the daughter of a Breton
ship's captain, who appears to have gained wealth in the
slave trade, and was able to marry the daughter of an important local personage, a judge; they were Royalist people
and religious, some of the feminine members of the family
being Ursuline nuns. Sophie, though not religious, shared
the Royalist feelings of the family, but does not seem to have
regarded this as any obstacle to her marriage with 'Brutus.'
She is described as *petite* and *mignonne*, with hands and feet
like a child's; she had no pleasure in Nature nor any inquisitive desire for knowledge; yet was not without a certain individuality of her own, as shown not only by her freethinking
tendencies, but also the rather active part she played — on
both sides, it seems — when the Terror came to Nantes. She
later acquired a certain virile authority as a result of her
husband's long absences, which eventually culminated in a
separation. Through her also came an element of nervous
weakness which was by no means without significance. She
is, again, significant from the fact of the difference of race;
the more or less Germanic people of Lorraine and the more or
less Celtic people of Brittany represent the two most opposed
elements in the population of France. Victor Hugo's mother
brought to him the racial instincts of a poetry-loving and sea-
faring people, which may well have served to give direction
to the more active and fundamental elements furnished on
the paternal side.

father was of aristocratic family and had inherited from the Middle Ages (and
passed on to himself) the title of Baron. As a matter of fact he had simply been
made a Spanish Count by Joseph Bonaparte, King of Spain, and he never used
this foreign title officially, as it was not recognised in France; in any case it was
personal and not hereditary, though his son liked to describe himself as Vicomte
and to assume that he was of ancient lineage.

Moreover, the mere fact of marked difference of race, of a kind of cross-breeding, is itself a source of the variational tendency, and cannot be passed over as a probable factor in the constitution of Victor Hugo's genius.

There was, further, an absence of congeniality, as well as a difference of race. It is not quite·clear why Sophie, who was two years older, was attracted to Captain Hugo, the *sans-culotte* Brutus, who was in social origin her inferior, and at the time living with a mistress who figured as his wife. Possibly the absence of a dowry made her more complacent. In any case, not long after the marriage she met a man, Colonel La Hoirie, who was not only at least her social equal, but shared her Royalist sympathies, and was in every way so congenial that she became his devoted mistress, aided him, and sheltered him when necessary, until for his part in a conspiracy he was court-martialled and shot. This domestic infelicity, the frequent absences from her husband, and the final separation, had their repercussion on the child Victor, who at one time was much devoted to his mother.[1]

Two children, both sons, were the first born of this marriage, and both were large and robust infants. Seventeen months after the birth of the second, on the 26th of February, 1802, at Besançon, was born the third child, Victor. At this time his father was twenty-nine years of age and his mother thirty-one. For some time before the birth of the child, his mother, we are told, was *singulièrement gênée*. Unlike his brothers, however, he was a small, delicate, puny child, and the doctor declared that he would never live; small and ugly, his mother described him, 'no longer than a knife.' This weakly tendency persisted through childhood, and was certainly an influence of the first order in turning the young Hugo's activities into imaginative rather than active channels. He was melancholy and languid, frequently found in corners crying, for no cause in particular. At school he was the smallest child there, and special care had to be taken of him; he was under the care of the schoolmaster's daughter,

[1] The life of Sophie Hugo, with the poet's misstatements corrected, has been written by Louis Guimbaud, *La Mère de Victor Hugo*, 1930.

and almost his earliest recollections were of being taken in the morning into her bedroom and placed on the bed, where he watched her put on her stockings and dress. This physical delicacy and languor was, however, only one aspect, though a significant aspect, of the silent, gentle, fragile child. On the other side he was reflective and intelligent, learning to read even before he was taught. His brain had gained through the inhibited activities of his body.

Yet it was Hugo's good fortune not to be permanently hampered by delicate health either of mind or body. On the contrary, when his early feebleness had performed its function by leading the shy and sensitive child into the path from which henceforth he could not retreat, eventually he acquired, and retained to the end, all the coarse robust vigour of his peasant ancestors. Rodin remarked that there was much of the Hercules about Hugo (Sainte-Beuve said Cyclops), and in every description of his physical appearance and habits the strength and vigour of his constitution and appetites are emphasised. Germain Sée, who examined him at the age of seventy-six, declared that he had the body and organs of a man of forty. Until his last illness, when over eighty years of age, his health was always perfect. He slept like a child; he rose at six and was able to begin work at once, and it was no fatigue to him to write standing. He 'ate like an ogre,' enormously, miscellaneously, and rapidly, yet he never suffered from indigestion; his teeth could crush peach-stones. His beard, said the barber, was three times tougher than anyone else's and destroyed all the razors. His eyesight was so keen that he could recognise friends from the top of Notre Dame and that he never required glasses even in old age. His good-humour, it need scarcely be added, was perfect, his gaiety colossal, and of Rabelaisian character. Dalou, the eminent sculptor, possessed a carefully made cast of Hugo's face, head, and neck, taken shortly after death, which has been studied by a well-known anatomist, Papillault. Hugo was of full medium height, solid and thickset, but so far as can be judged from the measurements of the head, his brain was by no means above the average in size; his face was unduly large and broad as compared to the head, and gave an impression of developed animality; there were many signs of lack of facial symmetry, and the lips and the nose were thick, the eyes small. The poet was evidently conscious of the animality of his face, and in his portraits was always accustomed to bend his head forward so that the forehead caught the light and looked very large, although in reality its dimensions were by no means remarkable.

At an early age Victor Hugo began to see the world. He was scarcely six weeks old when he was taken by his parents to Corsica, Elba, and the neighbouring places; a few years later he was in Rome. A more important journey, indeed one of the decisive influences of his life, took place at the age of nine, when he accompanied his mother to Bayonne (here for the first time falling in love with a girl a little older than himself), and on to Spain. He was now just old enough to obtain impressions which, while not precise or accurate, were yet strong to affect his childish imagination, and acted as a powerful ferment, developing with energy of their own and emerging later to give life to his work. Thirty years afterwards, when he saw once more the Spanish places he had known as a child, they seemed to him dull and commonplace.

Spain is not dull or commonplace even today, but Victor Hugo's experience was none the less significant. It was no accident that Spain, rather than France or Italy, should thus have exerted a definite influence on his childish imagination and on the shape and colour of his future work. Spain is the one European land in which, until yesterday, the spirit of medievalism still lived, in which the atmosphere of old romance might still be breathed. Whether or not, as Mabilleau, one of his most penetrating critics, believes, Hugo had a real affinity with the Spanish temperament, it was certainly the direct influence of Spain on this sensitive, moping child which moulded the romantic and medieval movement in which Victor Hugo was the great protagonist.

The world of books soon began to open before the eyes of the eager receptive child. His rather Voltairian mother was not among those who think that books are dangerous, so the young Hugo was free to devour Rousseau, Voltaire, Diderot, *Faublas*, Restif de la Bretonne, and at the same time that irresistible pushing ambition, which in other forms had stirred in the immediately preceding generations of the Hugo family, began to make itself felt. It was characteristic that Chateaubriand, with his rhetoric, his sentiment, and his exotic colour, was young Hugo's first idol. 'I will be Chateaubriand or nothing,' he said at fourteen, and at the same time gave himself up, as far as possible, to writing prose and verse stories, translations, odes, tragedies, epistles, elegies, idylls, epigrams. An accident which confined him to bed for some time served to foster the fever of poetic production, and at fifteen he was a laureate of the Academy.

These early years, from the age of puberty, when he first began to write, to the completion of adolescence, were of immense and permanent importance in their effects on Hugo's art. This child of a race of peasants and craftsmen, of laborious and impersonal workers, though circumstances had led him into a totally different field, still remained a craftsman, laborious and impersonal. The whole of his early work is in substance purely conventional; it reveals no personal emotion; even in his enthusiasm for Chateaubriand he feels nothing of the breath of personal emotion in Chateaubriand; it is the exotic *décor* which attracts him. Young Hugo had instinctively made poetry his craft, and he treated it strictly in the spirit of the craftsman. Even when, after adolescence was over — and possibly under the stress of his mother's death and of his love for Adèle Foucher, who afterwards became his wife — his work really grew more emotional, this element always remained a little bald, a little thin. Behind the magnificent products of his poetic craft, the artist himself was content to possess a simple and modest stock of personal emotions, which the humblest of his fellow-citizens could share, and to which, as in *L'Art d'être Grandpère*, he has sometimes given exquisite expression. In 1930 Victor Hugo was still, after Zola, according to the booksellers' sales, the most popular author in France. Nothing, it has been said, is more fascinating to the mob than truisms uttered in the language of the gods.

We have to bear this in mind when we are tempted to charge Victor Hugo with insincerity. There have been some poets who have concentrated in their works the quintessence of their personal emotion, who have cast the most intimate experiences of their lives to be crushed as grapes in the wine-press of their art. With such poets Victor Hugo had no sort of affinity. It was not merely that he was far too shrewd, at bottom far too stolidly self-possessed, to be anxious to subject himself to any such violently disintegrating process. Not only was the impulse absent, but, it may be said, the necessity for it was also absent. Hugo had acquired so splendid a mastery of his craft that a very small modicum of personal emotion was amply sufficient to set the craftsman at work, and the emotion was transformed into objective art, vast and exuberant, long before it could attain — even if it had the capacity to attain — any high or specialised degree of intensity. Thus it was that while at the periphery of his immense activities he fascinated his admirers by a splendour of utterance that seemed to them to rival Homer and Aeschylus, in the centre the possessor of this *âme aux mille voix* was seated in Olympian calm with *Le Petit Journal* beside him. To describe such an attitude as insincere is to misunderstand it altogether.

On the intellectual side Hugo was equally limited and equally sincere. He accepted with great seriousness his own mission as a thinker and a moralist, and with an easy and offhand manner he flung about jargon terms from metaphysics or science and the names of remote historical personages. But at every step he plunges into absurdity, and an intelligent schoolgirl can see through his science and his erudition. Probably no poet of equal eminence has ever been so far below the higher level of his day in intellectual equipment. Renouvier, the distinguished philosopher, who was an enthusiastic admirer, at the same time devotes a chapter of his book on *Victor Hugo le Poète* to his 'Ignorance et Absurdité.' It is to the limited character of his emotions and his small intellectual equipment — combined with immense self-confidence — that we must attribute that *sentiment de faux* which Renouvier, again, notes as marked in Hugo's work. The soul at the centre of the great

embodied voice is quite inadequate to the vast constructions
it called into being, so that in all his work there is a certain
unreality, a certain lack of correspondence to the actual facts.
Yet these limitations were the necessary conditions for the
attainment of the special qualities which Hugo's work displayed in so high a degree. The primitive and myth-making
character of his imagination, the tendency to regard meta-
phors as real, and to accept them as the basis of his mental
constructions and doctrines, these tendencies, which Hugo
shared with the savage, are dependent on rudimentary emotions and a high degree of ignorance regarding the precise relationship of things. Hugo's defects were an essential element
of his qualities.

Every poet must have a mind that is predominantly audi-
tive. Hugo was certainly indifferent to music, and could not
sing a single note correctly. But an ear for music and an ear
for verse are two quite distinct forms of the auditory mind,
and the absence of one in no degree interferes with a high development of the other. Every poet must have developed an
ear, whatever sense may come next in development. To be a
poet at all argues a predominant delight in verbal melody,
and this Hugo possessed in the highest degree; he was very
careful of sonority and consonance, of syllabic harmonies, a
master of rhythm and cadence; for notwithstanding that at
certain points he broke through the rules of classic verse he
retained a horror of licence and was a strict upholder of law
in verse as in grammar.

In Hugo's case vision was unquestionably the sense that
came second, so closely following his ear in importance that
some have declared it must be put first. That can scarcely be
admitted, but certainly vision modified and moulded the whole
of Hugo's art. In his early formative years this vision was
purely verbal and without any basis in actual observation,
but during 1826 and 1827, after his tour in Switzerland, and
when he had acquired the habit of going out in the evenings
to study the sunset effects around Paris, the vision quality of
his imagination began to become precise and self-conscious,
and it developed with increasing years. It was during 1826

and 1827 that he wrote the *Orientales*, and the idea of that volume came to him while gazing at a sunset.[1]

If we examine the special qualities of Hugo's vision we find that it is above all a sensibility to light and shade, whiteness and blackness, the opposition of sunshine and obscurity. It would seem that even the love of antithesis, which became eventually a marked and one might almost say morbid defect of his style, was really based on this sensory delight in the opposition of light and shade. There are no signs of any delicate sensibility to colour in his work. Although colour is by no means absent, it is not finely seen colour, but usually a delight in violent contrast, and really, one may say, a special case of antithetic opposition of light and shade. The extreme predominance of white and black in Hugo's work is brought out by an analysis of his colour words. I have made such an analysis in the case of a large number of poems from the *Orientales*, the *Feuilles d'Automne*, and the *Chants du Crépuscule*. In the order of decreasing frequency the chief colour words are found to be white (including 'argent') and black, both equally frequent to within one unit; then follow red (including a considerable variety of words), golden (and yellow), blue (and azure), green, finally at some distance purple, and lastly grey. So numerous are those colour words which really indicate the simple opposition of light and shade, that if we separate out the white, black, and golden groups we find that they considerably outnumber all the other colour words taken together. Such a result throws a significant light on Hugo's psychology, and is absolutely different from that which we obtain when examining the work of the French poets who have followed Hugo. In Baudelaire, indeed, there is the same abnormal predominance of black, but in his case it is an index of temperament and less a seen black than a felt darkness, nor is it accompanied by any antithetic whiteness, while in Verlaine,

[1] When later an exile in Guernsey (as I was told when there by an old inhabitant then occupying the Hugo country house) the poet would drive over the island in a pony carriage and at some attractive spot would say to his driver,' Stop now, Peter,' and begin writing.

the poet of *nuance*, both blackness and whiteness sink into the background and grey becomes predominant.

Hugo's tendency always to visualise his imagery precisely is easy to trace through his work. As one of his critics has pointed out, even sounds are sometimes in his hands described in terms of vision. The intense reality of vision, of the image, of the metaphor, lay at the foundation of all his mental constructions. For Hugo, as for the savage, the image evoked the idea, and was regarded as a sufficiently adequate cause of the idea. That, indeed, is the source of the primitive power and charm of Hugo's work. But it could only have arisen in a mind that was at once very acutely affected by vision and very deficient in the reserve of intellectual ideas which in the ordinary educated civilised man controls and modifies the impressions furnished by sight.

An indication of Hugo's tendency to regard the world as a vision is seen in his spontaneous and late-evolved love of sketching, which we may study in the fascinating and instructive Victor Hugo Museum in the Place des Vosges. Those amateurish drawings which he loved to execute — mostly fantastic old-world dreams of architecture — clearly illustrate his delight in white and black, in light and shade, and may well be described by two of the favourite adjectives which he often abused, '*sombre*' and '*mystérieux*.' Even more significantly, perhaps, we find his visual sense illustrated by his handwriting. Nearly all his manuscripts are in the Bibliothèque Nationale, and they have been carefully studied by Paul and Victor Glachant. At first his handwriting was slight and small, seeming to betray a sort of physical timidity, but during the course of his career it swells and rises, becomes almost hieratic; to a writer of the first order, he seems to say to himself, must belong writing of the first order, and to do justice to this writing he latterly always used thick blue paper of vast folio form.

This gradual expansion of Hugo's handwriting is significant, not only of the gradual expansion of his own self-conscious personality, but, as one may indeed say, of the whole history of the Hugo family. Beginning very humbly as peasant cultivators of the soil, the Hugos went on rising and swelling in their upward ambition through three generations to reach the inevitable goal of insanity. We seem to trace already a faint indication of coming mental disequilibrium in the pompous baptismal name of Hugo's father (such names, it is well recognised, being very significant of a tendency to mental unbalance), and the career of 'Brutus' Hugo himself, also, shows such traces. Actual insanity seems first to appear, however, in Victor Hugo's own generation; his elder brother, Eugène (the brother nearest in age to himself), who was warmly attached to him, sharing all his tastes but not his genius, went mad on the very day of Victor's wedding, and remained in an asylum until his death some years later. Victor Hugo's own daughter, Adèle, was ultimately consigned to an asylum, and others of his children showed signs of mental anomaly.

Victor Hugo himself remained unquestionably sane. But he showed a degree of megalomania going far beyond the bounds of vanity. There was no claim for himself that he was not willing to make or to allow others to make. He regarded himself as the real successor of Napoleon (did he know that his early idol Chateaubriand had also regarded his own career as parallel to Napoleon's?) and, coming to believe in metempsychosis, he held that in previous incarnations he had been numerous heroes of mankind.[1] He seems to have found a safe anchorage, partly in the immense and acquired pride of his own apostolic mission, and partly in the congenital inheritance of peasant stolidity which was so liberally bestowed on him. He was completely unable to tolerate or to comprehend any rival figure greater than himself. Sir Sidney Colvin tells that once in Hugo's presence the conversation turned on Goethe. Hugo rose from his seat, placed his hand on his heart, and said: 'For my part, I look upon Goethe as Joan of Arc would have looked on Messalina.' His pride was indeed abnormal and almost morbid. It forced him to be at every moment, as he himself put it, 'a torch'

[1] Details of Victor Hugo's arrogant megalomania are given by Cabanès in an essay on 'Victor Hugo Megalomane et Spirite,' *Grands Névropathes*, tome 11.

to humanity, to deny himself the pleasures of friendship since friendship could only be between equals, to become impervious to ridicule, to develop into a great master of *réclame*. But at the same time, it may well be, this pride served to give him serenity and equipoise, to balance the tendencies of his poetic temperament and so to guard him from that fate to which his brother succumbed. A curious proof of the beneficial effect which his pride had is still extant; like many others who live on the borderland of the abnormal, Hugo could write verse automatically, as he discovered at the age of fifty, by means of a spirit-rapping table. To some unbalanced persons this discovery would have been fatal; not so to Hugo; he never even published any of these verses, partly, as he said, out of respect for the mystery — for he took the phenomenon very seriously, being always credulous where the supernatural was concerned — but partly, as he added, out of respect for his own inspiration.[1] Not only by his pride was he safeguarded, but also, it must be repeated, by that quality of peasant and bourgeois temperament which on both sides he had inherited in such peculiarly large measure. He was always, one might almost say by hereditary instinct, a great craftsman rather than a great artist. 'If we take a higher idea of the artist and his art,' remarked Hugo's enthusiastic admirer, Renouvier, 'than that which attaches to skill of execution, we must say that Victor Hugo is not a pure artist.' The philosopher's observation is true and subtle. We have but to think of the English lyric poet who was drowned in the Mediterranean within a few days of the publication of the *Odes et Ballades* to realise the difference between the artist whose whole personality was fused into his work and the craftsman who, indeed, developed his craft on a scale of magnificence never before achieved in poetry, but yet remained a craftsman, strictly outside the high-strung rhetoric he produced, finding his

[1] Through his table-rappings he believed himself to be in touch with Jesus, Moses, and other great figures of the past, and he had a new theory of reincarnation. Professor Denis Saurat, who is an expert in this matter, considers that Hugo was influenced by the Cabala (*La Religion de Hugo*, and *A History of Religions*) and that he may be regarded as 'a mythological genius of the first order.'

own personal comfort and support in *Le Petit Journal*. Sainte-Beuve, the great critic who was Hugo's contemporary and friend, accepted in public the public estimate of Hugo whom at the outset he genuinely admired. But he wrote at last in his private *Cahiers*: 'Is Hugo of the true great family of poets? Yes, and no.' And an even more penetrating critic than Sainte-Beuve, Baudelaire, remarks in a letter that Victor Hugo is a proof that a man may possess a special genius and yet be a fool.

At the outset I alluded to Napoleon. When we survey the career of Victor Hugo and the various factors which, as we have seen, went to the constitution of his genius, it is difficult not to be reminded (as he was himself) of Napoleon's career and genius. Both were great conquerors in the fields they had chosen for the display of their energies, both made a great stir in the world, and both, having left their own mark on it, saw their direct influence speedily swept away by their successors. They were alike in being men of low birth who fought their own way unaided; they were alike in their pride and ambition, the overweening sense of their own mission; they were both great forces rather than lovable personalities; they both lived on the verge of insanity, and perhaps both were saved from falling over it by that element of common-place vulgarity which both alike possessed.

An examination of Victor Hugo, such as that here attempted, thus reveals an underlying affinity between the two greatest craftsmen, the two supreme figures, of modern France. But when we think of the supreme figures of European literature, as of Dante and Shakespeare and Goethe, we are left with a profound dissatisfaction. We can sympathise with the sentiment of André Gide, who is above all a penetrating critic. When asked who is the greatest French poet, it is reported, he replied: 'Victor Hugo — *malheureusement*.'

12

THE APPROACH TO VERLAINE

I

IF I were asked to say which among the persons of distinction I had met seemed to possess most of the primitive emotional temperament of genius I should reply: 'Verlaine.' There were some, possibly less rare, whose genius was primarily the expression of intellectual constitution; others in whom intellect seemed to conceal a highly organised emotional temperament; still others, more numerous, in whom an element of genius seemed inhibited or disguised by some foreign mask, a man of the world's, a moralist's, and so forth. But here genius was reduced to its simplest terms, naked and helpless to all the winds of heaven, all compact of imagination, the prey of its impulses. In all genius there is the child; Verlaine was a child on a colossal scale, with the child's eternal freshness, and the full endowment of those less innocent instincts which in some degree psychologists find to mark even the healthy normal child. A mass of living sensitive protoplasm open to every influence of Nature and humanity, he remained unconfined by that tough restricting hide which gives to most of us adults a certain stolid rigidity, a factitious indifference to our environment. He stood at the furthest remove from the pachyderms, more like those primitive molluscous creatures of the sea which zoologists have shown to be permeated all through by as yet undifferentiated and unprotected senses.

Thus Verlaine represents genius naked and helpless. All, or nearly all, the eminent French men of letters who were his contemporaries had some breastplate against the arrows of the world. Victor Hugo was saved, amply saved, by his colossal superiority-complex; Edmond de Goncourt held fast by the tastes and traditions, as well as the income, of a gentleman; Zola always cultivated the industrious habits of an accomplished journalist; Huysmans devoted much of the energy of his acute intellect to warding off the shocks of the world against his exquisitely sensitive organism; Rimbaud possessed a tough virile energy which more than balanced his genius; Villiers de l'Isle Adam, alone almost as helpless as Verlaine, was in some degree protected by his ability to merge the practical world in an ideal world. Verlaine, throughout, was by native constitution the world's absolute victim.

It sometimes seems strange that the same age and the same city should have seen Victor Hugo and Verlaine, Hugo before whom his contemporaries shuddered with awe as, from behind a big mask, he shouted through his magnificent trumpet, and Verlaine whose finest songs seemed simply a succession of broken musical sighs which few noticed. But we remember that in poetry, as in religion, the divine voice is ever a still small voice. There are poets who reach fame in a day, and die in a blaze of journalistic eulogy. One need not protest; it is well to be tender to a merry life that one knows will be short. Verlaine was a pilgrim throughout life, the victim of all the Fates, severely shunned by all respectable people, libelled as the head of a ridiculous coterie, twice the inmate of a prison, many times the inmate of hospitals; and at the end his death was recorded in a few lines of small type, among which one caught the words 'dissipation,' 'vice,' 'crime,' 'failure.' Certainly from the ephemeral point of view Verlaine was a failure. Even for his publisher, who would, however, occasionally advance a few francs, he can have been little better than a failure, and when I have seen the poet draw a two-franc piece from his purse, it seemed with a proud and joyful surprise. For the Church he was a failure, a depressing failure, for when he seemed at the point of becoming a miracle of saving grace he relapsed. From whatever worldly or social viewpoint we look at his life, it was a failure. But from another standpoint it has been possible to consider

him as the greatest success in French literature on his own
lines since Villon.[1]

Porché, the latest and best documented biographer of
Verlaine, presents a picture of the man which is often repulsive and has called forth the protests, justified or unjustified,
of many admirers. Thibaudet, perhaps the sanest and most
competent critic of French literature today, is among those
who have thus protested.[2] He considers that Porché has
attached undue weight to the recollections of Verlaine's
widow, Madame Delporte, whose very real grievances stood
in the way of an impartial picture with recognition of the
man's better sides. He was not, Thibaudet adds, so depraved
a drinker as Musset, and he fully expiated his faults. It was
his evil star (more accurately his bad reputation) that for an
incident which only called for a small fine he suffered a long
term of imprisonment. 'I have loved a hog,' Rimbaud said
in his *Saison en Enfer*, probably referring to Verlaine.[3] But
in one of his letters he expresses the more Christian sentiment,
'everyone is a hog.' I would not say, Thibaudet remarks,
that everyone is a hog in the manner of Verlaine; 'there are
many roofs in the devil's pigstyes.'

Verlaine's periods of religous adoration and humility were
as spontaneous and genuine as his more vicious impulses. The

[1] Verlaine has, indeed, receded in the estimate of some critics. So it may be as
well to quote the recent remarks of the greatest living French writer, who is also
the exponent of advanced poetic technique. 'Towards 1875,' writes Paul Valéry
(*Nouvelle Revue Française*, January, 1935), 'we saw born the names of Verlaine,
of Mallarmé, of Rimbaud, those Three Kings, the Magi of modern poetics, bearers
of treasure so precious, of aromatics so rare, that all the time since passed has
not affected their brilliance or the promise of their extraordinary gifts.'

[2] A. Thibaudet, 'Le Poëte Assassiné,' *Nouvelles Littéraires*, 15th July, 1933. I may
add here that Porché's biography, while more nearly final, should be taken in
association with the earlier and more sympathetic biography by Lepelletier, who
had the advantage of knowing the poet personally from boyhood. For the English reader Harold Nicolson's book on Verlaine's life and work (1921) is still in
general satisfactory.

[3] Verlaine, on his side, wrote on his own copy against *Sagesse IV*: 'About Arthur
Rimbaud, Arras, Sept. or Oct. 1875,' adding, 'I see afterwards that this might
apply to [in English] "poor myself." ' But though in the mood of this poem he
calls Rimbaud 'poétastre,' there is no doubt that he admired Rimbaud's strange
genius.

priest who received Verlaine's last confession is still living, and it is reported that, when directly questioned about Verlaine, his only reply is: 'C'était un Chrétien, Monsieur,' though Lepelletier states that he was not a believer, and that *Sagesse* was the expression of a passing mood, even that associated with *Parallèlement*. 'On our side,' concludes Thibaudet, 'we may settle the matter, with Mallarmé in his *Divagations*, by saying: "He was a poet." And a fine English critic, with the facts of Verlaine's life before him, Earle Welby, asks: 'Where else shall we find so complete an illustration of the qualities, personal and literary, which go to the making of the purest poetry? We see here the most completely poetical life lived by any modern poet.' Madame de Noailles went further:

> *Es-tu toujours simple et divin,*
> *Ivre de ferveur et de vin,*
> *Bon Saint Verlaine?*

We may seek the reconciliation in the mystery of genius. I recall, as I often have in other connections, the insight contained in the sayings of James Hinton who had pondered much on its nature: 'Genius is a cross between animal and Man, the re-uniter of Man and Nature; its face tells the tale. How should genius be afraid of hell and devils, being one of them?'[1]

So that if we must needs have the courage to face the picture (such as Marcel Schwob described it to Jules Renard), in a sordid room in a dubious house, of a man lying clothed on the bed, dirty boots protruding from the sheets, a filthy metal chamber pot beside it (also, indeed, a Racine), marks of mud on his face, and only able to articulate monosyllables, we must also remember that this was the poet who wrote lines which spring spontaneously to the lips in our moments of ethereal aspiration or deepest tenderness. We may recollect how the dying Remy de Gourmont, who knew all there was to know about Verlaine, in his last failing letter to his dearly loved Amazon, recalled brokenly the words:

> '*Voici des fleurs... voici des fruits.*'

[1] James Hinton, *The Law-Breaker*, pp. 150–69.

II

When approaching Verlaine, we thus encounter aspects seemingly in conflict, each of which we have to come to terms with before we can see him truly. Even if they may not seem so disastrous as to his contemporaries, we must recognise them in order to comprehend his significance.

In the first place, we have to realise that here is not the kind of poet we have learnt to expect in France. He was not even a poet the French expected. It was easy for a Frenchman to recognise Hugo and Gautier, or even Musset, as earlier it had been easy to recognise Boileau and Corneille. Even the genius of Baudelaire had remained more in touch with those accepted masters than this rebel, who yet owed something of his first inspiration to Baudelaire and others. He broke the traditional moulds of verse, he violated conventional modes of sentiment. His forms of verse and his ways of feeling were alike new. Several critics and poets of distinction, indeed, spoke words of admiration. Only, however, in 1888 — about a year before I met him and when most of his best work had already appeared — was there any clear and decisive recognition of Verlaine's genius or any attempt to analyse it.[1] Even then it came not from any critic of acknowledged authority, but from one of the new men, Charles Morice, a critic of singular receptivity for new influences and able to enter into the spirit of Verlaine, though he was himself a child of Provence and Verlaine characteristically a Northerner.

Morice in this little book, *Paul Verlaine*, which appeared just after *Bonheur* and *Parallèlement* had come out together and is still well worth reading, spoke with assurance. By his sincere humanity, his perpetual communion with the essence of things, the endless subtlety of his simplicity, this poet, Morice asserted, for those who can receive such spiritual joy, is 'the revelation of a new beauty.' While pointing out

[1] But I should like to point out that a by no means negligible study of Verlaine appeared in July, 1884, in the *Revue Indépendante*, by Louis Desprez, who recognised here 'a master for a small group of people of distinguished intelligence.'

his relationship to Baudelaire, Morice rightly observes that Verlaine's attitude is altogether different, full of pity and astonishment and forgiveness, a sad pity without disgust, since everything human to him is sacred. So that Verlaine unites — and here, Morice declares, his modernity lies — the two inspirations of mysticism and sensualism. 'He erects a statue of the Madonna in Sodom.'

It was Morice who first emphasised the conflicting elements of character — often dwelt on since — so well expressed in Verlaine's extraordinary face. Never was a human face, he remarks, more violently expressive of irreconcilable enjoyments than in the contradictory formation of this strange head: 'the high and broad brows which serve as the dome of powerful jaws — the forehead of a dreamy cenobite and the jaws of a voracious barbarian — in a struggle left to chance, an irregular head, without grace and yet of almost terrifying beauty,' the head of an immortal child.

It is pleasant to me to pay a tribute to the insight of Charles Morice who thus clearly set forth a critical estimate which was a daring novelty at the time, though now we take it for granted; it was Morice who first clearly grasped the genius of Verlaine, and his analysis of it has never been excelled. For an Englishman, however, it was perhaps easier than for a Frenchman to recognise the genius of Verlaine. And that not only because in our own island we have had poetic manifestations of allied character; in Burns, for instance, alike in his genius and his personality, we have, less extravagantly presented, those two conflicting elements. More deeply, Verlaine had a real affinity to the genius of England not to be found in any other French poet of the same eminence. He sprang from a latitude and a climate akin to that of England; his family belonged to the Ardennes from among a Walloon population by race and migration in touch with Celtic England; in early adult life he had spent several years in England; he had enjoyed and absorbed some of the most typical English poets, and, indeed, from the first he had a closer affinity with the Lake poets than with any French school.

Verlaine's relations to England have been specially studied

by Jean-Aubrey on the basis of previously unpublished documents. He came to England seven or eight times, once for two years together, the first visit in 1872 and the last in 1893: 'that joyous old England — Bournemouth, Lymington, Brighton — peace, rest, benediction, the charming and terrible sojourn of my years of exuberance.' He was first driven to England by circumstances — the difficulty over returning to his bureau at the Hôtel de Ville after the part, though slight and merely passive, he had played in the Commune, and grief over the separation from his wife who had left him — though it seems probably the vigorous initiative of Rimbaud, who accompanied him, which first brought him across. Now, actually on the spot, he was able to develop his interest in the English language and literature. There is no doubt that his association with England left a deep mark on his work. It was, indeed, in England that (putting aside the eighteen months he later spent in prison at Mons) he produced his best and most mature work. He had previously written little but the *Fêtes Galantes*. Here he wrote most of the *Romances sans Paroles* and it was an English girl whom he addressed with:

> *Voici des fruits, des fleurs.*

During the early period, when still in London, he sometimes wrote at midnight at a bar he frequented at the corner of Old Compton Street and Greek Street, the only place in London, he said, where he could get a glass of excellent white wine for twopence. Lepelletier thought that it was in England that Verlaine acquired drinking habits; this is denied by Jean-Aubrey; the temptation certainly came earlier, though Rimbaud's society and the desire to drown his love for his wife may have fostered the habit. When in prison at Mons, after his first visit to London, Verlaine's occupation was still chiefly English literature, and he wrote (in English): 'Of course I am to live in London.'

For the most part Verlaine's life in England was simple, innocent, rural; he lived quietly in the most respectable company as a teacher of French and drawing, all his spare time spent in writing and with books, in enjoyment of the English landscape. His temperament was really fitted for happiness under such conditions — for he had a deep love for the earth and an innate taste for peasant simplicity — and he was able to say of the year he spent at the little Lincolnshire village of Stickney that it was an '*enchantement.*' He reached Stickney in 1875, to teach French and drawing at a school where he quickly became friends with the young schoolmaster William Andrewes and his wife, as well as with the vicar, Canon Coltman, a man of superior culture and intelligence, the friend and school-fellow of Tennyson, whose work he greatly admired and made known to Verlaine, who thus acquired the taste for Tennyson which he never lost. At Stickney, where the '*paysage exquis*' in spring much attracted him, Verlaine wrote many of the poems in *Sagesse*, and remained till the following year when he left to settle as a teacher in neighbouring Boston, the friendship with Andrewes still, however, continuing, and lasting till the schoolmaster's death many years later.

Verlaine's last visit to England was in 1893. He came then under very different circumstances, by invitation, a famous poet to meet friends and admirers. But he was still the same simple child, as glad to lead a simple life, as ready to enjoy simple things. It so happened that I was away from London and unable to meet him, but owing to my absence, by arrangement with Mr. Arthur Symons who had been influential in bringing him across, he occupied my rooms in the chambers I shared with Symons at Fountain Court in the Temple, and while there he wrote his oft-quoted little poem about that '*coin exquis.*'

We have to realise this element of homely and childlike simplicity, with its affinity to the more idyllic sides of English life, if we are to understand alike Verlaine's essential temperament and that cleavage from the more typical poets of France which was often so hard to understand. There was another misunderstanding of the opposite kind, which was still more puzzling: Verlaine was not only the poet of rustic simplicity, he was the poet of 'decadence.'

That assertion, so often made, found ready acceptance in many quarters. Its champion was Max Nordau, whose name is still remembered. Indeed, he has even become magnified into a medical expert, and is sometimes referred to as 'Dr. Nordau.' He was simply a clever German journalist in Paris, who had the journalist's flair to concoct into a popular shape the not very scientific doctrine of 'degeneration' then floating in the air, and applying it to contemporary men of letters and art. He felt himself qualified for the task, he declared, because he had followed Professor Benjamin Ball's classes at the Asylum of Sainte-Anne. It was pleasant and instructive to follow that amiable Professor through the grounds of Sainte-Anne — as I know by experience — but one would like to hear what Dr. Ball would have said, had he lived, to such an experience being regarded as an adequate preparation for the condemnation as 'degenerates' of some of the chief writers and artists of the day. I do not know, but I well recall the bland and disinterested air with which he would listen to the *sottises* of his patients. So it came about that Verlaine was for the English and American public 'a decadent of the first water,' which meant to the ordinary man not only a reference to a particular form of art — which Verlaine himself was willing to accept, though he denied that he was a 'symbolist' — but a 'degenerate,' and carried with it the tone of both artistic and moral reprobation. 'In this man we find united all the physical and intellectual signs of degeneration,' wrote Nordau, 'and to no other writer of my acquaintance' — but it has been denied that Nordau ever even saw Verlaine — 'apply so exactly, trait for trait, the descriptions that at the clinics are designated those of the degenerate.' Verlaine laughed with good humour over this violent attack which appeared not long before his death; he had grown accustomed to the extravagances of the journalists and cartoonists, and even if the fantastic account of his appearance were correct, he remarked, 'Saint Vincent de Paul looked like a criminal, and many a real criminal has the face of an angel.'

We frequently see Verlaine's face described, usually by

people who never met him, as 'hideous.' It may be possible to say the same of the traditional image of Socrates (whom Verlaine somewhat resembled), though its irregularity was interesting and redeemed by its expressiveness. His mother, whom he is said to have resembled in features, was good-looking. In later years Verlaine's features in real life, while far from regular or handsome, could not fairly be called hideous, nor — putting aside caricatures — do they so appear in his portraits. But there is no doubt that an inborn irregularity and disharmony of feature was present — evidently associated with defective heredity — and that this was pronounced in early life. Verlaine's first and most sympathetic biographer, Lepelletier, a friend and early school-fellow, states that in youth he showed 'grotesque ugliness,' and mentions that when he first brought the boy Verlaine to his own home, his mother remarked afterwards that he looked like 'an orang-utang escaped from the Zoo.'

It is thus that the approach to Verlaine has been rendered difficult. Even for some early admirers 'decadence' seemed 'really a new and beautiful and interesting disease,' while more robust English critics, brushing aside these fantasies, were content to regard Verlaine as 'one of the chiefs of the Fleshly school,' and even in the same breath — with equal incongruity and absurdity — 'the hierophant of the Art for Art dogma.' So hard has been the approach to Verlaine!

III

We approach more naturally if we consider the stock and the environment from which Verlaine sprang. In the streets of Liège, the capital of the Celtic Walloon country, I have sometimes noticed men whose brows and eyelids, though less faun-like, recalled those of the poet, and I have seen the name Verlaine over a shop-front. It was not, indeed, directly from the province of Liège that Verlaine's family came. There is a place called Verlaine in this neighbourhood, and in ancient days there were, it is said, de Verlaines of high lineage, heralds of arms of the State. Verlaine's father was born in Luxembourg, which was then French, and he was probably the first French Verlaine in the family; he married a girl from Arras in Picardy; their son Paul was born at Metz, where his father, who had become an officer in the engineers of the French army, was then in garrison.

Taken widely, we may say that, by ancestry, by parentage, by birth, and by environment, Verlaine belonged to a district which receives its tone and colour from the Ardennes. But if we know and can recognise the racial ancestry, until recently we knew little or nothing of the precise organic psychological equipment which Verlaine received at birth, and he himself, indeed, appears to have known scarcely more. We learn new and instructive facts from Porché, his latest and most copious biographer, even when we put aside the rather uncertain ancestor of noble race, Gilles de Verlaine, in the sixteenth century.

Captain Nicolas-Auguste Verlaine, the poet's father, was only seven when his own father died, leaving three children; the widow soon married again and the children were placed with their maternal grandparents, the Grandjeans, whose son, a colonel in the engineers, persuaded Nicolas-Auguste to follow the same career. The Grandjeans were an old-fashioned family of rigid piety, and the orphans heard nothing about their father; they only knew he had been a lawyer. But it is now known that this man, Henry-Joseph Verlaine, early destined for the Church, speedily went to the opposite extreme; an ardent revolutionary in 1789, when the cross was torn down in the village he was one of the few who applauded. He was of violent temper and was called to account for insults uttered when drunk about Napoleon; it was, indeed, on this occasion that he suddenly died. This hot-headed drunkard had some literary pretensions and belonged to a local literary Academy. Moreover, his father, Jean Verlaine, the poet's great-grandfather, was also a disturbing figure, irascible and quarrelsome, fined for blasphemous oaths, and apt to go to law with his relations, even his father. There were others of similar type in the family, quarrelsome and unstable, though they succeeded in allying themselves with highly respectable families such as the Grandjeans, who produced many canons and priests. But this ancestry is in the highest degree significant; it must never be forgotten when we approach Verlaine. He came of a family with an unsound strain deep engrained and he carried it on; his own son Georges became alcoholic, and died, it is reported, in delirium tremens. It may also be significant that the poet's mother had three miscarriages before her famous son was born, though we may think it eccentric that she preserved the three resulting foetuses in alcohol, three bottles on a shelf in the cupboard, which were finally smashed by her son Paul in a fit of drunken rage.

These facts of birth and origin are highly significant in our investigation of the approach to Verlaine. It seems worth while to note also, in passing, that they are instructive in their bearing on the always actual problem of heredity *versus* environment. Certainly heredity and environment can never fail to co-operate in the making of any human being as of every other living thing. But the proportion varies. In Verlaine's case, environment, it is clear, played an unusually small part. He was brought up in a respectable and well-to-do family; he was the cherished child of tender parents, and his affectionate cousin Elise took the place of a sister. Though rather more of a child in boyhood, Lepelletier tells us, than age warranted, he was not led astray by boy comrades; there were many of sober and serious character among them, and he, rather than they, furnished the bad example. Useless to search the social environment for the explanation of the Verlaine we know, or, as some have done, his married life; certainly he ought never to have married, but his temperament was fixed long before that event, and to find its roots we must seek below the hereditary surface.

We note without surprise that at an early age the characters that were always to mark Verlaine's genius had already begun to develop. For if he was throughout to be, as has so often been said, a child, that can only be by the persistence of early traits. He summed himself up once (in a letter written in 1889, shortly before I met him) in words that are not quite accurate, but came near to a fair statement of the matter:

> What are my lapses due to? Shall I accuse my heredity, my education? But I was good, I was chaste. Ah! drink developed the bacillus, the microbe of lust in a body made to be normal and orderly. I lack judgment, for all my good sense. The result — which I do not like, for it stinks of simple physiology — is that I have a feminine temperament — which explains many things!

All those statements are significant, and in his *Confessions*, written some years later, he elaborates some special points which also are significant. In childhood, he there says, it was specially through the eyes that he was precocious.

> I gazed at everything; none of the visible aspects of things escaped me. No doubt I was hunting for forms and colours and shades. Daylight fascinated me, and though I was a coward in the dark, the night also attracted me. I seemed to seek in it something white or grey — I know not what, *nuances* perhaps.

Towards the end of his life he confessed that he cared little for sunshine, which caused him nausea; he remained a child of the North, and, indeed, only once in his life went further south than Paris. Even before he had an interest in poetry, he showed taste in drawing with ink, pencil, and colours. His sense of the music of speech, of which he says nothing, evidently came later and might even be regarded as a transformation of his visual concentration, a love of *nuances* in language. With it there was a curious love for the plastic moulding of speech. Sometimes, I well recall, one would hear him mouthing some strange new word over and over on his tongue, shouting it in different tones, emitting it with sudden explosive energy as though to catch unaware its spirit, not resting until he had gained a mastery of its vocal value. So a dog will sometimes lick round and round some morsel of dubious value until at last it gains a sweetness, not its own, which he has imparted to it, and he swallows it with gusto. It was thus, I am sure, that Verlaine had dealt with the various English words he has used as titles for poems, finding in them a beauty and expressiveness which for our ears they

PAUL VERLAINE

mostly lack. But to this habit of patiently testing the precise value of words in sound and their exact *nuance*, Verlaine owed his miraculous mastery of verbal enchantment, which seems so artless and instinctive.

By origin, as well as by the quality of his art, Verlaine singularly recalls Watteau, who also was of Walloon origin, and also born in France to come under French influences. There was the same kind of inspiration, the same style of genius, in both, and in both it was that of the Ardennes. The critic of Watteau insists on his delicate and sensitive realism, his love of *nuance*, the almost musical quality of his rhythms, his partiality for detached studies. We seem to be hearing about Verlaine in terms of a closely related art. And for both of them alike it is the *Fête Galante* — the title each chose — which expresses the ideal of life.

As will commonly happen, Verlaine's awakening to poetry, largely by the discovery of Baudelaire's *Fleurs du Mal*, came about with his sensual awakening, in his fourteenth year. His confessor enjoined on him prayers with clasped hands; there was what he called 'sensual childishness' with younger comrades, and later, at seventeen, he became drawn to women of the street. After the death of the beloved girl cousin whom he had grown up with, he sought to drown his grief in beer, and henceforth admits that drink was sometimes a 'mania' with him, especially in later days in Paris, when it appeared in the form of 'the atrocious green witch,' as he calls absinthe. Yet all through the troubles that later befell him by his own sins of weakness, there was always a vein of fundamental simplicity and homeliness. If Verlaine could have lived as he desired to live, he would have found it easy to be always the humble little bourgeois official, with a wife and home, which at one time he was at the Hôtel de Ville.

Even when he had lost his post, was separated from his wife, and his mother, who adored him and knew how to care for him, was dead, even when in bad health and in sordid lodgings, Verlaine could live in poverty, contented and cheerful. His friend Ernest Reynaud has described his life at this time, in a wretched lodging-house, looking out on a noisy and unsavoury courtyard. The furniture was of the poorest and shabbiest, but the poet had preserved a few of his most loved books among which, it is said, the works of Calderon filled him with ecstasy, and there were prints and lithographs which he cherished, even paintings, including to the end a portrait of his father. Here would assemble round the bed distinguished literary friends, as well as poets of the younger school. They were always delighted with Verlaine's cordial welcome, his good humour, and a cheerfulness which, in such dismal surroundings, was almost heroic. He was never heard to complain or to make an appeal for pity. His conversation might be desultory, but it was without slander or spite, wholesome and full of savour, yet always decent. And when he mixed familiarly, as he sometimes liked to do, with the workmen at the bar near-by, he still knew how to preserve his dignity, and was always treated with deference, even by the prostitutes. It was not only the foreigners among us who recognised in Verlaine the 'gentleman'; the evidence of his own fellow-countrymen who knew him better gives the lie to many idle stories invented by those who never knew him or only pretended that they had met him. During his last years, with increasing infirmities, he was inclined to avoid being known and to escape the importunity of disciples and admirers.

Two rival women, Philomène and Eugénie — each of whom and specially the second had in her something of the prostitute as well as the termagant — claimed his affection, as well as whatever money he received, and looked after him intermittently. He seems to have preferred Philomène, but confused them a little sometimes in an intoxicated mental haze; on one occasion, at all events, he began an affectionate letter to one of the rivals and concluded it to the other. Small contributions came from time to time to keep him alive, sent by friendly admirers, most constantly by the eccentric Comte de Montesquiou; they were quickly spent.

Verlaine was a child, a dreamer, who walked in his own remote world, putting together words that seem to be made of sighs, yet when they came from this magician's lips turned to music which haunts us for ever. He was not a good citizen, not an effective man in any relationship; it was possible to consider him vicious, and on one occasion even to treat him as a criminal; it was scarcely respectable to be seen walking down the boulevard with him. Yet of such is the Kingdom of Heaven, and it is not only in the New Testament that they are met.

He died in humble lodgings in the Rue Descartes. A little earlier he had felt himself failing and had sent messages to friends. They were unable or unwilling to come. At last, three days before the end, one faithful friend, Cornuty, came and stayed to the last. He died on the 8th of January, 1896, and the Verlaine family vault in the Batignolles Cemetery is the little known site of his remains. Money was owing to the landlady for rent, food, and medicine. The poet's belongings were said to consist of little more than a few clay pipes, a meerschaum cigarette-holder, and an old hat. But there were also a number of manuscripts of which the possession was disputed, until the law intervened to seal them up — 'for some antiquarian to discover in an official pigeon-hole a century hence,' thought a French journalist. And again an English journalist ended up a supercilious obituary notice with 'another sample of a certain kind of unsuccess which is the halo of the modern French poet.'

The halo has become more radiant even to the journalists now. Less than twenty years later the sale of a single volume of Verlaine's poems had passed one hundred thousand copies. He has exchanged his worn-out garments for more dignified raiment and looks down more imposingly than he was wont to in life from his monument in the Luxembourg Gardens, amid the roses and rhododendrons, and the chestnuts on the outskirts. Not too far away, yet not too indiscreetly near, he is accompanied by the indolent Silenus in bronze, riding among fauns and supported by naked nymphs. No spot in Paris could be more fittingly devoted to the memory of Verlaine, and here in autumn the mists that he loved and the purifying rain envelop him in their beneficent gloom.

13

IT MAY seem strange that the name of Elie Reclus should be included even in an unconventional and widely extended series of studies connected with the development of French literature. In any field, indeed, it may be accounted an unknown name. I recall that when *Primitive Folk*, the first book of his to be translated into English, and certainly his most characteristic, appeared from the hands of two sympathetic and excellent translators, in the Contemporary Science Series of which I was the general editor, a reviewer, in a serious scientific journal, unaware that 'Elie' is French for 'Elijah,' referred to the author as a woman, while it was common to confuse him with his brother Elisée. Today I doubt if even a scientific journal would review the book.

That, indeed, is one of the reasons why Elie Reclus's name should appear here. He was really an artist more than a man of science. He acquired in his day a considerable reputation as an anthropologist and ethnologist; he was a valued contributor to various important encyclopaedias. As a man of science he may be said to belong to the class of which Sir James Frazer is still the honoured head. I mean the class of those students of more or less primitive Man who spend a lifetime in their studies, patiently collecting data, new and old, from all available sources, and exercising their best skill in systematising and explaining them. They thus stand apart from the somewhat later school of workers — Professor Malinowski is of these a distinguished and brilliant representative — who, having first equipped themselves with the material of the study, go forth to make a searching and minute exploration of some special native race in its own habitat. There is a third class, of which Professor Westermarck might be regarded as almost the unique example, combining the traits of both the other classes, a man of the study who late in his career becomes a man of the field.

Elie Reclus belonged to the first class, and yet, by our standards of today, he was not an altogether satisfactory example of its qualities; his scholarship was wide rather than deep; his passion for collecting facts was even too comprehensive; his critical acumen was sometimes weak; his generalisations were lacking in precision. His chief significance was as a pioneer.

That significance, however, I would not belittle. It is in the eighteenth century that we must place the real discovery of savage Man (if we say primitive Man, we must always remember that no existing race is really primitive). Oceana, which until lately retained its reputation as the supreme haunt of Man relatively unspoilt by civilisation, had been laid bare by a series of discoveries due to adventurous navigators, French and English, of whom today the outstanding representatives are popularly Bougainville and Cook. It seemed to Europeans that the real natural Man had at last been discovered, Adam and Eve not yet driven out of the Garden of Eden. For Rousseau notably — and he was a more careful student of this discovery than he now receives credit for — this meant much. It meant so much that the subsequent reaction went too far. It seemed that the discovery was merely a baseless idealisation and that the earlier view of savage Man as ignorant and brutish was more reasonable. Even today that reaction survives among those unfamiliar with modern scientific research in this field. The study of native peoples in Oceana was left to the spare moments of devoted Christian missionaries like William Ellis and Turner.

But towards the close of the last century a return took place, on a higher and more enlightened plane, to the standpoint of the eighteenth century. The savage was no longer idealised as the survivor of an ancient idyllic world. But he was treated as a serious human being, with his own often highly complex systems of thought and feeling and life, to be studied in a scientific spirit, both for his own sake as a reasonable human being, however widely his ways might differ from our own, and also for the light that his various cultures might throw on our more highly evolved culture.

Elie Reclus was in at the beginning of this movement, not yet as a highly trained investigator nor as one equipped to study the savage in his native haunts, but in touch with the general scientific approach to Man, anxious to learn all he could from those who had lived among savages, and, perhaps above all, an enthusiastic lover of mankind, the disciple of an advanced school of social thought, eager to show that even the savage is a reasonable and lovable human being.

In addition, he was an artist in literary style, in a sense that his brother Elisée, who obtained greater scientific reputation as a geographer, never was. He had, as he told me once, soaked himself in the French classics of the sixteenth century, especially those, like Montaigne, belonging to his own ancestral region. It was the combination of all these qualities that made his chief book, *Les Primitifs*, so attractive and so influential. Thus it is that he was not only an interesting figure, who at one moment played a small part in human affairs, but also an artist, and as such coming before us here.

Elie Reclus was the eldest son in a large family of which his next younger brother Elisée is the most famous, alike by his great geographical works and his position as the apostle of philosophical anarchism. But there were twelve other children in this distinguished and robust family — all but one lived to over seventy years of age — and many of them were notable, such as Onésime as a geographer and Paul as a surgeon. It was an ancient Protestant family belonging to the southwestern region of France which throughout French history has produced so many daring fighters and adventurers, so many charming saints like Fénelon, and not a few great writers, of whom Montaigne, incomparably the greatest, is yet truly and genuinely typical. Here in 1827 was born Jean-Pierre-Michel, generally known as Elie, after the relative who was his godfather. His father was a Protestant pastor, issuing from a peasant family with a remote noble ancestry, and his mother Zéline was of noble family. This pastor father already practised some of the theories his sons preached. On one occasion, we are told, he found that potatoes had been dug up in his fields and stolen: thereupon he had more dug up and placed by the roadside so that they could be taken without being stolen. His sons did not approve of going so far as that, though of Elie we hear that once, when books of his were stolen, he remarked: 'It is well — I should never have given them!' The two brothers always remained closely attached and in sympathy with each other, although widely unlike both in appearance and temperament: Elisée, short and active and an incorrigible optimist; Elie, tall and dark and of slow movement, benignantly sceptical of human nature, but loving even its imperfections. He seemed to some to have an English air, and it is noteworthy that in Gascony in ancient days the relations with England were close.

The most significant event in the life of the child Elie was an accident which nearly killed him. At the age of two he crept through a hole, otherwise used only by cats and rats, in an attic of the large house then occupied by the family, and fell to the irregular pavement far below, cracking his skull, and taken up for dead. He survived with only a permanent scar to mark the event. But when at school he asked too intelligent questions, his teacher would make a gesture and say: 'Cracked!' Elie could recall a little later seeing tricolour flags hanging from balconies and trees, and believed at first it was a public manifestation of joy at the birth of his own younger brother. But it was the Revolution of 1830, and from that period Elie dated the slow evolution of his social and political views.

Elie is described by his brother Elisée as a gentle, quiet, dreamy child, sensitive to the Gascon country influences at Sainte-Foy on the banks of the Dordogne. But he was then still a child, and only dimly remembered the most decisive event of his childhood days. His father, a young and ardently devout Christian, with primitive and exalted conceptions of his religious mission, refused all offers of promotion and high position in the Church which his abilities had invited, and resolved to leave the sphere of worldly success. He seems already to have acted on Elie's favourite motto: 'Above all, my friend, above all, preserve yourself from success.' He abandoned his promising career in the luxuriant Dordogne Valley to accept the call of a little community of rather unorthodox Protestants, outside the Church and the Consistory, in a remote commune of France near Orthez in Béarn.

Elie could vaguely remember this journey of fifty leagues southwards, seated on horseback in front of his father's supporting arm, a child of four, through vineyards and fields and sands and heaths. The family settled in a succession of houses at Orthez and at Castétarbes, and the capable and accomplished young mother, whom in features Elie resembled, set up a school which eventually flourished. The wild and romantic scenery of this region doubtless fed the child's imagination, and here he probably began to acquire that interest in plants, at once poetic and scientific, which frequently occupied him in later life.

Pastor Reclus had developed a deep admiration for the Moravian Brethren; it seemed to him that their leader, Zinzendorf, represented the finest embodiment in later times of the spirit of Jesus. They had really become more docile, childish, conventional, even more time-serving, than at a distance he knew. He resolved to send Elie at the age of eleven, together with the elder girl Suzie, to the Moravian Brothers at Neuwied on the Rhine in Prussia.

Elie never became a meek disciple of the Moravians, but the stay of some years amongst them was of immense service to his development. He was thrown into an international environment well fitted to mould his original character into its adult shape. He learnt to acquire his own style, studying the mystery of language, and the various tongues of the pupils, chiefly Dutch and English, around him, as well as Latin, which in its resonance he always found attractive. At the same time his character was fortified by hostility; it was not yet thirty years since Waterloo was fought; national enmities still flourished in the playground of Neuwied; young Elie sometimes had to endure, his brother relates, the fisticuffs of the English boys and the kicks of the Germans. But hostility gradually gave place to friendship with members of both hostile nationalities, and mutual esteem grew up between Elie and his afterwards distinguished English school-fellow, George Meredith. Amid the still unspoilt scenery of the Rhine he was also able to cultivate his love of Nature. He always loved the open air, and throughout life he read and wrote as far as possible out of doors.

On his return home, a developed youth, Elie pursued his college courses with ease and enthusiasm, reading everywhere and always, leading an ideal life of imagination and aspiration. From the communal College of Orthez he proceeded to the Protestant College of Sainte-Foy and then in 1847 to Geneva University, to pursue a theological course. This was not, as might have been supposed, at the instigation of his austere father, who, on the contrary rightly feared that his son had no vocation for such a life, and, far from exercising authority over him, treated his views with almost timid respect. The 'Protestant Rome' in fact proved profoundly antipathetic to the young student, and in after life he seldom referred to the unhappy year spent in the uncongenial city. It was the 'black' year of his life, his brother says, and ever after he refused to visit again the city of ferocious Calvinism.

It was not merely the particular brand of religion which repelled his tender and sympathetic nature. The social disturbances which at the period were disturbing and changing the Genevan constitution also disgusted him. The middle-class elements calling themselves republican were attacking and overthrowing the ancient and wealthy patrician class which claimed to be liberal. The representatives of both parties were alike repugnant to Elie Reclus. He sought refuge in studies of the past. Especially he was attracted to the financially most unprofitable study of ancient devil-worship and magic. He became profound in the science of demonology and his playful scholarship in this field in later years delighted his audience at the Nouvelle Université of Brussels.

His misery was heightened by the natural feelings of a solitary youth in proximity to attractive and intelligent girls, who could appreciate his fine qualities but stood cautiously aloof from their poor and unworldly possessor, for he seemed to show little promise of success in any career. At night he would often wander along the streets desperately, at random.

He left Geneva to study at the more cheerful but still Protestant Faculty of Montauban, a Huguenot establishment of the State. Here the French atmosphere was congenial; life was easy; social conditions were hospitable; the influence of Paris could be felt. Elie was still vaguely cherishing the notion of a theological career. But here it was that that notion began to be gradually dispelled. The professional teaching was conventional and commonplace; Elie was already beyond it and seldom went to lectures. With his most congenial friends, his brother Elisée and Edouard Grimard, he was searching for deeper truths than the professors could reveal. They spent their time among the hills — at times wild and sublime, at times enchanting — where Elie would read Oken and Schelling and Leroux and Proudhon, make endless notes, and prepare his thesis. They had found a delightful spot where they were allowed to swing hammocks to the acacias and read or talk all day long.

As that reading shows, Elie was now reaching the field of social thought in which his own doctrines were to develop. The revolutionary year of 1848, with its republican struggles and Utopian dreams, had come and was gone, but left its ineffaceable mark behind. Montauban was within reach of Paris; ardent young apostles of the new social doctrine were able to run down, and their influence spread among the students. An attitude of negligence, if not rebellion, towards the official superiors of the Faculty began to be manifested; even in their dress the students revealed this attitude. The three student friends became the natural leaders. The authorities began to be worried. It was felt that here was a dangerous abscess in the academic body which, however painful the operation, must be opened. The Dean of the Faculty, though with regret, was compelled to send to our three student friends the official intimation that they were sent down.

Elie proceeded to Strasbourg, still French and still Protestant, though this time Lutheran, and here, among professors and students alike, he found for the first time a genuine
and vital spirit of learning as well as real friendships. Here in
1851 Elie concluded his official course in theology and sustained his thesis on 'The Principle of Authority,' which,
Elisée tells us, was severely blamed and would have led him
to the stake a few centuries earlier; but it was accepted. Elie
Reclus was now officially competent to be the shepherd of a
flock of Protestant sheep. 'But, above all, my friend, above
all, be careful to preserve yourself from success.' He chose
that moment to take the decisive step of definitely and for
ever renouncing the career of a Protestant pastor.

Before leaving Strasbourg, Elie awaited the arrival of
Elisée, who was in Germany, and with scarcely thirty francs
between them the brothers then set out to walk home across
France, sometimes sleeping in the hills, sometimes swimming
across rivers with their clothes wound turban-wise around
their heads, often evoking the suspicion of police and inn-
keepers, who were puzzled by the contrast between their respectable clothes and their vagabond ways, and scarcely paci-
fied by the display of University diplomas. In twenty-one
days they reached Montauban, where friends succoured them,
and they finally arrived at Orthez.

Here again trouble met them. The brief Republic of 1848
had been crushed by Napoleon's *coup d'état*, Orthez was sim-
mering with excitement. The Reclus brothers and a few friends
made a futile attempt to group themselves in resistance at
the Town Hall. The Mayor regretfully received notice from
the new authorities that he must avenge that little effort.
But he kindly warned Madame Reclus beforehand. She made
an effort to get together five hundred francs for her two sons,
more than they had ever possessed, and they at once put into
execution a scheme they had already formed of crossing to
England, to pursue there the apprenticeship to life and so-
ciological study. The journey to Havre was uneventful, and
though a 'dear brother in Christ' there who carried on an
evangelical correspondence with Pastor Reclus could not go

so far as to admit two republicans into his house, they found
an amiable old sea-captain who was willing to give them the
necessary certificate of good conduct, and on New Year's
Day, 1852, they reached London.

That was not the end of struggle. The conservative and
traditional England of those days admitted the strangers and
rebels of other lands, but with no warm welcome, unless they
arrived with gloves and swallow-tail coats and shiny hats,
equipped to enter its society as equals. Even John Stuart Mill
refused to receive Pierre Leroux. Elie endured some months
of misery, only finding joy and consolation — where so many
other distinguished exiles with Marx and Lenin have found
it — beneath the peaceful dome of the British Museum's
Reading Room. At length he obtained a post as tutor in a
titled family of friendly but old-fashioned manners and habits.
He could not adapt himself to their ways, nor they to his.
He had to transfer his services to an Irish middle-class family
of distinguished ability with whom he was able to spend
several happy years in Dublin and London.

Then Napoleon III proclaimed the amnesty of 1856 and Elie
Reclus was able to return to France, and the more gladly since
now he might marry his cousin Noémi Reclus with whom he
had long been in affectionate correspondence. She remained
throughout life his sympathetic and capable helpmate. About
the same time an influential friend of the family, a distinguished lawyer, procured for him a post in the secretarial
office of the Crédit Mobilier.

The directors of that financial institution, the brothers
Pereire, had ambitious aims, and regarded themselves as carrying on the practical Socialism of the Saint-Simonians. In the
confused complexities of the period the most contradictory
doctrines were put forward. Was not Napoleon III, it was
asked, for all his errors, in some degree a Socialist Emperor?
It seemed possible for the financiers to follow in the same
path, realising Saint-Simon's dream of a union of capital,
talent, and labour, which should bring harmony to mankind.
This movement failed to materialise, though it rallied to its
support the survivors of the earlier Socialist doctrines. To-

day, it seems to present to us an advance guard of that Fascist army which has since attained success in some countries of Europe.

Here was Elie Reclus's opportunity to study at close quarters, and in the penetrating and comprehensive way that was natural to him, all the prevailing schools of social doctrine. It is sometimes said that at this time he identified himself with Fourierism. This is denied by Elisée, who admits, however, that Elie had studied Fourier's works 'with enthusiasm,' and was interested in all the attempts to establish a phalanstery, the old home of the Fourierists, at Condé-sur-Vosges, being indeed one of his favourite holiday resorts.

The Crédit Mobilier Bank was successful, but in its success, as might be anticipated, it drew in its Socialist horns, and concentrated on capital. Elie refused to become the Director's secretary, and in consequence found it desirable to leave the concern. Now began that journalistic career which was henceforth to absorb a considerable part of his energies and to furnish him with a modest income. It was an important Russian review, later called the *Dielo*, which, then and for many years later, opened its pages to him, and allowed him to write, as freely as the censors might permit, on all the subjects that attracted him: contemporary political and social questions, history, art, science, even mythology. He sometimes wrote under a pseudonym, especially Jacques Lefrène (that is to say, the strong and supple ash tree to which he liked to compare himself), thus gaining an attached Russian public, and many friends, who were attracted by his wide outlook, his insight, and the erudition which his accomplished literary style rendered so living and so penetrating.

Owing to his association with Russian and other papers, and sometimes as their representative, Elie enjoyed much freedom of movement, including various interesting and instructive expeditions abroad. Thus he visited Russia as far as Moscow and Nijni-Novgorod, was in Spain during the revolutionary period, and was among the army of guests present at the inauguration of the Suez Canal in 1870. He took that opportunity to study sympathetically many of the remains of

Egyptian antiquity. Nearer home he spent several months every year with his brother-in-law, Alfred Dumesnil, who possessed an old and picturesque house, Vascoeuil, with a turret overlooking a fragrant and incomparable garden, the winding river Acrevon, and a vast horizon of hills and forests. Here in the intervals of work he could engage in conversation with friends on questions of philosophy and art, not to mention the inexhaustible study of botany.[1]

In Paris, meanwhile, he was much occupied in social propaganda, and in furthering schemes of co-operation which he regarded as an important step towards more radical social reform. With a few friends he threw his best energies into the foundation of a bank of Crédit au Travail, to help in financing societies of workers. At the same time he aided in the movement by founding and editing a journal called *L'Association*. Into the whole movement he put the best of his life and all his enthusiasm during several years.

But all Elie's hopes were deceived. The Crédit was too liberal in its advances to co-operatives, while some members also were drawn away by the fascination of private money-making. The concern had to be painfully liquidated, and the members were mostly transformed into mere small shop-keepers. It was perhaps the greatest grief Elie Reclus ever encountered. His love and devotion to the cause of public welfare had ended in failure. It was a turning-point in his life.

Not by any means that it turned him bitter. His faith in mankind, his love for humanity, never failed. But it made him sceptical regarding all attempts at speedy progress in social reform, though to the end he remained personally sympathetic, helpful, and hospitable, even to the most revolutionary propagandists. He was no longer a propagandist himself, nor, as his brother Elisée always was, a sanguine optimist in the revolutionary faith. There was henceforth a touch of benevolent mockery in Elie's attitude to revolutionary schemes.

[1] He was always interested in plant life and a volume of his papers on this subject has been translated from unpublished manuscripts by Rose Freeman–Ishill and issued by Joseph Ishill from his Oriole Press, 1931.

What was lost by the propagandist was gained by the artist and scientist. As student and author, Elie Reclus now developed more rapidly, and his literary style acquired its characteristic and delightful flavour. If he no longer believed in the possibility of any sudden revolutionary change in human nature, his tender passion for that human nature increased. The whole of human mythology — all the faiths and aspirations which have fermented in mankind — became ever more for him a subject of study. As his scholarly knowledge of the past increased, and his personal contact with explorers of the present, he detected an inevitable rightness and reasonableness under the conditions of all human beliefs, even the most seemingly absurd. He planned a great general work on human mythology. All the papers and lectures he was constantly producing, even to the end, were to contribute towards that work. But he never wrote it; he never even began it.

We need not regret the loss. Elie Reclus possessed all the inspiration needed to initiate so splendid a theme. But he scarcely possessed the equipment to complete it satisfactorily; indeed, even if his scholarship had been more profound and his critical acumen sharper, in his day, as he himself realised, the equipment had scarcely begun to be shaped. The scientific conditions needed for such work to be sound were only beginning to be established. In Sir James Frazer's *Golden Bough*, we may see carried out, with fulfilment of the conditions more lately demanded, a large share of the work Elie Reclus pioneered.

He is well revealed as a pioneer in his second book, *Le Primitif d'Australie*, published as far back as 1894, with the motto on the title-page: 'There is no science save that of the human soul.' In the Preface to this 'study of comparative ethnology' he sets out by stating that no human communities appear more abject and backward than those formed by the aboriginals of Australia, and none with more incongruous and absurd customs. But we put them side by side and they begin to illuminate each other, and when we reunite them the customs of Australia fall into line with those revealed by comparative ethnology in general. We even have the pleasant surprise that these indigenous savages of Australia throw light on the barbarous societies of the ancient world, and our own ancestors come to life in the disdained mist. 'What is more, this primitive folk takes on the shape of universal Man.' 'No one,' said DeGreef, the Rector of the Nouvelle Université, in an *Eloge*, after Elie Reclus's death, had 'a deeper sense of the continuity of racial development'; the errors Man makes in his upward course are all reasonable and necessary.

But we are looking ahead. In 1870, the Franco-Prussian War broke out, with the swift defeat and fall of the Empire, and the revolutionary republican movement in which Elie Reclus joyfully took part. An accident to the right hand, some years previously in the mountains, prevented him from being active during the siege of Paris, but he was for a time a stretcher-bearer, and was afterwards associated with André Lefevre (whom later I was to meet at the Ecole d'Anthropologie) in transcribing and classing papers in the Tuileries. Subsequently he offered his services to the Assistance Publique, happy to be helpful in succouring the poor and suffering.

Next year, during the brief episode of the Commune, Elie kept a full diary of the events that came under his notice. He states at the outset that he was not one of the 'personages' of the Commune nor even in their confidence, but merely a citizen, at most 'a thermometer hung in a corner,' registering the temperature of the days as they passed. The diary is full and instructive, but was not published until after Elie's death, in 1908, as a substantial volume, *La Commune de Paris au Jour le Jour*.

He was prepared to welcome the Commune; 'if thou art really what we believe,' as he rhetorically apostrophises it on the 29th of March in his diary, 'the New Era, the Republic of the United States of the World, the Universal Commune! O, live, dear child, the hope of heroes and martyrs, expected for generations!' But that note is not repeated. On the 4th May he writes: 'I am far from admiring the Commune.' On the 23d May: 'In the bloody conflict of fierce passions man is nowhere directly seen; he is too small in relation to the mass.

The presence of the proud and terrible insect is only revealed by clouds of smoke, white, blue, and blackish.... It is surprising that anyone can wish to be an actor in the great social drama; one feels how vain is combat, how ridiculously feeble is the will of the individual of upright conscience who seeks to intervene in a gigantic cataclysm.' And two days later: 'O Fraternity! what crimes thou hast cost us!' he exclaims as he sees 'brothers' firing pistols at 'brothers' who reply with bayonet thrusts in the belly.

Early in May he casually mentions that the Commune has 'given me an employment more honourable than important.' But I search in vain through the diary for an account of the post to which he was appointed, or of his activities. That post may not have been important from the Commune's point of view, but it was of the first importance from the standpoint of civilisation, and Elie Reclus seems to have carried out his duties with immense energy and complete success. Here we must rely on his brother's narrative, and his son's still later account.

The post offered to him at the end of April by the Delegate of Public Instruction was that of Director of the Bibliothèque Nationale.[1] It was a post of danger, but he accepted without hesitation, realising that some of the most precious things in the world were here threatened. Fortunately he could place trust in the National Guard of Paris, and was able, by energetic action in taking precautions to guard against falling shells and the risks of fire, not to mention the minor evil of illustrious savants, ever ready, especially in troubled times, to carry away secretly some valuable document. When the Versailles troops made an obstreperous entry, Elie Reclus escaped being shot and was concealed in a friendly family until, with the aid of false papers and a devoted guide, he found his way first to Italy and then to Switzerland, pursued by the Council of War's condemnation to perpetual detention in a fortress. He received no thanks for the services he had rendered, and the official history of the Bibliothèque knows not

[1] It is sometimes said that Elie Reclus was also put in charge of the Louvre at the same time. But I do not find this stated either by his brother or his son.

his name, a certain proof, his brother remarks, of his faultless management, for if he had committed the smallest mistake much would have been made of the atrocities of the Commune at the Bibliothèque.

Elie settled in Zurich as convenient for the education of his two sons, and from that time, though his views always remained substantially the same, his name was seldom mentioned in the advanced Socialist press. He was not a propagandist and he was never at any time chosen by election for any public office. But the Commune was the climax of whatever public activity he ever exercised.

At Zurich, Elie Reclus appreciated not only the educational advantages but the facility of access to books and libraries in a quiet Germanic atmosphere of scientific activity. He passed some peaceful years here and made valuable friends. Though little in touch with social politics, he came in contact with distinguished revolutionary thinkers, notably Bakunin, with whom, however, though their relations had long been friendly, he was not altogether in sympathy. The two brothers never closely associated themselves with Bakunin, who, however, retained always a high opinion of both. The Reclus brothers, and especially Elie, believed that the proletariat should join hands with the radical bourgeoisie for the ultimate economic and social transformation of society. That was not Bakunin's idea, though, towards the end of his life, his faith in his own creed seems to have wavered. Like so many over-sanguine saviours of the world, he echoed at last the words of despair and abandonment attributed to Jesus on the cross. In a remarkable letter dated 28 February, 1875, from Lugano, Bakunin wrote to Elisée:

To my great despair I have ascertained, and I ascertain every day afresh, that revolutionary thought, hope, and passion do absolutely not exist in the masses, and when these are absent we shall achieve nothing.... I have become too old, too ill, too tired, and, I must tell you, in many directions too disillusioned, to feel the desire and the strength to partake in this work. I have retired from the struggle and shall pass the rest of my days in contemplation. Since I have had to recognise that evil has triumphed, I begin to study the developments with a quasi-scientific passion quite objective.... Poor humanity! Never was European reaction so formidably aroused against all popular movements. Repression is made a new science taught systematically — and what have we got to attack this impregnable fortress? The disorganised masses. But how organise them when they are not even impassioned for their own salvation, when they ignore what they ought to desire, and do not want what alone can save them? These immense Military States must sooner or later destroy and devour each other. But what a perspective!

The faith of Elie Reclus never fell to this mood of despair. His love of mankind was deep, but far too tender not to be indulgent, ever ready to smile at human errors and mistakes, and therefore always remaining imperturbable. But he became ever less interested in politics, and here in Zurich he could devote himself more than ever to the study of ethnology and especially to the history of myths. The religious impulse of mankind had fascinated him from an early period and absorbed him more and more to the end.

In 1878, however, an unpleasant episode took place. The Russo-Turkish War had broken out, and was preoccupying Russian readers. So the editor of the *Dielo* insisted that Elie Reclus should carry on his duties by becoming a war correspondent with the Russian army on the Danube. Elie, however, not only detested the hideous spectacle of war, but objected to pander to nationalistic passions, and, with much regret, felt bound to separate from the old friends of the Russian review with which he had so long been associated. He set out for America, whence he had received a tempting proposal to write for a prominent magazine. He was naturally well received. But his very first article caused a disturbance. He was so 'immodest' as to write about the Goncourt brothers and their humanitarian book on prostitution, *La Fille Elisa!* The American editor declared that the moral purity of his readers forbade him to treat such a subject.[1] So Elie, after

---

[1] Strange as it may seem today, this harmless philanthropic book even shocked Paris on its first publication in 1876. Goncourt tells in his *Journal* how for a time he went about in constant dread of legal proceedings.

acquiring some impressions of the States in New York and Massachusetts, left America for that 'hospitable England' (as his brother terms it) where he had lived during his first exile.

This time he only stayed two years in London, for the amnesty had meanwhile been declared and he returned to Paris, joining his son who had just passed through the Ecole Centrale to become a civil engineer.

A really happy period of life followed for Elie. He received a small post as librarian to Hachette the publisher; here he could pass pleasant hours among fine books, and give advice to young students while pursuing his own special work; in the evenings there were friends with whom to discuss questions of science and literature and art. It was during these years in Paris that my own acquaintance with Elie Reclus began, a few years after the publication of his first book *Les Primitifs*, in 1885.[1]

His second book, indeed the only other original book published during his lifetime, appeared in 1894 and was entitled *Le Primitif d'Australie*. It may be regarded as a continuation of the earlier volume, and while, like that, a pioneering work, it is now largely out of date. It is more learned, however, more freely and widely ranging than *Les Primitifs*, more full of eager partisanship for the savage everywhere, together with playful irony, and sometimes eloquent indignation, at the brutal and hypocritical treatment of the savage by the civilised. If less scientific than the earlier book, it is more attractive. But, Elie ends up, do not let us waste our pity on savages who have vanished. Let us rather show our sympathy to the savages in the streets of our own cities and villages.

But shortly before this book appeared, another violent shock brought this happy period to an end. Elie Reclus was closely watched by the police. Their suspicions, however misplaced, were not altogether unnatural. Although in no way mixed up with any conspiracies, he was certainly the friendly and hospitable 'patriarch' of revolutionaries belonging to various

[1] It may be noted that his international reputation in his own field at this period is shown by the invitation to write articles on 'Ethnology' and 'Ethnography' for the *Encyclopaedia Britannica*.

lands. At this time anarchists were about with bombs. Public feeling was tense. It seemed a good opportunity for the police. They persuaded themselves that Elie Reclus's eldest son was manufacturing bombs, and he thought it best to get out of the way. Police attention was then concentrated on the father. A long since forgotten minister in the government of the time thought on the first of January, 1894, to make a welcome New Year's present to the good people of Paris by arresting Elie Reclus. He was carried away to the Conciergerie. The prison governor excused himself as best he could and opened to the prisoner whatever treasures his library contained. Elie asked for the Vulgate version of the Bible. 'Unfortunately we have not the book.' 'I am sorry, since an establishment like yours stands for authority. I will make a point of sending you this Bible when I no longer have the honour of living under your roof.' But he was released that very evening, and the 'good people' of Paris seem to have felt that the minister had gone too far.

No doubt disturbed by these events, and certainly by the absence of his son, Elie Reclus felt ready once more to leave Paris and live abroad. He hastened to accept the offer, which came at this time, of the chair of Comparative Mythology at the Nouvelle Université of Brussels then in course of formation. His brother Elisée had already been called there, and Elie speedily joined him. The work at Brussels came to him as the natural development of his studies, and he threw himself into it with enthusiasm, lecturing at the Institute of Advanced Studies for more than nine years, to the end of his life, without a break, on the History of Religions. He regarded the study of religious beliefs as of vital importance, since 'religion underlies politics and holds the key to history.' The sorcerer, as he liked to show, was the first 'intellectual.' It was because 'the religious idea has no place amid modern conceptions and belongs to a superseded state of things,' he held, that it is so necessary to study religion. At his death in 1904, William de Greef, the Rector of the University, said that 'no one had a stronger sense than Elie Reclus of the individuo-social being, hence his serenity, which was not Olympian like

Goethe's, but gentle and human. He saw his own existence linked with all preceding generations, even to the most primitive, and so, he knew, it would be linked in the same way to all future generations. The harmonious beauty of his life resulted from his personal conformity with the evolution of the whole race, the reconciliation of all social divergencies.' A student who attended Elie's lectures at this time, Thérèse Dejongh, has put on record her impressions:

> It was fine to see these two old men, full of mutual affection and respect, each in turn with the assiduity of a neophyte, occupying the chair in that hospitable Hall of Advanced Studies. They were well matched in science, kindness, intelligence, the sense of justice, and the worthiness of their lives — but very different in their turn of mind. Elisée spoke, as he wrote, with perfect purity and classic elegance. Elie — 'Old Elie' as we called him among ourselves with affectionate familiarity — had the more original turn of mind. He possessed a caustic quality which was, however, so tempered with good nature that it gave his hearers nothing but pleasure. He picked his words with the precision of a philosopher. He employed unexpected terms and archaic turns, with the most racy effect. His eye sparkled with quizzical kindness. It was an incomparable pleasure to see and hear him.

Of political questions we do not hear his students speaking. Elie Reclus may have been opposed to the political institutions of his time, but for individuals he was always tender. He realised human fragility and imperfection. 'Only time can modify mankind,' he said. He believed in unconscious rather than in deliberate and conscious progress, and in the need for reflection. He still summed up his wisdom in his early saying, 'Beware of success.' He had the greatest horror of the crowd of *arrivistes* and *parvenus* who thrust themselves forward in every field of modern life; and indeed he succeeded in remaining, as it was said, 'fairly well unknown' by being so often mistaken for his brother Elisée. He shunned success. His writings are fragmentary, though he had vaguely adumbrated a great work on human religious conceptions. He was, however, even too keenly aware that the field of folklore in which he was a pioneer was still shifting and formless, and that it was not yet possible to systematise clearly the palaeontology of the human soul.

So with his vast knowledge, his talent for collecting facts, and his excellent memory, he was content to deliver lectures which were little monographs on special questions at the point, far from final, which they had reached in his time.

From 1895 onward, his lectures on the evolution of religions were published in various journals and from time to time he would send me a reprint. I have about a dozen such: on funeral rites; on the soul as a breath and a shadow and a reflection; on the nourishment and physiology of shades; on the origin of spiritualism in spiritism, etc. They all tend to show the gradual evolution that has taken place from demonism, through spiritism, to the spiritual doctrines of civilisation, each stage still retaining much of that which went before.

It is interesting to note the optimism of the man who had known and felt so acutely the evils of the world. Near the end of a lecture of 1897 on the Shades we find:

Poor dead folk! we exclaim after our investigation. But how little we know how to appreciate what life gives us! Those who are deprived of it speak with regret of the pleasures the soul derived from the flesh — that 'flesh' so much abused by refined spiritualists, who make it a term of insult, an object of contempt and disgust. They are ill-advised! Through that happy flesh, a mantle of delights, an ideal garment woven of nerves with an intellectual apparatus, the seat of sensations sometimes sweet, sometimes painful, circulates a warm and vivifying blood from the fountain of the heart, even for those who know it best a mystery, an admirable mystery. Have you ever been present at a performance of *Orphée aux Enfers*? Then you remember the valet, John Styx, ex-King of Beotia, who only learnt what life was when he had lost it. How they abound, those Kings of Beotia! If in the gloomy Beyond they preserve any intelligence and memory — as many doubt — how sad they must be at having enjoyed so little their earthly life, to have profited so poorly by the extraordinary and incommeasurable chance of being born among men. But an ironical Fate has ordained that our suffering should be sensitive even in faintest traces, and that a crumpled rose leaf should irritate our skins.

He was free from all doctrinaire or dogmatic notions in his science as in the social questions which were equally near to his heart. When he was once asked the remedy for the social problem, he replied: 'Have you ever been hungry and not known when the next meal would come and where you would spend the night? No? Then the remedy will not spring from your heart and it is useless for you to approach the problem.'

His nephew, the distinguished critic, Elie Faure, who knew him well, has written with eloquent love and reverence of Elie Reclus as the embodiment of sweetness and knowledge and wisdom: 'The man who never met Elie has missed the chance of crossing, for once in his life, the path of Sakya-Mouni reincarnate.'

So it is that we may still find it worth while to contemplate for a moment the figure of Elie Reclus. He was one of the first to show that savage beliefs and customs, however outrageous or fantastic they may appear from the civilised point of view, have a demonstrable reasonableness and a justifiable morality when studied in connection with their environment. The spirit and attitude of his work is that which now marks all research having as its end the unravelling of the savage mind.

He was, we see, not only scholar and scientist, but also artist. His admirable literary style reveals his love for the rich and expressive language of the sixteenth century, and his writings show how profitably a modern man may enrich his vocabulary by a judicious study of Montaigne and the other great masters of that age. *Les Primitifs* carries no scientific authority today, but it remains a charming introduction to the study of the psychology of primitive peoples, while at the same time an intimately personal book, reflecting the author's quiet humour and grave irony, at every point suggesting his humane and profound philosophy of life.

The style was the man. Endowed with a singularly luminous intelligence, he has been described as the very type of the sages of antiquity. But no one was more simple, modest, unaffected. Even those who but casually met the old man, with the radiant face and the shabby coat, vaguely felt the presence of the gentleness and goodness, the universal benevolence, which had survived all the rough shocks of a lifetime. Those who knew him best loved him most; 'he was a man of infinite sweetness and goodness,' wrote to me one of his colleagues at the Nouvelle Université. Although he lost his early faith in revolutionary action, he never lost his sympathy with those who suffered, rightly or wrongly, in the cause of humanity.[1] In his little apartment in Paris, as afterwards in Brussels, men of science mingled with the outcast practical idealists of all nations. In the morning you might read in the papers how some revolutionary leader was being hotly pursued by a foreign government; in the evening you might find him in the person of some pale, silent little man sitting by the fire in

---

[1] I may possibly be permitted to regard as an illustration of this sympathy a letter (here translated) which I received from him in November, 1898, when I was about to start for a visit to Morocco with my wife immediately after the judicial condemnation of my *Studies in the Psychology of Sex* as 'obscene':

'Dear Friend, What a bolt from the blue has fallen on you! I had no idea of it, or I would have felt in honour bound to send you some words of sympathy and encouragement at the time of the trouble. But you have had the support of the great Milton [he is referring to the *Areopagitica*] and I congratulate you on such an ally.

'My regret is that England, whose justice, compared with the French, I have so often vaunted, should on this occasion have shown herself so foolish and scoundrelly.

'If you had accepted the martyr's part, or decided to "fight it out in the way Britishers do," you would have been perfectly right; but I consider you have been wiser to act as you have done. You have other tasks to perform than setting yourself up as a sort of official martyr for the Freedom of the Press. I feel acutely that you serve this cause best by the silence you have maintained since you referred the case to public opinion. Had you appealed, it would have been an admission that Her Majesty's judges were qualified to pronounce on questions of science, and especially of scientific morality. The judgment they have rendered is sufficient proof that such questions are not within their competence.

'Such a verdict reminds me of the Sultan, who, when his favourite wife was dangerously ill, sent for a physician:

' "You will prescribe for her through a lattice window."

' "But at least I must feel her pulse?"

' "If you touch her, you will be lucky to escape with a bastinado!"

'There it is! You have treated a question of social pathology? Very well! Be arraigned before a court!

'But are you really going to Morocco to dispel your ill-humor, by far too legitimate? Or is that only a joke? When jokes are serious as those cracked by your judge one does not know what to think.... Best regards from my wife. Ever yours, Elie Reclus.'

Reclus's salon. For every brave word and deed, in any country, which seemed to him a blow struck for social or intellectual freedom, he was, up to the last, full of a tender, appreciative, unworldly sympathy which could never be forgotten by those who had experienced it. Of himself and his own actions he rarely talked, perhaps it seemed to him that there was little to say. He was one of those men who are ranked among the criminals while they live, among the saints when they are dead.[1]

[1] The primary source for the facts of Elie Reclus's life is an anonymous pamphlet written shortly after his death by his brother Elisée for private circulation among friends, and later, an article by Elie's son Paul, in *Le Semeur*, Paris, 8 February, 1928. Much more comprehensive is a substantial volume entitled *Elisée and Elie Reclus: In Memoriam. Compiled, edited, and privately printed by Joseph Ishill*. Oriole Press, Berkeley Heights, New Jersey, U.S.A., 1927. This handsome volume, which we owe to Joseph Ishill's devotion, contains contributions from various relatives (including a portion of Elisée's Memoir), friends, and pupils. It is also well illustrated by numerous characteristic portraits of both brothers.

14

REMY DE GOURMONT[1]

I

ABOUT twenty years ago a junior assistant librarian of the Bibliothèque Nationale published an article, entitled 'Patriotism the Plaything,' in which he advocated an amicable understanding between France and Germany. It would not be easy for a French official to take this sensible view even today; at that time it was nothing less than a public scandal. Bureaucracy at once released the unpatriotic librarian from any further duty in the service of the State. He was free to devote himself to the career of literature and to develop his dangerous opinions at leisure.

I doubt whether many who can claim the privilege of being his friends at that time quite realised the position of authority in the intellectual world which Remy de Gourmont was slowly but surely to achieve. A simple, quiet, friendly man, born in a Norman château, he displayed more than the Norman's usual undemonstrative reticence. The strong fibre and tenacity of the Norman, his aristocratic individualism, lay beneath. But it was not obvious. Moreover, Gourmont was already a recluse, happiest when, slipping on a monk's robe for ease, he shut himself up in his book-lined cell in the Latin Quarter. He has displayed the restless daring of the Northman in the spiritual world, he has no passion for exploring the physical world. He is doubtless too cosmopolitan in temper, too universal in his curiosities, to adopt the saying of Malherbe, '*Hors de Paris, il n'y a pas de salut*'; but he lives in accordance

---

[1] An interval of years separates each of the three sections of which this essay is made up. The first was published in *The New Statesman* in 1913, an early attempt to discuss Gourmont in England, and here reprinted with only a few minor changes. The second was published in *The New Republic* in 1915, just after Gourmont's death. The third section was written in 1934.

with it and in the course of over twenty years he has changed his domicile but once and then by only a few yards.

On one side of his manifold temperament Gourmont is indeed something of a monk; a few centuries earlier he would have added fame to one of the great Benedictine foundations of Normandy. It is notable that his earliest large book was a vividly interesting study of medieval monkish verse, *Le Latin Mystique*, to which Huysmans contributed a Preface. Even his first novel, *Sixtine*, which belongs to the same period as *Le Latin Mystique*, reveals something of the same side of Gourmont's temperament. It is described as '*roman de la vie cérébrale*,' and that description may be applied to the novels and plays that have succeeded it. They are all evocations, phantasmagoric processions called into being by the fiat of a singularly vigorous brain. The fragrance of life, the breath of the actual world, the touch of real warm humanity, though not entirely absent, are rarely felt. Their intellectual insight has in it something of the aloofness of the cloister, and their sensual passion the daring analysis of the early theologians. Even in *A Night in the Luxembourg* this cloistered character remains, although we are here lifted to a height whence the aspirations of religions and philosophies are serenely regarded as harmonious manifestations of a new Trinity: Beauty, Strength, and Intelligence. The procession of variegated imagery that passed before the vision of Saint Anthony in the desert is the symbol of all these achievements in the imaginative field, and Gourmont has himself pointed out that we may regard Anthony's visions as, after all, not the least satisfactory method of experiencing life; at the worst, as a tumultuous passage towards spiritual peace. In the extravagances of the imaginative Gourmont we can find a clue to the clear-eyed sanity of the philosophic Gourmont.

Thus the spirit of the cloister in Remy de Gourmont is not accompanied by any attraction to the religious life. He is constitutionally incapable of that Catholic seduction which finally overcame his early friend Huysmans. His aloofness, indeed, is really an aloofness, not so much from the world as from the prejudices which seem to him to obscure and spoil the world. He is of the school of Goethe and Flaubert. He is a lover of life; intellectual freedom and spiritual independence are to him the prime necessaries of life. The monastery of his heart's desire would be no La Trappe, but rather an Abbey of Thelema. It is thus that he has become a great critic of life, a supreme master and critic of style.

It was less as a moralist than as an inquirer into the aesthetics of language, that Gourmont started on this career. Herein, we may well believe, he was stimulated by a strain in his blood, by a double tradition in his family. For, it is interesting to note, Remy de Gourmont is the descendant of the famous sixteenth-century printer, who was also a scholar, Gilles de Gourmont; while on his mother's side he is of the family which three centuries earlier had produced the great Norman lawgiver of French language and style, Malherbe. It is not surprising that he was peculiarly attracted to the art of using words, not only to words as jewels, but still more as the substratum of thought. He recognises that language is a vital growth. 'The beauty of a language is its purity,' but this is to be safeguarded, not by rigid rules, but by good sense, by a fine aesthetic feeling, which watches over growth, not disdaining even slang, but avoiding so far as possible foreign importations and classical neologisms, moulding all in accordance with the genius of the language itself. Such problems as these are discussed in a penetrative and stimulating way in *L'Esthétique de la Langue Française* and elsewhere in Gourmont's work.

The study of words leads on to the study of style, and Gourmont approaches style in the same spirit as words. Style in itself, he argues, is nothing. Whatever is deeply thought is well written; 'the style is the very thought.' In his literary predilections Gourmont may be said to be in the fundamental sense classically French. But for pseudo-classicality he has no taste, and just as little for romanticism; the one seems to him frigid, the other baroque. 'I feel at home,' he remarks, 'before Boileau and after Baudelaire,' though it must be added that his fine literary insight, his sense of justice, do not forsake him even when he is dealing with the pseudo-classical or the romantic period. But this aloofness from each of the opposed extravagancies of the French genius — linking the late nineteenth to the early seventeenth century, Verlaine to Ronsard and Mallarmé to Beroalde de Verville, a continuity of things that are vital, personal, and independent — imparts a rare quality to Gourmont's literary judgments. We feel that we are listening to one who speaks with authority, from the heart of the French genius, which is too alive to be cold, and has too fine a sense of measure to be excessive.

As a critic of literature Gourmont is supreme, and it would be hard to point to any living writer who could produce a volume so decisive and so masterly, so mature in its balanced and mellow judgments, as the latest volume of the *Promenades Littéraires*. If it were necessary to furnish any demonstration of this critic's insight into literature, one need only refer to his *Livre des Masques*. Nothing is so difficult as to estimate the literary quality of people the critic himself moves among, still for the most part at the outset of their careers. This is what Gourmont attempted twenty years ago in the brief and firm sketches included in his *Livre des Masques*, and it is doubtful whether a single judgment there recorded needs seriously revising today. Here and throughout his critical work, Gourmont has been aided by his peculiar intellectual aloofness. He can penetrate to the core of the aesthetic product before him unmoved by those secondary considerations which so easily dim the vision of the less unattached critic. The ruthless energy of his criticism may sometimes seem too destructive — as when he declares that of the whole naturalistic period nothing survives but a few stories of Villiers de l'Isle Adam and Guy de Maupassant; but we realise, in the end, that we are in the presence of one who lives habitually with great literature and will tolerate nothing that falls short of perfection. Life is too brief, after all, for the unessential things.

Remy de Gourmont is more than a critic of literature. He is a critic of ideas. He was first led to philosophy and science, he has himself indicated, by the study of words regarded as the substance of thought. But it is clear that, whatever the avenue of approach, his searching and independent spirit was bound, sooner or later, to undertake the task of examining and appraising the current notions of the time. He has devised a doctrine of the dissociation of ideas and what he calls a law of intellectual constancy as clues in these fields, wherein he has approached the most various and the most fundamental problems, not excluding that of sex. In science and in philosophy he is the heroic amateur, lacking in training and in equipment, but never failing in keen penetration. The *Revue des Idées*, of which he is the founder and editor, reflects the extent of his curiosities and the thoroughness of his research.

Above all, Remy de Gourmont is, in the wide and deep sense, a moralist, a great critic of life. A thinker with so powerful an impulse to weigh and to test, to search out the essential things, he could not fail to be profoundly interested in human action. This interest, already pronounced in the *Chemin de Velours*, has steadily developed, growing at the same time more tolerant and many-sided, for he never forgets that 'the true philosopher always smiles.'

Gourmont the moralist may best be studied in the successive volumes of the *Dialogues des Amateurs*. Here questions and incidents of the day, as they occur, are discussed, playfully or gravely, but always with reference to fundamental principles, by the man in the street and the man of the fireside, M. Delarue and M. Desmaisons, who but thinly disguise Gourmont's own attitude. He is a sceptic in the face of social panaceas — 'to live,' he says, 'is to grow in wisdom and in scepticism' — but he is always an optimist and on the side of joy in life.

The problem of the supposed antagonism between social organisation and individual liberty has for him no difficulties; his tradition of order, his instinct of freedom, are alike too strong. He values social organisation, but he values it as the guardian of liberty. 'Society is an apparatus to protect the individual.' 'And all progress worthy of the name,' he declares, 'is progress in liberty.' From this standpoint, and with all the resources of his wit and irony and sanely balanced intelligence, he castigates the darling sins of his age, those most deplorable sins of all, which believe themselves to be virtues. In the Latin world Remy de Gourmont thus performs much the same function as our own Bernard Shaw performs in the so-called Anglo-Saxon world, with the inevitable differences involved by the possession of another temperament and the need to react vitally against another group of social prejudices.

II

The death of Remy de Gourmont has evoked little comment. In this great crisis of the world's history the quiet departure from life of a literary man in Paris might, indeed, well seem an insignificant event. One doubts, however, if it would have been very different even in normal times. Gourmont has sometimes been compared with Anatole France, and these two writers, however they may have held aloof from each other — the Parisian bookseller's son and the Norman of old aristocratic family — represented the fundamental French qualities in a greater degree than any other Frenchmen of recent times. Both approaching the world from an almost professionally bookish point of view and both great masters of language, they both slowly acquired a vivid personal interest in life, both became daring sceptics yet cheerful optimists, and both alike have been consummate ironists. But here the resemblance ends. Anatole France, with a more limited range, concentrated himself on the story-telling form of literature, and by that concentration has obtained a great and legitimate success; he has also, in a way that was impossible to the more deeply sceptical Gourmont, taken a definite side in the questions of his own day, and along both these lines has come into close touch with the man in the street. Gourmont, whose genius was of more daring and more masculine quality, yet throughout his whole life held himself aloof from the world in which he was so passionately interested. He was, indeed, always a recluse, who never took part, or sought to take part, in any public functions. His personal life was always simple, regular, and unobtrusive, lived chiefly in his own little apartment, at first in the Rue du Bac, where I can recall him at his desk in a

monk's frock surrounded by his books, and afterwards, somewhat more commodiously, but still on the same left bank of
the Seine close to the quays, in the quiet Rue des Saints Pères,
where he remained until the end. He was, from its inception,
actively associated with the *Mercure de France*, at one time the
most vital, alert, and comprehensive of the world's literary
reviews, and probably had a hand in every number of that
review until its temporary suspension on the outbreak of the
war. In 1903, as his interests ever grew less purely literary,
he started on his own account a review of wider range, the
Revue des Idées, devoted to science, philosophy, and general
criticism, in which he was able to publish a great variety of
valuable studies by eminent authorities in many fields. Gourmont's reputation slowly increased, both in France and
abroad, and to a special degree in the Latin countries. Those
who had the privilege of knowing him and were best able to
follow his development could not fail to realise that his individuality was ever growing stronger, his outlook wider, his
criticism more penetrating, his philosophic and moral outlook
more pronounced and assured. This development proceeded,
however, with no sudden and startling shocks. It is not surprising that, while the books of Anatole France are easily accessible in English, of the thirty-seven or more volumes which
Gourmont published, only one has so far, been, with difficulty,
introduced to the English reader, though that volume, admirably rendered, *A Night in the Luxembourg*, is the most brilliant of his philosophic fantasies.

We need not dispute the justice of the popularity which
Anatole France has achieved. At the same time it should be
recognised that Remy de Gourmont's spirit was of wider scope
and deeper penetration. At the outset, indeed, his interests
appeared narrowly literary, highly specialised, even esoteric.
This is indicated by the writers who seem chiefly to have influenced his early efforts, Baudelaire, Mallarmé, Flaubert in
The Temptation of Saint Anthony, Villiers de l'Isle Adam, Huysmans, Maeterlinck. Moreover, in his early more imaginative
work, and to some extent throughout — as also in the work
of Anatole France — we are conscious of a cloistered quality,

an inspiration that proceeds from literature rather than from life, the creative effort of a parthenogenetic energy, Gourmont himself seems to have realised this as in *Sixtine* and in *Le Latin Mystique*. But the whole of his mental growth throughout a quarter of a century was more and more away from this cloistered and bookish seclusion, towards Nature, the open air, simplicity, and the delicate and ever enchanting play of the human heart and intelligence. We see this plainly in his later stories such as *Un Coeur Virginal* and in such of his poems as the charming *Simone* series. It is even more clearly seen in the freely ranging discussions of a long series of studies, more or less loosely associated in his books, over the most various fields of life and thought. An immense erudition is always perceptible, but it is henceforth subordinated to fruitful discussion and reflection. Throughout this process we may observe how Gourmont's classical attitude becomes ever more clearly affirmed. The French genius has from time to time turned towards romanticism and thereby been enriched, but it is fundamentally classic, instinctively following, that is to say, the paths of simplicity and clarity, of order and self-control. Gourmont began his career under predominantly romantic influences; there was a certain violence in his sensibilities — wherein we may perhaps trace the primitive Norman — which predisposed him to such influences. But the fundamentally classical temperament in Gourmont ever becomes more firmly pronounced. Herein he has been true to the best and most ancient traditions of France, and may well stand before us as the most complete representative in our time of the essential French spirit.

It is characteristic of Gourmont's searching and inquisitive nature that his transition to the wider questions of life may be said to have been effected by his impulse to probe into literary problems, into the history of words and the nature of style. We see this transition effected in his volume *Esthétique de la Langue Française*. A little later, in *La Culture des Idées* and *Le Chemin de Velours*, he is frankly emancipated from merely literary preoccupations and ranges freely in the realm of ideas, among the problems of philosophy and morals. A little later still we find him grappling with the most difficult problems of physiological psychology, especially in his book on the sexual instinct, *Le Physique de l'Amour*. The treatment of such a subject by one who had no training in biology could scarcely be altogether adequate; Gourmont's discussion is too individual for a scientific topic, but his penetrating sagacity, wide knowledge, and daring frankness of presentation still render this a notable book.

Henceforward Gourmont's philosophic and literary activities proceeded side by side. Volumes of the *Promenades Philosophiques* and the *Promenades Littéraires* would appear alternately. To many, if not indeed to most of his readers, however brilliant and suggestive the first series of volumes, it is the second series which gives most satisfaction. For in criticism Gourmont was a supreme and unquestionable master, whose hand was ever firm, delicate, and unfaltering, equally so whether he was dealing with his own contemporaries and friends or with the dawn of literature. He was not only a critic of books, but a great critic of life. This we see especially in the volumes, all belonging to the later years, entitled *Epilogues* and *Dialogues des Amateurs*, which are mostly comments, often of a highly caustic character, on events of the day. Some may imagine that Gourmont was not interested in morals, but to be interested in life, as Gourmont was ('The wise man has only one country, Life,' he said), is necessarily to be concerned with morals. He was well aware that 'virtue is only beautiful if one never talks of it,' but he was none the less a moralist, of however individual a type, perpetually examining and analysing human action; and, with the critic of literature, it is probably the critic of life in his books which gives them deepest and most abiding interest.

When Remy de Gourmont died on the 29th of September, 1915, he was in his fifty-eighth year. It has been said that he was killed by the war. That is scarcely true.[1] His health, never very robust, was already failing when he left Paris, a

---

[1] Since this was written, Voivenel has stated that Gourmont died at the same age as his mother, whom he much resembled, and from the same cardio-renal affection.

month before the war broke out — and 'very innocently,' as he put it — for his beloved Normandy, and in the disturbed state of the country he was too much of an invalid to be able to travel back to Paris until October. At this point begins his last book, a kind of diary, *Pendant l'Orage*. It is only too easy to see here how deeply he had been hit by the war. A few years earlier, in one of his *Dialogues des Amateurs* he had made his *alter ego*, M. Desmaisons, say to his friend Delarue: 'I should not dislike a new Deluge.' 'Can you swim?' asks M. Delarue. 'No, but I would take refuge in the Mountains of Irony; I would remain faithful to my philosophy which is to contemplate the movements of life with an innocent eye.' The innocent eye is here, but we are far indeed from the Mountains of Irony in these simple, grief-laden notes in which the great critic sets down impressions of the day which are scarcely distinguishable from those of his most ordinary fellow-citizens. He has abandoned his radiant and challenging individualism. He no longer exclaims, as of old: 'A man must be himself. If he is a German, let him be very German.' Now it seems to him that 'between my present and my past there is a curtain of mist which with a gesture I sometimes try to dissipate.' It seems to him, indeed, that the past has never existed, and that he is merely a phantom floating in the air. Every rich and vigorous nature must sometimes fall into inconsistencies, and Gourmont was often inconsistent. But this great final inconsistency in the face of a desolated world was one which, surely, he would not himself have corrected, even if he could, and none will account it to him even as a weakness.

III

When we look back, less than twenty years after his death, we clearly realise that Remy de Gourmont belongs to an age that is past. That is not by any means to say that he has ceased to possess significance or that his work — his best work — is no longer worth reading. It is, indeed, notable that only since his death have his writings to a considerable extent been rendered available in English. For those who turn to them, there are books of Gourmont's always worth reading; he deals with the essential stuff of life, and he deals with it in the medium of intellect which never dies. But it remains true that, while he appealed sympathetically to the foremost and most daring spirits of his own generation, he answers no pressing questions of the generation of today. Yet that generation is far from having made up its mind about him. He is not placed in any unquestioned niche, for respect or for indifference. Indeed, the extraordinary variety of opinions concerning his place might be held to show that he is still very much alive.

I could quote a great number of variegated and often completely contradictory estimates of Gourmont, put forth since his death. He was 'too vast to weigh or measure,' 'a universal critic,' 'a novelist rather than a critic' (that was Souday, who no doubt regarded him as a dangerous rival in criticism), 'an amiable Benedictine,' 'the author of the Bible of Epicurism' (*A Night in the Luxembourg*), 'a wanderer from the eighteenth century,' 'the representative critic of the immediately pre-war period,' 'still extraordinarily modern.' But Rouveyre, a notable artist who is also a penetrating if capricious critic, and had once bestowed high and subtle praise on Gourmont, comparing him to his advantage with the academic and narrowly classical Anatole France, seemed in 1924 to turn on himself and to render equally subtle dispraise. Gourmont had made the great moral mistake of confusing ethics with aesthetics; he had prettified to infinity the vulgar formula, 'Art is life'; he founded all his personal development on a discredited commonplace, thereby for ever shutting himself out from the company of great thinkers and encountering the fate of Phaeton. And when, a few years ago in Paris, I was discussing the critics of today with one of them — certainly noted for his malicious wit — he dismissed Gourmont as 'esprit de concierge.' I made no comment. But it seemed to me, and still seems, that the thinker who was once considered almost too subversive and dangerous to mention was at the furthest possible remove from the mentality of the porter's lodge.

There has appeared, as I write, another and more balanced estimate of Gourmont, though not notably sympathetic, from a distinguished critic of today, Thibaudet. He denies to Gourmont any large outlook; he was occupied with the trees, not with the forest; he belongs to the nineteenth century, while Gide, who was of the same generation, belongs to the twentieth. But Gourmont remains, Thibaudet adds, 'a Sainte-Beuve of decadence,' the great critic of symbolism. His work has strongly and solidly conquered its place on the shelf of great criticism. It is a too sober estimate, but it touches some actual points.

The reference to Gide recalls to mind that Gide himself — whom I would regard as, like Gourmont, a critic rather than novelist — has criticised Gourmont at length even during his lifetime (in *Nouveaux Prétextes*, 1911). Gide as a critic proceeds from a totally different position and approaches life at a totally different angle. It is this that makes his pages on Gourmont illuminating, even when unsympathetic. Not that Gide underrates the power of Gourmont's purely literary criticism; he remarks that he reads the *Promenades Littéraires* (caring less for Gourmont's early work) as he would wish his own books to be read. But: 'Ah! if he only wrote that!' It is in such books as *Dialogues des Amateurs*, where Gourmont goes beyond literature to reflect on life, that Gide becomes devastating. 'If M. de Gourmont pleases me when he is good, he only really excites me when he becomes detestable.' And in approaching this aspect of Gourmont, he applies to him what Carlyle says of Voltaire: that the first question with him always is, not what is true, but what is false, not what is worthy to be loved, but what is to be derided, and pushed with a jest out of the door. Voltaire, in attacking religion, was supported by his age, but Gourmont, by attaching himself on this side to the Encyclopedists, had less excuse today for declaring that 'religious literature is dead' and that 'the word of God is only tolerable in music.' Gide sarcastically comments: 'What a musician M. de Gourmont must be!' 'Scepticism,' he adds, 'may sometimes perhaps be the beginning of wisdom, but it is often the end of art.' Gide strongly suspects that Gourmont only loves science so much in order the better to hate religion, for there is nothing disinterested in his love; he only seeks in science a provision of arguments, no matter of what sort; even in the most scientific of his books, *Physique de l'Amour*, he is moved by two passionate hatreds, in the first place that of modesty, in the second of Christianity. 'No, no, you know as well as I do, Remy de Gourmont: religions are neither "ugly" nor "foolish"; they are what you make of them.'

But we must supplement this judgment of Gide's by that put forward by Jules de Gaultier, belonging to the same generation and a personal friend, who, if not a critic, is yet a highly distinguished thinker and in touch with the thought of today. In his preface to *Esthétique de la Langue Française* (1927) Gaultier claims that Gourmont, too, was a great thinker, a typical representative of *intelligence* in the best sense, and one who successfully followed the difficult path between the superstition of old days and the popular ideologies of our day, which are also superstitions. He might treat dogmas in a frivolous spirit — 'religion is for me a fairy-land,' his M. Desmaisons says — but he did not oppose them with the truisms of a crude rationalism; prayer was for him an essentially human fact, and beneath the most naïve fables and beliefs he saw hidden the psychic elements which determine the spontaneous evolution of human life. A great sceptic, Gourmont was completely disinterested and free from all personal ambitions. Gaultier, as we know, defines 'metaphysical sensibility' as the power to enjoy things without possessing them, the power of discovering in their mere beauty a source of the highest joy. In this power Gaultier would see the Overman, *homo estheticus*. 'It is possible that the salvation of the world is bound up with the coming of men of this high lineage, that of Intelligence attaining the stage of perfection at which beauty is born. Of this class of men Remy de Gourmont is one of the purest representatives.'

When I turn from these widely divergent and often wildly conflicting views of Gourmont, put forth especially since the Great War, and turn to my own first essay, I feel reassured.

It had seemed probable to me that my opinions would now need considerable revision. I find certainly that various qualifications are needed. But the miscellaneous estimates of Gourmont more recently put forward seem to furnish no adequate ground for any fundamental modifications.

The changes to be made are in non-essentials. A great critic, but it is true that there were pronounced limitations to the range of his critical powers. He remained always an individualist with his penetrative insight concentrated on individual personalities. So that in spite of his interest in ideas he was not interested in movements. Many-sided, like Voltaire, with whom Gide significantly associated him, he accepted, like Voltaire, his own age and the movement, however narrow, along which he was borne, as a foundation not to be questioned. It is, indeed, interesting to observe Gourmont's attitude to Voltaire. No doubt he was always naturally drawn to *Candide*, but his early attractions to his symbolist contemporaries and friends rendered Voltaire disturbing, if not repulsive. His growing interests in life more and more modified that attitude, and in the end completely reversed it. A year before his death Gourmont wrote: 'After having detested nearly everything of Voltaire's, I now like nearly everything, for I perceive, in reading him, that the man is a great writer, and the very type of the sage. His was the vastest mind I know, and the least superficial. If he spoke of everything, it was because he knew everything.' Gourmont was not the peer of Voltaire; they were both, in the first place, men of the study, but Voltaire was also, almost in the first place, in the full and complete sense a man of the world; one need scarcely say, for instance, how significant for his development was his early visit to England. Gourmont was never in any sense a man of the world, content to spend his whole life in Paris, with occasional visits to his native Normandy; even in Paris he cherished his dislike of society and desired to mix with none but congenial friends with whom he could be almost silent. It was the result of these habits of mind and life that, while Gourmont was from the first completely emancipated from the prejudices of

patriotism, his critical skill was never operative outside
France. He was interested in some foreign literatures, notably the English and Spanish, as we might indeed anticipate,
since England and Spain are in France the traditional lands
of individualism and could not but appeal to a professed
individualist. But he was never at home in those literatures,
and scarcely made even the attempt to approach them as a
critic.[1] In this he was true to the French spirit of his day
and generation. Nearly every notable French writer of that
day was rooted in the Boulevards of Paris. It is almost the
last place where one expects to find French writers of the
post-war generation, who scatter themselves over the world
and seek to absorb the spirit of every land.

When a few years ago I was walking in the Bois de Boulogne
with a prominent young writer of today, I smiled to myself
at the contrast between the French men of letters I had known
of old and this representative of a new age, striding along
beside me, fair-haired and hatless, eagerly inhaling the
breeze, as became one who is at the front in physical culture
as well as in fiction and criticism.

Certainly it is necessary in any case to recognise that for
the generation of today Gourmont has not the immediate
message which he had during his life for his own generation.
That is inevitable. Every generation makes its own special
demands which are never those of the immediately preceding
generation. Gide responds to the needs of today as Gourmont
does not, but we cannot be sure that if Gourmont had lived
on to the post-war period, like Gide, he would not have been
alive to its new needs. A remarkable fact about Gourmont
was his constant growth and development, so that, when in
1914 the war broke out, he was really at his best. When I
first met and knew him twenty-five years earlier, near the
beginning of his independent career, after being cut adrift
from the Bibliothèque Nationale, I was not attracted to his

[1] 'I have so little English poetry that I am ashamed,' he wrote to the Amazon
in 1911: 'and it is the first that I loved, or at all events that I *felt*.' Reference
may be made to Gourmont's essay of 1908 on Dante, Beatrice, and the amorous
Italian poetry of the thirteenth century as exceptional, since he here not only
goes outside France, but deals with a whole movement.

work, and indeed found antipathetic the cerebrally sexual
fantasies often conspicuous in it. Gradually, however, as his
work developed in ever wider scope, I found it growing more
attractive, more penetrative in its criticism, nearer to life in
its sympathies.

There is one aspect of Gourmont, indeed, to which I had
made no reference, for it was only revealed towards the end
and not clearly to the public until after death. I refer to that
expressed in *Lettres à l'Amazone*. So I may say something
about it here.[1]

Most writers on Gourmont have recognised, for it is fairly
obvious, the cerebral sensuality which is the note of his early
romances. It is love as dreamt of in the solitary cell of a pagan
cloister that we seem here to encounter. This attitude was
one with Gourmont's general attitude, that of a recluse who
lived with books in his study, seldom coming out save to
visit publishers or booksellers. Indeed, to the end his friends
were accustomed to say that the spot where they were most
likely to find him was among the bookstalls along the quays
close to where he lived.[2]

But in the course of his gradual but very real development,
it became more and more the life mirrored in books, rather
than the books themselves, which fixed his attention, and his
criticism became ever less of literature and more of life. Even
the most casual inspection of the long list of his books shows
how the stream of his literary activity thus broadened out to
a wider comprehension of life, however reserved and individualistic he may himself have remained.

That secluded life is frequently put down to the disfiguring
affliction which at one period even induced him to wear a

[1] Gourmont's attitude to love has been well and fully discussed by Paul Es-
coube, *La Femme et le Sentiment de l'Amour chez Remy de Gourmont*.

[2] But from time to time, as in his letters to the Amazon, Gourmont refers to his
love of the country, which meant the districts round Rouen and Coutance, the
district where he was born and where he spent his vacations. Gaultier, who had
sometimes accompanied him, refers to the unforgettable gleam of his blue eyes
('Eyes golden like an autumn leaf,' his brother Jean describes them) as he would
bend down to recognise weeds or insects, or gaze, a descendant of the Viking race,
at the distant vision of the sea.

veil over his face, and led certain clients of the Duval Restaurant he frequented to request the manager to forbid his
entry, though in the end it was said that his ravaged features
displayed a certain beauty. But when I knew him, long before
he was attacked by this persistent complaint, he was already
just as much of a recluse as afterwards.[1] Indeed, one might
say that if a victim for this affliction must somewhere be
chosen, no one more temperamentally fitted to bear it could
well be found. I would not even seek here a key to the unreality of Gourmont's later love-stories which if, like *Un Coeur
Virginal*, they have lost the mythical and fantastic character
of his early romances, remain thin, only faintly in touch with
real life.

It would appear, however, that the cerebral and unreal
character of Gourmont's attitude to love in his books, while
largely due to his temperament, which Voivenel describes
as 'at once chaste and perverse, two aspects which are really
complementary,' was largely also due to his extreme reserve
where he was himself concerned. He was physically robust
(at college he won the prize for gymnastics); apart from his
facial disfigurement for a long period he was considered personally attractive, and at all times he had devoted women
friends. Voivenel, moreover, hazards the statement that to
the end he was capable of amorous adventures. By nature,
however, Voivenel adds, love with him took the form of
tenderness, which is unfavourable to the manifestation of a
Casanova's sexual prowess.[2] The question of a marriage
never seems to have arisen, and in this matter Gourmont's
ideals appear to have been conventional and rigid. He was

[1] When, as has often been done, Gourmont's life has been compared to that of
a cloistered monk, we do well to remember that such a life is not the solitude which
Gourmont loved. In one of the finest of his *Epilogues*, entitled 'Solitude,' Gourmont
himself points out that life in a monastery is an infinite series of petty obediences,
so that the monk is never left alone: 'Monastic life has never been anything but a
machine to crush individual wills.'

[2] Dr. Paul Voivenel, *Remy de Gourmont vu par son Médecin* (1924). This little book
is rambling, fragmentary, and careless, rather injured by an affectation of literary
style; but it is indispensable for some aspects of Gourmont's life, and has a touching
Preface by Remy's brother, Jean.

opposed to divorce and shocked by Léon Blum's book on marriage.

Since his death much has been made clear by his brother Jean and by the publication of the early *Lettres à Sixtine*. It had not before been seen that Sixtine was a real being of flesh and blood whom Gourmont had once adored and who was devoted to him, early recognising his genius. The novel was the cerebral transposition of real love.[1]

It was not until the last six years, however, when his strength seems already to have diminished, that Gourmont is clearly revealed in a relation of human affection outside his own family, and during these latter years he was much in touch with his brother Jean and Jean's wife, Suzanne. The chief outcome was the *Lettres à l'Amazone*. We owe gratitude to the American woman who evoked that book and evidently did so much to soothe the almost final period of the secluded thinker's life.

The Amazon type seems to have been Gourmont's feminine ideal. Long before, he had written to Sixtine: 'You seem to me like a proud Amazon, intelligent and sensual.' The *Lettres à l'Amazone* are, however, not real love-letters. They were inspired by the Amazon, they were written for her, they reveal a genuine and moving attitude towards love. But, nevertheless, old habits persisted. Gourmont wrote too much for the press to be anything but laconic in his correspondence (as I know by personal experience) and the *Lettres à l'Amazone* were deliberately intended for publication, and were so issued, first serially, and then in a volume. It is a book to be read at

[1] The identity of 'Sixtine' is veiled, at first by Gourmont's reserve in personal matters, and still in the published *Letters*. It is only by vague indications in Voivenel's book that I have realised that 'Sixtine' was the Madame Berthe Courières (sometimes called de Courières) whom I knew in Paris in 1890, sometimes in her tiny salon, sometimes with Huysmans, but never with Gourmont. The love-letters all belong to 1887 and end with coolness on Sixtine's part and continued devotion on Gourmont's, friendly relations not absolutely ceasing. I never heard of this love-affair, but I did hear of some unexplained estrangement between Gourmont and Huysmans. At some later period Sixtine's affection for Gourmont revived. She was his devoted nurse at the end and died shortly after him, first placing the letters for publication in the hands of his brother Jean, who speaks with tender regard of her 'inspiration' for Remy and her 'Olympian heart and face.'

leisure and enjoyed, by many held to be Gourmont's most beautiful book.

But there is another volume of letters, never intended for publication, and only given to the world by their recipient in a limited edition more than ten years after Gourmont's death: *Lettres Intimes à l'Amazone*. They date from 1910 until a few months before the end of his life, though by that time, it appears, the Amazon has admitted that 'they had not much more to say to each other.'

The first of these more intimate letters are formally addressed to 'Mademoiselle' and are written in the proper tone of a celebrated author who receives from a young feminine admirer the little volume of poems (in French) which she is publishing, and finds something there which seems worthy of his approval. But this feminine author, thus encouraged, attempts to see her literary idol, and the letters soon begin to take on a more personal note. We find that he has been walking in her garden, and in the course of a few months she has become the *tendre amie*, and he signs his letters 'R.' He regrets that he had not known her in earlier years. 'Perhaps you will enable me to find again an interest in life I no longer possess.' She desired to be called, latinizing her name in a more masculine shape, Natalis. He is delighted with the name. He writes a pretty little poem on the portrait of Natalis, and numerous subsequent poems. He sends her brief letters almost daily, for a time even twice a day. 'It is a great pleasure for me, I who so little like writing letters.' Certainly, he adds next day: 'I do not want to write to you more than two or three times a week, though I feel the need much more often.' And a little later we find: 'I must tell you that I take a long time to write you two little pages and often raise my head to dream between the words, delaying over them. Each phrase, before going to you, has stayed a long time with me. It is a way of holding your hand in a dream.' She has now become his 'divine friend.' 'I live in you.' 'My altogether dear friend, I cannot leave you. I profit by a respite in my life to say to you the words that I say so badly when I am with you. You notice it; you refer to my "silence."

My silence — a relative silence — my friend, is adoration. Do you not like me to adore you? And then I have to look at you. I have looked so little at you yet, and you are so beautiful a landscape!' And a little later he compares himself with Stendhal, who when he reached the woman he loved always forgot the beautiful protestations he had prepared on the road. 'That is constantly my history. I am only eloquent at a distance. I treat people in their presence rather like a picture or a statue to which one has no idea of confiding the pleasure their presence gives you.' Again, later, telling of his extreme reserve, he continues: 'I am considered hard and insensitive, and I like to be thought so, but not by you. I have so much wished to repress and dominate my sensibility, that I have sometimes succeeded too well. At other times it escapes me. I must be writing incoherent things. It is because I am much troubled, I would like to hold your hand, I would like to kiss you.' He even fears that she might unduly influence his work: 'Since you read the *Epilogues* regularly, I congratulate myself on not writing them for you. You have so invaded my thoughts that I feared I might be seeking to please you by giving them the turn you like. You also will congratulate me. You love me enough for that, do you not?' The relationship grows more and more to him, ever more the satisfaction of his own deepest needs. 'I am secret. I am solitary. I love you because with you I can be in very truth myself. It is indeed only with you that I can be myself, that I can yield to that serious tenderness which is the best of my nature.' Again and again he refers to his solitary temperament, his inability to tolerate anyone whom he does not like, 'that is to say hardly anyone,' that 'bearish nature like mine.' Now and then he refers to the *Lettres à l'Amazone*, 'destined for the public, though I hope it won't understand much in them,' and often the proofs go to the Amazon before publication.

As the years pass, he sometimes begins to fear that the Amazon no longer needs his tenderness. His health becomes more impaired, at times it is difficult for him to walk as far as the Boulevard Saint-Michel. He seems to find that she has forgotten what his letters contain. But his own tenderness, at all events, never fails and is there to the end. 'There is something at least I can offer you, sweet friend, the love accumulated day by day in my heart.' These are the last words.

I have dwelt on the *Lettres Intimes*, since, never intended for publication, this volume, like the much earlier *Lettres à Sixtine*, throws light on the genuine Remy de Gourmont. Here we see him, not standing in proud independence on the 'Mountains of Irony,' but simple, human, loving, even clinging.

Remy de Gourmont is among the great critics of the French nineteenth century. We need not claim for him the miraculous certainty of Baudelaire's occasional eruptions into this field, nor that equable and far-spread, almost impersonal sympathy which (save for his own age) Sainte-Beuve displayed. His reputation need not fear any other competitors. He meant much yesterday: he may mean little today: he will mean more tomorrow.

15

HENRI DE RÉGNIER

I

IT WAS long ago. Mallarmé lived in the Rue de Rome, with his family, in a small flat reached by many flights of stairs. The oblong dining-room was correspondingly small and almost filled by the long narrow table. Up to this sanctuary, on Tuesday evenings, when Mallarmé received his friends and disciples, there used to climb a few young men whose names have since become, for the most part, well known to Fame in France and some in the world. They talked, quietly, episodically, never magisterially — least of all the courteous and unassuming host — perhaps of the premature death of a young poet, of the new book of another, of the technical qualities of some foreign poet, of the great principles of art. As they talked, they pushed up and down the table the porcelain bowl of tobacco which symbolised their host's hospitality, and was the only form of hospitality within the means of the man who was then the most significant and influential figure in French literature. That, indeed, mattered little to those who knew and loved him. Among these one would at this time scarcely fail to miss, seated next to the host, his preferred disciple, a tall, slender young man, with long and elegant fingers, an eyeglass in his weak left eye, a drooping moustache, a powerful chin, and a general air of rather languid aristocratic distinction, a calm, correct, observant air, more suggestive, on the whole, of a young diplomat than of a man of letters, the mask, one divined, of a highly sensitive temperament.

It was long ago, and I have never seen Henri de Régnier again. But I have followed with interest and enjoyment the course of this rare, wayward, and delicious genius. He is now near the end of that course, having many years ago

HENRI DE RÉGNIER

achieved the pinnacle of conventional success by entering
the portals of the Academy — which Mallarmé, who turned
over a whole new leaf in literature, never sought, and might
well have disdained, to enter — and it is not too early to
speak generally of his work. It is possible to do so with the
more confidence, since that work, with all its subtle and even
strong artistry, is at bottom the work of a child and a dreamer,
unlikely, as it was even from the first, to yield those new
developments which may sometimes come with age to richer
and robuster natures.

I think, indeed, of the genius of Régnier as a perpetual
child. There is the child's fresh and unspoilt vision, noting
new aspects of familiar things, sometimes the things which,
one might say, no adult would notice, or at all events mention.
There is the inconsequence and spontaneity of the child,
obedient to its own caprices, wandering at its own will
through the variegated field of the world, not even so much
as seeing the things which fail to interest it. There is, again,
the child's innocence of morals, no deliberate immorality,
indeed, and a delicate horror of grossness save when it fascin-
ates by its strangeness, yet sometimes a certain mischievous-
ness and even a touch of delightful impertinence. In all these
ways the genius of Régnier is a child, while at the same time
he is a conscious, deliberate, and highly accomplished artist
in the control of that genius.

If the spirit of Régnier's genius is a child's spirit, his
inspiring Muse is certainly an Undine. There are few things
that so mark the true child as the love of water. All his life,
one can well believe, the visionary Muse that has beckoned
Henri de Régnier through the world is a creature of fountains
and streams, a wayward and lovely Undine who has scarcely
yet acquired a soul. All the forms of water in Nature are
beautiful to this poet. The seashore and the river, lakes and
ponds, springs and fountains and the basins they fall into,
beautiful vases and glasses for water or for wine, mirrors
that are like still pools — all these things and the like, and
many others in which the charm of water in the world is
more elusively presented, pass before us in the pages of

Régnier, alike in his poems and his novels, and always with
a fresh touch of poetry or observation to make them delightful. Even the meeting of lovers comes to him with the divine
freshness of living waters:

> *Tu viens de la fontaine, et je viens de la source.*

The places of which he has written most, and most lovingly,
are the places of waters, and among cities, especially Versailles and Venice. To Versailles he has been strongly attracted from an early age. It appears again and again in his
novels, and he has devoted to it at least one series of poems,
La Cité des Eaux. They are, indeed, scarcely among his happiest poems, for though he knows how to seize the more exquisite aspects of Versailles —

> *La grandeur taciturne et la paix monotone*
> *De ce mélancolique et suprême séjour,*
> *Et ce parfum de soir et cette odeur d'automne*
> *Qui s'exhalent de l'ombre avec la fin du soir*

— he is not quite able to suppress that dreary and pompous
conventionality which is too obvious for most of us; for
Régnier, clearly, Versailles has its supreme charm as the background of that ancient life which he loves to evoke with so
intimate a sympathy; and even in realising this aspect of
Versailles he has never been so happy — the remark has
been made before — as Musset, certainly attempting less,
in the unforgettable stanzas 'Sur Trois Marches de Marbre
Rose.' Venice is the city of waters which later took the
first place in Régnier's affections, and what he has written of
Venice is always and altogether happy, sometimes among
his most exquisite work. Many poets have written of Venice,
but few have been more temperamentally fitted to appreciate
her beauty. There is only one form of water which is repugnant to Régnier, and that is rain. He takes indeed an
interest in rain, but it is a purely malevolent interest. He
regards it as a chastisement, and views it with disgust,
distress, and revolt. He has written an essay on 'Jours de
Pluie,' one of the most important subjects, he declares, that
anyone can write about. But 'just as rain has always seemed

vexatious to me, so water has always appeared beautiful,' and even his anathema of rain becomes a paean in praise of water.

The love of all forms of water which runs through Régnier's work is the chief and most distinctive element in a wider affinity for all the sylvan aspects of Nature, for woods and for gardens, for flowers and for fruits. Fruits, especially grapes and peaches and pears, play an unusual part in Régnier's work, and are described with a rare love and felicity, wherein, again, we may see the child in this poet. One recalls, for instance, that the Abbé Hubertet especially loved the season of autumn, and not least because it is the season of pears, which, with their slowly developed maturity and beautiful individuality, filled that season for him with delicious surprises. Very notably, fruit plays a symbolic part in Régnier's work. The beauty of a fruit is for him almost the beauty of a woman, and he notes it with almost as delicate and tender an appreciation. It is, therefore, meet to be the symbol of a woman's offer of herself, a temptation playful or serious, as was long ago dimly realised when Eve was represented as offering sin to Adam symbolised as a fruit. In Régnier's work it is the grape which fills this place. In the tragic comedy of M. de Galandot's life, narrated in *La Double Maîtresse*, the offer of love in youth and again in age is flung to him with a grape. To the timid boy, the challenge of his charming cousin came in vain; forty years later the same challenge came once more, and this time it made M. de Galandot the hopeless slave of an insolent Roman girl of the gutter.

Autumn, especially September, is thus, with April — and before April — the season which Régnier peculiarly loves. It would often appear, indeed, that there are only these two months in his year. He is drawn to the things which move gaily with light feet over the threshold of life in the dawn, and still more to the things which in mellow maturity move towards the twilight, tender and melancholy, exuberant and sombre, beautiful with a beauty which is heightened because it is fleeting. These things become habitually imaged to the poet's eye as Sylvans and Nymphs, Centaurs and Centauresses, Fauns of the rivers and Satyrs of the sea. For him such figures are not classical conventions, but fresh emanations from living Nature, and yet mixed with humanity. The siren whom he sings of in *Aréthuse* has the form of a woman, and the seaweed is in her hair, and the odour of all the forest in her breath, and the fountains in her eyes, and the bees in her laughter. These figures which he has evoked, a whirlwind of the forces of Nature, dance madly around the artist — as he has himself told in one of the finest of his poems, 'Le Vase' — and gravely he takes up his chisel and reproduces them in a spiral around the great marble vase he carves for idle spectators to gaze at. The spectators do not know that it is himself he has put into his work. As we read in another poem:

> ... *vous disiez: il est habile;*
> *Et vous passiez en souriant.*
>
> *Aucun de vous n'a donc vu*
> *Que mes mains tremblaient de tendresse,*
> *Que tout le grand songe terrestre*
> *Vivait en moi pour vivre en eux,*
> *Que je gravais aux métaux pieux*
> *Mes Dieux,*
> *Et qu'ils étaient le visage vivant*
> *De ce que nous avons senti des roses,*
> *De l'eau, du vent,*
> *De la forêt et de la mer,*
> *De toutes choses*
> *En notre chair,*
> *Et qu'ils sont nous divinement.*

I quote that poem because it shows Régnier as sensitive to what has often been charged against him, that he presents an executive ability no deeper than virtuosity. He says nothing, harsh critics have declared, though he says it with perfection. The poet was justified in the warmth with which he claimed a genuine and deeply felt inspiration, even though it may have been of slender substance. He could, indeed, hardly have exerted the influence he possessed over the younger generation of his day by force of mere virtuosity.

Jean de Gourmont, in a thoughtful booklet, *Henri de Régnier et son Oeuvre*, published in 1908, remarked of Régnier's poems: 'I do not know any poetry that has done more to reveal me to myself.' That remark becomes significant when we recall how two youths of high distinction, Alain Fournier and Jacques Rivière, till then indifferent to literature as taught at college, were suddenly awakened to life when their professor chanced to read in class, by way of relaxation, a poem of Régnier's. This poet of a generation close to their own had moulded a new shape of poetic art, linked on one side to that of the Parnassians and on the other to that of the Symbolists, but with an order and harmony of its own, and with it he had expressed the emotions to which the new generation — weary of their fathers' Zola-esque naturalism and crude scientific materialism — were ready to make an eager and heartfelt response. Today Giradoux, perhaps a less exquisite and original artist, has made for the post-war generation a rather similar appeal.

Yet those who were critical of Régnier's excessive virtuosity, and doubted the degree of substance behind it, do not appear completely in the wrong. It is undoubtedly true that Régnier's genius has, in a sense, never matured, and that it scarcely ever offered the promise of maturity. The work that he has produced during the last twenty years and more, alike in verse and prose, while the old accomplishment of style is scarcely diminished, is so thin in substance that it can only evoke the tamest admiration. It may wisely be neglected by those who desire to savour the quality of the real Régnier.

And yet it is the final outcome of the man's temperament and his deliberate philosophy:

> *Le vrai sage est celui qui fonde sur la sable,*

and he has emphasised this doctrine by pointing out that everything is vain, and that even love is 'no more durable than the breath of the wind or the colours of the sky.' Such a philosophy necessarily excludes the artist from ever attempting to express any of the strongest emotions, or championing any of the great human aspirations. In 1919, apparently moved by an unfamiliar sense of the duty of being patriotic, he published a volume of poems about the war, entitled *1914–1916*. He would have done well to suppress them, for they could add little to the credit even of a third-rate poet, so completely is the subject outside Régnier's scope, while the tone of them is sometimes unpleasant even for a reader with no pacifist tendencies. More recently (1929), under the title of *Lui*, appeared a little volume mainly consisting of two groups of maxims (*Demi-Vérités* and *Donc*) which we might expect to find rich with the deep reflections of an old man who has lived among some of the chief figures of his time in the centre of European culture. It is readable enough, but shallow and cynical, with little in it to carry away and store in the mind, not to be mentioned among the noble collections of *pensées* which French literature holds. Perhaps the most interesting of Régnier's latest writings is the volume of sketches (*De Mon Temps*) published in 1934 — admirably just and firmly critical yet always urbane — of the distinguished men of letters he knew in earlier life.

It is interesting to compare Henri de Régnier in this respect with Anatole France, who also spent most of his life as a detached artist, indifferent to popular creeds, and, to a greater degree, ostentatiously contemptuous of ordinary human aspirations. But as old age approached, he seemed to feel that such a spirit towards life was sterile, and he turned with considerable energy against his old self to adopt in turn various of the prominent isms of the day, from Dreyfusism to Bolshevism. In advocating them, he tried to convince himself, yet, as Janko Lavrin has remarked, 'his voice sounded more convincing when he had no convictions.' De Régnier, too, with age, seems to have become conscious of sterility, but, being of different temperament from France, and less intellectual, he turned to none of the popular isms (except for a while patriotism) and seems to have been content to make rather ineffective efforts to stimulate and revive his native impulses.

HENRI DE RÉGNIER

II

Henri de Régnier was born in 1864 at Honfleur, and spent his early childhood in that old town at the mouth of the Seine which probably lingers chiefly in the memory of those who have visited it for the sake of its fascinating little Norman Museum and the homely charm of its ancient wooden church: rather a decayed town nowadays, it looks lazily across from its quays towards the dreary upstart city of Havre which has more than replaced it in the world. Here the poet's father was an official in the Custom House. Both father and mother, neither of Normandy, were of anciently noble stock, one from Picardy and the other from Burgundy, and this fact has not been without influence in determining the personality of the poet and especially the novelist who has so often re-created the atmosphere of the days when his forefathers were brilliant soldiers. The early life of the sensitive and rather nervous child at Honfleur is brought before us in 'Le Trèfle Blanc,' included in the volume entitled *Couleur de Temps*. He was still a child when the family removed to Paris, where he passed through the usual school and college career, more brilliantly than Georges Dolonne, whose educational and sentimental experiences are described in *Les Vacances d'un Jeune Homme Sage*. Young Régnier was intended for the diplomatic service and for a short time he was in the Ministry for Foreign Affairs. But his literary vocation soon affirmed itself; and diplomacy was abandoned.

At an early age he had begun to write verse, accomplished verse, even in the first stage, rich, jewelled, exotic, and complex. His early admirations were largely for Hugo and Sully-Prudhomme. But Hugo was too strident to accord with his refinement, and Sully-Prudhomme too tamely correct for his vagrant freedom. Régnier exhibited a feminine receptivity to the manifold inspiring poetic forces of his time. But the artist in him has always possessed a delicate plastic strength to mould this sensibility and to hold it aloof from alien disturbance. All the various influences he underwent in his developmental period were fitted to aid his own personal temperament. He fell under the influence of Mallarmé and

Verlaine, and his verse soon became simpler, more variously musical, more intimately personal in its spirit. A little later he began to know Edmond de Goncourt, the discoverer of the art of the eighteenth century, which to Régnier also is 'l'époque delicieuse,' and in the last volume of the *Journal* Goncourt often refers to his young friend and his 'conversation full of charming images and acute remarks and delicate ironies.' He also became intimate with Heredia, the 'prince of the sonnet,' whose artistic perfection could not fail to attract and influence the younger poet; from Heredia, moreover, he received what he has described as 'the dearest and most beautiful gift of my destiny,' in 1896 marrying the elder poet's daughter Marie, herself a writer of verse and stories under the name of 'Gerard d'Houville,' and to her Régnier has dedicated several of his best novels and many of his poems. In the meanwhile he was beginning to attract the attention and the applause of a wider public, not only through his poems, but by his *contes*, and since 1900 the long list of his novels, of which between *La Double Maîtresse* and *La Pécheresse* there are at least a dozen. He lives quietly, it is said, partly in Paris, partly in the country, and, as his writings show, he has travelled considerably. He may be said to have shown a fine artist's taste in his selection of sites and cities to visit. He loves the old Cities of Dreams, which are also usually the Cities of Waters, such as Bruges, Aix in Provence, Arles, Aigues-Mortes, and, 'beautiful above all,' Versailles. He loves Constantinople 'the city of fountains,' Corfu, New Orleans, Damascus 'the city of fruits,' and, with a love which has grown with familiarity — and found expression through novels, *contes*, essays, and poems — Venice.

III

Régnier is, no doubt, most widely known as a novelist, but he is first, if not last, a poet and published seven volumes of verse before any volume of prose, though in his prose, firmly sound as that prose is, we still feel the poet. It is easy to trace his growth. His poetic work has been divided into periods, but any such division is artificial, for there are no sharp boundary lines. Putting aside the early work, in which, however accomplished and interesting, the poet has not yet attained full individuality, it may be said that Régnier's earlier manner is best represented in *Jeux Rustiques et Divins* and his later manner in *La Sandale Ailée*.[1] In the first we see to perfection the peculiar wayward world, sylvan, pagan, and melancholy, which Régnier has created; in the second he has attained the full expression of his directly personal, lyric, and sometimes rather philosophic emotion, the mood of the Stoical Epicurean who declares that the truly wise man, knowing that all things are fleeting, builds upon the sand. The *Jeux Rustiques et Divins* contains the best of Régnier's poems in *vers libres*. To his special temperament *vers libres* could not fail to appeal, and it is generally agreed that no other poet has used this kind of verse in a more masterly fashion. If *vers libres* appealed to Régnier because of the careless freedom and caprice they lend themselves to, he is too severe an artist to abuse those aptitudes, and retains much of the harmonies and even the metre of regular verse. It is significant that he has no sympathy for the later poetic technique of Valéry (though admiring Valéry's prose) and has declared that poetry must become 'anti-Valérian.' It is also significant for those who are not enthusiastic concerning the possibilities of *vers libres* that Régnier finally abandoned this kind of verse; there is little of it in *La Sandale Ailée*, and none at all in *Le Miroir des Heures*, where the note is graver, and there is even a sombre reserve. In Régnier's poems it is usually possible to divine that the poet was transforming into the forms of art — as it were clay or marble or metal, to use his own favourite images — the emotions and moods that stirred himself, his own special vision of the world. Now, at last, he declares,

> *Je ne livrerai plus aux passants du chemin*
> *Le clé des beaux palais de ma mélancholie.*

At an early period in his career it was Régnier's ambition

[1] These poems have been well translated by the late Mrs. Flora Hamilton.

to write a novel. But with the fine judgment which has seldom failed him he knew that a young man is not likely to attain success in this field; his first novel was published at the age of thirty-six. In the meanwhile, he had written many *contes*, now further increased in number and collected in several volumes. The earlier of these *contes*, such, for instance, as 'M. d'Amercoeur,' form a transition between the poems and the novels. The atmosphere of poetry prevails even when they present some tragically dramatic situation; they are laden with rich imagery, there is a languorous or melancholy trail in the complicated sentences. But, as had happened with the poems, they tended to grow simpler and more direct, and the way was then opened to the novels.

Although it may not be the most skilfully achieved, the first of these, *La Double Maîtresse*, will remain the most curiously characteristic, as it certainly is the most elaborately wrought, of all Régnier's novels. It came to him, he has told in recent years, from a bizarre terra-cotta figure of an eighteenth-century Burgundian gentleman, seen at the Restrospective Art Exhibition of 1889, and around this figure the story slowly grew up in his mind. The story is double and is told in an inverted manner which at first seems more awkward than perhaps it really is. Within this framework we find a whole gallery of delightfully sketched persons and a long succession of gracious, piquant, and poignant scenes. Here and in the later novels, Régnier reveals a delicate power of observation, an enjoyment of rare human types, and a fine skill in presenting them by a few strokes, with an apparently effortless ease. Régnier has stated in recent years that he had been greatly impressed by Elemir Bourges's work: 'Without *Le Crépuscule des Dieux* I would not perhaps have written *La Double Maîtresse*,' but it is not easy to trace in Régnier a kinship with the deliberately firm and masculine grip of Bourges's style. Most of these early novels are historical in the sense that it is not difficult to realise that they are placed in the late seventeenth or early eighteenth century. Yet nothing could be further from the conventional pattern of the historical novel. There are never any tedious descriptions of definitely real historical events, places, or personages, at the most but a swift momentary glimpse. They are written by one who has clearly absorbed the atmosphere of that old life with intimate love and an artist's perception, and who writes of it as if evoking his own early memories. This evocation of a picture as though it were a vision drawn from remote recollection, with the fragrance of personal emotion still clinging to it, is, indeed, a special element in the charm of Régnier's novels, as often of his *contes*, but in the novels it is effected with a finer ease and simplicity. There is no elaborate and self-conscious poetic prose here; we move, indeed, in the atmosphere of poetry and at every turn we are conscious that we see the details of the story through that atmosphere. But the artist always takes care that this fact shall not be too obtrusive.

It is significant that Régnier seems to move with greater freedom and with a fuller development of his own personal qualities in the stories he places two centuries ago than in the stories of today. Sometimes, indeed, as in *Le Passé Vivant* — by some critics held to be his masterpiece — he ingeniously seeks to throw back the interest of the present into the past. But, on the whole, by what is no doubt a sound artistic instinct, when he concerns himself with modern life, he at once falls into modern conventions. The special qualities of his genius are thereby obscured or dissipated. The appreciative admirer of Régnier can often only feel a very tepid interest in the sentimental or amorous stories of these elegantly commonplace modern persons. Even the vein of nonchalant libertinism running through them makes a different impression when we are no longer concerned with the wanton or fantastic persons on whom the Great Monarch had once shone in the gardens of Versailles. Yet it must be admitted that in these later novels, such as *La Flambée* and *L'Amphisbène*, Régnier is still moving on his artistic career. They grow swifter and more direct, evidently inspired by a definite ideal; the novelist, one perceives, is seeking to suppress, altogether if possible, all literary conventions, dramatic artifices, mechanical surprises, only concerned that the action of a story should be simple, supple, various, moving with ease and always close to Nature.

Yet in the later novels one cannot but feel that craftsmanship predominates over inspiration. I do not find that my memories of any of them are mingled with that subtle fragrance, those tones melancholy or grave, which come back to me from the earlier novels. Perhaps Régnier has himself been conscious of something amiss, for in the best of the later novels (but it was begun in 1900 though not finished until 1915), *La Pécheresse*, undoubtedly a fine piece of work, he seems to have made an almost painfully elaborate effort, yet still incompletely successful, to capture the spirit of his early novels. Some of his latest *contes* appear to be woven, with the most exquisite workmanship, around nothing. Similarly, and beginning at an earlier period, in the later poems, with all their meticulous care and precision, we generally find aridity. That, indeed, is a quality often admired in the Waste Land poets of a later generation, but it is scarcely characteristic of Henri de Régnier.

At the best, Régnier's novels reveal an objective psychological skill in the concise presentation of subtle traits of character which his poems never lead us to suspect. They also reveal, throughout, another trait equally organic yet equally absent from the poems, and that is a continual slight irreverence. In face of all the conventional verities, we constantly detect, not the solemn uplifting of the eyeball we anticipate, but rather a mischievous uplifting of the nostril. It may perhaps surprise us at first in one who, as so stern a critic as Remy de Gourmont declared, has written the sweetest love-poems of his time. But while it is in the novels and not in the poems that this trait prevails, we may yet trace it to the poet's instinctively close intimacy with Nature. His irreverence to the make-believes of men is the outcome of his belief in reality. His attitude is that of the child in the fairy-tale who alone had the vision and the courage to declare that the Emperor had no clothes on. To the most impudently delightful of his books, *Les Rencontres de M. de Bréot*, Régnier has set a Preface in which he briefly says what he has to say on this aspect of his work. He is quite content, he declares, to be engaged in 'the delicious and always novel pleasure' of a useless occupation, and if his pleasantry may seem a little offensive to respectable feelings he is far from wishing to offend; it may find an excuse, he believes, in its 'joyous and wholesome good humour.' And then he strikes a deeper note by quoting Ninon de Lenclos's sentence: 'They are much to be pitied who need a religion to guide themselves by, for there can be no surer proof that one's mind is very narrow or one's heart very corrupt.' There we have a clue to the artist's temperament in Régnier, the wayward and original temperament, equally insusceptible to the external restraint of social conventions which to ordinary people mean religion or to the mysticism which appeals to more penetrating minds like Jules de Gaultier, yet firmly controlled by its own delicate judgment and its own instinctive sense of measure.

Anyone who is still inclined to find an offence to good taste in such adventures as these of M. Le Varlon de Verrigny, or such an attitude towards life as that of M. Armand de Bréot, may well feel a doubt on which side the lack of taste lies when he realises how exquisite an artist we are here concerned with. Régnier has, indeed, no wish to thrust his vision of life upon us. He is the least insistent of fine artists, content to assure us that he writes only to please himself. Has he not entitled one of his earliest groups of stories *Contes à Soi-même*? He knows that, as he wrote long ago, in an essay on Mallarmé, 'an understanding between the reader and the writer can only come about slowly: one has some chance of being understood by one's contemporaries; afterwards one is only understood by tradition; and, to tell the truth, one has never been understood at all except by oneself.'

Understood or not, it would scarcely seem that the gay irreverences, social, moral, or religious, which play through the novels of Régnier has done him serious disservice even in his own time; except possibly on his first attempt to enter the Academy when it was a source of scandal to some that he had presented in *La Double Maîtresse* a grotesque picture of a Roman cardinal. In playing with cardinals, however, Régnier was in good company, and had Stendhal on his side. The name of 'that free and delicious spirit,' as Régnier has termed him, may here be fittingly recalled, for if we are to seek any germs anywhere for the novel developed by Régnier, it should probably be mainly in Stendhal, whose *Chartreuse de Parme* has been from an early period one of the later writer's most cherished readings. In both we may see something of the same disdainful independence of spirit, the same faculty of reminiscent vision, psychological aptitude, and delicate dramatic presentation, which makes *La Chartreuse de Parme* so rare and so fascinating a book for certain readers. The difference is that Stendhal had in him a trace of the soldier and much of the man of the world, indifferent to literary style, while Régnier, whatever else he may be, is always poet, dreamer, and artist. There is thus a fundamental difference of temperament. Stendhal curiously united with his pungent intellectual analysis a slight affectation of the swashbuckler and a touch of the ambitious vulgarian. In Régnier, on the other hand, the poetic dreamer, there is, rather, an excess of sensibility. The beauty of the world has for him a mysterious terror: '*J'ai peur*' occurs again and again in his poems, even though he sometimes seems inclined to a pantheistic conception of the universe, an instinctive naturalistic pantheism like that of Maurice de Guérin, with whom he has a real affinity. *La Peur de l'Amour* is the title of one of his novels, and a sensitive apprehension before the mystery of life, different indeed from the attitude of Julien Sorel or even Fabrice, frequently marks the heroes of Régnier's novels; in M. de Galandot he has made that attitude extravagant and pitiful, but he has done so not only with the artist's instinct but the poet's sympathy. In Régnier's attitude there is no failure of courage, and he has never turned away from his vision of the world to the narcotics and stimulants in which so many writers of his own and the immediately succeeding generation in France have sought consolation, a submissive Catholicism or a propagandist morality or a narrow patriotism or a zealous anarchism. It is scarcely even easy to tell what this isolated guardian of pure art, as he has been called, thinks of these things. 'I forget Bismarck when I read Goethe,' he remarks in an early essay. 'D'Annunzio hides Crispi, and in a Shakespearian drama I think less about Mr. Chamberlain.' I wish he had maintained that same attitude during the war, but for the most part he has certainly been content to find the reconciliation of men's jarring ambitions in the serene world of art wherein he has himself seen so much loveliness and evoked so many dreams. For his day Régnier represents the most exquisite embodiment of the French spirit in literature, as Debussy, to whom he is akin, may be said to represent it in music, and as once Watteau immortally embodied it in painting. It is a spirit of joy, of freedom, of wantonness, but also of discipline, of self-restraint, even of sadness. Régnier has himself noted how restless and troubled a spirit guided the hand that painted the *Embarquement pour Cythère*, and perhaps there must always be an element of melancholy in the creation of beauty more exquisite than the world holds.

It is sometimes said in France that the art of Régnier is so intimate an expression of the French spirit that it cannot be understood outside France, and must presumably be impenetrable to the English mind. One may be permitted to doubt. Watteau has always been appreciated in England and Debussy found here some of his most ardent admirers. The author of the *Mémoires de Grammont*, who may be said to be, on the prose side, at the source of the tradition Régnier carries on, was Scotch; Stendhal, who influenced Régnier so deeply, was known and read in England perhaps earlier than in France; Verlaine, whose '*l'art poétique*' he embodies, has the closest affinities with the English spirit. Régnier himself, his friends think, has in him something of the Englishman. Still, even if the doubt is unjustified, and this poet-artist is not for the many, the few among us may perhaps venture to associate ourselves with the sentiments of that robust old-world Englishman, Thomas Tobyson of Tottenwood, in *La Double Maîtresse*, who had spent twenty years exhaling his boredom along the highways of Europe, having sworn never to return home so long as Mrs. Tobyson lived, though it was the dearest wish of his heart to see once more the soft rain falling on London Bridge. 'We English, sir, value men who carry out to the utmost their duty or their passion or their whim. That, sir, is why I claim to admire you. To do what one has willed to do — that is everything.' And then the postilion mounted and he entered his coach, having sought in vain to carry away M. de Galandot, who had not 'the honour of being an Englishman,' from his slavery to Olympia. Happier than Galandot, when that Undine who is his Muse flung the last grape of her bunch at his lips and made him captive for ever, Henri de Régnier was led into a Paradise of freedom and delight. Here with a fine skill and even a fine courage, subtly weaving reality into fresh symbols, he has carried out to the utmost his own passion and fantasy, in forms of harmonious beauty and unalloyed art, evoking a new dream into which the life-stained traveller may awhile wander, to inhale the perfume of its flowers, to gather its fruits, to drink of its unfailing streams. '*Faire ce qu'on veut, tout est là.*'

16

I

THE reputation of *Le Grand Meaulnes* has been of slow growth even in France. A quiet story of rural life — as on the surface it seems to be — put forth by an unknown author on the eve of the catastrophic episode of recent history in which he himself perished, it was not likely to make much stir in men's minds. Acclaimed from the first by a few fine judges, like Péguy, Madame Rachilde, and Julien Benda, it was only by a gradual process of penetration, when the war was well over, that *Le Grand Meaulnes* began to take the high place which at length it has won.[1] There is no doubt now about the reputation of this book. Thus Jaloux, a most competent critic of the modern novel, has repeatedly described it as one of the masterpieces of our time and a chief source of inspiration to contemporary literature. In Belgium, where strains of temperament congenial to the spirit of Fournier may be found, the influence of this book on the new writers of today is pronounced, a delicate and mysterious work, bathed in so intimate and profound an illumination of silence, as one of their young writers puts it, that one almost dreads for it the noise of fame. '*Le Grand Meaulnes*,' the Belgian novelist, Thialet, has written, 'remains in my mind and my heart as at once the most beautiful memory of a whole epoch that none has understood, and the most impassioned hope for the novel of tomorrow.' In Holland, a little more afield, but again on a soil we can well believe congenial, Dirk Coster, a notable Dutch author of today, remarked to M. Frédéric

[1] In English, *Le Grand Meaulnes*, translated by Françoise Delisle, under the title of *The Wanderer*, was published in 1929 with the present essay, in substantially the same shape, as Introduction. In revising it I have profited by some comments kindly supplied by Madame Isabelle Rivière.

Lefèvre in the course of an interview: 'There is a beautiful novel — I do not know what you think of it in France, but everyone knows it here — which I had the luck to read when it appeared, *Le Grand Meaulnes*. It is like a child's smile, like a ray of sunshine on the face of a youth. This book of adolescence awakes in me the same impression as the paintings of Douanier Rousseau; it reveals the freshness of soul as of a child who, by some marvellous chance, possessed the power of expression of a man and of a great artist.' Put in another way, we see in this book the work of a man, a great artist, who had still retained the vision of youth.

So it is that we may best approach *Le Grand Meaulnes* by knowing something of the man who stands behind it and wrought it out of the substance of his own spirit. Today we can come near to the elusive personality of Alain-Fournier through the publication, in four substantial volumes, of his intimate correspondence with his lifelong friend Jacques Rivière, who later became editor of the *Nouvelle Revue Française*, and until his premature death was one of the most interesting figures in contemporary French letters. By the *piété* of Madame Isabelle Rivière, sister of one of the friends and wife of the other, the letters of both have been brought together and published, seemingly in full. It is a fascinating record of the development in character and experience of two sensitive youthful figures, one at least an exquisite artist, who stood at the centre of the revolutionary change in the orientation of the French literary spirit which took place during the first decade of the present century.

II

Henri Fournier — to use the name by which he first comes before us [1] — was born on the 3d of October, 1886, at Chapelle-d'Angillon, a small place to the north of Bourges in the

[1] Fournier is a common name in France, and, as there were already two noted persons of the name of Henri Fournier, the novelist was induced (Madame Rivière informs me) to make for himself a name of good old sound by adding to his own the pen-name of Alain Chartier, the Paris professor whose influence on the younger French literary generation has been so marked.

department of the Cher, on the border of Sologne. The Sologne, a region between the Cher and the Loire, is a land of marshes and ponds, thinly populated under unhealthy conditions, but also a land of tender and delicate solitudes, with many a more or less decayed old mansion or château still marvellous and exquisite amid the wild scenery. In recent years there has been a movement for draining and reclaiming this district; it has become healthy and more populous, though still a favourite country for people who go to shoot wildfowl. We have to note these traits of the Sologne, for it was a background predestined for the adventure of Meaulnes, 'the country of my dreams,' wrote Fournier in later life of Nançay in the Sologne, 'the country from which I was exiled.'

It was at Nançay that Fournier's father, a school-teacher, was born (as Madame Rivière tells me) while his mother was born at Vailly-sur-Souldre in the same department of the Cher. She is said to have possessed unusual powers of expression and wrote charming poems and stories for children. She came of a mother of peasant stock united to a man of aristocratic family from the south. That family history of aristocratic decay links itself in the mind with episodes of *Le Grand Meaulnes*. But it was more especially the small village of Epineuil, at the extreme north of the department of the Cher, where his parents were for a long time the village teachers, that young Fournier passed his childhood and boyhood, leading the life of a little peasant. This region, in the centre of France, the old province of Berry, is in its southern portion the literary land of George Sand. But Fournier was in the north of it, a region of different aspect, quieter, a land of alders, rushes, and reeds, in a horizon which, it has been said, recalls the miniatures in the old French Books of Hours with their delicate little pinnacles against the sky. It was the region which alone Fournier knew in early life and it made on him a profound impression. He loved it, but in some mysterious way, while far from the sea and from international routes, it was the background which favoured the ardour of his adventurous spirit.

We know how that flame was fed. At the beginning of

July, every year, the books arrived which were later to be distributed as school prizes. These books Henri and Isabelle carried up to the attic to devour greedily beforehand. It was in this way probably that he first read *Robinson Crusoe*, a book that always meant much for him, though at first merely as a story of actual adventure, and this was the beginning of his attraction to England, which was for him the land of adventure. Naturally it was towards the ocean that his thoughts were directed (it was by no accident, as Pilon remarks, that Frantz de Galais belonged to a family of sailors) and at the age of thirteen he resolved to become a naval officer. After a short period at school in Paris, he went to Brest to prepare for his career. But here, although he had done well in mathematics, he seemed to have found the work uncongenial and felt out of sympathy with his surroundings. He left Brest with regret, but with his adventurous temper unquenched, and throughout his work we catch subtle suggestions of ships and the sea. Henceforth his adventures in real life, even for those who most sensitively follow his career and his intimate letters, were largely beyond exact analysis; we catch glimpses, there is a far music in our ears, we inhale a delicate fragrance — and that is all. 'Perhaps I am not altogether a real person,' said Benjamin Constant, and we are told that when Fournier came on that remark it was with a shock; he felt it applied to himself. 'But,' he said, on reflection, 'perhaps I am able to pass where you see only an abyss.'

It was from lack of anything better rather than from any inordinate sense of vocation that Fournier turned from the sea to letters, thinking, no doubt, that all his early dreams had gone for nothing. It was not so. We do not understand Fournier unless we remember Bougainville, the great French navigator who found and fascinatingly described a paradise in the Pacific, and unless we bear in mind the scheme of *Robinson Crusoe*, the great English epic which is the prototype — however remote it may seem — of the adventure of Meaulnes in Sologne, in the heart of France.

At the age of seventeen, then, in 1903, Henri Fournier went to a well-known secondary school, the Lycée Lakanal, delightfully situated to the south of Paris, with the idea of preparing for the Ecole Normale Supérieure. Here his independent temper quickly manifested itself in revolt against various antiquated regulations and humiliating obligations; he placed himself at the head of a group of rebels, and circulated revolutionary petitions aimed at the scholastic officials. Jacques Rivière, who from Bourdeaux had entered the Lycée at the same age and the same time and with the same object, observed his comrade's proceedings with interest, even with secret sympathy, but his own temperament was different and his character more timid. These dissemblances at first held them apart. But before long a revelation, which came to both at once, served to bring them together.

When we are young we do not immediately know where we shall hear those voices of our own time to which our virginal hearts will deeply and instinctively respond. They must come from figures of our own time, older than we are or they would not have found expression, but not old enough to have 'arrived,' so that we do not at once learn of their existence. Our teachers, as well as popular fame, thrust upon us the figures of the last generation, by whom they had themselves been inspired in youth, and these are, in general, precisely the figures to whom our instincts are most rebellious — though later we grow able to estimate them better — while the great figures of the past can only be genuinely understood when we have ourselves reached maturity. Young Fournier seems to have discovered nothing of literature or art at Epineuil, and at Lakanal the figures that came before him — Racine, Rousseau, Chateaubriand, even Flaubert — had nothing to say to his heart, for the great masters presented in a scholastic framework can scarcely make any strong appeal to the young mind. But one day a professor read to the class Henri de Régnier's *Tel qu'en Songe*.[1] A new note struck both boys at once. They turned towards each other and from that moment were friends.

[1] This professor, Francisque Vial, has since recorded the incident in an interesting illustrated volume, *Hommage à Alain-Fournier* (1930), to which many more or less distinguished writers have contributed. Vial remarks that Fournier and Rivière were not among the pupils in the class who were '*forts en thème*' and that these latter merely showed astonishment at a poet so unlike Boileau.

'We came upon words,' as Rivière later put it, 'chosen expressly for ourselves, without even knowing before that such existed, chosen words which not only caressed our sensibility, but revealed to us ourselves. An unknown spot was touched in our souls; a harp, we had not suspected within us, awoke and replied.' It was the process of religious 'conversion' which so often occurs in youth. With Rivière, who was less of a poet and artist, the process was not final; a spirit of disquiet, receptive and yet always quickly critical of what he received, he was much troubled in later years over more specifically religious problems. But with Fournier — though he, too, was at one period touched by religion — the experience was decisive; he had found the path to his own heaven, once and for all.

Henri de Régnier is perhaps the most exquisite poet of the so-called Symbolist Movement which at that moment reached its full expression in French literature. It was natural that these two youths should respond harmoniously to the spirit of their own time. But it must not be concluded that Fournier (or Rivière either) is to be classed among the Symbolists. Symbolism was the porch through which Fournier entered to take possession of his own mysterious domain, but while echoes of the Symbolists' delicate music linger about that domain, it has a vigorous life of its own completely independent of the fashions of a movement which had in it too much that was tenuous and evanescent to live, though it opened a new hope of the soul for young poetic natures at the end of the last century. We are not surprised to find the youthful Fournier, who had not yet discovered Mallarmé or Verlaine or Rimbaud or even Baudelaire, reading with congenial enthusiasm Henri de Régnier, Maeterlinck, and Viélé-Griffin, but more especially Laforgue and Jammes. These two really embodied aspects of his own temperament, and if at this time they may seem to have excited a certain degree of formative influence over him, while Rivière was at first carried away by Barrès whom Fournier found antipathetic, they were merely aiding him to discover his own path. In Laforgue he found a temperament closely allied to his own, tender, timid, proud,

ALAIN-FOURNIER (HENRI ALBAN FOURNIER)

This photograph, the only picture in existence of the author of 'The
Wanderer,' was taken shortly before he was reported missing in the
World War

ironical ('ironical because wounded, and only on that account'). Physically, Rivière remarked, Fournier was far from being timid, but he had a deeper timidity of the spirit, in the sense that, while he was strongly attracted to women, he could not endure the idea of being disconcerted or ill-used, and required for the development of love the perfection of purity and innocence. In this way, as will happen to the idealist, he manifested the cruelty of those who demand more than life will yield.

At this period of youth he formed a relationship, of quite innocent nature, with a girl student who became his companion on Sunday excursions and whom he tried to form to the shape of his ideal. But he suffered from the limits she imposed to his imagination; he desired more sincerity, more openness, and her little feminine coquetries hurt him.

Francis Jammes was a rather later but still youthful influence; he appealed to Fournier on the naturalistic side, to that sensitive realism which was never submerged in his idealism. Fournier was enchanted by Jammes's close and fervid grip of Nature and the felicity with which he had sometimes been able to incarnate the very scent and colour and shape of things in verse which, it has been said, 'may sometimes be grasped like a pole and sometimes be crushed between the fingers like a sprig of mint,' while Jammes's great maxim, 'We do not separate art from life,' was adopted by Fournier and carried to a point of exquisite perfection which Jammes never attained. It was at this time — while absorbing Gide and Claudel and Rimbaud and Ibsen — that Fournier began to seek after his own personal style in the art of writing. Now also, at the age of nineteen, he began occasionally to write verse, always in free form, and while personal and genuine, hardly the utterance of a born poet. But it remains interesting to us precisely because it is personal and genuine; some poems have been printed since his death and are important because they record (especially 'A Travers les Etés,' one of the earliest) the precise germ of the future *Grand Meaulnes*.

One day (it was Ascension Week in 1905), Rivière narrates, while walking in Paris along the Cours-la-Reine, Fournier met a marvellously beautiful girl whom he was impelled to follow. He even succeeded by some lucky ruse in obtaining her name and address. The next time he saw her, although her air was extremely reserved, he approached and spoke. Strange to say, for she appears to have been of superior social class, he was favoured with some words of response which led him to think he was not altogether disdained. He felt that this lovely apparition was exerting an effort over herself to say, 'We must separate; we have been foolish.' She left Paris; Fournier had the greatest difficulty in finding her traces. At last, in 1907, he learnt — on the very day after he had unexpectedly failed to pass his Ecole Normale examination — that, as he at once wrote briefly and in deep grief to tell his friend Rivière: 'Mademoiselle de Q was married last winter. What is now left to me, dear friend, but you?' That corollary was wrong. The great adventure of Alain-Fournier's life was indeed over. But Meaulnes had set forth to seek Yvonne de Galais, and a masterpiece of art was slowly growing beneath the surface.

The woman who incarnated for Fournier the essence of a mysterious domain which was hardly of this world (in his later letters he always refers to her as Yvonne de Galais) continued to live in his memory, though there were episodes in his life, we clearly discern, which left behind an oppressive burden later to be echoed in *Le Grand Meaulnes*. But the anniversary of the day on which he met the young girl in the Cours-la-Reine was a sacred season for Fournier. Later, the year before his death, he met her again, married and more inaccessible than ever, and wrote to Rivière: 'That was really the only being in the world who could have given me peace and repose. It is now probable that I shall never achieve peace in this world.'

III

We have gone a little ahead in the story of Fournier's life. Another significant event belonged to the year 1905. From childhood he had felt an attraction to things English; now he resolved to spend the summer holidays — from July to September — in London, and secured an easy post as French correspondent for a London merchant, into whose house he was admitted as a boarder on friendly terms. All the impressions of this episode are duly recorded in letters to Rivière. They are mainly favourable; indeed, in many respects England and the English made an intimate appeal to the French youth.

When we read the detailed reports of his impressions we note a touch of critical amusement from time to time, but always mixed with sympathetic appreciation. He lived in the western suburb of Chiswick within easy reach of Kew Gardens and Richmond, and was delighted with the green freshness of England and the pleasant little villas, with white-curtained windows, each in its own garden, so unlike Paris. He quickly began to observe English girls, with whom he came in touch both at the office and in the house, and the impression they made on him was not altogether favourable. He seems to have felt that — 'with their masculine gestures and their noses in the air' — they were often incompletely aware of the fact that they were women and only concerned to be good comrades. They were too far away from the Frenchwoman, whom he describes as 'unknown beneath her veil, silent and remote, shut up in her distant salon, and so femininely enwrapped in her dark dress.' 'There are exquisite young girls in England,' he remarks, 'but they become at once too comradely.' He himself, on the other hand, seemed to them cold and reserved.

England, he said later, enlarged his vision of life. He studied a new national temperament. He learnt to love Coleridge, Wordsworth, Shelley, Rossetti, and Morris. He grew seriously interested in painting. He was especially drawn to the Pre-Raphaelites. Today there is a revulsion of feeling against that wrongly named movement, and it is no longer easy to realise the new revelation of beauty and naturalism which Burne-Jones and his fellow-workers brought to the youth of forty years ago, disgusted with the dead academic conventions of the epoch. For Fournier it was still new, and it embodied in painting something of the same union of realistic detail with dreamlike vision which he himself was already foreseeing in his novel. His favourite in contemporary French art at this time, Maurice Denis, may be said to have similar points of affinity. Fournier left England (in excellent repute with his hosts) 'with much tenderness of heart,' for in many points I resemble these English'; and he carried away not only the memory of exquisite countrysides, but a new confidence and serenity in the road he was himself to follow.

Next year Fournier settled in Paris with his grandmother and sister and attended as an external pupil the upper courses at Louis-le-Grand. His aim was still the Ecole Normale, but when the day of examination arrived he was suffering with brain-fatigue from the strain and he failed in the oral. The career he had aimed at was definitely closed to him. 'I do not see you a professor,' Rivière had written to him, and on looking back after Fournier's death he wrote that the design was mad, for to a spirit of that temper 'no paths could be easy save those that had never been explored.'

In 1907, Fournier wrote and published in the *Grande Revue* (with a dedication to Maurice Denis) his first personal little essay in prose, though still a rather poetic prose, 'Le Corps de la Femme.' With that indifference to 'pure beauty' which Rivière said he hated in his friend, Fournier here revolted against the classic image of woman, the nude pagan idol which he associated with Taine and Louys and Gourmont, and celebrated a more modern ideal which had passed through centuries of Christianity, and come out frail and tender, yet with something of the simplicity of the peasant and the fragrance of nightfall in spring, all the delicate essence of her body expressed in her garment. In 1907 also he began his two years of military service and endured the miseries, fatigues, and forced oppressive comradeship which that life brings to men of his temperament. He emerged at the end as a sub-lieutenant, and carried away with him not only an enlarged knowledge of the France he loved (there are exquisite passages of description in his letters), but a precious familiarity with the lives of the men of the people, his comrades.

At one moment of discouragement Fournier proposed to go out to China to enter the Customs Service under Sir Robert Hart, and at another he almost accepted a post in an English school at Margate. Through everything he became increasingly occupied with the criticism of contemporary letters and art and music. At an early period he recognised that his own field was the novel, and realised, with remarkable lucidity in self-judgment, the precise nature of the art he was bringing to the novel. That art was so natural to him that we cannot discern the moment at which *Le Grand Meaulnes* began to grow in his mind, though we may follow its development and modifications for five or six years before it was finally completed and published.

But a definite step in the growth of the book took place in 1910. He had not yet completely left Symbolism behind and was struggling with a method which he felt to be difficult and artificial. At this time he was much impressed by Marguerite Audoux's *Marie-Claire* and R. L. Stevenson's *Treasure Island*; they gave him a new impetus towards a method he already felt within him, and now he writes to Rivière: 'In the end I have scrapped it all, for, one fine evening, I found my *road to Damascus*. I began to write simply, directly, as in my letters, in little tight voluptuous paragraphs, a simple history which might be my own. Now it goes by itself.'

Fournier lived in the Observatory Quarter of Paris in a quiet and isolated street recalling the streets of Bourges, and his room, we are told, was simple and neat and orderly. He might often be seen in the Luxembourg Gardens, a slender young man dressed in black, with a dark, serious face and slight moustache, 'the face of an imperious young prince,' it has been called. Pilon says he recalled the figures described by Pater in his *Imaginary Portraits* when dealing with Watteau. 'He was a miraculous creature whom one could not help loving,' said his friend, Madame Simone, the actress and novelist. 'You could not see him without loving him,' said Paul Fort. But they had no intimate knowledge of the man they found so lovable; to come near to Fournier may sometimes have been a difficult experience; his sensitive tenderness was not incompatible with hardness and violence. There was a certain awkwardness in him, even in his hands, we are told — and he lacked patience. 'Only women who have loved me,' he himself said, 'know to what point I can be cruel. Because I want the whole.' 'You see,' he adds, 'my hero Meaulnes!' And Valentine in the story, I may further add, was based on Fournier's personal experience; in a letter to his sister he narrates the episode with the real Jeanne B, whom he treated so badly. Fournier mentally prescribed to women, as Rivière says, the angle at which they were to enter his life, and at the smallest lapse on their part he would overwhelm them with reproaches for their innocent failure to attain his ideal. The ideal demand, he himself remarks in 1907, which he would make of his wife, was 'audacious initiative' blended with 'superhuman tact.'

He formed various literary relationships during the last years of his life, the most notable being with Péguy whom he first met in 1910. Péguy, for all his obstinate temperament, was often influenced by Fournier and always ready to follow his counsels. Fournier on his side found in Péguy the most congenial of contemporary writers. He felt a strong sympathy with his instinctive, childlike, peasant's nature; he admired his spiritual materialism ('a Rabelais of ideas,' he calls him), and with that tendency to find the miraculous in everyday life which Péguy carried to so high a point, Fournier was entirely at one. Péguy was not without influence on *Le Grand Meaulnes* and, during Fournier's last years, seems to have been his nearest friend. He regarded Fournier, Madame Simone says, as an exceptional being, gifted with peculiar graces, for whom there was no boundary between the visible and invisible worlds. When asked where was that invisible so near to him and so far from others, Fournier smiled and replied: 'Stretch out your hand and you will feel it there.' Rivière's sympathy with Péguy was only partial, and at this period the correspondence between Fournier and Rivière begins to languish. The old personal ties always subsisted, but the profound temperamental difference was becoming more clearly revealed. Rivière admits that Fournier's attitude sometimes 'got on his nerves,' while Fournier jealously guarded his own spiritual integrity and could not be moved from his own path. But to Rivière we owe a sensitively appreciative account of Fournier's life which cannot be superseded.

Over the last years we seem to feel a hovering obscurity. Rivière in after days reproached himself — though the reproach was unnecessary — with a neglect that led his friend to fall, we gather, into what Rivière regarded as evil courses and to come under disturbing influences. Amid episodes with women which brought him no satisfaction because, as he said, with Shelley, he had 'once met an Antigone,' we find Fournier still actively pursuing his aims in literature, and with the promise of success. But often we only see him through an atmosphere of melancholy. He realises that he has lost his childhood's vision of the world, and at times he is inclined to recover what he has lost by turning to religion. He obtains a copy of the Bible and is touched by incidents in the Gospels; he is deeply impressed by Dostoievski, especially by *The Idiot*. At one moment it even occurs to him that he would like to enter a religious Order and seek new adventure as a missionary.

When the Great War broke out in the summer of 1914, Fournier happened to be in the south of France. Like others — like Rivière, also in the south and who chanced to be in the same army division — he was hurried among many hardships to the front, and found himself eventually in the Meuse, near Vaux-les-Palameix, at a later period of the war occupied by the Americans. Fournier's captain was an unintelligent man whose one idea, against the better judgment of his lieutenants, was: 'Hunt out the Boches!' Fournier, 'timid but fearless,' for whom life was 'a great game,' never drew back. The inevitable end swiftly ensued. Fournier led a company, the captain was in command. On the 22d September at Saint-Remy a vague figure was seen in the enemy's lines. The captain rushed forward, revolver in hand, followed by Fournier, but only a small number of men. They were being led into an ambush on the edge of a wood. Most of them were shot down. Fournier fell struck in the forehead, according to the only report that could be obtained, but his body was not recovered. Until the end of the war his friends cherished the hope that, like his friend Rivière, he had been imprisoned and conveyed to Germany. When, after the war, Rivière came to search the ravaged and desolate ground for traces of his friend, he found little memorials set up by the Germans — some 'to a French hero' — but they were all of later date than Fournier's disappearance.

Five years earlier he had written in a letter: 'I am seeking for the key to these escapes into desired lands — and perhaps it is Death, after all.'

IV

There are people to whom *Le Grand Meaulnes* seems a simple and insignificant story, merely the adventure of a truant schoolboy, just as there are people who inhale in vain the most exquisite fragrance of flowers, or, to keep within the sphere of art, find only trivial the music of Mozart which transports others beyond the earth. For, as Racine said, in defending his *Bérénice* from critics who could see nothing in it but bald simplicity, all creation is out of nothing. And while Jehovah on the seventh day beheld everything he had made as very good, for an unseeing eye it may still have been chaos.

That is why it has seemed worth while to trace the career of Alain-Fournier with some care. It is worth while, that is, to give the reader the clue to the process of creation here achieved. Fournier disliked intellectual abstractions; he moved in the sphere of the intangible. Yet he was an acute critic with the most precise knowledge of the subtle course of his own mind. Although receptive to outside influences, he only admitted such as were akin to his own temperament. He knew from an early period his exact aim, and the exact equipment he possessed for attaining it, although he was not at first sure of the path by which it was to be reached. The letters written to Rivière from school days on to maturity — besides being one side of a most notable record of friendship — form a fascinating document of the sensitively self-conscious evolution of an original artist and are a real contribution to the psychology of art.

The posthumous volume of Fournier's fragments is entitled, in accordance with the headings of some of them, *Miracles*, and that title chances to indicate the nature of his work. In a supreme masterpiece of literature which describes and symbolises what are called 'miracles,' it is told how the divine artist may turn simple water into wine, or make a little every-day bread suffice to feed a multitude. Such always is the miracle of the finest art, stupendous only in its simplicity. *Le Grand Meaulnes* holds us, not as a brilliant achievement of rural romance such as George Sand accomplished in the same region of France with *La Mare au Diable*, nor as a fantastic fairy-tale allegory such as Theodore Powys has presented so finely in *Mr. Weston's Good Wine*. Alain-Fournier put forth no magnificent effort. He remained true to his early maxim of the unity of life and art. It is possible to say that there is nothing in *Le Grand Meaulnes* from one end to the other but the trivial details of real life as its author had known life. Only they had fallen slowly from childhood on a peculiarly sensi-tive and vibrant organism, and when at last they were trans-formed into art a miracle was achieved and the water had become wine.

We realise the fidelity to his own life of the episodes and the atmosphere in Fournier's novel when we read the cor-respondence. Not only is he himself in the narrative all through, so that, as he once remarks, he hardly knew whether he was Meaulnes or young Seurel or Frantz or the writer of the book, but we may note how in the smallest details he seeks to come as close as he can to his own personal life. The place-names of the book are, with little or no change, those around his early home. So are the personal names; Fournier's father was Auguste, and Meaulnes, after some changes, was finally called Augustin; Uncle Florentin, with his large family and large shop, corresponds to the real Uncle Florent of Nan-çay ('the land of my dreams'), as described in Fournier's letters. The sounds and sights and odours that sank into the

sensitive spirit of the real youth — all the traits of this remote and lonely spot of old France — live again transposed in
the novel. Nor must we conclude that Alain-Fournier was
merely a regional novelist. His outlook was too wide for this;
his alert intelligence and emotional sensibility were equally
alive in the totally different atmosphere of cities. He pro-
jected a novel in which he would do for Paris, his later home,
what he was doing in *Le Grand Meaulnes* for his early home;
he had planned, and even began, several novels, and a fragment
of one (*Colombe Blanchet*) has been published; this was to be the
story of the love-affairs of a young teacher (with an English
mother 'full of charm') in a small provincial French town,
scarcely more than a village, torn by political rivalries.

Some critics have been disposed to deny to Fournier the
name of 'novelist,' and to insist on the doubtless higher title
of 'poet.' Certainly we are obliged to introduce frequently
the term 'dream' in speaking either of this writer or his work.
But there is no need to refuse the title of novel to *Le Grand
Meaulnes*. Jaloux, who is both an acute critic and an accomplished practitioner of the novel, has quoted with approval
the saying of Herder that 'the essence of the novel lies in its
resemblance to a dream,' and adds that this is true of many
great realistic novels, as of Dickens and of Dostoievski. *Le
Grand Meaulnes*, whatever its method, is certainly a novel in
the same sense.

Rivière has somewhere remarked that it is not easy to
describe the method of Fournier in words that might not
equally apply to the method of Maeterlinck's early plays.
The methods are, however, totally different. Maeterlinck's
structures were of romantic material, heightened by the skilful
use of silence, even (to use the phrase of Villiers) a *crescendo*
of silences. Fournier's structure was severely realistic in every
detail, and it was the interstices of the structure itself that
were subtly interpenetrated with dream-life. Rivière, always
a severe critic of his friend, told him in early life that he had
too much '*sensiblerie*'; that he was inclined to be sentimental,
and to find everything 'touching'; too much in the vein of
Dickens's *David Copperfield* and Goncourt's *Germinie Lacerteux*.

That certainly was the danger for Fournier; but he was saved by his own acute self-criticism, in spite of his profound contempt of the intellect, and, above all, by his instinct as artist, for, as he himself replied to Rivière, '*sensiblerie* could not come in where perfect art was attained.'

All his life he was haunted by dreams, but it was his good fortune to be instinctively aware that, as Paul Valéry has put it, 'to tell one's dreams one must be infinitely awake.' Fournier has been called the brother of Gérard de Nerval, and it is probably true that Nerval is the one figure in French literature with whom Fournier may be instructively compared. Gérard de Nerval was a fascinating and original dreamer, but there was this profound distinction that he was never fully awake and that his final suicide was the natural outcome, not only of his life, but of his art. Fournier himself found Gérard de Nerval's *Sylvie* rather conventional and artificial. Charles Nodier, of whom Jaloux considers him 'the direct-descendant,' he may not have known at all, though he certainly knew Gide, whom the same critic refers to in this connection as 'the creator of the literature of evasion.' But it must be remembered that Fournier, in spite of his eager interest in all that books may yield, had a deep distrust of 'literature,' and felt that it was his own business as an artist to hold aloof from it. 'Every effort to bend my thoughts to literature, ancient or modern, is vicious.' While as to abstractions and formulas, 'the formula must unroll itself as slowly as life.' But this attitude involved neither an insensitiveness to what others were doing — that must already be clear — nor any egotistic concentration on himself. 'The novel that I have carried in my head for three years,' he wrote as early as 1905, 'was at first only me, me, and me, but it has gradually been depersonalised and enlarged and is no longer the novel which everyone plans at eighteen.' And again, in the same year, he explains that his aim in seeking to express tangible life in the form of a novel, is to produce, not himself, but 'the rich treasury of accumulated lives' he already held within him in the form of a moving 'dream' — and such dream must embody everything in the vision of the people described which is not mere social or animal mechanism. With all his vivid sensibility to the subtle facts of real life it was by his 'dream' that Fournier was led, and that dream, as he explained, was at once the reality of the past and the desire of the future, since we are made of old memories, and impressions that are unconscious, so that Desire is Recollection. 'Behind every moment of life,' he wrote in 1907, 'I seek the life of my Paradise; behind every landscape I feel the landscape of my Paradise. I am content.' Or, as in another mood he puts it: 'If I have been childish and weak and foolish, at least I have, at moments, had the strength in this infamous city to create *my life*, like a marvellous fairy-tale.'

In every poet — in the heart of everyone who shares in the poet's spirit — there is a certain restless homesickness of the soul for which each seeks to find his own expression; Poe, for instance, in 'To Helen,' Shelley over and over again, and once at least in the record of a personal experience, *Epipsychidon*. Alain-Fournier was similarly inspired by his own life, and if we seek in prose an expression of this nostalgia of the soul, we can perhaps nowhere find it so well expressed as in a book which may now be counted among the permanent human possessions, *Le Grand Meaulnes*.

17

IN SEARCH OF PROUST

NIGHT before last we dined with R.... and his mother, and as we were leaving his house a little after eleven, he asked if we would drop him at the home of his friend Porel, son of Réjane, as Porel was giving a party. Next day, when we saw R...., he gave us a most interesting account of the party at which many of the Paris circles were represented, from Cécile Sorel to Marcel Proust. Proust, it seems, arrived at two in the morning, during a pause in the concert being given extempore by one of the new pianists of the Stravinski school. The doors opened, and an apparition made its appearance which was Proust. It was, R.... said, "saisissant." Proust gave the impression of an exhumed corpse in remarkable preservation, in all black clothes, of the cut of 1890, hanging much too large on his emaciated figure. His dead black hair was worn too long, the great dark rings round his eyes and his waxlike long hands which he does not fold, the fingers as straight as if they were not articulated, and his whispering voice — all made an impression which actually for a time threw a chill over the gathering. R.... conversed with him for a half-hour or more, and in all that time Proust evidently talked genealogy (R....'s family counts all the quarterings and also a Saint); he knows all the family trees in France, who married who, and so on; but his information stops somewhere round 1885. He is vague and uninformed and difficult to interest in anything modern; affects to have scarcely ever heard, even cursorily, of Debussy, Stravinsky, or the new painters; and to compliment the musician of the evening asked him if he would be good enough to go on playing until eight or nine in the morning. He made this mild request towards four A.M., when most of the guests were very sleepy, some taking French leave and others saying good-bye; but of course it was midday for Proust, who was beginning to be wide awake. (When he gives people appointments the hour is always round four A.M.) Strangeness is what most expressed him for R.... But apart from the pose of being ill-dressed (he was the only man who was not in dinner clothes, and he is definitely rich), he looked very much a person of consequence, and with an abundant reserve of vitality, as if he might live to be really old; he is not over forty, if he is forty [he was really fifty], and does not look more than his age.

'R.... left round four o'clock; and, as you may imagine, it is not the easiest hour at which to find a taxi; but seeing a very shabby vagrant one, with a piratical black cover over its flag — one of those unreconstructed war cars that belong to no taxi federation, but prowl alone, owned by the driver — he thought it was waiting on the chance of a fare before returning to its garage in the Fortifications, so he went up to the sleepy driver inside the vehicle, and made his request. But when the driver woke sufficiently, he said he couldn't oblige, as he was "le taxi de Monsieur Proust." For R...., it was a final expression of Proust's strange personality. Also it appears that Proust lives alone, with only a young butler sixteen years old to wait on him and run his housekeeping. Somehow, I can't summon up any vision of a butler of sixteen; but I suppose butlers are born and not made.'[1]

After a separating interval of over a century it is possible, with an effort, to realise what Rousseau was like and what, for good or evil, he effected in the world. As at this distance we view his influence — putting aside the crowd of those who have misunderstood it — we may say that what he has done

[1] The letter here quoted is only dated '20 January,' but on recently consulting the writer of it she confirms my supposition that the year was 1922, so that we here see Proust ten months only before his death. It is as he appeared to a stranger who happened to belong to the aristocratic order Proust found specially attractive. The best picture known to me of Proust as seen by a more intimate friend is furnished by Madame Scheikévitch in her recent volume of reminiscences, *Souvenirs d'un Temps Disparu* (translated under the title of *Time Past*), while there are briefer records of interest in the special number of the *Nouvelle Revue Française* for January, 1923, 'Hommage à Marcel Proust.'

is to modify the air which we all have to breathe. There are various great and definite achievements to be placed to his credit or discredit. But, above and beyond those, there is one undesigned achievement far rarer: he has changed the spiritual and emotional atmosphere of our Western world. We feel and think a little differently because Rousseau lived. This does not mean that he was absolutely original; many others were moving in the same direction. But it was Rousseau who, by some natural personal quality, effected the general change.

The change is so general that we have long since become unconscious of it, and that it is even possible to deny its existence. We are not trained to take tracings of the spiritual respiration, or even to apply a sensitive finger to the pulse of life.

The rare men who at the interval of centuries exert this miraculous effect on the respiratory activities of the spirit are by no means necessarily the kind of men whom we like to count 'great.' That is why their influence is often denied, and they themselves vituperated. They are not the men whom, like Shakespeare, we easily venerate, men who, if not at every point approved, are regarded as splendid and well-balanced humans, supreme examples of the possibilities of our species. But, even on that very account, we bow before them; they have heightened humanity but remained normally human. They have not added any new peculiarity to the human reaction to life and the universe.

That can only be done by an abnormal man who is, almost inevitably, an imperfect man, under-developed on one side if over-developed on another. It is only such a man who is forced to approach life from a new angle. There may possibly be millions so forced. But when it happens that a man thus made comes along in an age peculiarly fitted to respond to the vision from this new angle, and uniquely gifted with the power to express it, he will win for himself a place among those immortals who create the world.

I come to Proust.

As may already be detected, I suspect in Proust — with

whatever hesitation I may still feel over the problem — something of that same type of genius which Rousseau illustrates. Not by any means that Proust displayed it in so splendid and overpowering a degree. The revelation itself was less overwhelming, and, moreover, not of a nature to appeal at first to more than a limited section of human beings.

Yet it may have been of the same nature in this essential respect that here a man was born into the world who saw and felt in it something that had not been seen and felt before, or at all events not seen and felt in so convincing a way that the world itself became conscious of the revelation. We see evidence of this in the fact that there was at first an almost complete blindness to what Proust brought; even the publishers who later were glad to accept his work at first rejected it. New books and essays about Proust are now constantly pouring out from the press. They say all sorts of different things. But their abundance shows that here is a phenomenon that we have to grasp, and explain as we may.[1]

Thomas Hardy's friend, Sir James Barrie, said of him that he 'could scarcely look out of the window in the twilight without seeing something hitherto hidden from mortal eye.' In some degree or in some respect that is the gift of all genius. Proust possessed it in a high degree and in many respects.

If further I am asked to state explicitly what I mean by suggesting that Proust has brought a new vision of the world, it may suffice for the present to bring forward one small example from his work. It is indeed possibly an example to which he

[1] The books about Proust I am myself best acquainted with are: Léon Pierre-Quint, *Marcel Proust: Sa Vie, son Oeuvre*, 1925, indispensable for the primary facts; the *Nouvelle Revue Française* for January, 1923, containing a number of sometimes significant contributions from friends, admirers, and others; Pierre Abraham, *Proust*, with many illustrations; Arnaud Dandieu, *Marcel Proust, Sa Révélation Psychologique;* Albert Feuillerat, *Comment Marcel Proust a composé son Roman*, 1934; this is an elaborate study, partly based on the recovered first proofs of Proust's early volumes, and the results are rather devastating for some conceptions of Proust's genius. It may be added that Proust's work is not easy to read, and for English readers there is available a translation, by C. K. Scott-Moncrieff, which is said by competent judges (I have not myself examined it) to be the remarkable achievement of a certainly most difficult task.

himself attached significance, since he published it beforehand in *La Nouvelle Revue Française* as 'La Regarder Dormir.' [1]
The comparison of the two versions, it may incidentally be
remarked, is of considerable interest, for it helps us in the
study of Proust's literary technique. We find him transposing
passages, making little additions or omissions, and changing
expressions, nearly always for the better, more simple and
more direct, as when the simile of '*un être analogue à un végétal*'
becomes '*une plante*.' More curious is the change in the name
of the sleeping girl, who is also the chief heroine of the whole
narrative, from Albertine to Gisèle. It may be recalled that
Gisèle was one of Albertine's girl companions at Balbec.
I gather from the photographic reproduction of pages of
Proust's manuscript by Pierre Abraham that 'Albertine' is
the name there used, and why it was changed for magazine
publication remains obscure. [2]

It had not been left to Proust to make the first record of a
lover's reactions as he gazes at the beloved in sleep. It may
often have been done before. It was very memorably done in
England even three centuries before Proust, by Sir Kenelm
Digby. That remarkable man, a belated English representative of the Renaissance, recorded in after years, like Proust
drawing from memory, the picture of the famous beauty,
Venetia Stanley, who afterwards became his wife, as he one
day came upon her asleep on her bed. The description is brief,
hardly more than a page, but it is marvellous in its direct
freshness and intimacy and poetic symbolism, excelling
Proust, though produced by the same method, one of a *Temps
Perdu*. [3]

[1] *La Nouvelle Revue Française*, November, 1922, and next year in *La Prisonnière*,
I, pp. 92–99.

[2] The final result of Proust's constant and unceasing elaboration of his work
until the last minute when it left his hands is not satisfactory when we examine
into details, while careless printers and negligent proof-reading have added to
the errors made by Proust in setting down contradictory statements concerning
his characters and forgetting what he had previously written. A number of such
errors were brought together by E. Marsh, 'The Text of Marcel Proust,' *London
Mercury*, May, 1923. Every reader can easily add to them.

[3] It is contained in Digby's *Memoirs*, never published until the early nineteenth
century, and even then with this and some other passages excluded from the

Yet never before Proust can so simple and familiar a phenomenon as a sleeping woman beneath her lover's eyes have been described in detail so elaborate, with so far-ranging a resource of simile and metaphor, with so minute an attention to the emotional reverberations of the scene as in these seven pages. Here, moreover, it is not, as in the fascinating vision recalled by Digby, an isolated fragment from past life, but a coherent portion of a prolonged record which is throughout of the same texture. As our perception of what has here been achieved grows clearer, we realise that we are in the presence of a new revelation. Here, as never before, a man has sought to draw from the vast recesses of a singularly observant and reminiscent psychic organism, a coherent record of the matured impressions cast on it in the past by its experiences in the environing world.

It is worth while to quote, from the reminiscences of his friend Reynaldo Hahn, a small example of Proust's method of direct observation. They were walking together in the country garden of a friend to whose house, it happened, they had both been invited, though at that time Hahn knew little or nothing of Proust's literary interests.

'Would you mind,' asked Proust in his childishly gentle and rather sad voice, 'if I stay behind a moment? I want to look again at those little rose trees.' I left him. At a turn in the path I glanced behind. Marcel had made his way back to the rose trees. I proceeded to stroll round the mansion, and then found him still at the same spot, gazing fixedly at the roses. His head was bent, his expression grave, his eyes winking, his brows rather frowning, as if by an effort of impassioned concentration, with his left hand pushing his little black moustache between his lips and biting it. I felt that he heard me coming, but did not wish to speak or move.

volume, but printed in a separate private supplement, so as not to shock the too prudish British public. It thus came about that the first partial publication of the passage was made by me, incidentally, in *Affirmations*, and later in full in the life of *Sir Kenelm Digby and his Venetia* (1932) by Mr. E. W. Bligh, who mentions that my book first revealed Digby to him. The English seventeenth century, awaking to so many new expressions of life, seems to have been specially impressed by the image of a beloved mistress asleep. We find it dwelt on again in a charming poem by a minor poet, Richard Leigh, quoted in William Kerr's anthology of *Restoration Verse*.

I passed without saying a word. A minute later he called, and rejoined me running, hoping that I was not angry.... How often [Hahn adds] have I later assisted at similar scenes! At such moments Marcel was in total communion with Nature, with art, with life, his whole being concentrated on a transcendent work of penetration, alternating with aspiration, entering, so to say, into a state of trance, reaching to the roots of things and discerning what none could see.

In the last pages of his work Proust complained that even those readers who were sympathetic to the ' truths' he had set down, looked upon them as having been discovered by the ' microscope.' He had really, he protests, ' used a telescope, to perceive things which were indeed very small, but situated at a great distance and each a world.' In reality, neither the microscope nor the telescope is here a helpful image. We are concerned with a task of penetration and revelation which is better described in the words used by Hahn, since things that are near and things that are far are brought together to be pierced by a vision in search of a more ultimate truth beyond. In seeking to define ' style' to Bois, Proust himself put it as ' a quality of vision, the revelation of the particular universe which each of us sees and others fail to see. The pleasure the artist gives us is that of enabling us to know another universe.'

Yet another aspect of this attitude, belonging to a much later period, is reported by Stephen Hudson, the translator into English of the final section of Proust's work. Céleste, the devoted *bonne* who looked after Proust at the end, told Hudson that he only observed things around him when he found in them some special beauty or interest. But if, for instance, the sun happened to light up some corner of the room in a way that pleased him or to give a fantastic tint to some object — it might be a cup of coffee or a glass of beer half full — his eyes would be fixed on it for an hour or more, and he would not allow it to be removed even at night, in the hope of renewing the impression.

We are reminded — and the analogy may not be superficial — of Jacob Behmen, the mystic, who would similarly gaze at the glistening pots and pans in his kitchen, to find there divine illumination. There is a real analogy here, for Proust, with however different a creed from the mystic, was doing precisely what was done by Behmen: he was deliberately seeking beneath external and visible forms the inner and invisible essence of which the external things are merely the symbols: 'gates opening on the Great Mystery.' And Proust might have said with Behmen that 'Paradise is still in the world, but man is not in Paradise until he is born again'; that is, until his vision is purified. To 'regain the flowers of Paradise in the new man' is ever the revealing task of genius. When we transcend the creeds by which at the surface the mystics — Christian, Moslem, or other — may sometimes be entangled, we find that beneath they are at one.

The power of receiving impressions was accompanied in Proust by the power to imprint them in memory. Jacques Blanche the painter, who knew him well, refers to 'the exceptional quality of the registering apparatus which enabled him to fix fugitive sensations and perceptions which for most of us have fled when scarcely caught, to recall them at will, to seize their most distant analogies.' And to yet another friend he seemed to have those many-faceted eyes we attribute to insects, a sort of polygonal vision.

He showed the same quality in his attitude towards his friends, a penetrating perspicacity. You could not deceive him; he saw through you. 'This disconcerting psychologist photographed you with X-rays,' says Jacques Blanche. He once had the fancy to have his fortune told by a palmist. After glancing at his hand she looked up into his face: 'What do you expect of me, sir? it is rather you who should reveal my character.' With this penetrating insight and endlessly detailed observation of Nature and man there went, as indeed an essential part of it, the prodigious memory of which so many of his friends have spoken. He himself was accustomed to say, Paul Morand has noted: 'The Muses are the daughters of Memory; no art without recollection.'

If he thus, like Rousseau before him, yielded a new revelation, it was certainly a revelation completely distinct from

Rousseau's. For Rousseau's sensitive psychic organism — acting as a totality among people who reacted to life only in separate compartments whether intellectual or emotional — responded at once and manifoldly to his experiences, so that, even if nothing more, he was the most genuinely alive man of his time, and taught the world by his example how to respond in a more or less similarly total fashion. To the French society of the mid-eighteenth century Rousseau offered the astonishing spectacle of a man for whom the external world really existed, as Charlier has remarked. That world of matter, so vile and so neglected by an age of classicism, he took up and made his own, therewith casting contempt on urban civilisation and its superrefined minions. His success was so overwhelming because he was simply expressing — and marvellously well — the latent aspirations of the time, for he was (as Brunetière put it) 'one of the most sensitive and impressionable beings that ever existed.'

Rousseau lived and responded — incoherently it may indeed often have been — in a world with which he was in actual contact and by it often buffeted. Proust lived in a *camera obscura*; he was occupied with an immense world of reflections he had accumulated from afar. When a friend quoted to him the saying of Gourmont, 'One only writes well what one has not lived,' he jumped up, exclaiming: 'That is the whole of my work!'

Here we may recall Montaigne who has been invoked as the great revealing influence before Rousseau. Montaigne's supreme discovery was the interest of one's self. It was a revelation which naturally came before either Rousseau's or Proust's. Montaigne had lived in the large world, but was now apart from that world, shut up with himself, and he found infinitely interesting the shifting ideas and emotions of his intimate personal self in that seclusion. Naturally the influences that came to him were ultimately from outside, whether in the present or the past. But while Rousseau was concerned with his direct vital reactions to the living outside world, and Proust with the elaborate investigation of the past as mirrored in his conscious and unconscious mind,

Montaigne was directly concerned with himself. He was revealing the ego, not with any design of magnifying himself, for it was an ego in which we may all have part; he was revealing the rich significance of personality. That was a revelation which must naturally come before either Rousseau's or Proust's.

In however summary and imperfect a form, it is necessary to state the nature of the task laid on these three memorable men, since without some such bird's-eye vision of our spiritual world, it is impossible to understand where our civilisation in its intimate developments today stands. How essential that is we may realise when we find that, even at the present time, there are many who seem to have only the crudest notions, or none at all, of what even Rousseau stands for. They have not yet advanced beyond Montaigne, if so far. They are even shocked when, four centuries later, Whitman reasserts in a more grandiloquent shape, the message of Montaigne.

The men who bring these revelations are necessarily abnormal, since they are doing something which the normal man has never, so completely or at all, been able to do before. Montaigne's task was the most wholesome, and, when once accepted, the easiest; he was able to carry it out in freedom from outside impediments. We cannot consider him a strikingly abnormal person as was Rousseau, and, perhaps still more, Proust.

There is always a tendency to idealise the people who bring great spiritual messages to the world. They seem to their humble admirers to take on a semblance of divinity harmonising with the messages they bring. But even the most devout admirers of Proust find this idealisation difficult, and are sometimes brought to a more qualified estimate. This seems to have happened to Ramon Fernandez, a French critic of distinction, who evidently at first experienced an unqualified cult for Proust and undertook to edit *Les Cahiers Marcel Proust* with the idea of printing every smallest fragment from his pen, down to the most insignificant notes to acquaintances, in the belief that every word he wrote would throw light on his genius. But more recently Ramon Fernandez, while still recognising Proust's importance, has displayed a much more critical attitude. Thus, in reviewing Pierre Abraham's *Proust* in 1931, he highly praised the writer for having completely liberated himself from the 'Proustian religion.' That book is indeed remarkable in its combination of a high estimate of Proust's genius with an outspoken attitude towards his personality.

The details of Proust's life, Abraham frankly states, contribute to form of him 'a representation infinitely troubling and infinitely unpleasant.' Another critic, and of distinction, Denis Saurat, well remarks of Proust's correspondence as published in recent years (and still more, he adds, that which is shown without being published) that 'it leaves a bad taste in the mouth.' 'Proust's letters,' he adds, 'are so disagreeable because they reveal so fully the defects and vices of his personality, an extraordinary man, one of the most charming in some respects, but one of the most repugnant in others.' When I was in Paris not long after his death, I heard sordid details of Proust's life which may have been malicious gossip, but they circulated in quarters likely to be informed. I am reminded, once again, of James Hinton's conception of genius: a weak creature, not able to withstand the inrush of Nature, and, with Nature, the animal and the devil entering in.

We have always to remember that Proust was an invalid, from the age of nine until his death. His affliction happened to be one which is not incompatible with high artistic and intellectual power. But being a disorder of the nervous centres it is apt to be associated with other nervous and psychic peculiarities, these, however, differing with the individual and not always resembling those noted in Proust. But always they tend to affect the general routine of life, implicating at last the whole personality, and demanding a readjustment of life. They peculiarly hampered Marcel Proust's life, even, it seems, to an exaggerated degree, and the son of the distinguished professor who had done so much to introduce hygienic reform in the French State, lived the most unhygienic life, for the most part shut up tightly in his room and spending much of the day in bed, to go out, if at all, at night.

Certainly, of those narrowed opportunities he made an extraordinarily profound use. He learnt to know more of the world, of society and men and Nature and art, than those who are free to move among them all. That was where his genius came in, though we may well believe that it was the limitation of his disease that gave concentration and penetration of insight to his genius.

He was also no stranger to the world of books. Indeed, it was here that we first definitely trace the presence of his sensitive temperament, receptive and irregular. As a boy of fourteen, when asked to fill in the page of an English album, in reply to the question: 'Your favourite prose authors?' he wrote 'George Sand, Aug. Thierry'; and in reply to: 'Your favourite poets?' 'Musset.' That represented a youthful taste, though there was perhaps always something a little unbalanced in Proust's literary admirations, and rightly so. He was drawn by a sound intuition to the writers who, by their subject, their attitude, or their style, best furthered his own task. His *Pastiches*, done at a rather early stage in his career, present writers whose manner he was seeking in some degree to absorb: such as Balzac, Flaubert, Henri de Régnier, the Goncourts, Renan, and above all, Saint-Simon, whose name has since often been mentioned in connection with Proust's method.

His method in these *Pastiches* is really characteristic. He is always in the first place receptive; he lets his spirit soak into what he contemplates; in seeking what is essential he emphasises it, he becomes a little caricatural, so that in the end there is ridicule as well as reverence in his attitude, not ridicule only or reverence only, but, subtle and sometimes mystifying, a blending of both. That is his attitude towards life throughout his great work; that is his attitude towards great stylists in *Pastiches*.

There is an exception in his attitude towards Ruskin, who is not in the *Pastiches*, but is dealt with at much length in the *Mélanges* that follow. His name is not mentioned in the novel, but it has been supposed that we may partly identify him with Bergotte who exercises so much influence over the hero. Proust was conscious of some affinity with Ruskin, and reverence here overweighs ridicule. He had studied Ruskin extensively and minutely; he had actually (though his knowledge of English was very imperfect) translated part of his work, notably that study, late in life, of Amiens Cathedral which Ruskin entitled *The Bible of Amiens*. In front of the Cathedral Proust recalls the four great prophets of Israel: 'There is one more who is not here, and yet we cannot say that he is absent, for we see him everywhere. That is Ruskin: if his statue is not at the door of the Cathedral, it is at the entrance of our hearts.' And elsewhere he refers to the 'divine head' which had borne, and incarnated in living books, so many immortal ideas for the instruction of posterity.

In seeking to describe, as again and again he attempts to do, the method of Ruskin, Proust was clearly expressing his own ideal in art. For Ruskin, he says, is expressing, under the dictation of Nature, a part of her secret, and 'it is the artist's first duty to add nothing of his own to that divine message.' For Ruskin, he insists, there is nothing 'ancient'; everything that exists is 'actual' and can be related to our daily thoughts. In what may well be the most eloquent passage Proust ever wrote, he describes in these *Mélanges* how, as he believed, he had come across at Amiens, among the thousands of images, a worn little figure, some ten centimetres high, which Ruskin had gazed at for days, described, and drawn. So that the crumbling little figure placed there by the artist centuries before, now again, as at the trumpet of the Last Day, sprang to life for a man to whom what has lived is still alive and matter is nothing.

It was with intellectual sincerity, Proust continues, that Ruskin reflected the universe by the aid of a magical native gift for revealing and loving a new aspect of Beauty, even though an element of 'idolatry' may sometimes have crept in, the artist's own invention, to mar that direct sincerity. So that, after all, Proust's critical temper awakes even where Ruskin is concerned, and he finds at the root a certain element of falsehood, a confusion in Ruskin's opposed ethical and aesthetic ideals. 'I need not add,' he concludes, 'that if I make, as it were in the abstract, a general reserve, less with

regard to the works of Ruskin than to the essence of their inspiration and the quality of their beauty, he is for me none the
less one of the great writers of all ages and all lands.' [1]

If it is instructive to investigate Proust's attitude towards
books, it is even more so to observe his attitude towards the
actual persons he knew. The copious publication of his letters
in recent years has made this easy, and has thrown much light,
however ambiguously, on his way of thought and feeling.

We may specially note his correspondence with the Comtesse de Noailles, perhaps the most distinguished writer
with whom he was during many years (about eighteen) in
relations of personal friendship, though there seems to
have been little contact during the later years. These letters
were published in 1931 by Madame de Noailles herself in
a volume of over two hundred pages, and they are a remarkable, even if disconcerting, revelation of their writer's personality. So fine a critic as Denis Saurat (reviewing the book
in the *Nouvelle Revue Française*) finds them altogether revolting
and abominable. They reveal so fully those defects and vices
which in Proust's work become sublimated to an integral
part of his genius. An extraordinary man, charming in some
aspects this critic admits, he was most repugnant in others.
He possessed 'a really Satanic capacity for lying' and an
extraordinary aptitude for sentimental violence, these two
leading defects acting together to produce every form of
treacherous flattery. Proust's greatest pleasure was to make
fools of his friends and he found a malicious joy in catching
them in the traps he laid. He regarded all individuals, as
well as all moments of life, as standing separate and alone

---

[1] It may be noted here that Proust showed a special predilection for English
and American writers. In 1910 he wrote to his friend Robert de Billy: 'I have just
been reading a very fine thing which unfortunately resembles a little (though a
thousand times better) what I am doing, Thomas Hardy's *The Well-Beloved*.
There is not even lacking that grotesque touch which belongs to all great works.
It is curious that in all the different fields, from George Eliot to Hardy, from
Stevenson to Emerson, there is no literature which has over me a power comparable to English or American literature. Germany, Italy, very often France,
leave me indifferent. But two pages of *The Mill on the Floss* bring me to tears.
I know that Ruskin execrated that novel; but in the Pantheon of my admirations
I reconcile all these hostile gods.'

and aloof. 'Proust treats his friends as if they were as foreign as Patagonians and as inferior as slaves.'

There is an element of truth in this critic's attitude. But his judgment is too unqualified. Proust treated his friends as he treated the characters in his books. He had real affection for the people whom, consciously or not, he made ridiculous, whether his friends or his creations, just as it has been said of Dickens that 'he had a boy's love for the persons who afforded him opportunities for horse-play.' And there was much of the child in Proust. Yet we do not find his imaginary characters altogether unsympathetic, and it is certain that Proust's numerous friends never regarded themselves as 'Patagonians' or 'slaves' in his eyes. They usually make deductions or qualifications of one kind or another when describing him as a friend, but the final estimate is appreciative. So also was the judgment of his social inferiors in close touch. 'Madame,' said to Madame Scheikévitch his faithful *bonne* Céleste after his death, 'when one has known Monsieur Proust everyone seems vulgar.' Saurat's austerely Puritanic condemnation of Proust's 'Satanic' qualities in friendship seems to rest on a failure to understand his peculiar temperament. It was the temperament demanded for his work, and it was so intimately his own that it entered even into his closest relationships. He evidently possessed a deep craving for friendship; he was much absorbed in his friends as even his frequent quarrels and misunderstandings with them — often due to what Madame de Noailles calls 'the suspicious sensibility of this restless heart' — should suffice to show, and that was a chief source of those extravagancies which can hardly be dismissed as treachery. The sentimental violence was a real trait, and it was fortified by a failure of judicial balance in criticism, for Proust's extraordinary insight was not accompanied by any corresponding power to weigh and balance. He entered into the spirit of his friends; it was a real joy to him to appreciate their caricatural possibilities, with no thought of depreciating them, and, as so many of his friends have noted, he was an admirable mimic.

I cannot agree that he was deliberately making a fool of

Madame de Noailles in these fantastic letters which, some years after his death, she was innocent or courageous enough to publish. He certainly had a genuine admiration for her work, which he also expressed elsewhere than in the letters, and shared with other eminent writers of the time. It was the natural impulse of his violently sentimental and critically unbalanced temperament when in contact with his friends to push that admiration to fantastic extremes of expression. Again and again, almost constantly, he quotes from the poet's work lines and phrases which for the most part we may fairly regard as of complete banality and enthusiastically declares that they are worthy of the greatest poet of any age. It would seem that at first Madame de Noailles had been ready to accept Proust's eulogies seriously, though when she finally printed his letters she introduces various withdrawing comments concerning the 'magnificent verbal distractions' of his 'precious sympathy.' It must have been an irresistible temptation for his peculiar sensibility — and not requiring any touch of 'Satanic' vice — to pour out these cajoling extravagancies which were so gratefully received. We do not know that he ever bestowed them on objects for which he felt no real regard.

Before condemning Proust's 'capacity for lying,' we must understand his own attitude in the matter. He has been quite honest about it. We find his creed on this matter plainly set forth in 'Albertine Disparue.' The hero condemns himself here for having believed what he now considers to have been Albertine's falsehoods. 'Why have believed her? Lying is essential to mankind. It perhaps plays as large a part as the search for pleasure, and, besides, it is required by that search. One lies to protect his pleasure, or his honour if the revelation of the pleasure is contrary to honour. We lie all our lives, even especially, perhaps only, to those who love us.' It can hardly be satisfactory 'to those who love us,' but the motive is not 'Satanic.'

It may suffice to quote a single illustrative passage from these letters, though it happens to be one not altogether typical, since the laudation is here ingeniously indirect.

This evening [he writes in 1904] I dined with Montesquiou, and with an almost morbid exaltation in his high-pitched voice, emphasised by gestures which need to be imitated, he said: '*Exhortation* [a story by Madame de Noailles then just published] is not only sublime, marvellous, ravishing, it is *the most beautiful thing I have ever read;* I tell you, from the height of my competence in matters of taste and the breadth of my culture, that it is, pre-cisely, *the most beautiful thing ever written!*' And then he began to *recite it right through*, exclaiming, again and again; 'What genius! what genius!' And when we came out into the street he suddenly stopped, raised his arms to the sky, and murmured: 'The sky that evening was of a colour that cannot be described,' causing the passers-by to stop and me to catch cold, while he himself, electri-fied by the shock of the phrase he had just quoted, stamped on the pavement as if to break his heel, and threw himself back. That was not all. Before that he had spoken to our hosts of 'The Prayer to the Sun,' and, assuming an oracular tone, had said: 'I will tell you *exactly what that is: it is the finest thing written since the Antigone*. What sublimity! *It is even finer* than Sophocles!'

But, even here, Proust cannot resist the temptation to play up to the exalted Count:

Dear friend (pardon, Madame) [he adds], do not imagine that I consider all this worth mentioning, it is the inevitable echo of your divine accents on every human ear made to understand them. But it fills me with such joy, every time I allow my own admira-tion an instant's silence, to hear a momentarily fraternal voice take up the song in unison.

And the gratified poet adds a footnote, murmuring something about 'extravagance,' but desiring to be allowed to record her 'emotion and gratitude.' Ah, well!

I was led to quote this passage, not only in illustration of the correspondence, but because it introduces a characteristic figure we cannot avoid when we set out in search of Proust. We meet the Comte Montesquiou-Fezensac, not only by reason of his long, if disturbed, friendship with Proust, but because he is the figure so frequently mentioned as chiefly serving to make up that most memorable of Proust's creations, Charlus.[1]

[1] Montesquiou finally wrote and published a volume of *Mémoires*, which throw a most interesting light on Proust's conception of Charlus. Pierre-Quint remarks

Montesquiou belonged to another generation. I remember in Paris, in 1890, before Proust's days, one heard of Montesquiou as of an accomplished but highly eccentric personage, on the aristocratic outskirts of the literary world. He was commonly spoken of as having furnished traits for the aesthetically fantastic Des Esseintes of Huysmans's *A Rebours*, especially the tortoise with the bejewelled carapace. I recall turning over the pages of a volume of his poems, not thinking them sufficiently important to read with any care, but amused at their elaborate and peculiar virtuosity.

Recently Henri de Régnier, who moved in the same world and was of much the same generation, has in the course of his interesting reminiscences, *De Mon Temps*, set down the history of his own relations with this eccentric personage. Régnier is of urbane temperament, and always considerate of others' feelings, but even his relations with Montesquiou had been stormy. He first heard of the Comte Robert de Montesquiou-Fezensac, in connection with *A Rebours*, as a singular figure, descendant of an illustrious family, a dandy with sensational waistcoats, a poet who only revealed his choice productions to privileged friends, but who occasionally condescended to associate with the ordinary vulgar literary tribe. Mallarmé was among these until Montesquiou accused him of communicating personal traits to help build up the figure of Des Esseintes. Blanche the painter also fell into disfavour and would afterwards refer to Montesquiou, whose enmities were fierce and tenacious, with an amusing mixture, says Henri de Régnier, of terror and admiration. It was not till after the actual publication at last of a volume of verse, full of fantastically elaborate platitudes, *Les Chauves-Souris*, that Régnier was permitted to enter the presence of the author of these poems. He saw a tall and lean figure, most elegantly dressed, carrying high a small head with yellowish complexion and bright eyes, a personality at once courteous and insolent. He talked incessantly, sometimes incisively and

on the strange irony of life by which these *Mémoires*, written in self-justification, render inevitable the identification of their author with the ambiguous figure of Charlus.

wittily, in a voluble voice that was high almost to falsetto, and what he said revealed not only erudition, but a boundless pride and an equal vanity. This curious and slightly comic figure was usually escorted by his secretary, one Yturri of uncertain origin, Argentine by nationality, it was said, and of disquieting appearance. We cannot but see here the suggestion for Charlus and possibly for Morel, though it appears that Montesquiou actually had a protégé who was, like Morel, a musician. By his marriage with the poet Heredia's daughter, Henri de Régnier came into closer relations with the Count. One day when they were both present at a highly aristocratic afternoon tea party, they chanced to leave the drawing-room together and exchanged what De Régnier thought were a few insignificant remarks. Next day, however, to his surprise, he received a challenge to a duel on account of remarks said to have been ' insulting.' The seconds, duly appointed, could not settle the matter, so the duel was fought, with swords. De Régnier, without experience in this matter, took a few lessons in fencing beforehand and succeeded in slightly wounding his adversary's hand. This brought to an end both the contest and all future relations between the two former friends. Montesquiou had been accused of cowardice at the disastrous Charity Bazaar fire shortly before, when, it was said, he made his escape through a struggling crowd of fashionable women by a liberal use of his cane, and Régnier thinks he may have felt it necessary to retrieve his reputation for courage by a duel, the more readily as he was an accomplished fencer.[1] But he was evidently a difficult friend, and it is the more notable that Proust's relations with him, even though sometimes disturbed, lasted

[1] Montesquiou gives his own account of the incident, somewhat differing from Régnier's, in his *Mémoires*, vol. III, pp. 144 and 294. These *Mémoires* were published in 1923, after Montesquiou's death. He had died in 1921, and was buried at Versailles beside his friend Gabriel de Yturri, 'beneath the Angel of Silence.' He often refers in his *Mémoires* to 'my dear Yturri,' but the references to Proust, who was still living, are vague and rather ambiguous. He had never known that he was to live in human memory, not by any achievement of his own, but as having furnished traits for the caricatural use of the two chief French literary artists of his time in their two chief figures.

for some twenty-eight years. They began in 1893 when Proust was twenty-two, and only ceased towards his death. The meetings began at the house of a mutual friend, and in Proust's first letter he signs himself 'your very respectful, fervent, and charmed Marcel Proust'; in the second he already describes Montesquiou as 'the sovereign of eternal things.' Before the end their relations had become cooler, and in his last letter Proust has to explain that his silence was not due to indifference, but to illness. After Montesquiou's death, Marcel's brother Robert succeeded with some difficulty in securing the letters and has published them (together with a few addressed to the Count's faithful friend and secretary Yturri) in a volume of Proust's *Correspondance Générale*.[1]

Proust, as his friends have often remarked, was a clever mimic; even his warmest admirations tended to take a caricatural aspect as he so shockingly revealed in his letters to Madame de Noailles. But Montesquiou was a magnificent subject for mimicry and Proust delighted to mimic him. This the haughty Count Robert resented as 'disrespectful,' and so arose frequent quarrels which, however, seem always to have been composed, no doubt by Proust's boundless facility in adulation. It is certain that Montesquiou made a profound impression on Proust by a personality so abnormal, so fantastic, so aristocratic. He combined all the traits needed to appeal to that modern Saint-Simon whom so many of his admirers find in Proust. At first, when the figure of Charlus appears in the pages of *La Recherche*, Montesquiou was not its sole inspiration but he becomes more and more so as *Sodome et Gomorrhe* progresses, so that Montesquiou may be said to be the key to Charlus in a sense in which no other character in the work can be said to have a single key.

That is why Montesquiou is of interest, for Charlus — when we are content to look upon Proust's work simply as a gallery of portraits — is Proust's supreme creation. No

[1] Dr. Proust had perhaps realised that his brother's letters have sometimes tended to give an unfavourable impression of the writer, and latterly refused permission to Madame Rivière to publish her husband's correspondence with Marcel Proust, though it might prove interesting, especially as presenting the letters on both sides.

doubt he felt that himself and therefore clung to his creation in spite of the reaction he foresaw that Charlus would arouse. He protested against conventional 'taste.' 'In art,' he said, 'taste is a reactionary element.' He knew that he was bringing a new theme into literature and he realised that in such a task there lay something grand and audacious. 'When M. de Charlus comes out,' he groaned (Pierre-Quint tells us), 'you will see, all will turn their backs on me, and especially the English. Though I seldom leave my bed people still invite me. Open that drawer in front of you and you will find an invitation from the Duchess of C. whom I scarcely know. (I show it you almost in confidence.) Tomorrow none will invite me any more. On every side I shall be driven out.'

He was not far wrong as regards the English, at all events for a time. Without any delay, in 1922, A. B. Walkley, dramatic critic of *The Times*, as fine a representative of respectable English conventions as one could find, at once proceeded to verify Proust's prophecy. He was by no means an Anti-Proustian, but he could not stomach M. de Charlus. That 'filthy brute and amazing cad is,' he declares, 'one of the most repulsive brutes ever conceived by a novelist'; it almost spoilt the whole work for him. He would have been surprised to know that in a few years' time that same Charlus would be regarded by some critics as one of the chief figures in literature, on a level with Don Quixote. That is certainly an extravagant estimate. Charlus is not with the supreme figures of literature, with Ulysses and Don Quixote and Robinson Crusoe. But it is not easy to find any figure in French fiction to put beside him. Walkley brings in the criterion of moral approval where it is altogether out of place. We do not feel approval of Falstaff who moves in the same circle of Art's Heaven as Charlus, though we may find his vices more amiable. But to refuse to enjoy such superb creations as Falstaff and Charlus on the ground of moral disapproval is merely to show that one has not yet taken the first step over the threshold of the House of Art.

But we must not yet leave this so significant volume of Proust's letters to Montesquiou, for it is impossible to over-

rate its importance in the search for Proust. As we turn over
the pages we find no limit to the extravagance of the language which Proust addresses to his correspondent, or to the
depths of his admiration for his artificial and pretentious
poems. He assures Montesquiou — and the assurance seems
badly needed — that he is 'an admirer who is candid, tender,
respectful, and truthful.' But we move in so fantastic an
atmosphere that it is even a pleasure to come on so simply
human an episode — this happens to be addressed to Yturri
— as Proust's description of how he is staying at a primitive
hotel in Finisterre where there are no *cabinets*, so that one cannot always repeat the prayer of Vigny to be left alone with Nature, and goes on to complain of 'the excessive zeal of the nettles' on such occasions. Proust had been fascinated by Yturri
from the first; Régnier, as we know, describes him as a disquieting figure. Proust writes in an early letter to Montesquiou:
'I have fallen under the charm of his spiritual graces, how
civilised! how delicate! and what a wildcat! what gentleness!
what bounds!' He is always full of compliments whenever
he writes to Yturri.

No one fails to note Proust's attraction to the aristocracy.
The son of a successful professional man possessing a high
reputation in hygienic science, and with a Jewish mother,
Marcel belonged to a prosperous family of good social standing, but hardly with any native connection with the ancient
aristocracy. Yet it was to that select social layer of Parisian
society that from the first he was irresistibly drawn. At a
very early age he began to be allowed a seat in the drawing-
rooms of society, alike in its aristocratic and in its unconventional assemblies. On the one hand he could study the Bonapartist nobility in the salon of Princess Mathilde, and on the
other hand he seems to have been little more than a boy when
a celebrated courtesan presented him with a book bound in
silk from her petticoat.

Proust has often been called a 'snob' in the English sense.
But his snobbery was of so special and peculiar a character
that the accusation has no sting. He took a genuine delight
in aristocrats of ancient race, and had among them genuine

friends. There was, for instance, the Duc de Luynes, three years his senior, as fine an aristocrat of ancient lineage as could well be found, who also happened to be a lover of literature; he showed his friendly and enduring regard by his presence at Proust's funeral. Honoré-Charles-Marie-Sosthènes d'Albert, tenth Duc de Luynes, Duc de Chevreuse, Duc de Montfort, Prince de Neuchatel, Comte de Tours, and de Dunois, Marquis d'Albert, whose mother was a daughter of the Duc de Doudeauville, his wife the daughter of the Duc d'Uzès, premier Duke of France, and who was descended from a godson of Henri IV, was indeed a figure after Proust's own heart. It was his delight to lose himself in the *Almanach de Gotha* and to trace out the ancestries and the relationships and the heraldry of the exalted persons therein recorded. A friend found him one day laughing over the *Gotha*: 'Did you know that Madame X is related to the Zs? It is too amusing!'

'A marvellous source of compliments and mockeries,' said, after Proust's death, Maurice Barrès who had known him fairly well. But in his art that attitude was transformed. The warm spirit of ingratiation combined with the cold spirit of cynical criticism to produce a penetrating attitude of scientific observation.

It used sometimes to be said that Proust's conception of character had put the art of his predecessors in fiction out of date. He conceived a figure in the round, in all its vital complexity, while their representations are flat and superficial; he himself told Bois that he had tried to establish a three-dimensional psychology, and some critics have accepted this view, or we might say that he tried to effect in fiction something of what Cézanne strove after in painting. Dr. F. C. Green put it that the difference between Proust and previous novelists is that feebly suggested by the difference between looking at a photograph through a stereoscope and with the naked eye. Feuillerat's exploration of Proust's manuscripts has now, however, discounted this estimate. He shows that Proust's opinion of his characters tended to change progressively as his work advanced. So that the new dimensional character is not so much a deliberate method of the artist as simply an added complexity accidental to his changing view. We need not throw aside Stendhal and Flaubert because we also have Proust, any more than we need throw aside Pascal because we also have Rousseau.

Many of Proust's characters, indeed, appear, as a result of their confused complexity, thoroughly unsatisfactory, and would hardly do much credit to a third-rate novelist. Even Albertine, who fills so large a place, less, it may well be true, for her own sake than for her action on the hero of the story, never — though I admit a difference of opinion on this point — becomes a vitally real person. She is supposed to have been built up from some half-dozen models of girls with whom Proust had come in contact, and we can well believe it; indeed, at the end of his work he as much as says so himself. Elstir, again, is equally vague, though, since he appears as a painter rather than as a man, this may be of little moment; he is composed, as Feuillerat reasonably considers, of Monet, a little Manet, and much Whistler, from whom probably his name.

The progressive change in the characters is largely due, Feuillerat finds, to Proust's growing disposition to pessimism. His retouches always tend to degrade his characters, and make them less likeable, more malevolent, even Françoise, even Saint-Loup. 'Formerly I believed in friendship; now it no longer exists for me,' he wrote in latter years to Lucien Daudet. It was a significant confession for the man who had justified deception and practised so much insincerity even in his genuine friendships.

It is nevertheless generally agreed, however the result may be attained, not only that Proust's figures — those that are best achieved — stand out in the round, but that he has admirably realised the tone of the society in which they move, even if he cannot sometimes help caricaturing it. No doubt it is the figures themselves that in the end remain in memory, and we can never too much admire the delicate skill with which this scientific entomologist of the aristocratic salons gently captures these creatures and pins them on the cardboard of his novel.[1] 'Every social condition has its interest,' Proust wrote in an article in the *Figaro*, 'and the artist may perhaps feel as curious to show the ways of a queen as of a dressmaker.' He felt the seduction of the people of the world, but his final judgment of them was severe; he was never their dupe. 'What idiots they are!' we are told he often exclaimed, as the outcome of this malicious sympathy. Yet there is the devil in it all!

That, however, is but another way of saying that the key to Proust's personality is of pathological nature. To turn ferociously against Proust the man may be on the surface natural and justifiable. But it is only so when we assume that we are concerned with a normal man, of ordinary healthy constitution, leading the average human life of his social class. We are concerned with a man who fulfils none of these conditions. Nor will heredity suffice to explain him. Rousseau's heredity we can study; it is full of illumination on Rousseau the man, though his genius remains, as it always will, a mystery. But the Proustian heredity most naturally leads us by no means to Marcel, but to his younger brother Robert, following in his father's footsteps, and attaining to distinction in his profession.[2] In Marcel we have to recognise an exasperated sensibility which is morbid in origin, and we cannot find the key by approaching it in a mood of moral vituperation, but rather of tenderness. Even Albert Feuillerat, in one of the most penetrating and accomplished studies of Proust's genius, concludes that the principal element in the special combination of conditions which make Proust's work original is of pathological nature.

We have to attempt to define that pathological foundation. As is known, the complaint which moulded the outward shape of Marcel Proust's life, and furnished the conditions

[1] 'A far less sentimental Fabre, repeating the doings of human dung-beetles,' I find a recent American critic describing Proust. But that is too prejudiced on account of the situation. It is more legitimate to say, with a more penetrating critic, that Proust had the spirit of the surgeon, and that in some of his volumes we seem even to be seeing the bright gleam of the scalpel making its incisions.

[2] Professor Robert Proust's death in 1935 evoked the highest testimonies to his professional skill and his personal character.

for his whole life-work, was spasmodic nervous asthma, allied to and often associated with the slighter form of the same disorder commonly called hay-fever. Since Proust's death this has become generally regarded as one of a group of disorders, having elements in common and tending to be associated, now going under the name of allergy. The allergic group of disorders especially includes asthma (with hay-fever) and some skin complaints, with which it may be interchangeable. They are technically described as showing one common aetiological characteristic: hypersensitiveness to proteins or other substances that are innocuous to ordinary people. The symptoms come and go suddenly, though in severe cases there is more or less illness during the intervals. The nature of the attacks indicates disturbance of the autonomic nervous system. When repetitions are frequent, the attacks are liable to be brought on by very slight causes, sometimes only psychical. Thus, while the provocation comes from without, the origin of the allergic condition is in an insecure internal metabolism, a sensitive autonomic nervous system. The victim of the allergic disorder is sometimes termed an 'autopath.' [1]

It is held that the source of the allergic condition is usually in some hereditary unbalance. This is not obvious in Marcel Proust. His father seems to have been vigorous and robust; we hear nothing against the mother's constitution; the only brother, Dr. Robert Proust, active and distinguished in professional work, was apparently a normal man. I am inclined to find a clue in the differences of race; the father belonged to central France, the mother was Jewish. Such racial blends of rather unlike genes certainly lead to unusual psycho-neurotic conditions, as is shown by the frequency with which an unusual level of ability is found in the offspring. We may quite reasonably expect the resulting condition sometimes to be pathological in character.

Not only were his parents healthy, but the boy Marcel seems himself to have enjoyed good health. It has been found,

[1] C. Paget Lapage, 'Allergy, Metabolism, and the Autonomic Nervous System,' *British Medical Journal*, 11th December, 1934.

however, in England by the Asthma Research Council (Report for 1934), not only that the level of intelligence in asthmatic children is superior to that of normal children, but that the disorder specially tends to occur among those who are over-protected and fussed by their parents, and both these conditions were probably present in Marcel's case.[1] One day suddenly, after a walk in the Bois de Boulogne with parents and friends, he was seized by a terrible fit of suffocation. It was the first attack of that asthma by which he was tortured during the whole of the rest of his life. As is usual in these allergic cases, the attacks were intermittent, but always liable to occur, while in the intervals health was frequently impaired. Great care had always to be exercised, since even the open air, the country, the odour of trees, and the fragrance of flowers were liable to prove asphyxiating. The general nervous state became exasperatingly tense, and the senses abnormally acute. Hence it was that Proust lived in his room with a cork lining to deaden sound, and in hotels would sometimes engage the neighbouring rooms to avoid disturbance. After the death of his father in 1903, he became wealthy, and was thus able to live as he liked and adopt every precaution, even every whim, which he chose to find desirable.

It is possible for me to understand Proust's pathological state, since I had the opportunity of observing closely a similar allergic situation in another victim who was also predestined by natural genius to be an artist: I refer to Olive Schreiner. In many features of mental and emotional character she was very far removed from Proust. But in pathological respects, as well as by a highly sensitised psychoneurotic nature, she was nearly allied to him. Her history, moreover, suggests instructive parallels. At the outset there was a similar origin from two fine and healthy stocks of a level above the average. Similarly, also, the two stocks were racially rather remote, in this case Swabian German and Northern English. This anomaly — in both cases the only

---

[1] At the age of fourteen, in reply to the album question, 'What is your idea of unhappiness?' he put: 'To be separated from Mamma.'

hereditary anomaly known — confirms my suspicion that we have here a source of allergy. Similarly, again, the allergic symptoms only appeared in one among the offspring while the general level of these products of racial blending was very high. Several of Olive Schreiner's siblings achieved some degree of distinction, but it is perhaps significant that alike in the Proust and the Schreiner families, it was in the member with artistic genius that the allergic manifestations alone appeared. Both seemed of vigorous and robust constitution until the first attack occurred, in Olive Schreiner at eighteen and when the artistic tendencies were already clear, but whether they had also appeared in Marcel Proust before his first attack at a much earlier age must remain doubtful. The chief difference may be said to be due to the longer early period of health enjoyed by Olive Schreiner, who had acquired adult activities before she was attacked (and, moreover, was never fussed by parents at home), while Marcel Proust, being attacked before puberty, was more completely moulded by the allergic state, and, by his good financial position, was better able to adapt his life to that state. So we may say that Proust's work was largely conditioned and even developed by his pathological state, and in Olive Schreiner it was an almost unrelieved handicap. Otherwise the pathological conditions in both were closely similar.

I must not be understood to assert that the form of Proust's genius was entirely and directly shaped by allergic conditions. It was even more precisely shaped by the indirect results of that condition, arresting development when he was still a child.

In genius, as I have often had occasion to observe, we seem to trace what we conventionally regard as elements of the child, the woman, and the man, the sensibilities of the child, the emotions of the woman, the intellect of the man. I would say that this held true of Olive Schreiner. It is still more clearly pronounced in Marcel Proust. One need not go so far as Jean Prévost, who compares Proust to the child in the womb, folded on itself, and only able to view the outside world with suspicion. But one may clearly recognise that the arresting influence of disease at the age of nine retained young Marcel for an unduly long period, and to some extent permanently, in the protected position of the child. Those ways and feelings which we commonly consider feminine were also fostered by his life, and in the concentrated will-power by which he was attached to his work, we may perhaps find — in the absence of any obvious evidence of virile qualities of character — the chief proof he furnished of what is considered masculine energy.

It was Dandieu who first emphasised the significance in Proust of his schizoid tendency, the tendency towards that rupture of contact with reality which in its extreme degree constitutes the form of insanity termed schizophrenia.[1] This rupture I would associate with an inner division of personality, the presence of the infantile element carried into adult life. For the schizoid tendency to rupture of contact between the personality and external life may be said to have its origin in an initial rupture within, between the infantile element unable to contact with reality and the struggling adult tendency towards such contact, which in Proust is specially associated with fetiches (like the cup of tea) serving to evoke that deeper infantilism which, as Dandieu says, is 'the secret alike of Proust's weakness and his genius.'[2] Such a schizoid tendency, representing a stage on the way to schizophrenia, is thus not altogether remote from the cycloid tendency which represents a stage towards the insane manic-depressive state, for we might say that the alternate depressed and exalted moods of the latter condition are represented in the schizoid condition by opposed moods existing side by side.

We are thus led to various manifestations of ruptured vital contact with reality, marked in Proust as well as in Rousseau, the extreme sensitiveness, the morbid susceptibility, the

[1] Dandieu devotes especially the last section of his book, *Marcel Proust*, to an illuminating discussion of the implications of this tendency.

[2] The relation of the concrete fetich to the inner unconscious world of memories, which for Proust is the real world, is rendered admirably clear in the early pages of the second volume of *Le Temps Retrouvé*. Here, more than anywhere, Proust furnishes the key to his work.

aptitude for suspicion (associated in Proust with extravagant adulation), which made relations with friends, and sometimes even with strangers, so difficult. We may say it was the pressure within of the child element for ever needing defence and seeking for protection. His absurdly exaggerated politeness was really, as Pierre-Quint remarks, a method of protecting himself. In this connection we may remember that, as has been said in connection with Proust's genius, the power of observation only develops highly in the individual who has a personality to defend. And in the same connection we may also recall that need, on which Proust (like Rousseau) so often insists, of solitude, as well as the flight from the present. Dandieu has noted that his reduction of space to time is only apparent, since he really (as Fernandez also argues) spatialises things, recollections and perceptions alike, and as Minkowski, for instance, shows in his book on schizophrenia, this tendency is precisely a trait of the schizophrenic subject.[1] In the same connection Dandieu refers to the significance of Proust's systematic pessimism in love, and finally in friendship, and his belief in the necessity of pessimism as well as solitude for artistic creation. They rest on the schizoid lack of personal contact with external reality, the affirmation of a sole subjective reality, with the consequent incommunicability of human beings. 'The artist who sacrifices an hour of work for an hour's conversation with a friend,' said Proust, 'knows that he is sacrificing reality to something which has no existence.... The only reality, for everyone, is the region of his own sensibility.'

When we seek to explore Proust's philosophy from a severe

---

[1] Some writers have emphasised an influence of Bergson on Proust. But Proust himself, while declaring that he would have no objection to calling his novel Bergsonian if it really were so, denied that it was. 'My work is dominated,' he said to Bois in 1913, 'by a distinction which not only does not figure in Bergson's philosophy, but is even inconsistent with it. For me voluntary memory, which is specially memory of the intelligence and the eyes, only brings us unfaithful images from the past, while an odour, a taste, recurring again under quite different circumstances, awakes the past in spite of ourselves, and we feel how different it was from what we thought it to be, when depicted by voluntary memory, as by a painter using wrong colours.' But in general philosophic outlook Proust was more influenced by Bergson than he here admits.

critical and intellectualistic standpoint, we meet with much confusion and contradiction. He enters blind alleys, he follows aims that are not those of his genuine temperament, he returns again and again on himself. Even in so simple matter as that of friendship, on which I have just quoted an opinion, we see that there is really no place for it in his philosophy. His own self is the only reality for the artist; no communication is possible with other things, to attempt it is sheer waste of time. Yet, as we know, Proust had many friends, and we might even say that the whole of his life not devoted to his work was given to cultivating, with the most anxious and hyperaesthetic sensibility, his relations with these friends.

I do not propose to enter the thorny path of Proust's philosophical conceptions expressed or implied. It has been well investigated by Arnaud Dandieu whose early and lamented death occurred only three years after the publication of his *Marcel Proust*, which is the most critical and penetrating study of the subject known to me. He discussed Proust's various and often contradictory tendencies and his conclusions may seem at first damaging. But he suggests how the schizoid condition throws here a constant illumination, as by the combined hyperaesthetic and anaesthetic tendencies found side by side in the subjects of schizophrenia.

In the end Dandieu triumphantly shows how Proust's defects and confusions and weaknesses contributed to the magnificence of his psychological revelation. He never disengaged himself from a radical subjectivism which was a kind of suicide. But without that suicide we could never have had his revelation. He has given us a new conception of individual reality, even though there is, we may say necessarily, a dynamic lack, on the moral side notably the lack of 'charity' which, Dandieu remarks, is rather than as Mauriac thinks, the lack of 'grace,' Proust's moral failure. His infantilism involved anarchy by its defect of force, though it brought creative magic by an excess of force. When all is said that can be said against Proust by literary critics, we must still conclude, Dandieu finally affirms, that here was a writer who 'escaped from literature to re-create literature.'

It is the miracle of genius — even from of old vaguely
apprehended — that through an incomplete, defective, if
not infantile instrument, the voice of wisdom is heard.
We must not say that in Proust disease was the actual cause
of genius. We may, however, say, with Martin-Chauffier,
who knew him, that he courageously seized and utilised his
disease to exploit his prodigious gifts. Forget the man Proust,
and as we turn the pages of the sixteen volumes of his great
novel [1] we perpetually come on passages which reveal a profound insight into the mysteries of life, at the same time often
expressing that insight in forms of new and singular beauty,
mingling, in his own phrase, the dust of reality with magic
sand.

Proust has remarked that the man who is often sleepless
knows more about sleep than he who sleeps well. That, indeed, was a subject of which he had had much experience, and
his meditations on it occupy the very first pages of his work.
I am here reminded afresh of his remark, for might we not
say that the man who is abnormal knows more about normality than the normal man himself? We tend to become unconscious of what is habitual; the normal man feels no impulse
to contemplate his own normality. At the most he only sees
normal things from the outside, and Proust has declared that
the observer who only sees things from the outside has seen
nothing. The abnormal man is fascinated by normality;
he sees it from his own angle, he meditates on it; he as it
were gets behind it; he is able to embody it; in his vision the
normal becomes flesh. It is so when he gazes even at living
things of a lowly class. I have noted, for instance, the passage
where Proust describes asparagus as it was never described
before. Such a passage as that, indeed, might almost have
been written by Huysmans, whose genius was somewhat akin
to Proust's (I do not know that Proust ever recognised this
kinship), but the angle at which Huysmans viewed the
world often tended to make the normal appear abnormal,
while Proust's vision tended to make the abnormal more
normal, and to reveal a new universe.

[1] As published from 1913 onwards (not 1914 as printed on volume I).

It may seem to some that the vision thus obtained is, if not arbitrary, capricious and insignificant. Certainly it may be. Proust himself has remarked that any novelty in art, simply because it wanders from our conventions, will seem artificial and fatiguing.[1] But Croce is on firm ground when he insists that there are no objective standards of judgment. It is useless to approach a work of art with our rigid laws and categories. We must comprehend the artist's own values, and only then are we competent to judge his work. That, Croce adds, is why criticism is immensely more difficult than is commonly supposed. That is also why the search for critical equilibrium in the estimate of Proust has taken so long between the too unbalanced extremes: that of those critics who found his work 'boring' and 'exceptionally dull,' to say no worse, and those who set up a 'Proustian religion.'

It may seem to some rather extravagant to couple Proust with so immensely significant a figure as Rousseau, though it is not here suggested for the first time.[2] Certainly from the moral point of view — I mean, of course, in their relation to social life — they are not even on the same plane. Proust was consciously above all an artist. He was concerned, as he said to Bois, with a quality of vision, the revelation of the particular universe, within the individual, which other individuals fail to see. 'The pleasure that the artist gives is that of enabling us to know another universe.' Rousseau was a great artist in literature, and he realised that, as indeed Proust has said, style is not mere adornment, but the very stuff of the medium in which the artist works, but he was not primarily

[1] So sensitive a spirit as Boylesve could make nothing of Proust's work at first, though he afterwards became a warm admirer. Anatole France, even when Proust was growing famous, said: 'I can't understand his work. I have tried hard, but I cannot succeed.' Gide remarks how interesting it is that the two writers of our time most sure of fame, Proust and Valéry, almost of the same age and with closely parallel careers, took little interest in each other and indeed seemed incapable of understanding each other.

[2] It is noteworthy that, even before Proust's death, the parallel was suggested by Mr. Middleton Murry in the *Quarterly Review*, July, 1922. Proust's work, he declares, marks the arrival of a new sensibility to which the only parallel is Rousseau's *Confessions*.

a conscious artist and was contemptuous of the *gens d'esprit*. The fountain from within which he released brought a new vision, but it was primarily an impulse to action, and one which could stir the masses and alter not only the quality of human sensibility, but the shape of the human world. For the masses of men, who are aesthetically blind, the world remains the same as before Proust appeared. It is the finer spirits for whom it can never again be quite the same.

'Every generation believes,' Marcel Arland has remarked, 'that with it the world is awaking from a dream.' That is emphatically true, as we know, of the generation of today, which often seems to us to be awaking very vigorously. But vigour may be blind as well as impotent. It is not every generation for whom the dawn brings a new vision of the world.

It happens now and again. Then we feel that a veil has been lifted from Nature to reveal secrets before unseen. Many such veils have, indeed, been removed in the space of Man's life on earth. And before the last is lifted, Man himself will be no more.

THE END

INDEX

INDEX

399

INDEX

INDEX

INDEX

INDEX

INDEX

INDEX

INDEX

INDEX

effect of, on modern world, 364–65; Proust compared with, 395–96
Rousseau, Jeannette, 154–55
Rousseau Revisited (Murry), 142–43
Rubens, Peter Paul, 77
Ruisdael, Jacob, 77
Ruskin, John, 90–91, 374–76

Sabran, de, Comtesse, 183
Sacy, birthplace of Restif de la Bretonne, 150, 151
Sade, de, Donatien Alphonse François, Marquis, 100, 111, 172
Sagesse (Verlaine), 271, 275
Sainte-Amaranthe, de, Emilie, 204–06
Sainte-Amaranthe, de, Madame, 205–06
Sainte-Beaume, 72, 90
Sainte-Beuve, Charles Augustin, 15, 87, 147, 258, 267, 327
Saint-Evremond, de, Charles, 41
Saint Gothard Pass, 78
Saint-Lambert, de, Jean François, Marquis, 132
Saint-Leu, 136
Saint-Pierre, de, Bernardin, 99, 109
Saint-Preux, character in *La Nouvelle Héloïse* (Rousseau), 100
Saintsbury, George Edward Bateman, 171
Saint-Simon, de, Duc, 191, 292, 374
Saison en Enfer (Rimbaud), 270
Sales, de, François, 21
Salisbury Plain, 79
Salter, Emma Gurney, 76
Sand, George, 36, 101, 374
Sandale Ailée, La (Régnier), 337
Sarcey, Francisque, 5
Saul of Tarsus, 123
Saurat, Denis, 266, 373, 376, 377
Savoy, characteristics of, 19–23; as refuge for Rousseau, 26; effect of, on Rousseau, 27–30; Chambéry in, 30; as land of poets, 33; biographers of Madame de Warens in, 35; Rousseau leaves, 55
Scheikévitch, Madame, 364, 377
Schelling, von, Friedrich Wilhelm Joseph, 290
Schiller, von, Johann Christoph Friedrich, 147
Schinz, Albert, article by, 30; his opinion of Rousseau, 103
Schmid, Oswald, 186, 189
Schopenhauer, Arthur, 106, 144
Schreiner, Olive, 389–90
Schweizer Studien zur Geschichtswissenschaft (Schmid), 188

Schwob, Marcel, 271
Scotland, 61–62
Scott, Walter, Sir, 90, 241
Scott-Moncrieff, C. K., 366
Seasons (Thomson), 90
Sée, Germain, 258
Ségur, de, Joseph Alexandre, 183, 186
Seillière, 13
Sells, A. L., 27
Senancour, de, Etienne Pivert, 87, 101
Seneca, Lucius Annaeus, quoted, 59, 69, 72
Senecterre, de, Marquis, 203
Sentiment de la Nature en France, Le (Mornet), 83
Sévigné, de, Madame, 64–65, 128
Sexualpsychologische Bibliothek (Bloch), 243, 246
Shakespeare, William, 90, 128, 162, 174
Sharpe, Sutton, 193, 194
Shaw, Bernard, 312
Shelley, Percy Bysshe, 33, 36, 85, 90, 91, 106, 362
Siddons, Sarah, 203
Silva Gadelica (O'Grady), 62
Simler, Josias, 78
Simone, Madame, 355, 356
Sinai, Mount, 59
Sir Kenelm Digby and his Venetia (Bligh), 368
Sixtine (Gourmont), 308, 314
Smith, Robertson, quoted, 60–61
Social Contract (Rousseau), 98, 105, 142, 143
Sodome et Gomorrhe (Proust), 382
Sofa (Crébillon), 109
Soirées de Neuilly (Dittmer and Coué), 195
Solothurn, 180
Soul of Spain (Ellis), 72
Souvenirs d'un Page (Hézecques), 199–200
Souvenirs d'un Temps Disparu (Scheikévitch), 364
Souvenirs et Portraits (de Lévis), 186
Spengler, Oswald, 16
Spleen and other Stories (Besenval), 187, 188, 189
Staël, de, Madame, a follower of Rousseau, 33; attitude of, toward Nature, 82, 85, 109; a writer about Rousseau, 101, 107; Restif de la Bretonne's opinion of, 164
Stendhal (pseudonym of Marie Henri Beyle), discussion of, by Bourget, 6; aversion of, toward Romanticism, 101; appreciation of Besenval's *Mémoires*, 187, 188, 192; comparison of,

INDEX